Physics Galaxy

Lecture Notes on

OPTICS & MODERN PHYSICS

JEE (Mains + Advance) | BITSAT | NEET

Vol. IV

Physics Galaxy

Lecture Notes on

OPTICS & MODERN PHYSICS

JEE (Mains + Advance) | BITSAT | NEET

Vol. IV

All Notes with Video Explanations!

Ashish Arora
Mentor & Founder

PHYSICSGALAXY.COM
World's largest encyclopedia of online video lectures on High School Physics

G K Publications (P) Ltd

CAREER LAUNCHER INFRASTRUCTURE (P) LTD.

Edition 2020-21

© AUTHOR

No part of this book may be reproduced in a retrieval system or transmitted, in any form or by any means, electronics, mechanical, photocopying, recording, scanning and or without the written permission of the publisher.

ISBN　　: **978-93-90187-45-4**

Typeset by : *CLIP DTP Unit*

Administrative and Production Offices

Published by : **CLIP**

A-45, Mohan Cooperative Industrial Area, Near Mohan Estate Metro Station, New Delhi - 110044

Marketed by : **G.K. Publications (P) Ltd.**

A-45, Mohan Cooperative Industrial Area, Near Mohan Estate Metro Station, New Delhi - 110044

For product information :

Visit **www.gkpublications.com** or email to **gkp@gkpublications.com**

**Dedicated
to
My Parents, Son, Daughter
and
My beloved wife**

In his teaching career since 1992 Ashish Arora personally mentored more than 10000 IITians and students who reached global heights in various career and profession chosen. It is his helping attitude toward students with which all his students remember him in life for his contribution in their success and keep connections with him live. Below is the list of some of the successful students in International Olympiad personally taught by him.

NAVNEET LOIWAL	*International GOLD Medal in IPhO-2000 at LONDON*, Also secured **AIR-4** in **IIT JEE 2000**
	PROUD FOR INDIA : Navneet Loiwal was the first Indian Student who won first International GOLD Medal for our country in International Physics Olympiad.
DUNGRA RAM CHOUDHARY	**AIR-1** in **IIT JEE 2002**
HARSHIT CHOPRA	*National Gold Medal in INPhO-2002* and got **AIR-2** in **IIT JEE-2002**
KUNTAL LOYA	A Girl Student got position **AIR-8** in **IIT JEE 2002**
LUV KUMAR	*National Gold Medal in INPhO-2003* and got **AIR-3** in **IIT JEE-2003**
RAJHANS SAMDANI	*National Gold Medal in INPhO-2003* and got **AIR-5** in **IIT JEE-2003**
SHANTANU BHARDWAJ	*International SILVER Medal in IPhO-2002 at INDONESIA*
SHALEEN HARLALKA	*International GOLD Medal in IPhO-2003 at CHINA* and got **AIR-46** in **IIT JEE-2003**
TARUN GUPTA	*National GOLD Medal in INPhO-2005*
APEKSHA KHANDELWAL	*National GOLD Medal in INPhO-2005*
ABHINAV SINHA	*Hon'ble Mension Award in APhO-2006 at KAZAKHSTAN*
RAMAN SHARMA	*International GOLD Medal in IPhO-2007 at IRAN* and got **AIR-20** in **IIT JEE-2007**
PRATYUSH PANDEY	*International SILVER Medal in IPhO-2007 at IRAN* and got **AIR-85** in **IIT JEE-2007**
GARVIT JUNIWAL	*International GOLD Medal in IPhO-2008 at VIETNAM* and got **AIR-10** in **IIT JEE-2008**
ANKIT PARASHAR	*National GOLD Medal in INPhO-2008*
HEMANT NOVAL	*National GOLD Medal in INPhO-2008* and got **AIR-25** in **IIT JEE-2008**
ABHISHEK MITRUKA	*National GOLD Medal in INPhO-2009*
SARTHAK KALANI	*National GOLD Medal in INPhO-2009*
ASTHA AGARWAL	*International SILVER Medal in IJSO-2009 at AZERBAIJAN*
RAHUL GURNANI	*International SILVER Medal in IJSO-2009 at AZERBAIJAN*
AYUSH SINGHAL	*International SILVER Medal in IJSO-2009 at AZERBAIJAN*
MEHUL KUMAR	*International SILVER Medal in IPhO-2010 at CROATIA* and got **AIR-19** in **IIT JEE-2010**
ABHIROOP BHATNAGAR	*National GOLD Medal in INPhO-2010*
AYUSH SHARMA	*International Double GOLD Medal in IJSO-2010 at NIGERIA*
AASTHA AGRAWAL	*Hon'ble Mension Award in APhO-2011 at ISRAEL* and got **AIR-93** in **IIT JEE 2011**
ABHISHEK BANSAL	*National GOLD Medal in INPhO-2011*
SAMYAK DAGA	*National GOLD Medal in INPhO-2011*
SHREY GOYAL	*National GOLD Medal in INPhO-2012* and secured **AIR-24** in **IIT JEE 2012**
RAHUL GURNANI	*National GOLD Medal in INPhO-2012*
JASPREET SINGH JHEETA	*National GOLD Medal in INPhO-2012*
DIVYANSHU MUND	*National GOLD Medal in INPhO-2012*
SHESHANSH AGARWAL	*International SILVER Medal in IAO-2012 at KOREA*
SWATI GUPTA	*International SILVER Medal in IJSO-2012 at IRAN*
PRATYUSH RAJPUT	*International SILVER Medal in IJSO-2012 at IRAN*
SHESHANSH AGARWAL	*International BRONZE Medal in IOAA-2013 at GREECE*
SHESHANSH AGARWAL	*International GOLD Medal in IOAA-2014 at ROMANIA*
SHESHANSH AGARWAL	*International SILVER Medal in IPhO-2015 at INDIA* and secured **AIR-58** in **JEE(Advanced)-2015**
VIDUSHI VARSHNEY	*International SILVER Medal in IJSO-2015 to be held at SOUTH KOREA*
AMAN BANSAL	**AIR-1** in **JEE Advanced 2016**
KUNAL GOYAL	**AIR-3** in **JEE Advanced 2016**
GOURAV DIDWANIA	**AIR-9** in **JEE Advanced 2016**
DIVYANSH GARG	*International SILVER Medal in IPhO-2016 at SWITZERLAND*

ABOUT THE AUTHOR

The complexities of Physics have given nightmares to many, but the homegrown genius of Jaipur-Ashish Arora has helped several students to live their dreams by decoding it.

Newton Law of Gravitation and Faraday's Magnetic force of attraction apply perfectly well with this unassuming genius. A Pied Piper of students, his webportal https://www.physicsgalaxy.com, The world's largest encyclopedia of video lectures on high school Physics possesses strong gravitational pull and magnetic attraction for students who want to make it big in life.

Ashish Arora, gifted with rare ability to train masterminds, has mentored over 10,000 IITians in his past 24 years of teaching sojourn including lots of students made it to Top 100 in IITJEE/JEE(Advance) including AIR-1 and many in Top-10. Apart from that, he has also groomed hundreds of students for cracking International Physics Olympiad. No wonder his student Navneet Loiwal brought laurel to the country by becoming the first Indian to win a Gold medal at the 2000 - International Physics Olympiad in London (UK).

His special ability to simplify the toughest of the Physics theorems and applications rates him as one among the best Physics teachers in the world. With this, Arora simply defies the logic that perfection comes with age. Even at 18 when he started teaching Physics while pursuing engineering, he was as engaging as he is now. Experience, besides graying his hair, has just widened his horizon.

Now after encountering all tribes of students - some brilliant and some not-so-intelligent - this celebrated teacher has embarked upon a noble mission to make the entire galaxy of Physics inform of his webportal PHYSICSGALAXY.COM to serve and help global students in the subject. Today students from more than 180 countries are connected with this webportal and his youtube channel 'Physics Galaxy'. Daily about more than 35000 video lectures are being watched and his pool of video lectures has cross and sutdents post their queries in INTERACT tab under different sections and topics of physics.

Physics Galaxy video lectures have already crossed 27 million views till now and growing further to set new benchmarks and all the video lectures of Physics Galaxy can be accessed through Physics Galaxy mobile application available on iOS and Android platform.

Dedicated to global students of middle and high school level, his website also www.physicsgalaxy.com has teaching sessions dubbed in American accent and subtitles in 87 languages.

PREFACE

For a science student, Physics is the most important subject, unlike to other subjects it requires logical reasoning and high imagination of brain. Without improving the level of physics it is very difficult to achieve a goal in the present age of competitions. To score better, one does not require hard working at least in physics. It just requires a simple understanding and approach to think a physical situation. Actually physics is the surrounding of our everyday life. If you wish to make the concepts of physics strong, you should try to understand core concepts of physics in practical approach rather than theoretical. Whenever you try to solve a physics problem, first create a hypothetical world in your imagination about the problem and try to think psychologically, what the next step should be, the best answer would be given by your brain psychology.

This book of Lecture Notes is designed for quick reference of video lectures available on 'Physics Galaxy' youtube channel which can be accessed in an organized step by step approach through our website www.physicsgalaxy.com or by 'Physics Galaxy' mobile app. If a student has attended/watched a lecture carefully and later whenever these reference notes are viewed again, complete lecture can flash in memory as it is a proven fact that audio visual memory of human brain is having stronger retention then the content which is read through text books. In case of any confusion in understanding, students can scan the QR code using any 'Android' or 'iOS' device printed on each page of notes to quickly open the respective video lecture to understand the concept better.

The handwritten format of the screenshots gives a clear understanding of the application of concepts explained in the lecture which helps in quick grasping and revision of the concepts.

In this book of compiled screenshots of the video explanations, I have tried my best to make the content error free but owing to the nature of work, inadvertently, there is possibility of errors left untouched. I shall be grateful to the readers, if they point out me regarding errors and oblige me by giving their valuable and constructive suggestions via emails for further improvement of the book.

Date : August, 2018

Ashish Arora

PHYSICSGALAXY.COM
B-80, Model Town, Malviya Nagar, Jaipur-302017
e-mails: ashisharora@physicsgalaxy.com
ashash12345@gmail.com

CONTENTS

6.   Diffraction of Light   107 – 114

Lecture Notes Modules

7.   Polarization of Light   115 – 122

Lecture Notes Modules

8.   Photometry   123 – 128

Lecture Notes Modules

Chapter 1
Geometrical Optics I - Reflection of Light

Lecture Notes Modules

Module-1 Geometrical Optics or Ray Optics

Geometrical Optics or Ray Optics:

It is the branch of physics which describes the light-prop in terms of "light ray" which are used to theoretically demonstrate rectilinear prop of light.

Rect Prop of Light: (RPL)

The tendency of light is only to travel in straight line path in homogeneous medium.

Scan for Video Explanation

Web Reference at www.physicsgalaxy.com

Module-2 Light Ray and Light Beam

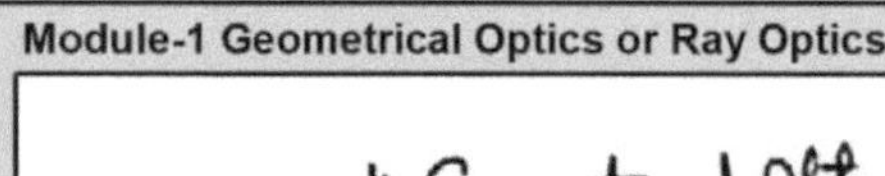

Light Ray and Light Beam:

Light Beam: It is a bundle of several light rays

Light Ray: A very narrow beam of light

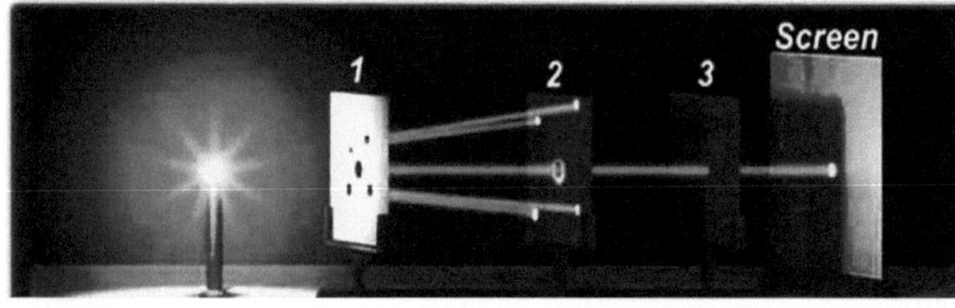

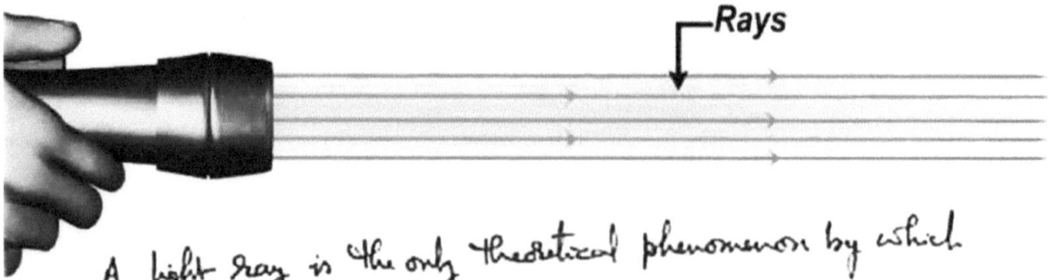

A light ray is the only theoretical phenomenon by which we can analyze RPL in details.

Scan for Video Explanation

Web Reference at www.physicsgalaxy.com

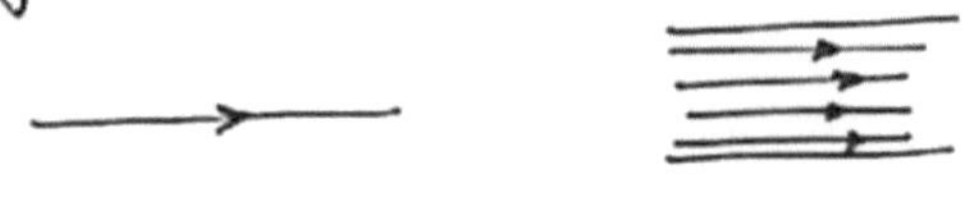

Module-3 Reflection of Light

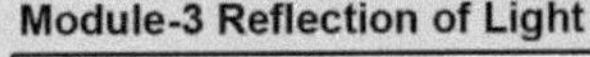

Reflection of Light:

NOTE: At every boundary of two media always reflection takes place according to __laws of Reflection__.

Module-4 Laws of Reflection

Laws of Reflection:

Two law:

(1) Angle of incidence = Angle of Reflection

$$i = r$$

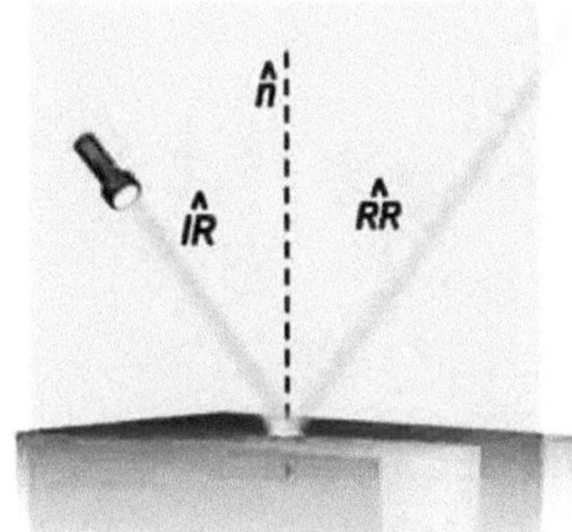

(2) IR, N & RR all lie in same plane $\perp$ to boundary of two media.

vectorially

$$\hat{IR} \times \hat{n} = \hat{RR} \times \hat{n}$$

Module-5 Types of Reflections from a Surface

Types of Reflections from a surface:

① Specular/Regular Reflection:

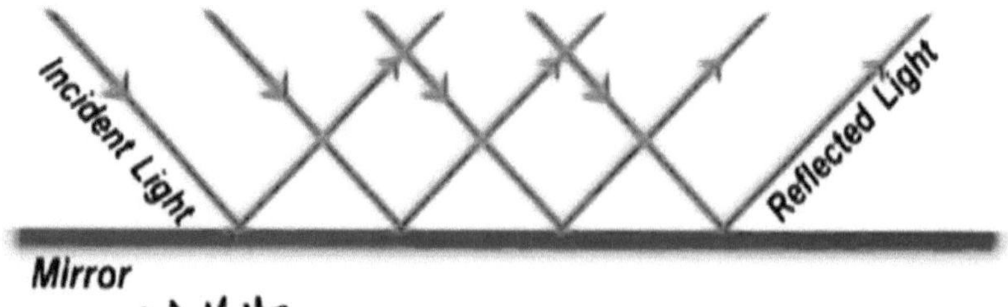

② Diffused Reflection:

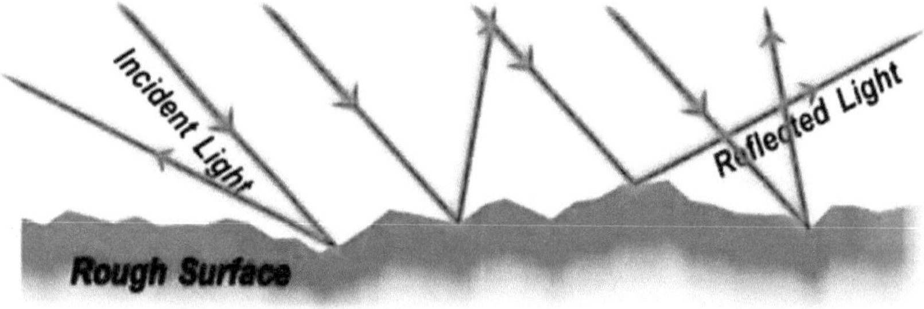

Scan for Video Explanation

Web Reference at www.physicsgalaxy.com

Module-6 Objects and Object Types in Geometrical Optics

'Objects' and object types in Geometrical Optics:

In G.O. an object for an optical device is defined as the point from where all incident rays appear to come.

OR.

An object for an optical device is the int pt of all IRs on the device.

Based on types of IRs on an O/D object can be classified in 3 ways —

① When IRs are Div. ② When IRs are Conv. ③ When IRs are ||

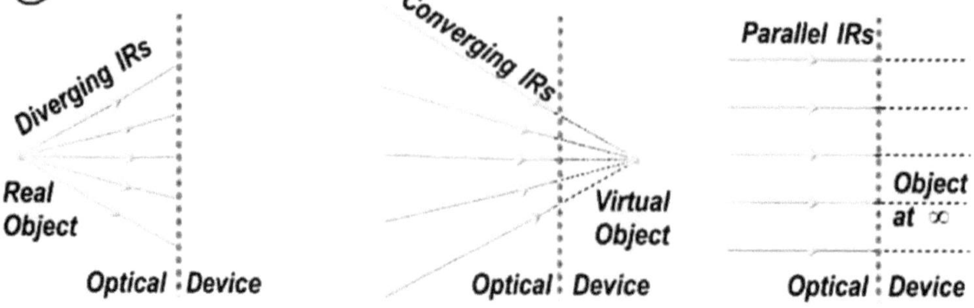

Scan for Video Explanation

Web Reference at www.physicsgalaxy.com

Module-7 Images and Image Types in Geometrical Optics

Image and Image types in Geometrical Optics:

After incidence on an O/D light rays reflect/refract and move away from the O/D. For this O/D intersection point of these RRs can be taken as image for this device.

Based on types of RRs, images can be classified in 3 ways -

① RRs are Converging ② RRs are Div. ③ Parallel RRs.

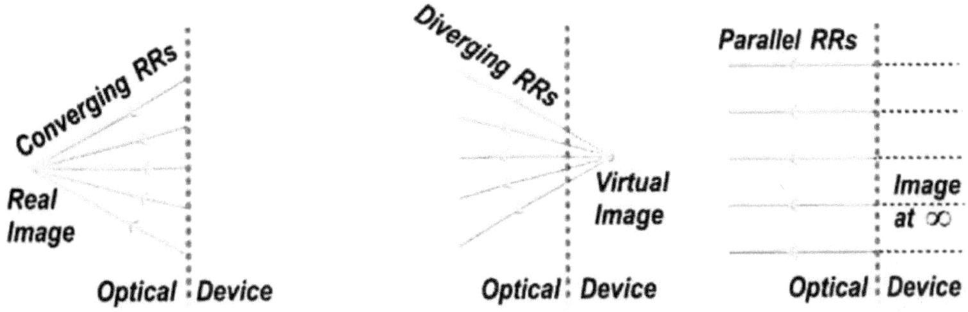

Web Reference at www.physicsgalaxy.com | Scan for Video Explanation

Module-8 Plane Mirrors

Plane Mirrors:

It is a piece of flat glass with a reflecting coating on one side, and it reflects a light beam only in one direction as specular reflection.

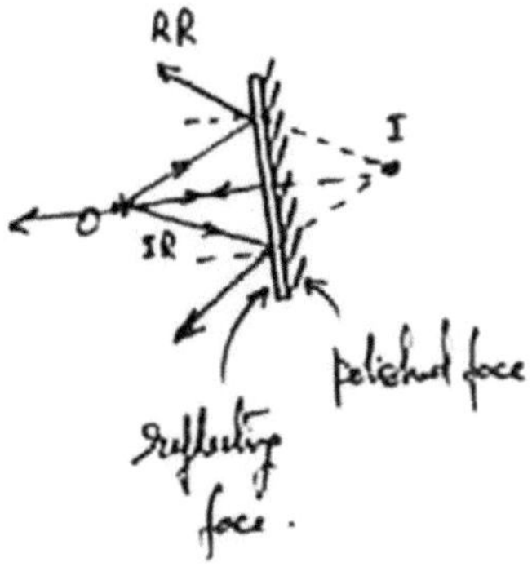

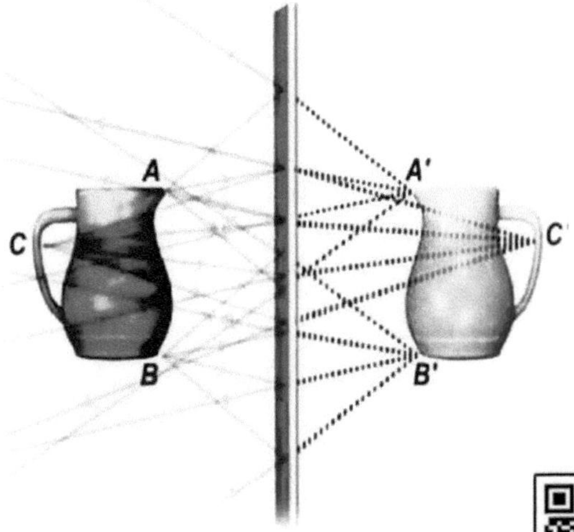

Web Reference at www.physicsgalaxy.com | Scan for Video Explanation

Module-9 Properties of Image Formation by a Plane Mirror

Properties of Image formation by a Plane mirror :

1. Image distance is equal to obj distance from mirror

2. Image formed is laterally inverted

ABC   ЭBA

3. Nature of Image is always opp to that of object.

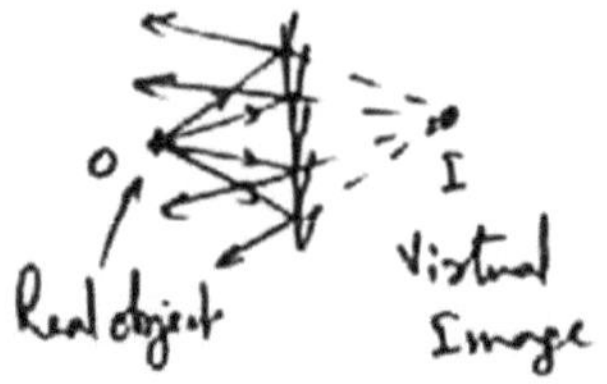

Real object — Virtual Image

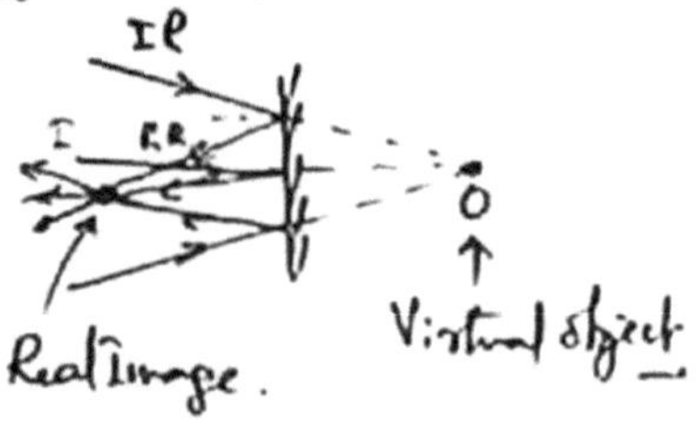

Real Image. — Virtual object

Module-10 Field of View of Image in a Plane Mirror

Field of View of Image in a Plane Mirror :

(Field of View of Image)

FOV of Image.

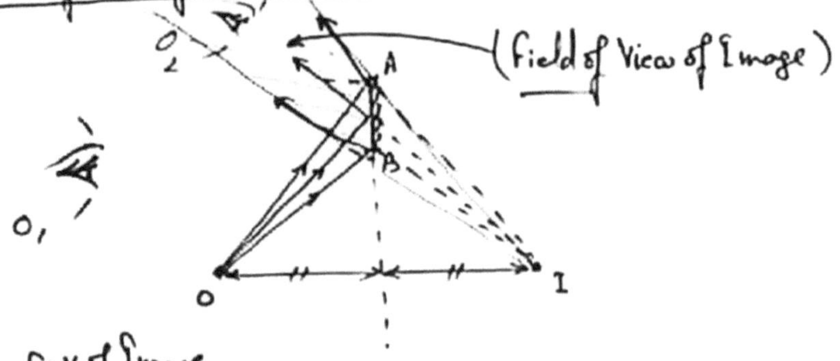

NOTE: Every Plane mirror irrespective of its Size always produce complete image of the object but with Size of mirror field of view of Image increases.

Module-11 Field of View of an Observer in Plane Mirror

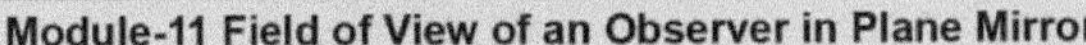

Scan for Video Explanation

Module-11 Field of View of an Observer in Plane Mirror

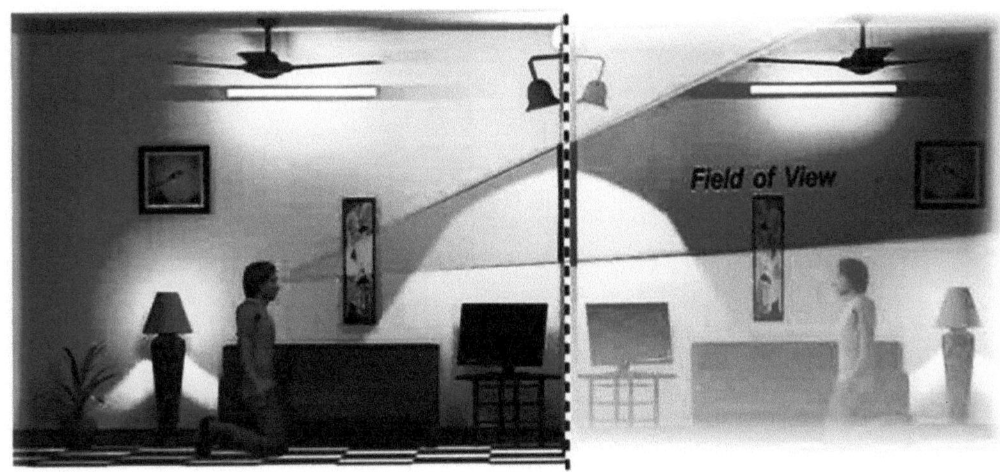

Scan for Video Explanation

Module-12 Minimum Length of Mirror Required to See Self Image

\# Minimum Length of mirror required to see self image:

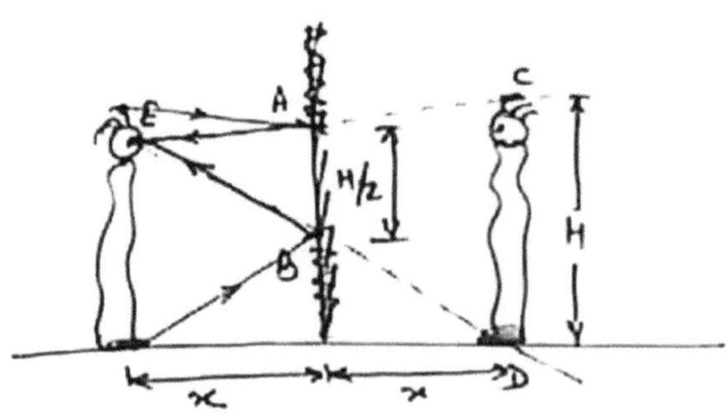

$$\text{in } \triangle ECD \longrightarrow AB = \tfrac{1}{2}CD = \tfrac{H}{2}$$

NOTE: Min length of mirror reqd for a man to see his Complete image is half of his height.

Module-13 Effect of Rotation of Object on Image Formed by Plane Mirror

\# Effect of Rotation of Object on Image formed by Plane Mirror:

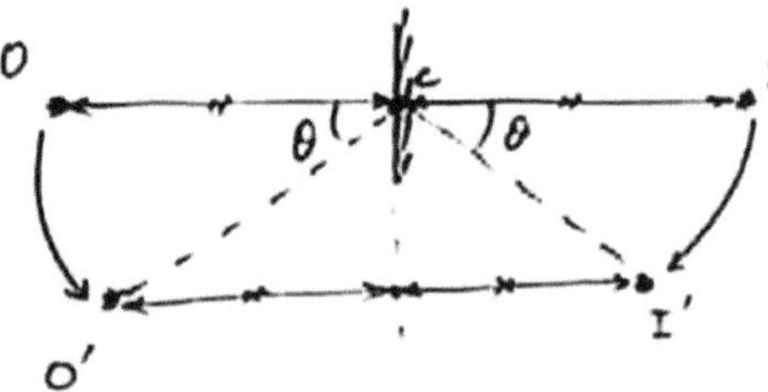

NOTE: If object position rotates by some angle then image position will also rotate correspondingly by same angle but in opposite direction.

Module-14 Effect of Rotation of Mirror on Image

Effect of Rotation of Mirror on Image:

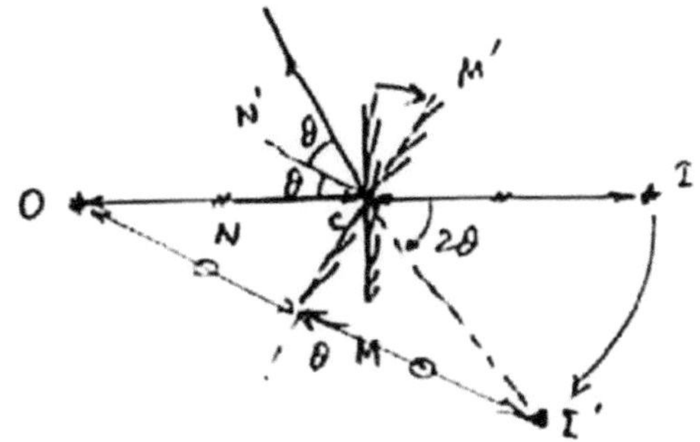

NOTE: If mirror rotates by an angle θ then image position rotates by angle 2θ in the same dir of rotation of mirror.

Scan for Video Explanation

Module-15 Image Formation by Multiple Reflection by Inclined Mirrors

Image formation by multiple reflections by inclined mirrors:

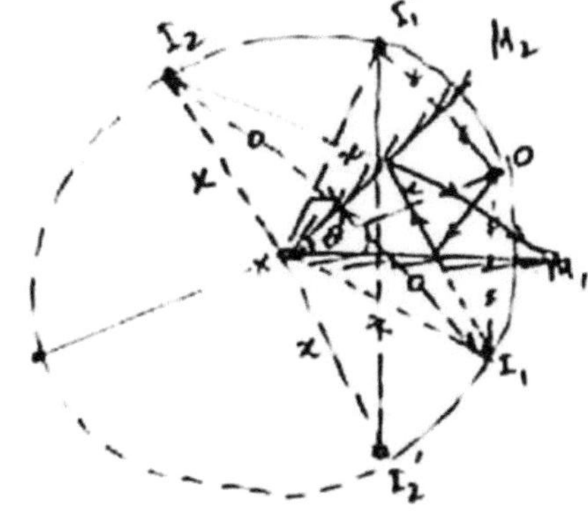

If $\dfrac{180}{\theta} \in I$ then total no. of images obtained $\boxed{N = \dfrac{360}{\theta} - 1}$

NOTE: Due to multiple reflections all images obtained by inclined mirrors lie on a circle with centre at the pt of intersection of mirrors.

Scan for Video Explanation

Module-16 Effect of Motion of Object on Image Formed in Plane Mirror

Effect of motion of object on Image formed in Plane mirror:

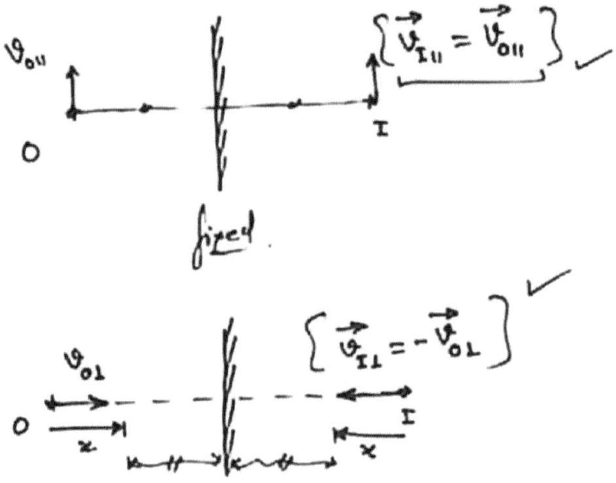

$$\left\{ \vec{V}_{I\parallel} = \vec{V}_{O\parallel} \right\}$$

$$\left\{ \vec{V}_{I\perp} = -\vec{V}_{O\perp} \right\}$$

fixed.

Module-17 Effect of Motion of Mirror on Image Formed in Plane Mirror

Effect of motion of Mirror on Image:

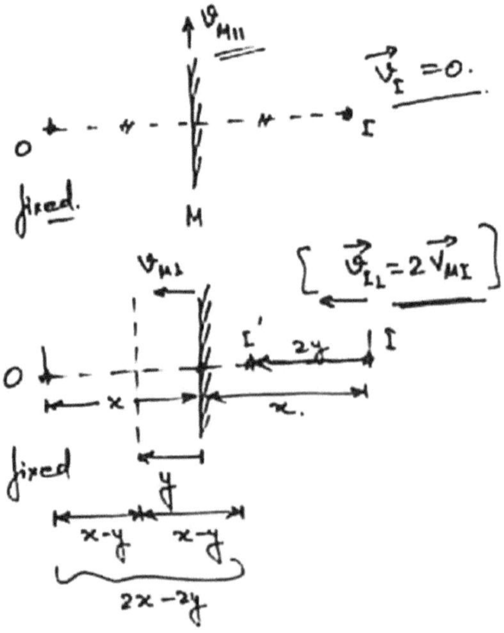

$$\vec{V}_I = 0.$$

fixed.

$$\left\{ \vec{V}_{I\perp} = 2\,\vec{V}_{M\perp} \right\}$$

fixed

$$2x - 2y$$

Module-18 Solved Example-1

Ex : Figure shows a mirror M on which a light ray incident at an angle 40° from normal. If the ray is rotated by 10° clockwise find the change in angle of deviation of light after reflection.

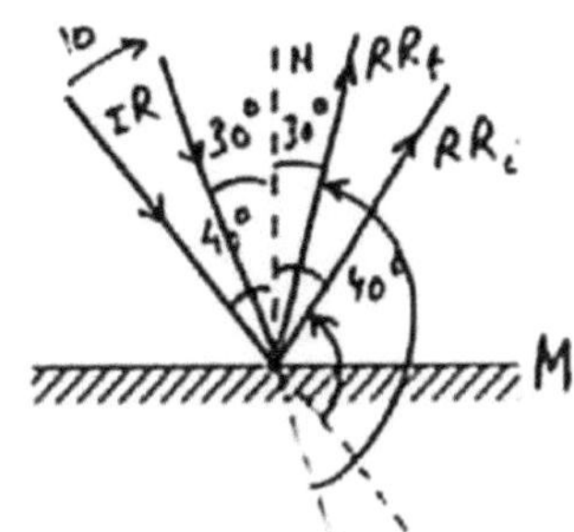

Sol^n:

Initial deviation angle $\delta_i = 180 - 80 = 100°$

Final deviation angle $\delta_f = 180 - 60° = 120°$

Change in deviation angle $\Delta\delta = \delta_f - \delta_i = \underline{20°}$ Ans.

Scan for Video Explanation 

Module-19 Solved Example-2

Ex : In figure shown a light ray 1 after getting reflected from mirror M_1 strikes another mirror M_2 and reflected as ray 2. If angle between M_1 and M_2 is 60° find angle 0.

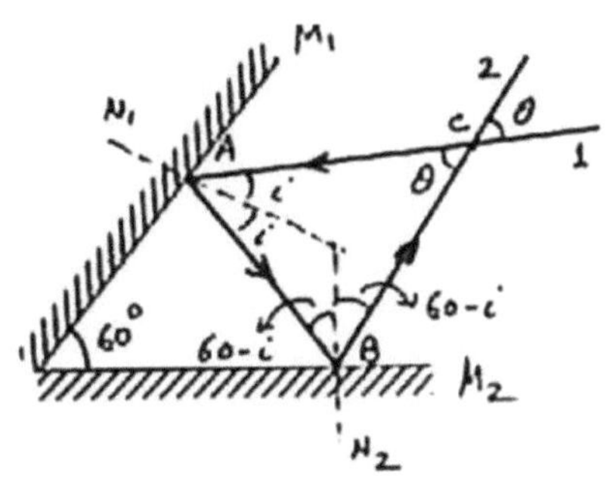

Sol^n: In $\triangle ABC$ we have

$$2i + 2(60-i) + \theta = 180°$$

$$120° + \theta = 180°$$

$$\theta = \underline{60°}\ \text{Ans.}$$

Scan for Video Explanation 

Ex : In figure M_1 is a mirror inclined at 45° to horizontal and passing through point (0, 1) as shown. There is a point source S located at point (1, 0). Locate the position of image of S in mirror.

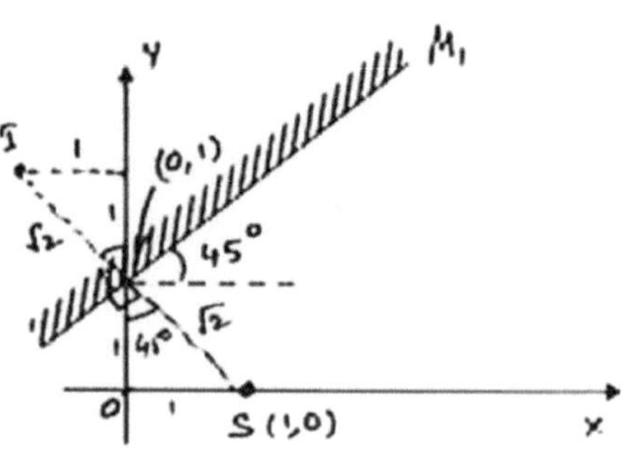

Sol :

Image position the given situation is

$$I\,(-1, 2)\ \text{Ans.}$$

Ex : A person's eye is at a height of 1.5 m. He stands in front of a 0.3 m length plane mirror bottom of which is 0.8 m above ground. Find the length of his image he will be able to see in this mirror.

Sol :

by Similarly in triangles ABC and DEC

$$\frac{l}{0.3} = \frac{2x}{x}$$

$$l = 0.6\,m\ \text{Ans.}$$

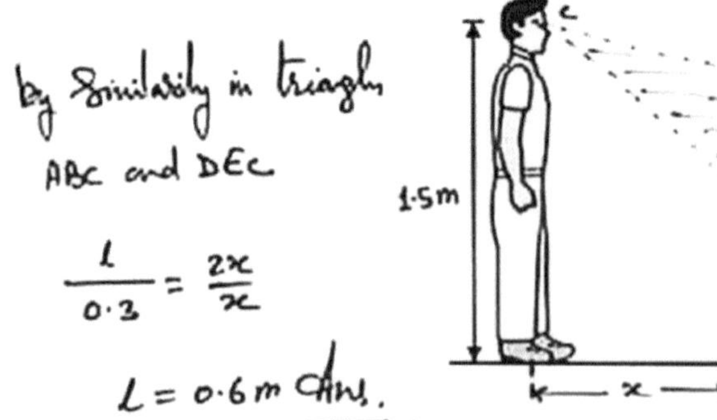

Module-22 Solved Example-5

Ex : A man is standing in a room of length 20m and height 3m at a distance 5m from one wall. On the facing wall a mirror is hanging. Find the minimum size of mirror required in which man will be able to see complete height of wall behind him.

Sol^n:

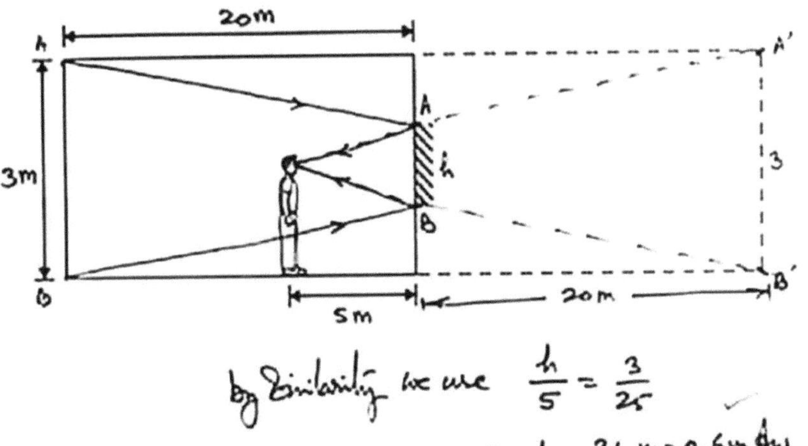

by Similarity we are $\dfrac{h}{5} = \dfrac{3}{25}$

$\implies h = 3/5 \, m = 0.6m$ Ans.

Module-23 Solved Example-6

Ex : In a 3D coordinate system a plane mirror is placed parallel to XY plane and above the mirror a point object is moving at velocity $\vec{v}_0 = 5\hat{i} - 3\hat{j} - 11\hat{k}$ m/s. If mirror is also moving parallel to itself at velocity $\vec{v}_m = 2\hat{i} + \hat{j} - 3\hat{k}$ m/s, find the velocity of image produced in mirror.

Sol: Due to object motion, image vel components parallel to mirror remain same

$$\vec{v}_{i_x} = 5\hat{i} \ m/s \quad \& \quad \vec{v}_{i_y} = -3\hat{j} \ m/s.$$

In dir $\perp$ to mirror (along N) image vel is given as-

$$\vec{v}_{i_z} = 2\vec{v}_{m_z} - \vec{v}_{0_z}$$

$$= 2(-3\hat{k}) - (-11\hat{k}) = +5\hat{k}$$

Vel of image $\vec{v}_i = 5\hat{i} - 3\hat{j} + 5\hat{k}$ m/s Ans.

Module-24 Spherical Mirrors

Spherical Mirrors: These are pieces of hollow glass spheres which are polished on one side.

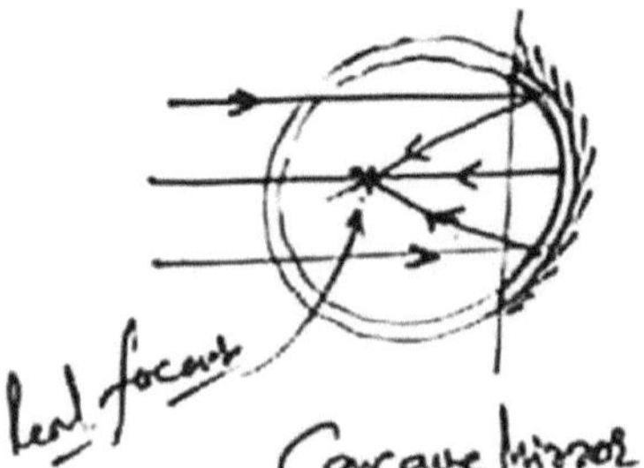

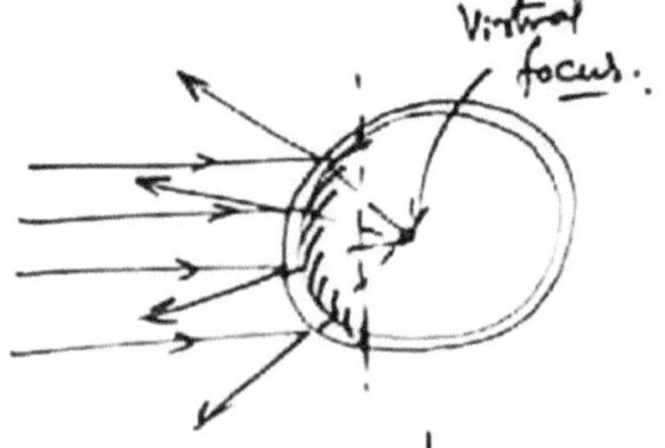

Concave Mirror.
Also known as
Converging Mirror
(in respect to ॥^{l} Its omit)

Convex Mirror
Also known as
Diverging Mirror
(in respect to ॥^{l} I Rs omit)

Scan for Video Explanation

Web Reference at www.physicsgalaxy.com

Module-25 Some Definitions About Spherical Mirrors

Some definitions about spherical mirrors:

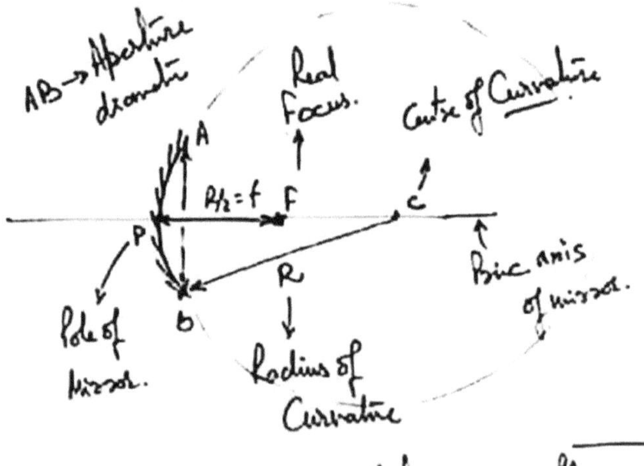

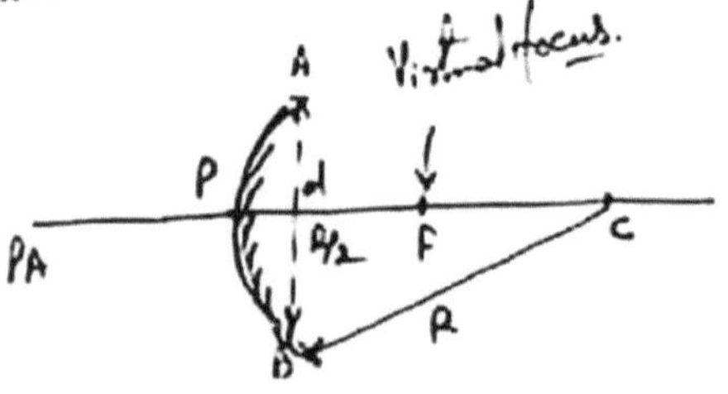

$f = \frac{R}{2}$ is Called focal length of mirror

Scan for Video Explanation

Web Reference at www.physicsgalaxy.com

Module-26 Paraxial Incident Rays on Spherical Mirrors

\# 'Paraxial Incident Rays' on spherical mirrors:

- IRs which are very close to PA of mirror are called paraxial rays.

- Only paraxial rays incident on spherical mirrors which are parallel to PA pass through focus after reflection.

$$f = R/2$$

<u>NOTE</u>: Focus of a spherical mirror is only defined for paraxial rays.

Module-27 Reflected Rays Corresponding to Standard Incident Rays

\# RRs corresponding to standard IRs:

for sph mirrors there are some std paraxial rays which are used for image formation.

Concave Mirrors

Convex Mirrors

① ② ③ ④

Module-28 Relative Position of Images Formed by a Concave Mirror

Relative Position Images formed by a Concave Mirror:

Case-I: When O is at ∞
I is formed in f-plane, real, highly diminished.

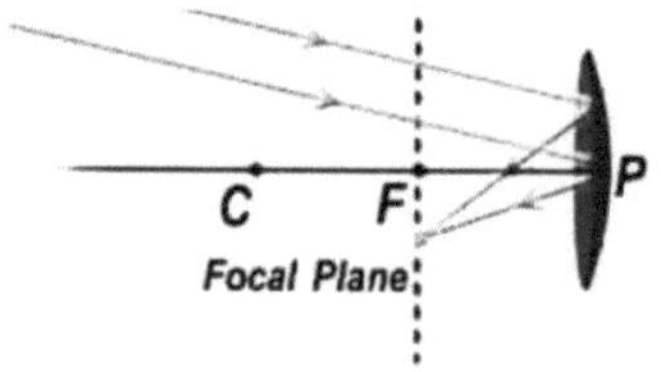

Case-II: When O is at beyond C
I is formed betwn F and C, Real, Inv & diminished.

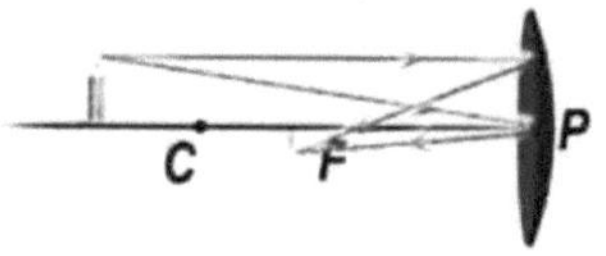

Case-III: When O is at C
I is formed at C, Real, Inv & same sized.

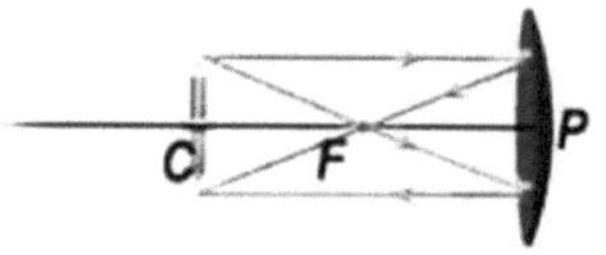

Case-IV: When O is betwn F and C
I is formed beyond C, real, inverted, enlarged.

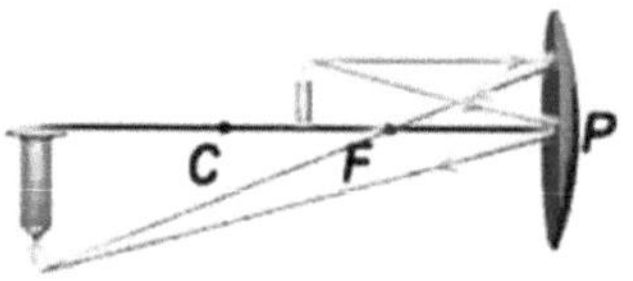

Scan for Video Explanation

Module-28 Relative Position of Images Formed by a Concave Mirror

Case-V: When O is at F
I is at ∞, highly enlarged.

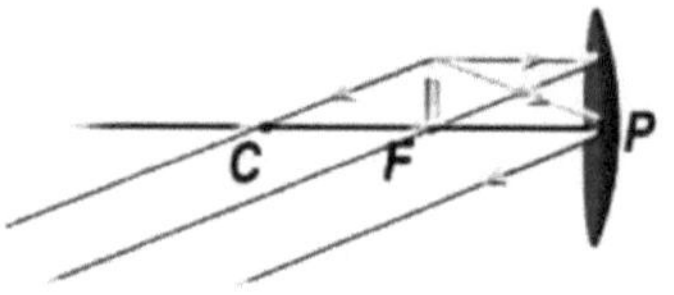

Case-VI: When O is betwn F & P
I is formed behind mirror, Virtual, erected & enlarged.

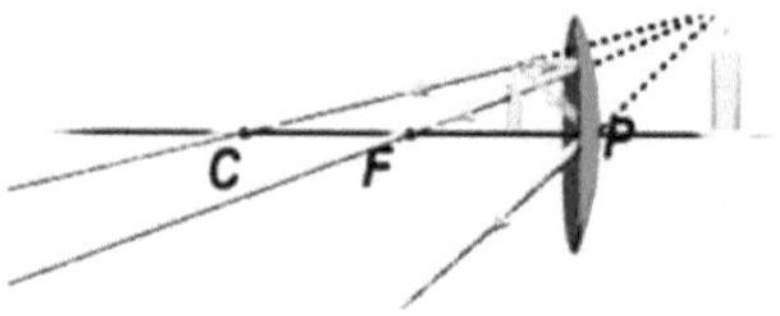

Scan for Video Explanation

Module-29 Relative Position of Image Formed by a Convex Mirror

\# Relative Position of Images formed by Convex mirror:

Case-I: When O is at ∞.

I is formed in f-plane.

Virtual & highly diminished.

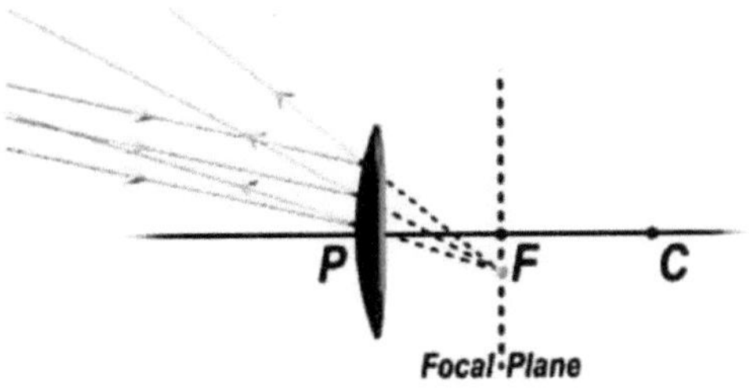

Focal Plane

Case-II: When O is placed any where on PA at finite distance

I is formed between F and P.

Virtual, erected and diminished.

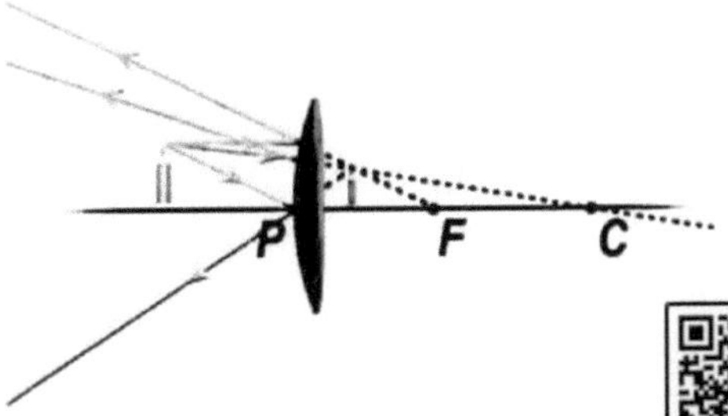

Scan for Video Explanation

Module-30 Analysis of Image Formation by Spherical Mirrors

\# Analysis of Image formation by spherical mirrors:

For a given object, a spherical mirror produces its image for which four parameters are analysed. These are—

① Exact location of image $\longrightarrow$ obtained by "mirror formula."

② Nature of image $\longrightarrow$ obtained by nature of RRs.

$\quad$ Conv RRs $\Rightarrow$ I is Real

$\quad$ Div RRs $\Rightarrow$ I is Virtual.

③ Size of image

④ Orientation of image $\longrightarrow$ obtained by "Magnification formula"

NOTE: In G.O. whenever O and I both are of same nature always image is produced on opp side of PA and when O & I are of opp. nature the image is always produced on same side of PA.

Scan for Video Explanation

Module-31 Mirror Formula and Magnification Formula

\# Mirror Formula and Magnification Formula:

used to locate exact pos of I formed

used to find size/height of I abr PA.

Mirror formula:
$$\frac{1}{u} + \frac{1}{v} = \frac{1}{f}$$

$u \rightarrow$ o distance from pole of mirror
$v \rightarrow$ I distance from " " "
$f = \frac{R}{2} \rightarrow$ focal length of mirror

* The abv formula is only applicable for paraxial rays. (O size should be small)

generalisation of mirror formula

$$f = \frac{uv}{u+v}$$
$$v = \frac{uf}{u-f}$$
$$u = \frac{vf}{v-f}$$

NOTE: In mirror formula we always substitute values of u, v and f with proper signs acc. to Sign Convention used.

Magnification formula:

magnification $\rightarrow$ $m = \left|\frac{v}{u}\right| = \frac{\text{Image distance}}{\text{object distance}}$
produced by mirror.

Image height abv PA below. $= m \times$ Object height abv PA below.

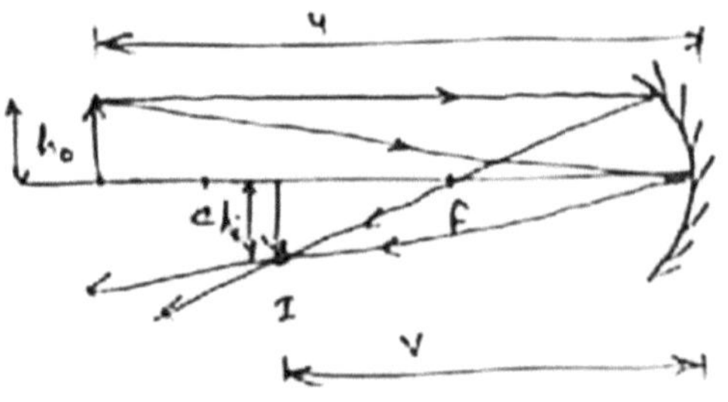

$$h_i = \left|\frac{v}{u}\right| \times h_0$$

Module-32 Sign Convention for Mirror Formula

Sign Convention for Mirror Formula :

Mirror formula $\qquad \dfrac{1}{u} + \dfrac{1}{v} = \dfrac{1}{f}$

here u, v and f are used with proper signs acc. to the sign convention used.

Sign Convention -1.
— Taking pole of mirror as origin
— Consider dir of IR on mirror as +ve dir.

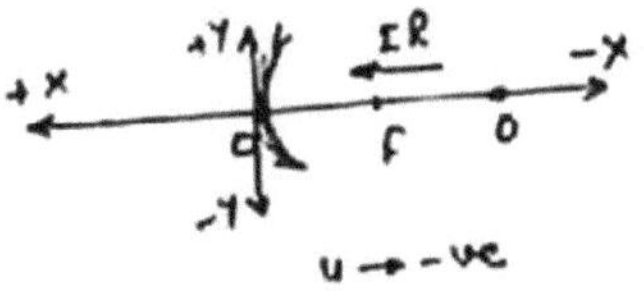

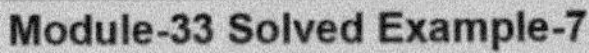

Sign Convention -2
— Taking pole of mirror as origin
— Consider any dir as +ve & other −ve.

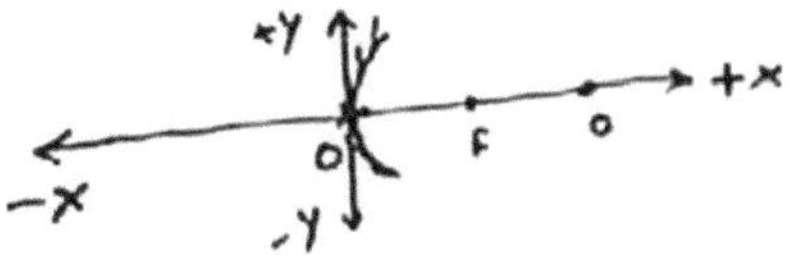

Module-33 Solved Example-7

Ex : A point object is placed at a distance 30 cm in front of a concave mirror of focal length 20 cm. Find the nature and location of image obtained.

Sol^n: Here we can take

$u = -30\,cm.$

$f = -20\,cm.$

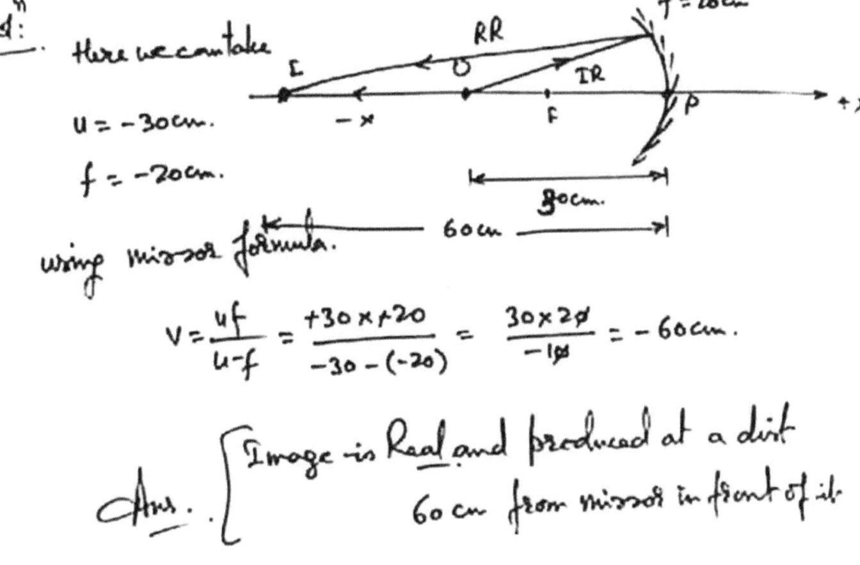

using mirror formula.

$$V = \dfrac{uf}{u-f} = \dfrac{+30 \times +20}{-30 - (-20)} = \dfrac{30 \times 20}{-10} = -60\,cm.$$

Ans. $\Big[$ Image is Real and produced at a dist 60 cm from mirror in front of it.

Module-34 Solved Example-8

Ex : In figure shown find the distance from P at which when a plane mirror is placed, image produced by both mirrors will coincide.

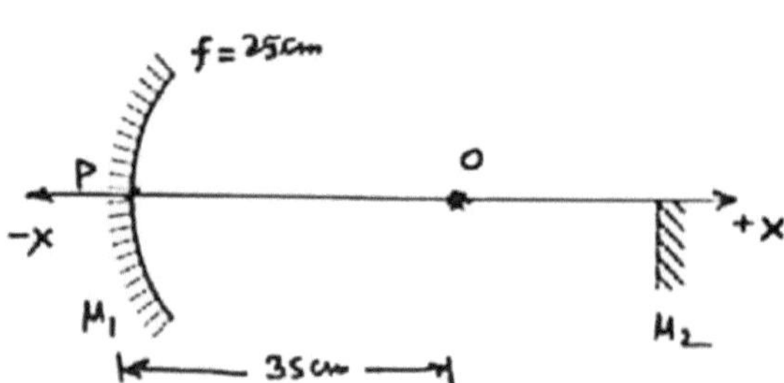

Sol^n: Here we use

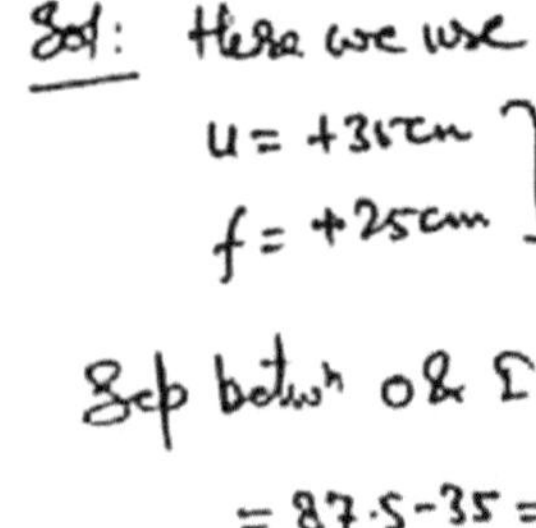

$$u = +35\text{cm} \;\Big] \quad V = \frac{uf}{u-f} = \frac{35 \times 25}{10} = +87.5\text{cm}$$
$$f = +25\text{cm}$$

Sep betw^n o & I is

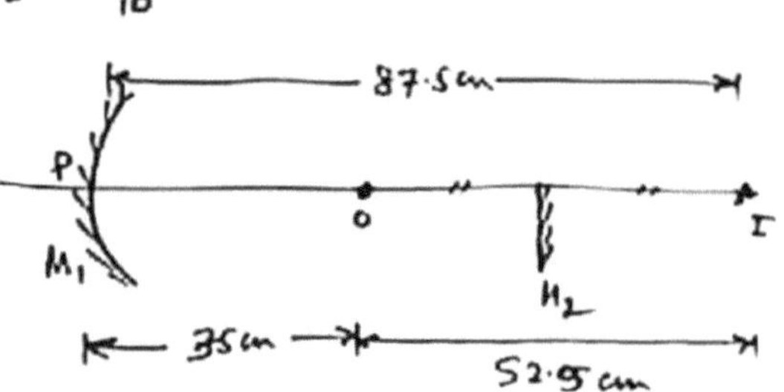

$$= 87.5 - 35 = 52.5\text{cm}.$$

position of M_2 from object is

at o distance $= \dfrac{52.5}{2} = 26.25\text{cm}.$

distance of M_2 from P $= 35 + 26.25 = 61.25\text{cm}$ Ans.

Module-35 Solved Example-9

Ex : Find the distance from a convex mirror, of focal length 60 cm where an object of height 12 cm should be placed so that its image is produced at 35 cm from mirror. Also find the height of image.

Sol^n:

Here we use

$$V = +35\text{cm}$$
$$f = +60\text{cm}$$

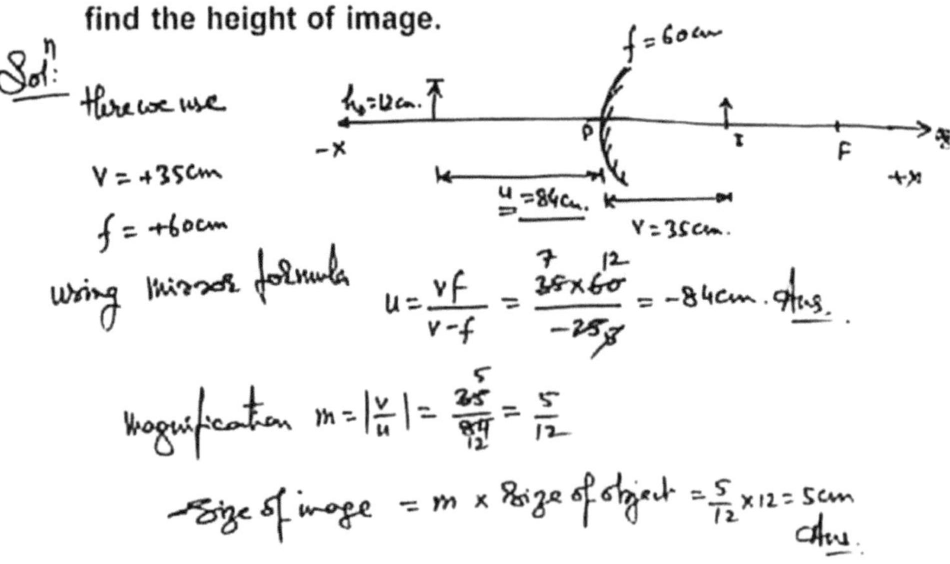

using mirror formula

$$u = \frac{vf}{v-f} = \frac{\overset{7}{35} \times \overset{12}{60}}{-25} = -84\text{cm}.\text{ Ans.}$$

magnification $m = \left|\dfrac{v}{u}\right| = \dfrac{\overset{5}{35}}{\underset{12}{84}} = \dfrac{5}{12}$

Size of image $= m \times$ Size of object $= \dfrac{5}{12} \times 12 = 5\text{cm}$
$$\text{Ans.}$$

Module-36 Solved Example-10

Ex : A coverging beam incident on a concave mirror of focal length 40 cm in such a way that intersection point of the incident rays is located at a distance 40 cm on principal axis behind the mirror. Find the location and nature of image produced.

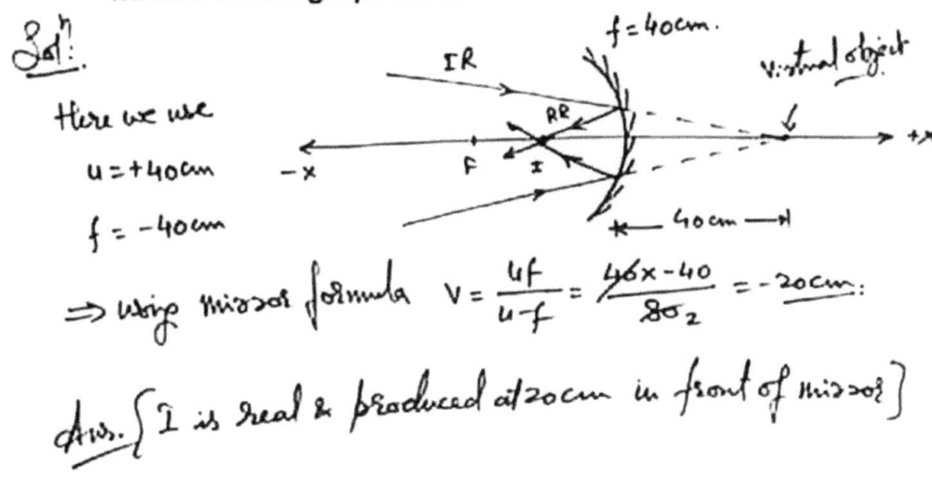

Solⁿ:

Here we use

$u = +40\,cm$

$f = -40\,cm$

$\Rightarrow$ using mirror formula $V = \dfrac{uf}{u-f} = \dfrac{40 \times -40}{80_2} = -20\,cm.$

Ans. {I is real & produced at 20 cm in front of mirror}

Scan for Video Explanation

Module-37 Solved Example-11

Ex : A man uses a concave mirror for shaving and sees his 2 times enlarged image in mirror when his face is at a distance 40 cm from mirror. Find focal length of mirror.

Solⁿ:

using mirror formula.

$$f = \dfrac{uV}{u+V} = \dfrac{-40 \times 80}{-40+80} = \dfrac{-40 \times 80}{40} = -80\,cm.$$

$f = 80\,cm$ Ans.

Scan for Video Explanation

Module-38 Solved Example-12

Ex : Figure shows two spherical mirrors M_1 and M_2 on same optical axis at a separation of 50 cm. A point object O is placed midway between mirrors on optical axis. Find location & nature of its image after two successive reflections first at M_1 then at M_2.

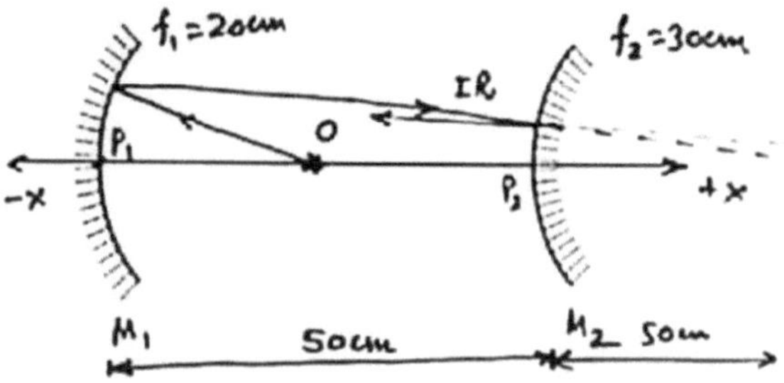

Sol^n: I reflection $u = +25cm$. & $f = +20cm$.

Using mirror formula $v = \frac{uf}{u-f} = \frac{25 \times 20}{5} = 100cm$.

II reflection $u = +50$ & $f = +30cm$. | $v = \frac{uf}{u-f} = \frac{50 \times 30}{20} = +75cm$ Ans.

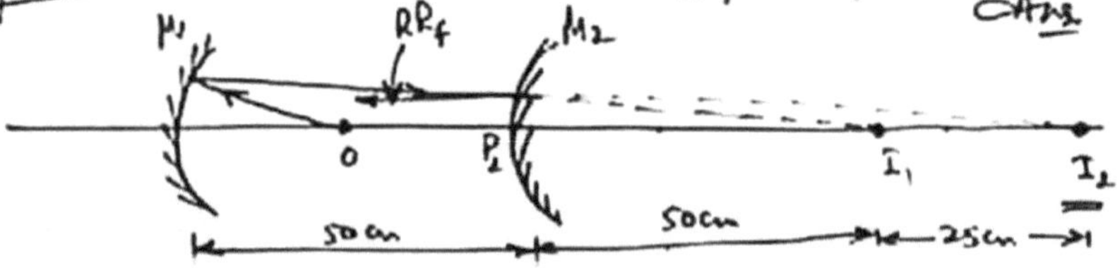

Scan for Video Explanation

Web Reference at www.physicsgalaxy.com

Module-39 Longitudinal Magnification by Spherical Mirrors

Longitudinal magnification by spherical mirrors:

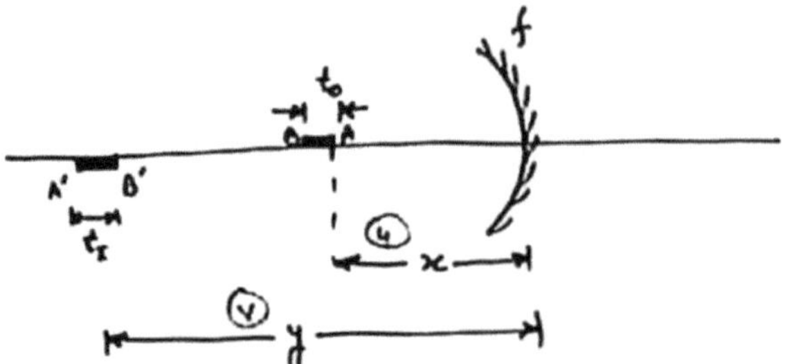

using mirror formula we have $\frac{1}{x} + \frac{1}{y} = \frac{1}{f}$

differentiating this exp $-\frac{1}{x^2}dx - \frac{1}{y^2}dy = 0$

$$\frac{dy}{dx} = -\frac{y^2}{x^2}$$

In magnitude for small t_0

$$\frac{t_I}{t_0} = \frac{dy}{dx} = \frac{y^2}{x^2} = \frac{v^2}{u^2} = m^2 \rightarrow m_L \text{ longitudinal mag.}$$

Image width $= m^2 \times$ object width.

Scan for Video Explanation

Web Reference at www.physicsgalaxy.com

Module-40 Velocity Magnification by Spherical Mirrors

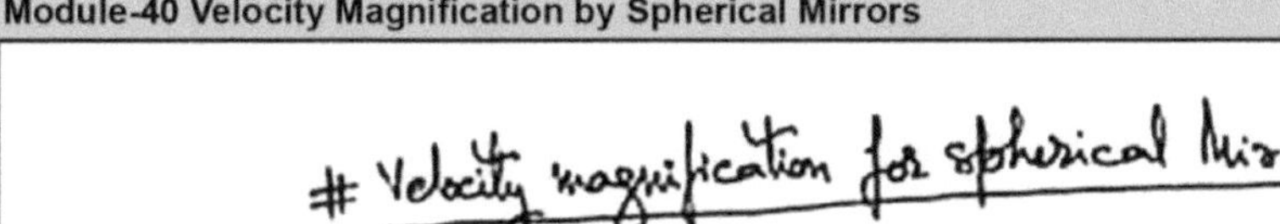

Velocity magnification for spherical Mirrors:

Case-I: When O vel is $\perp$ to PA

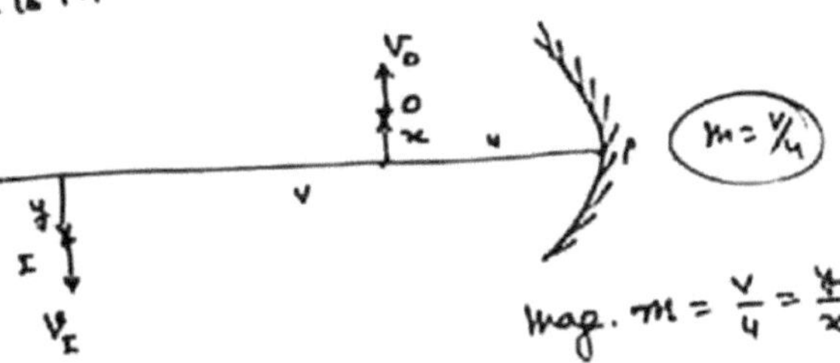

As object vel is $V_0 = \dfrac{dx}{dt}$

Image vel is $V_I = \dfrac{dy}{dt}$

here we have $y = mx$

$V_I = \dfrac{dy}{dt} = m\dfrac{dx}{dt}$

When V_0 and V_I are $\perp$ to PA.

$$\boxed{V_I = m\,V_0}$$

Module-40 Velocity Magnification by Spherical Mirrors

Case-II: When O vel is along PA.

As we know here $\dfrac{dy}{dx} = -\dfrac{v^2}{u^2}$

$$\dfrac{dy}{dt} = -\dfrac{v^2}{u^2}\cdot\dfrac{dx}{dt}$$

In magnitude $$\boxed{V_I = m^2\cdot V_0}$$

when V_0 and V_I are along PA.

Chapter 2

Geometrical Optics II - Refraction of Light

Lecture Notes Modules

Refraction of Light:

When a light travels through a boundary of two trans media from one med to another, the phenomenon is called Refraction of light.

— In diff media speed of light is different and it is associated in terms of Refractive Index of medium.

R.I of medium (n) $\mu = \dfrac{\text{speed of light in free space}}{\text{speed of light in medium}} = \dfrac{c}{v}$

$$v_{med} = \dfrac{c}{\mu} \qquad (\mu \geq 1)$$
$$\mu = 1 \longrightarrow \text{for free space}$$

If $v_{med\,I} < v_{med\,II}$ then med I is considered as optically denser med w.r to med II (optically rarer)

NOTE: When a light travels from one med to another unless it incidents normally the path of light can also change either toward normal or away from normal

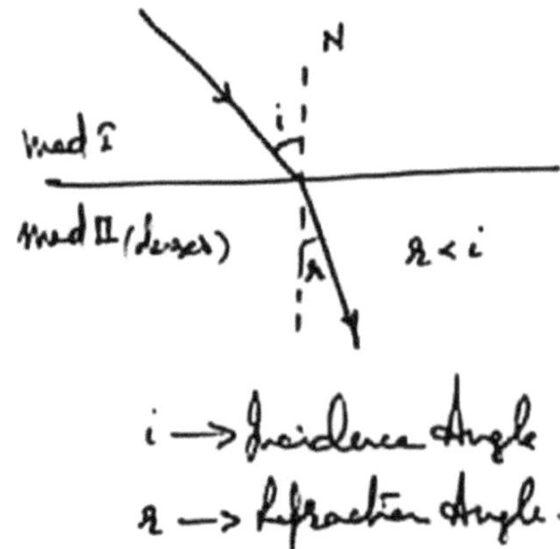

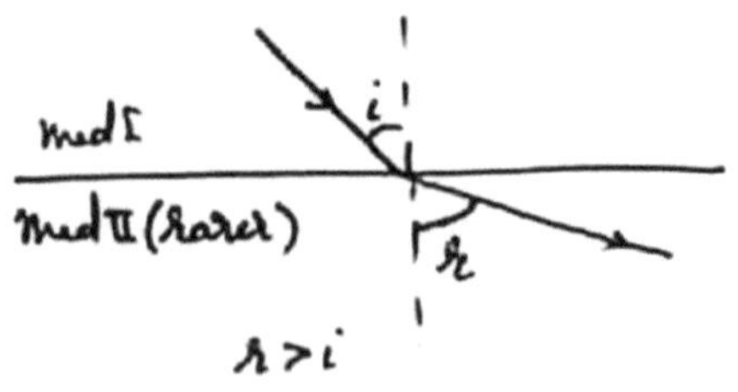

$i \longrightarrow$ Incidence Angle
$r \longrightarrow$ Refraction Angle.

Module-2 Laws of Refraction

Laws of Refraction:

These are laws acc. to which refraction of light from one kind to another is governed. These are called Snell's laws.

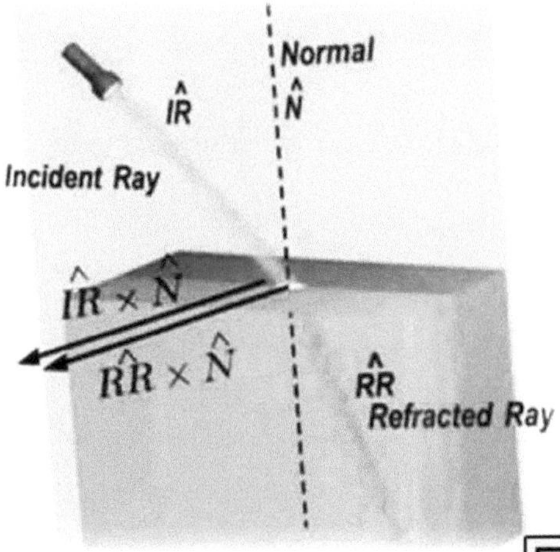

Law-I: Product of sine of the angle made by light ray with normal and RI of medium is a Constant.

$$\mu_1 \sin \theta_1 = \mu_2 \sin \theta_2 = \text{Constant}$$

Law-II: IR, N and RR lie in Same plane.

$$\mu_1 \left(\hat{IR} \times \hat{N} \right) = \mu_2 \left(\hat{RR} \times \hat{N} \right)$$

Scan for Video Explanation

Module-3 Refraction of Light Through a Glass Slab

Refraction of Light through a glass slab:

Acc. to Snell's law

1. $\sin i = \mu \sin r$ ✓

lateral displ $\Delta = BC$

$$= AB \sin (i-r)$$

$$= \frac{AD}{\cos r} \cdot \sin (i-r)$$

$$\boxed{\Delta = \frac{t \sin (i-r)}{\cos r}}$$

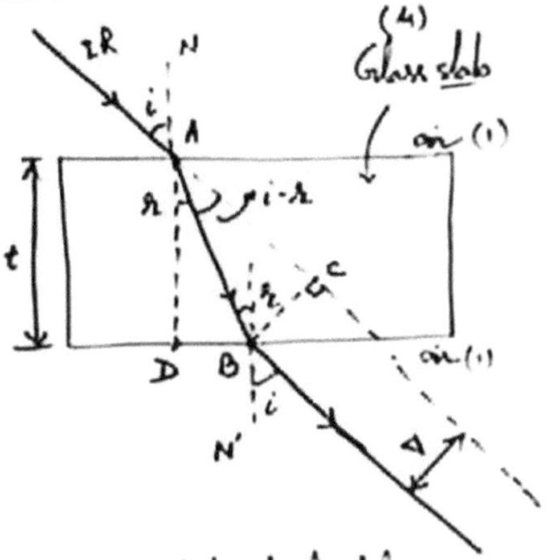

$\Delta \to$ lateral displacement of light ray.

Scan for Video Explanation

Module-4 Lateral Displacement by Multiple Refractions

Lateral displacement by multiple Refractions :

by Snell's law :

$$\mu_a \sin i = \mu_1 \sin \vartheta_1 = \mu_2 \sin \vartheta_2 = \mu_3 \sin \vartheta_3$$

Total lateral displacement along dir of I R is

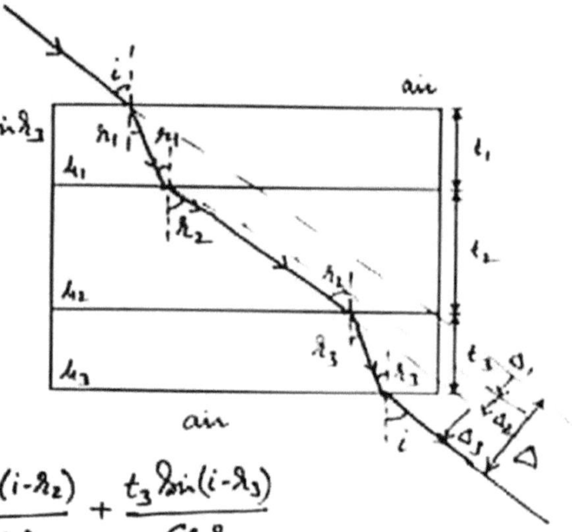

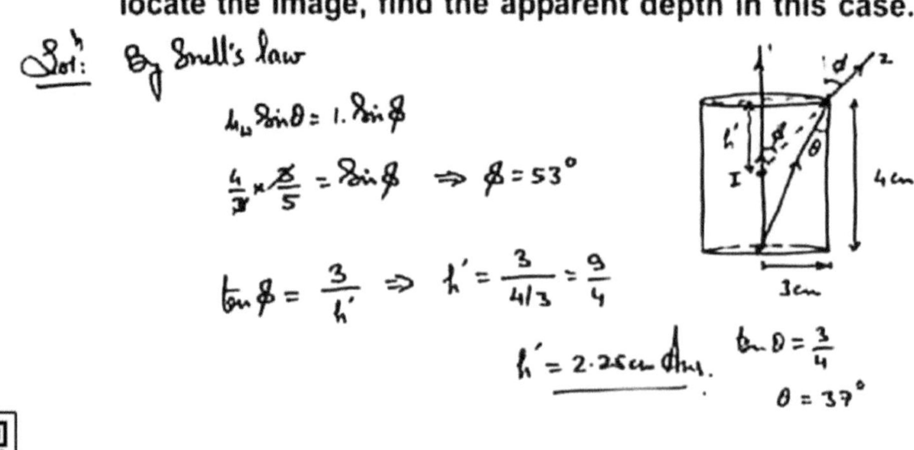

$$\Delta = \Delta_1 + \Delta_2 + \Delta_3$$

$$\Delta = \frac{t_1 \sin(i - \vartheta_1)}{\cos \vartheta_1} + \frac{t_2 \sin(i - \vartheta_2)}{\cos \vartheta_2} + \frac{t_3 \sin(i - \vartheta_3)}{\cos \vartheta_3}$$

Module-5 Solved Example-1

Ex : A small object is kept at the centre of bottom of cylindrical beaker of diameter 6 cm and height 4 cm filled completely with water ($\mu = 4/3$). Consider the light ray from object leaving the beaker through a corner. If this ray and the ray along the axis of beaker is used to locate the image, find the apparent depth in this case.

Sol: By Snell's law

$$\mu_w \sin\theta = 1 \cdot \sin\phi$$

$$\frac{4}{3} \times \frac{3}{5} = \sin\phi \quad \Rightarrow \quad \phi = 53°$$

$$\tan\phi = \frac{3}{h'} \quad \Rightarrow \quad h' = \frac{3}{4/3} = \frac{9}{4}$$

$$\underline{h' = 2.25\,cm}\ Ans.$$

$$\tan\theta = \frac{3}{4}$$
$$\theta = 37°$$

Module-6 Solved Example-2

Ex : A light ray incident at a point on the surface of a glass sphere of $\mu = \sqrt{3}$ at an angle of incidence 60°. It is reflected and refracted at the farther surface of sphere. Find the angle between reflected and refracted ray.

Sol^n: By Snell's law

$$\sin 60° = \mu \sin\theta$$

$$\sin\theta = \frac{\sin 60°}{\sqrt{3}}$$

$$\sin\theta = \frac{\sqrt{3}/2}{\sqrt{3}} = \frac{1}{2} \Rightarrow \theta = 30°$$

$$\alpha = 180 - 60 - \theta$$

$$\alpha = 120° - 30°$$

$$= 90° \text{ Ans}.$$

Module-7 Solved Example-3

Ex : A light ray falling at 60° angle with the surface of a glass slab of thickness 1m and is refracted at angle 75° with the surface. Calculate the time taken by the light to cross the slab.

Sol^n: light speed in glass.

$$v = \frac{c}{\mu}$$

by Snell's law -

$$1 \cdot \sin 30° = \mu \sin 15°$$

$$\mu = 2\cos 15°$$

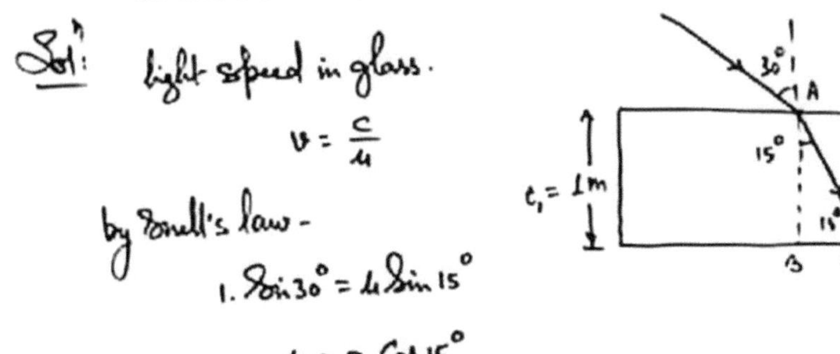

time taken by light to cross the slab

$$t = \frac{Ac}{v} = \frac{t_1/\cos 15°}{c/\mu}$$

$$t = \frac{1}{\cos 15°} \times \frac{2\cos 15°}{3\times10^8} = \frac{2}{3}\times10^{-8} \text{ sec} \quad \text{Ans}.$$

Module-8 Solved Example-4

Ex : A ray of light is incident on a parallel slab of thickness t and refractive index μ. If the angle of incidence is θ then for small θ show that the lateral displacement of light ray will be

$$\Lambda = \frac{t\theta(\mu - 1)}{\mu}$$

Solⁿ: lateral disp of light due to a glass slab

$$\Delta = \frac{t\sin(i-r)}{\cos r}$$

$$\Delta = \frac{t[\sin i \cos r - \cos i \sin r]}{\cos r}$$

$$\Delta = t\left[i - \frac{\theta}{\mu}\right] = \frac{t\theta(\mu-1)}{\mu}$$

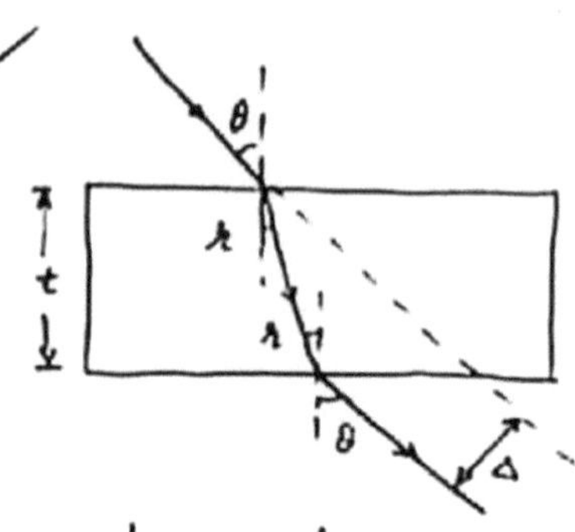

by Snell's law

$$\sin\theta = \mu\sin r$$
$$\theta = \mu r$$
$$r = \theta/\mu$$

Module-9 Total Internal Reflection

Total Internal Reflection :

This ph can take place only when a light ray travels from a denser med to rarer med.

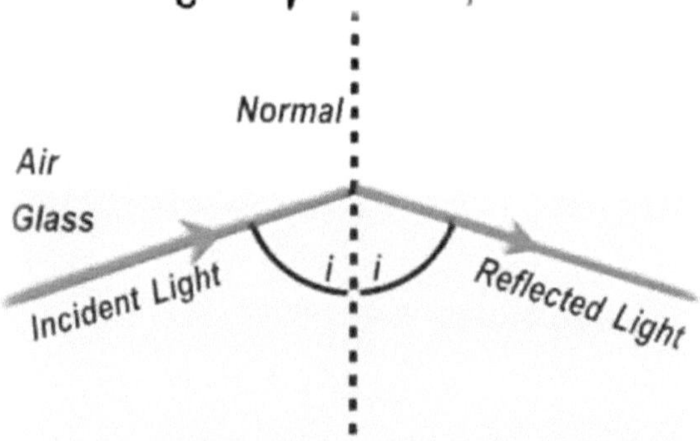

$$\mu_g \sin i = \mu_a \sin r$$

For $i = \theta_c$, $r = 90°$

$$\mu_g \sin\theta_c = \mu_a$$

$$\boxed{\theta_c = \sin^{-1}\left(\frac{\mu_a}{\mu_g}\right)}$$

Critical angle for air-glass interface.

for $i > \theta_c$ light is internally reflect at the boundary of two media.

Module-10 Escaping Light From a Medium Interface by a Point Source

Escaping light from a medium interface by a point source:

Solid angle of Cone
with half angle θ_c is

$$\Omega = 2\pi(1 - \cos\theta_c)$$

Power which is escaping
from water to air is

$$P_{esc} = \frac{P}{4\pi_2} \times 2\pi(1 - \cos\theta_c)$$

$$\boxed{P_{esc} = \frac{P}{2}\left(1 - \sqrt{1 - \frac{1}{\mu^2}}\right)}$$

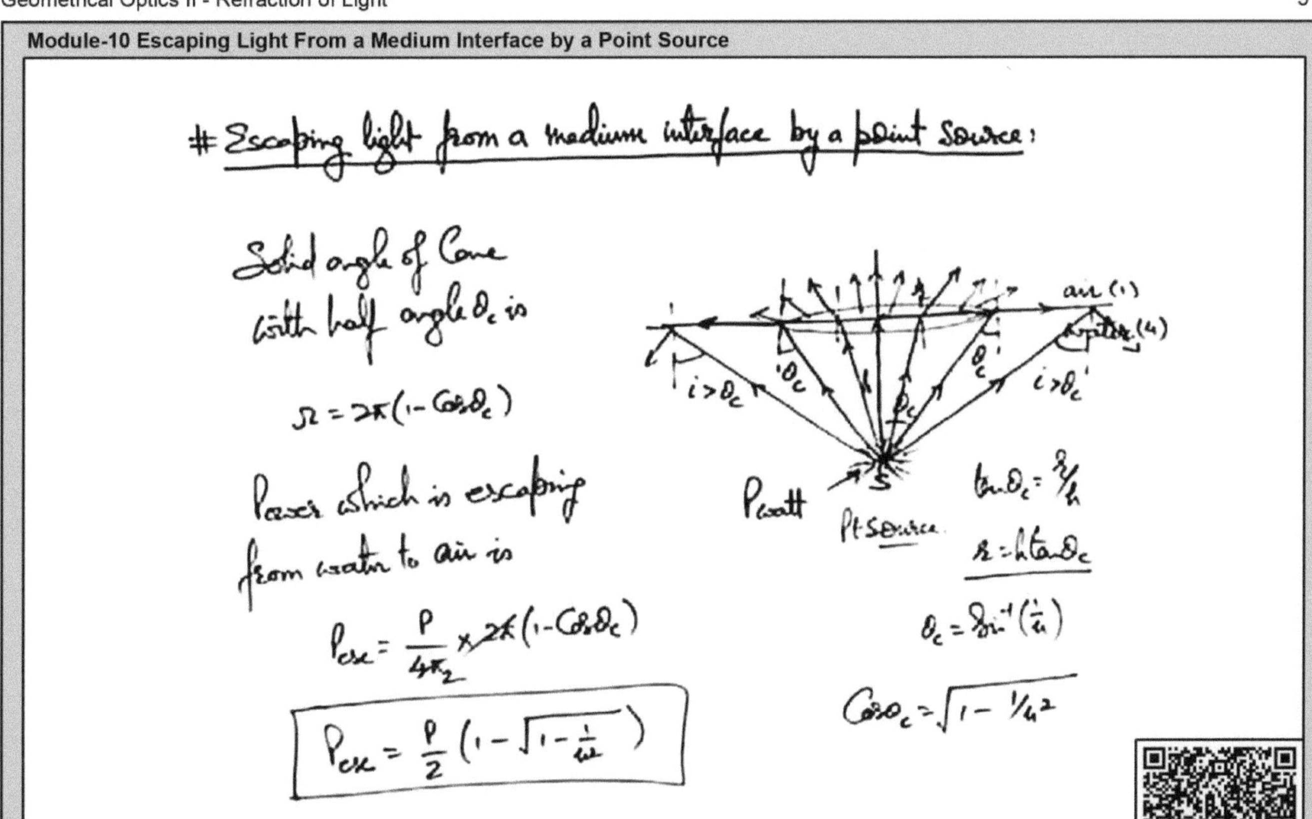

Module-11 Grazing Incidence of Light on an Interface of Two Media

Grazing Incidence of light on an interface of two media:

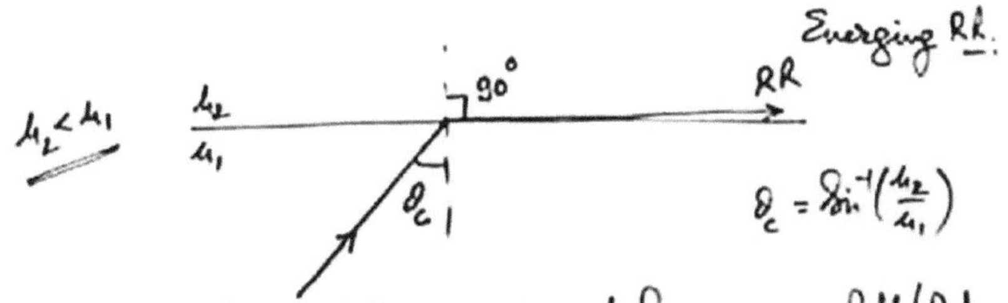

Law of Reversibility of light: Path of light ray in Refl/Refr is Retraceable.

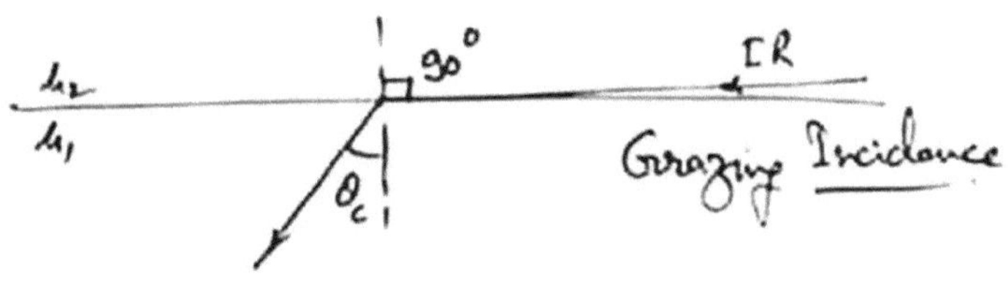

Module-11 Grazing Incidence of Light on an Interface of Two Media

Case-I: Grazing Incidence from denser medium.

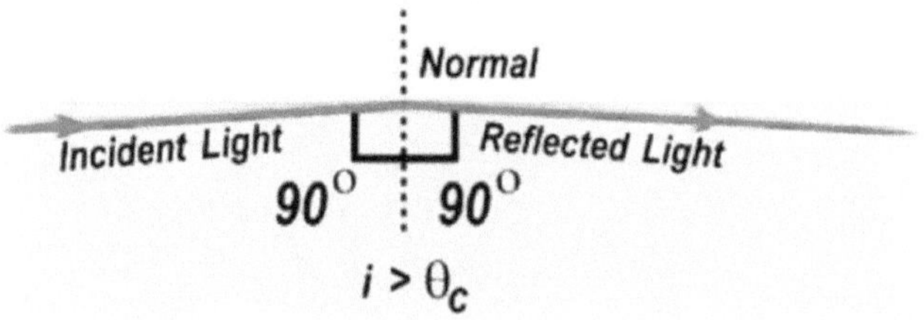

Normal

Incident Light | Reflected Light

90° | 90°

$i > \theta_c$

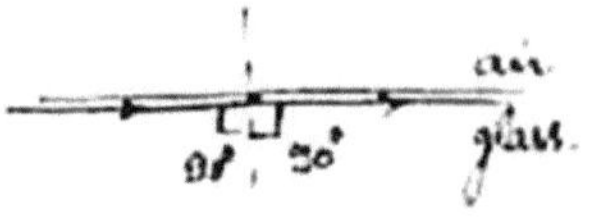

air
glass

Case-II: Grazing Incidence from Rarer medium.

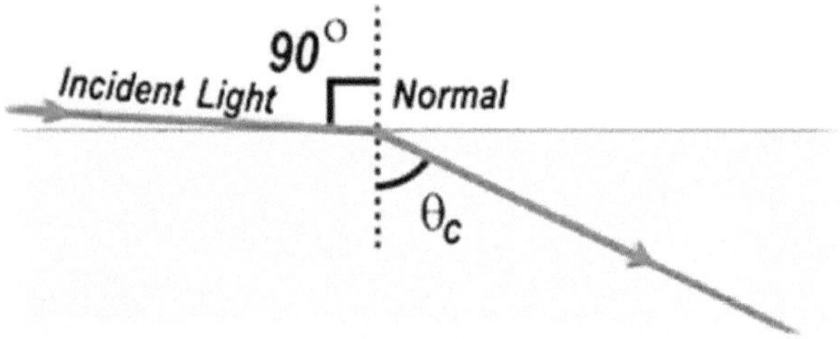

90°

Incident Light | Normal

θ_c

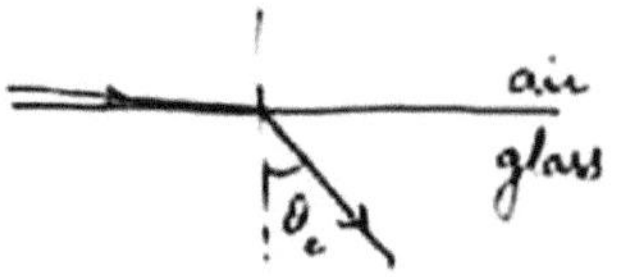

air
glass

θ_c

Scan for Video Explanation | Web Reference at www.physicsgalaxy.com

Module-12 Solved Example-5

Ex : A light ray incident from glass $\left(\mu = \dfrac{3}{2} \right)$ to air interface.
Find the angle of incidence at which deviation angle of light will become 90°.

Sol^n: for δ to be 90°

$i > \theta_c$

$\delta = r - i$

air
glass

i

When

$\delta = \pi - 2i = 90^\circ$

$i = \dfrac{\pi - \pi/2}{2} = \dfrac{\pi}{4}$

$\underline{i = 45^\circ}$ Ans.

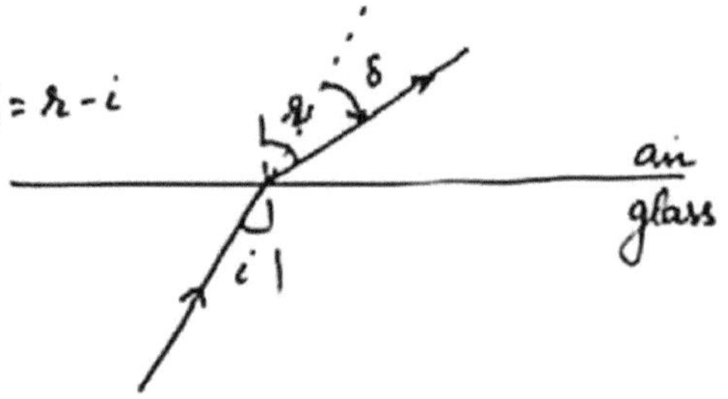

$\delta = \pi - 2i$

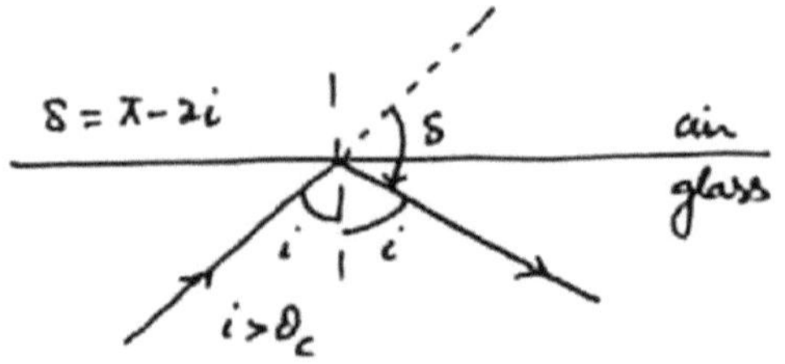

air
glass

$i \quad i$

$i > \theta_c$

Scan for Video Explanation | Web Reference at www.physicsgalaxy.com

Module-13 Solved Example-6

Ex : A point source of light is placed directly below the surface of a lake at a distance h from the surface. Find the area on water from which the light will come out from water.

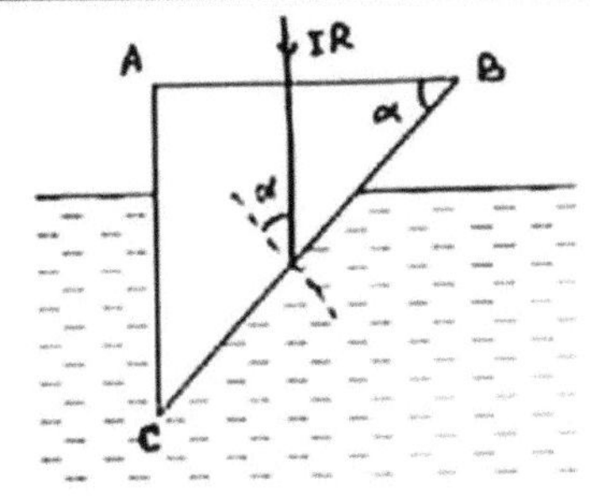

Sol^n:

here $\tan\theta_c = \dfrac{r}{h}$

$r = h\tan\theta_c$

Area of circle through which light comes out from water is

$\sin\theta_c = \dfrac{1}{\mu}$

$A = \pi r^2 = \pi h^2 \tan^2\theta_c$ **Ans.**

Scan for Video Explanation

Module-14 Solved Example-7

Ex : Figure shows a right angled prism ABC having refractive index $\mu_g = \dfrac{3}{2}$ lowered into water $\left(\mu_\omega = \dfrac{4}{3}\right)$. Find angle α so that the incident ray normal to face AB will be reflected at face BC completely.

Sol^n: for light ray to reflect at face BC completely

$\alpha > \theta_c$

$\alpha > \sin^{-1}\left(\dfrac{\mu_\omega}{\mu_g}\right)$

$\alpha > \sin^{-1}\left(\dfrac{4/3}{3/2}\right)$

$\alpha > \sin^{-1}(8/9)$ **Ans.**

Scan for Video Explanation

Module-15 Solved Example-8

Ex : Find at what angle a fish inside a lake will see a rising sun. (Take $\mu_\omega = 4/3$)

Sol^n:

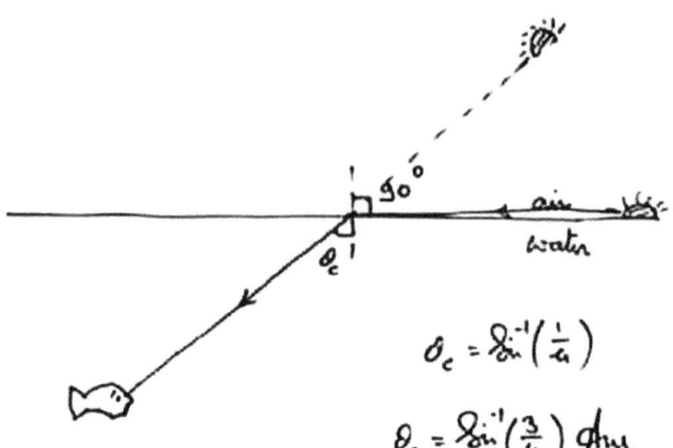

$$\theta_c = \sin^{-1}\left(\frac{1}{\mu}\right)$$

$$\theta_c = \sin^{-1}\left(\frac{3}{4}\right) \text{ Ans.}$$

Module-16 Refraction at Spherical Surfaces

Refraction at Spherical Surfaces:

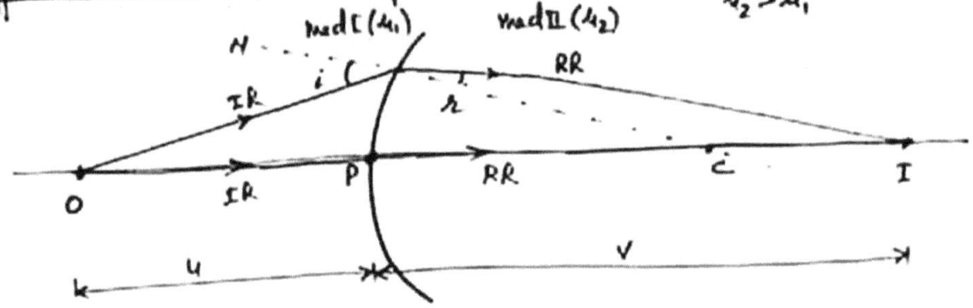

Image formation by Refraction at spherical surfaces can be analyzed by spherical "Refraction formula" used for paraxial IR on med. boundary. It is written as —

Rfn. formula.

$$\frac{\mu_2}{v} - \frac{\mu_1}{u} = \frac{\mu_2 - \mu_1}{R}$$

$u \rightarrow$ Object dist $\mu_1 \rightarrow$ RI of med of IR

$v \rightarrow$ image dist $\mu_2 \rightarrow$ RI of med of RR.

$R \rightarrow$ Rad of curvature.

Module-17 Magnification for Refraction at Spherical Surfaces

Magnification for Refraction at Spherical Surfaces:

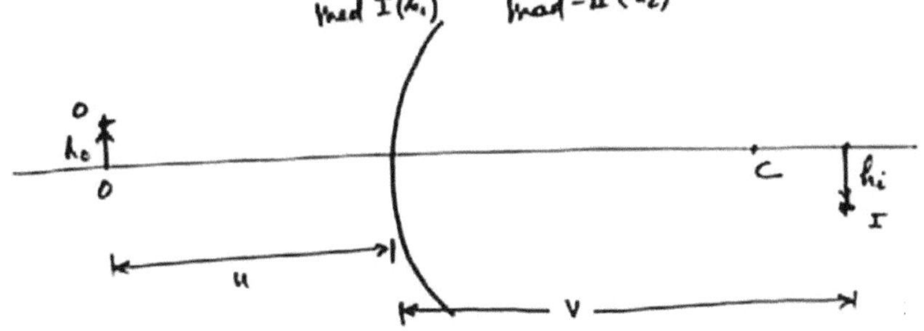
med I (μ_1)
med-II (μ_2)
O
h_o
O
C
h_i
I
u
v

$h_o \rightarrow$ object height above OA.

using Ref formula. $\left.\dfrac{\mu_2}{v} - \dfrac{\mu_1}{u} = \dfrac{\mu_2-\mu_1}{R}\right] \Rightarrow v = ----$

Magnification $\boxed{m = \left|\dfrac{\mu_1 v}{\mu_2 u}\right|} = \left(\dfrac{\text{height of image abv OA}}{\text{height of object abv OA}}\right)$

$\{h_i = m \times h_o\}$

Web Reference at www.physicsgalaxy.com | Scan for Video Explanation

Module-18 Longitudinal Magnification for Refraction at Spherical Surfaces

Longitudinal Magnification for Refraction at Spherical Surfaces:

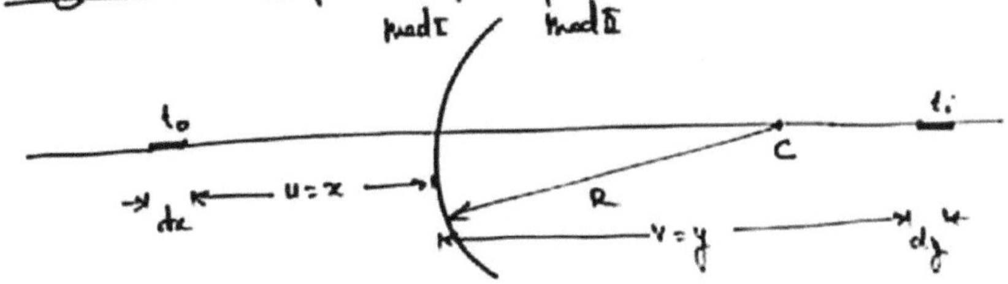
med I
med II
l_o
l_i
C
dx
$u = x$
R
$v = y$
dy

by refr. formula we use

$$\frac{\mu_2}{y} - \frac{\mu_1}{x} = \frac{\mu_2-\mu_1}{R}$$

differentiating, we get

$$-\frac{\mu_2}{y^2}dy + \frac{\mu_1}{x^2}dx = 0$$

width of I along OA $= m_L \times$ width of O along OA. $\leftarrow \boxed{m_L = \dfrac{dy}{dx} = \dfrac{\mu_1 y^2}{\mu_2 x^2} = \dfrac{\mu_1 v^2}{\mu_2 u^2}} = \dfrac{l_i}{l_o}$

Web Reference at www.physicsgalaxy.com | Scan for Video Explanation

Module-19 Velocity Magnification for Refraction

Velocity magnification for Refraction:

For motion of object $\perp$ to OA we define image vel by normal magnification as -

$$\text{vel of image } \perp \text{ to OA} = \left|\frac{\mu_1 v}{\mu_2 u}\right| \times \text{vel of object } \perp \text{ to OA}$$

For motion of object along OA we define image vel by longitudinal magnification as -

$$\text{vel of image along OA} = \left(\frac{\mu_1 v^2}{\mu_2 u^2}\right) \times \text{vel of object along OA}$$

Module-20 Solved Example-9

Ex : Figure shows a glass sphere of radius <u>10 cm</u>. Along its diameter AB from one side a parallel beam of paraxial rays incident on it. What should be the refractive index of glass so that after refraction all rays will converge at opposite end B.

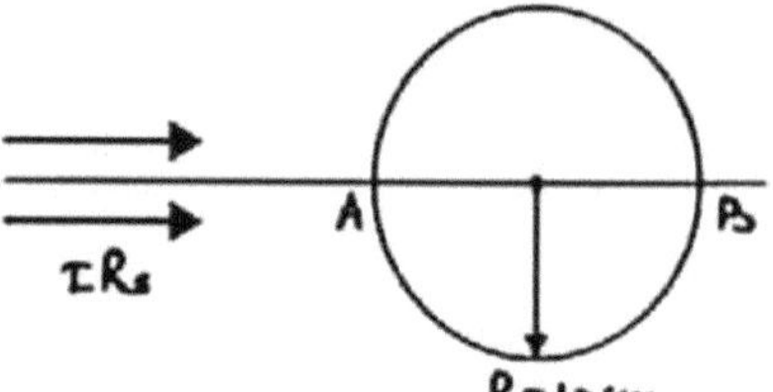

Sol^n: For $\mu\mu$ formula we use

$$u = \infty$$
$$v = 2R = +20\,cm$$
$$R = +10\,cm.$$
$$\mu_1 = 1$$
$$\mu_2 = \mu$$

$$\Rightarrow \quad \frac{\mu_2}{v} - \frac{\mu_1}{u} = \frac{\mu_2 - \mu_1}{R}$$

$$\frac{\mu}{2\emptyset} = \frac{\mu - 1}{1\emptyset}$$

$$\mu = 2\mu - 2$$

$$\Rightarrow \quad \mu = 2 \underline{\text{Ans}}.$$

Module-21 Solved Example-10

Ex : A spherical surface S separates two media 1 and 2 as shown in figure. Find where an object O is placed in medium-I so that the light rays from object after refraction becomes parallel to optic axis of this system.

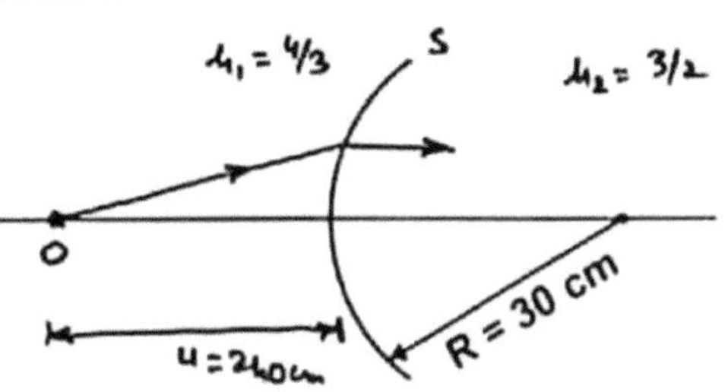

Sol^n: We can use in ref formula.

$$u = ?$$
$$V = \infty$$
$$\mu_1 = 4/3$$
$$\mu_2 = 3/2$$
$$R = +30\,cm.$$

$$\frac{\mu_2}{V} - \frac{\mu_1}{u} = \frac{\mu_2 - \mu_1}{R}$$

$$\frac{3/2}{\infty} - \frac{4/3}{u} = \frac{3/2 - 4/3}{30}$$

$$\frac{4}{3u} = -\frac{1}{180}\; 60$$

$$u = -240\,cm \quad \text{Ans.}$$

Module-22 Solved Example-11

Ex : Figure shows a glass hemisphere placed on a white horizontal sheet. A vertical paraxial light beam of diameter d incident on the curved surface of hemisphere as shown. Find the diameter of the light spot formed on sheet after refraction.

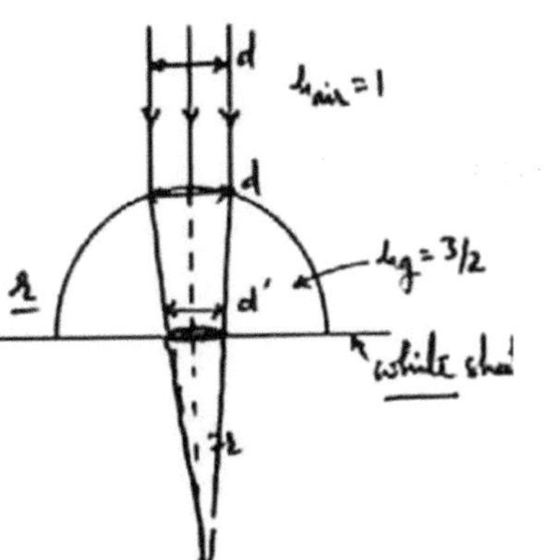

Sol^n: For ref formula we use

$$u = \infty$$
$$\mu_1 = 1$$
$$\mu_2 = 3/2$$
$$R = +r$$

$$\frac{\mu_2}{V} - \frac{\mu_1}{u} = \frac{\mu_2 - \mu_1}{R}$$

$$\frac{3}{2V} = \frac{3/2 - 1}{r} = \frac{1}{2r}$$

$$V = +3r$$

by similarity, we can write

$$\frac{d}{d'} = \frac{3r}{2r}$$

$$d' = \frac{2d}{3} \quad \text{Ans.}$$

Module-23 Solved Example-12

Ex : Figure shows a small object M of length <u>1 mm</u> which lies along a diametrical line of a glass sphere of radius 10 cm and $\mu = \dfrac{3}{2}$ which is viewed by an observer as shown. Find the size of object as seen by the observer.

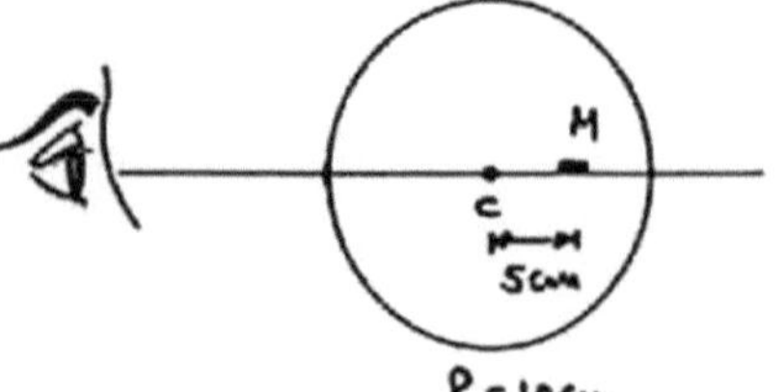

Sol: In ref. form we use

$u = +15\,cm$
$R = +10\,cm$
$\mu_1 = 3/2$
$\mu_2 = 1$

$$\frac{\mu_2}{v} - \frac{\mu_1}{u} = \frac{\mu_2 - \mu_1}{R}$$

$$\frac{1}{v} - \frac{3/2}{15} = \frac{1 - 3/2}{10}$$

$$\frac{1}{v} = \frac{1}{10} - \frac{1}{20} = \frac{1}{20} \Rightarrow v = +20\,cm$$

longitudinal mag.

$$m = \frac{\mu_1 v^2}{\mu_2 u^2} = \frac{3/2 \times (20)^2}{1 \times (15)^2} = \frac{1.5 \times 400}{225} = \frac{8}{3}$$

Image Size $= \dfrac{8}{3} \times 1 = \dfrac{8}{3}\,mm$ Ans.

Module-24 Solved Example-13

Ex : Figure shows a fish bowl of radius 10 cm in which along a diametrical line a fish F is moving at speed 2 mm/sec. Find the speed of fish as observed by an observer outside along same line when fish is at a distance 5 cm from the centre of bowl to right of it.

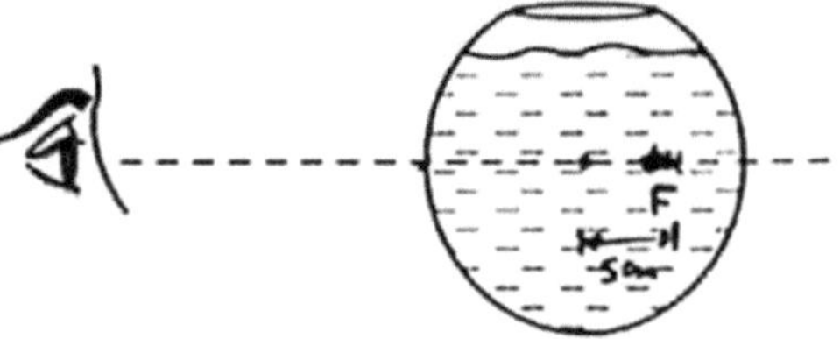

Sol: For refr. formula, we use

$u = +15\,cm$
$\mu_1 = 4/3$
$\mu_2 = 1$
$R = +10\,cm$

$$\frac{\mu_2}{v} - \frac{\mu_1}{u} = \frac{\mu_2 - \mu_1}{R}$$

$$\frac{1}{v} - \frac{4}{3 \times 15} = \frac{1 - 4/3}{10} = -\frac{1}{30}$$

$$\Rightarrow \frac{1}{v} = \frac{4}{45} - \frac{1}{30} = \frac{1}{18} \Rightarrow v = +18\,cm.$$

vel mag. along optic axis $m = \dfrac{\mu_1 v^2}{\mu_2 u^2} = \dfrac{4/3 \times (18)^2}{1 \times (15)^2} = 1.92$

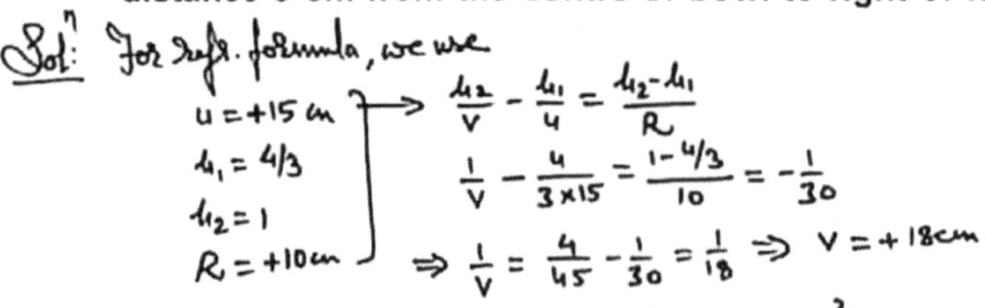

vel of image of fish $= 1.92 \times 2 = 3.84\,mm/s$ Ans.

Module-25 Image Formation by Refraction at Plane Surfaces

Image Formation by Refraction at Plane Surfaces:

for Plane Surfaces, we use $R = \infty$

By Refr. formula we have

$$\frac{\mu_2}{v} - \frac{\mu_1}{u} = 0$$

$$\frac{\mu_2}{v} = \frac{\mu_1}{u}$$

$$\boxed{v = u\left(\frac{\mu_2}{\mu_1}\right)}$$

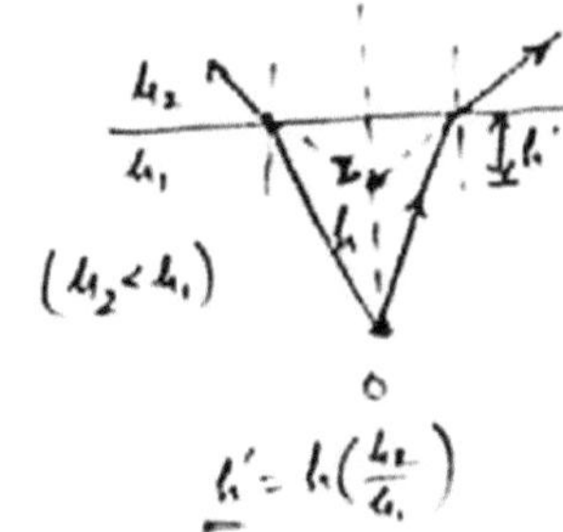

$$(\mu_2 > \mu_1)$$

$$(\mu_2 < \mu_1)$$

$$h' = h\left(\frac{\mu_2}{\mu_1}\right)$$

$$h' = h\left(\frac{\mu_2}{\mu_1}\right)$$

If
$$\left.\begin{array}{l} u \to +ve \Rightarrow v = +ve \\ u \to -ve \Rightarrow v = -ve \end{array}\right\} \Rightarrow$$
by refr at plane surfaces always Image is produce on same side of object.

Scan for Video Explanation

Module-26 Shift of Object due to Refraction at Plane Surfaces

Shift of object due to Refraction at Plane Surface:

Case-I: When O is in denser medium

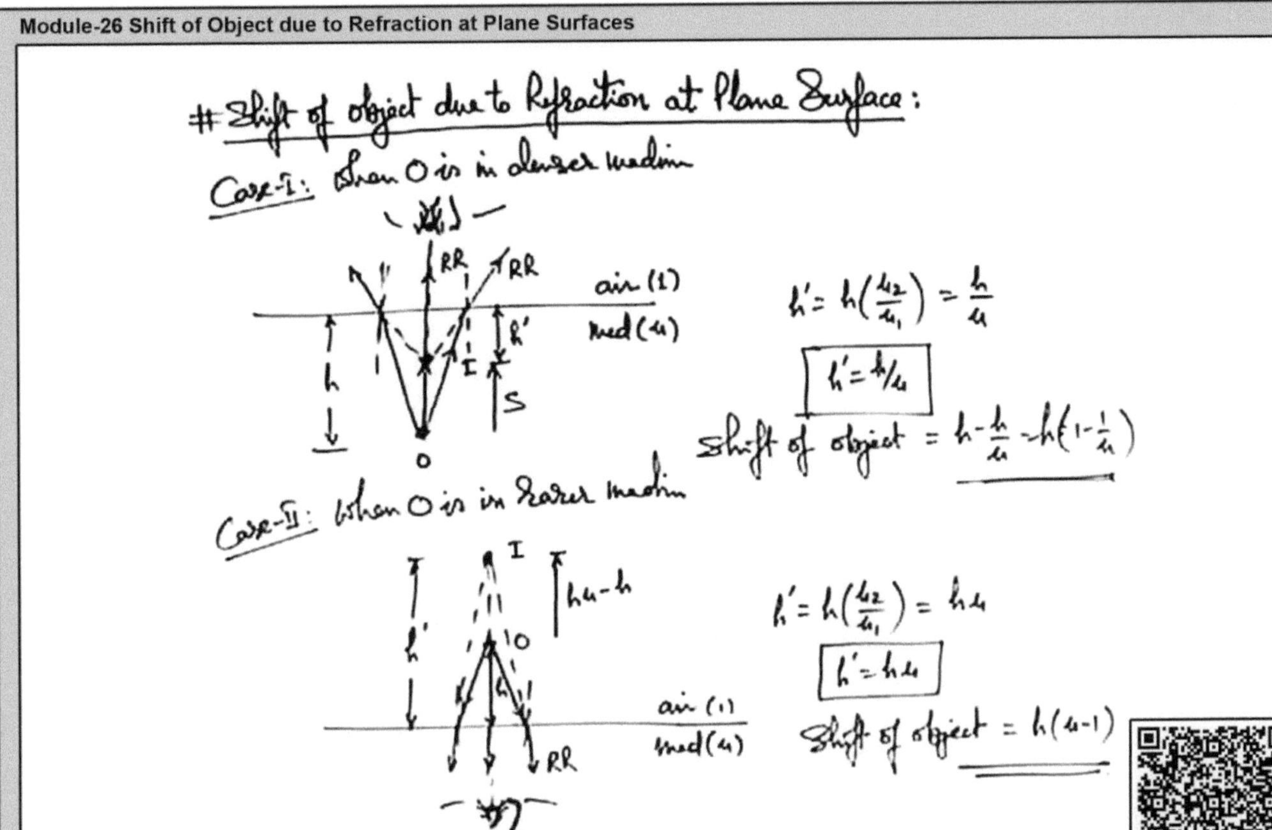

$$h' = h\left(\frac{\mu_2}{\mu_1}\right) = \frac{h}{\mu}$$

$$\boxed{h' = h/\mu}$$

Shift of object $= h - \frac{h}{\mu} = h\left(1 - \frac{1}{\mu}\right)$

Case-II: When O is in rarer medium

$$h' = h\left(\frac{\mu_2}{\mu_1}\right) = h\mu$$

$$\boxed{h' = h\mu}$$

Shift of object $= h(\mu - 1)$

Scan for Video Explanation

Module-27 Shift of Object due to a Parallel Sided Glass Slab

Shift of object due to a parallel sided glass slab:

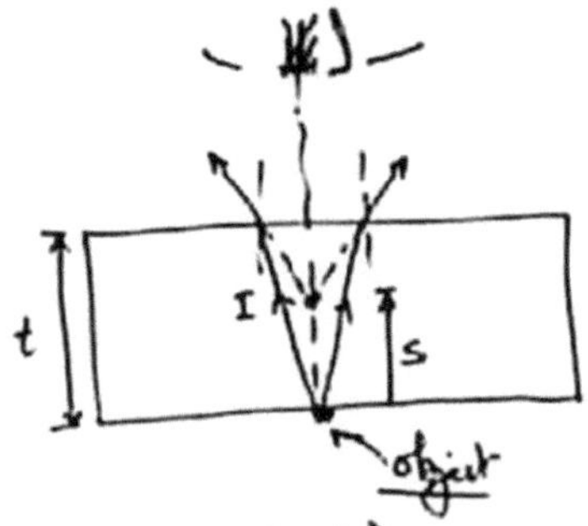

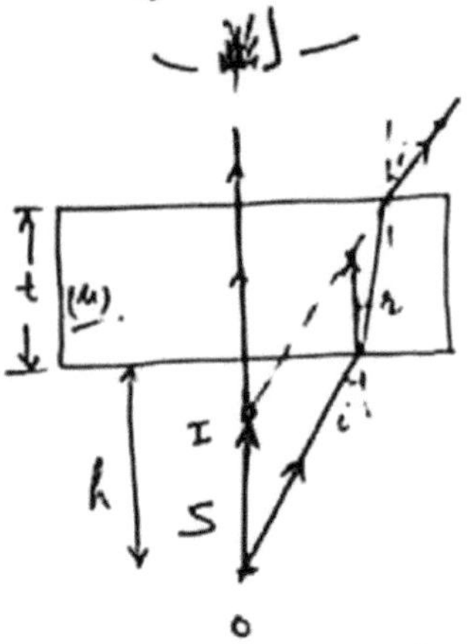

Shift $S = t\left(1 - \frac{1}{\mu}\right)$

NOTE: The shift of object as seen by observer for paraxial rays is independent from the distance of observer from glass slab & it is $\boxed{S = t\left(1 - \frac{1}{\mu}\right)}$

Scan for Video Explanation

Module-28 Shift of Object due to Multiple Slabs

Shift of object due to multiple slabs:

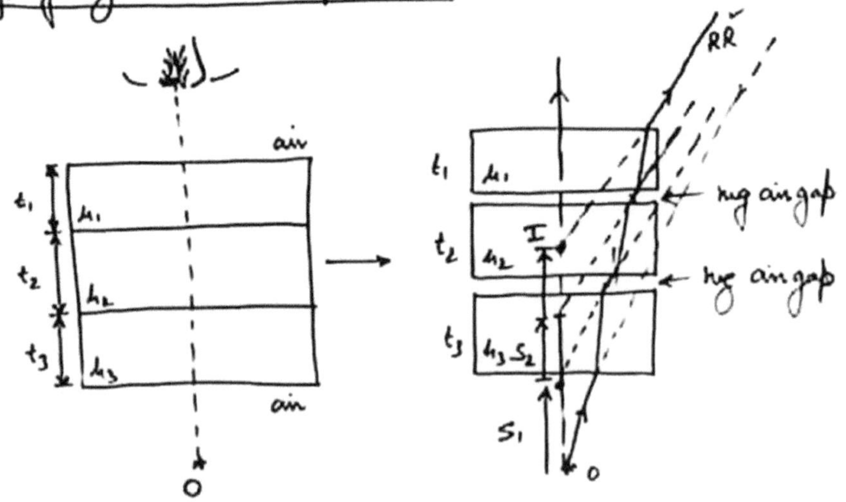

Total shift of object $S = S_1 + S_2 + S_3$

$$S = t_1\left(1 - \frac{1}{\mu_2}\right) + t_2\left(1 - \frac{1}{\mu_2}\right) + t_3\left(1 - \frac{1}{\mu_3}\right)$$

Scan for Video Explanation

Module-29 Solved Example-14

Ex : Find the apparent depth of an object O placed at the bottom of a beaker as shown in which two layers of transparent liquids are filled.

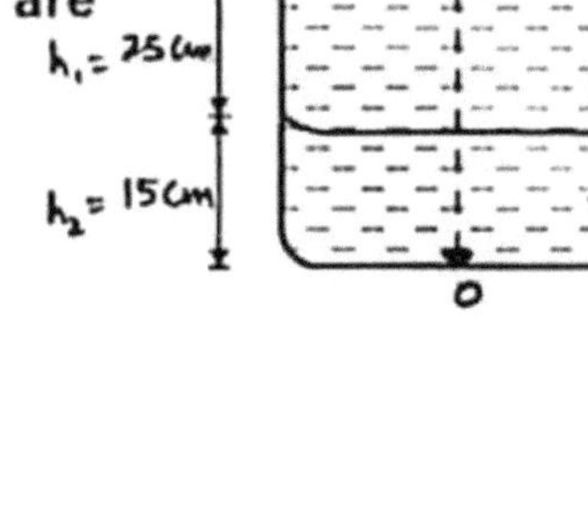

Sol^n : Apparent depth due to Refraction by $\parallel^l$ Sided slabs

$$h_{app} = \frac{h_1}{\mu_1} + \frac{h_2}{\mu_2}$$

$$= \frac{25}{1.5} + \frac{15}{2.5} = 16.67 + 6 = 22.67\,cm \quad \underline{Ans}.$$

Scan for Video Explanation

Module-30 Solved Example-15

Ex : A converging beam of light rays incident on a glass-air interface as shown. Find where these rays will meet after refraction.

Sol^n : for plane Surface we can use Refr. formula as

$$\frac{\mu_1}{u} = \frac{\mu_2}{V}$$

$$\left.\begin{array}{l} \mu_1 = 1 \\ \mu_2 = 3/2 \\ u = +20 \end{array}\right\} \longrightarrow \quad \frac{1}{20} = \frac{3/2}{V}$$

$$\Rightarrow \quad V = +30\,cm. \quad \underline{Ans}.$$

Scan for Video Explanation

Module-31 Solved Example-16

Ex : Figure shows a concave mirror of focal length F with its principal axis vertical. In mirror a transparent liquid of refractive index μ is filled upto height d. Find where on axis of mirror a pin should be placed so that its image will be formed on itself.

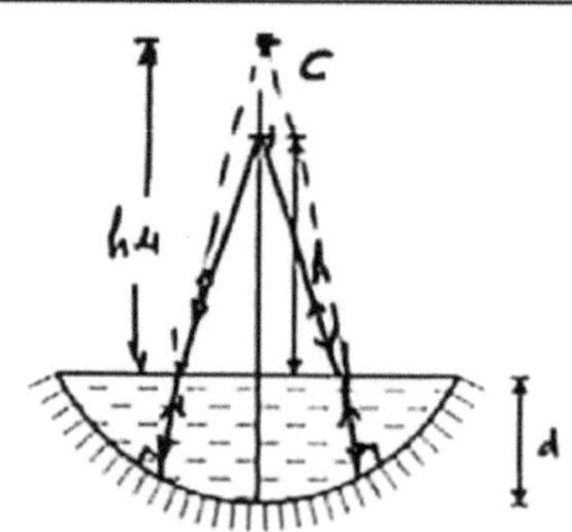

Sol: For image of pin to be produced on itself we use

$$h\mu + d = R$$

$$R = 2F$$

$$\underline{h = \frac{2f - d}{\mu}} \quad \text{Ans.}$$

Module-32 Solved Example-17

Ex : How much water should be filled in a container of height 21 cm so that it will appear half filled when viewed along normal to water surface. (Take $\mu_\omega = 4/3$)

Sol: Contain appear to be half filled when

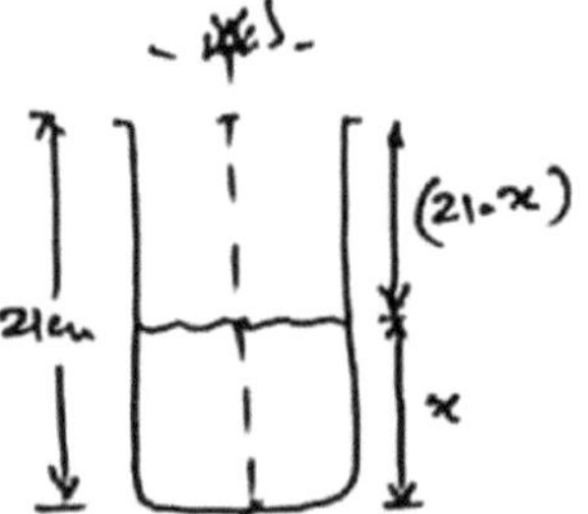

$$\frac{x}{\mu} = 21 - x$$

$$\frac{3x}{4} + x = 21$$

$$\frac{7x}{4} = 21$$

$$x = 12\,cm \quad \text{Ans.}$$

Module-33 Solved Example-18

Ex : Figure shows a glass hemisphere M of $\mu = \dfrac{3}{2}$ and radius 10 cm. A point object O is placed at a distance 20 cm behind the flat face which is viewed by an observer from the curved side. Find location of final image after two refractions as seen by observer.

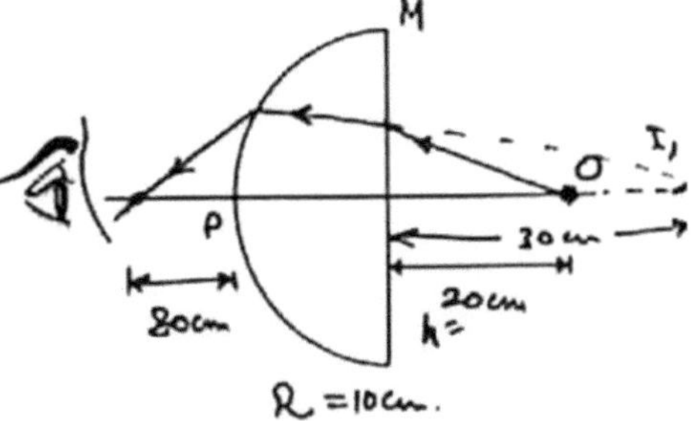

Solⁿ : after I ref image is produced at a distance $= \mu h = \dfrac{3}{2} \times 20 = 30 cm$

for II ref at sph surface we can use

$u = +40 cm$
$R = +10 cm$
$\mu_1 = 3/2$
$\mu_2 = 1$

$\dfrac{\mu_2}{v} - \dfrac{\mu_1}{u} = \dfrac{\mu_2 - \mu_1}{R}$

$\dfrac{1}{v} - \dfrac{3}{2 \times 40} = \dfrac{1 - 3/2}{10}$

$\dfrac{1}{v} = \dfrac{3}{80} - \dfrac{1}{20} = -\dfrac{1}{80}$

$v = -80 cm.$ **Ans.**

Module-34 Introduction to Prism

\# **Prism** : It is a transparent region bounded by some rect surfaces and two identical polygons.

Trihedral Prism.
2 - triangles
3 - rect faces

Pentahedral Prism
2 - Pentagons
5 - rect faces:

Hexahedral Prism

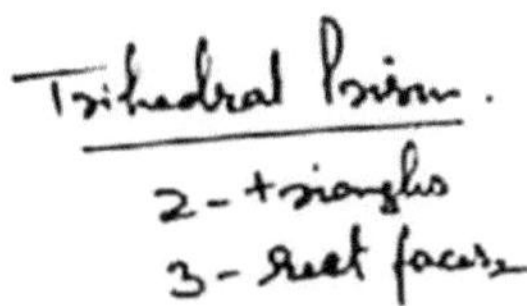

Trihedral Prism

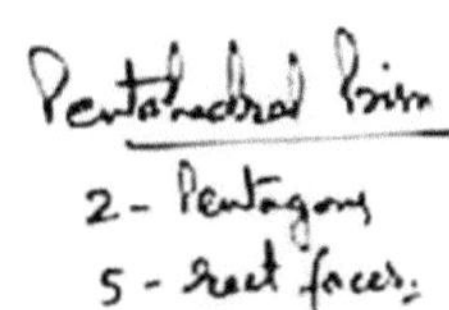

Pentahedral Prism

Octagonal Prism

Module-35 Refraction Through a Trihedral Prism

Refraction Through a trihedral Prism :

A (Prism Angle / Refracting angle of prism)

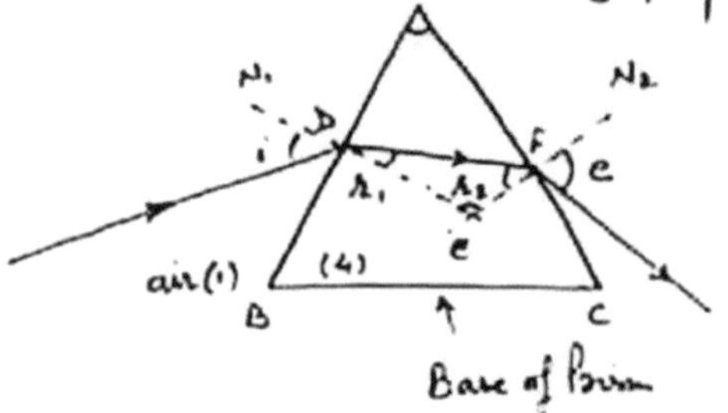

air (1)

Base of Prism

$AB/AC \rightarrow$ refracting surfaces of Prism

By Snell's law at faces AB and AC –

$$\left\{ \begin{array}{l} \sin i = \mu \sin r_1 \\ \sin e = \mu \sin r_2 \end{array} \right\} \quad\text{———}\quad ①$$

In cyclic quad ADEF we use – $\quad A + E = \pi \quad$ ——— (A)

In $\triangle DEF$ we have $r_1 + r_2 + E = \pi \quad$ ——— (iv)

$$\boxed{A = r_1 + r_2} \quad\text{———}\quad ②$$

Module-36 Angle of Deviation of Light Ray Through a Prism

Angle of deviation of light ray through a Prism :

$\sin i = \mu \sin r_1$

$\sin e = \mu \sin r_2$

$(A = r_1 + r_2)$

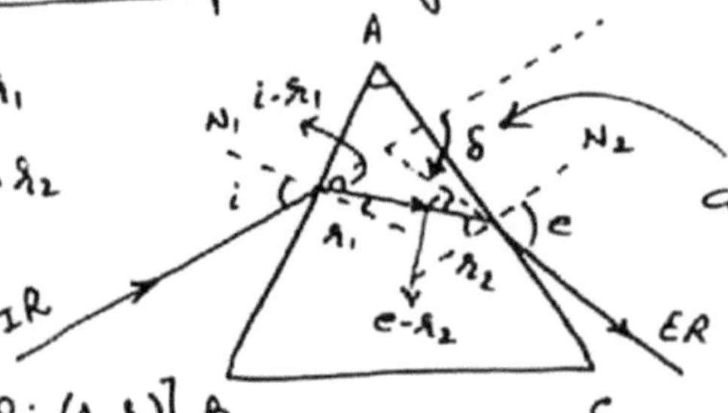

Angle of deviation

$e = \sin^{-1}\left[\mu \sin (A - r_1) \right]$

Angle of deviation $\delta = i - r_1 + e - r_2$

$$\boxed{\delta = i + e - A}$$

$$\delta = i - A + \sin^{-1}\left[\mu \sin \left(A - \sin^{-1}\left(\frac{\sin i}{\mu} \right) \right) \right]$$

$$\underline{\delta = f(i)}$$

Module-36 Angle of Deviation of Light Ray Through a Prism

$\delta = f(i)$

δ will be min when $\frac{d\delta}{di} = 0$

on analysis of this exp we find that $\frac{d\delta}{di} = 0$ when light ray passes through the prism symmetrically $\Rightarrow$ when $i = e$ & $r_1 = r_2 = A/2$

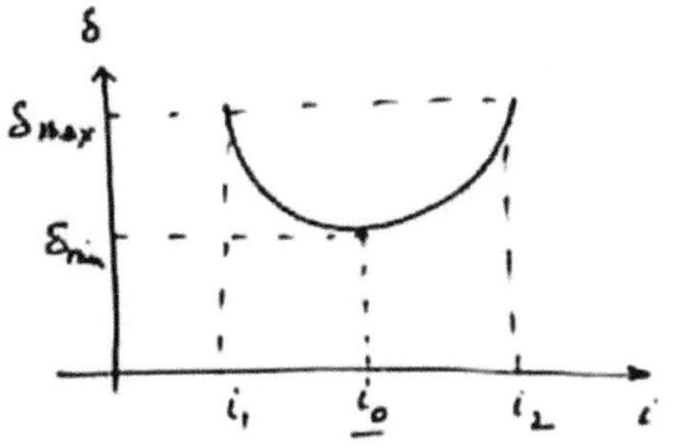
δ
δmax
δmin
i₁
i₀
i₂
i

As $\delta = i + e - A$

$\delta_{min} = 2i_0 - A$

$i_0 = \frac{\delta_m + A}{2}$

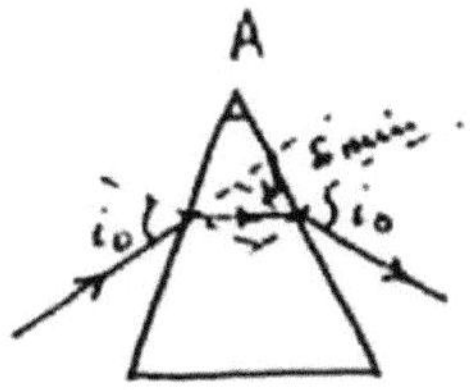
A
δmin
i₀
i₀

by Snell's law

$\sin i = \mu \sin r_1$

$\sin i_0 = \mu \sin A/2$

$$\sin\left(\frac{\delta_m + A}{2}\right) = \mu \sin(A/2)$$

Web Reference at www.physicsgalaxy.com | Scan for Video Explanation

Module-37 Maximum Deviation of Light by a Prism

Maximum deviation of light by a Prism:

There are two conditions under which deviation is max.

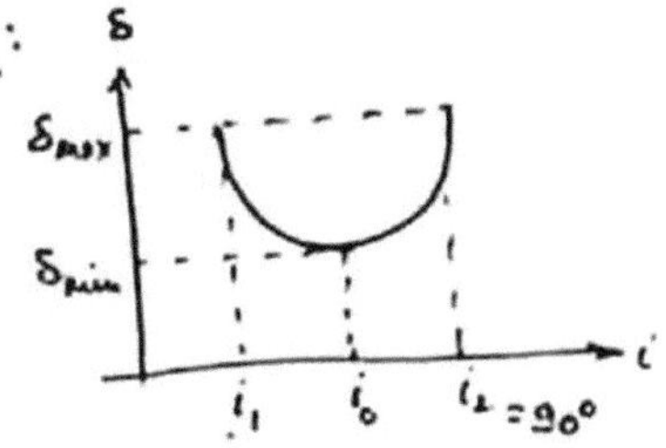
δ
δmax
δmin
i₁
i₀
i₂ = 90°
i

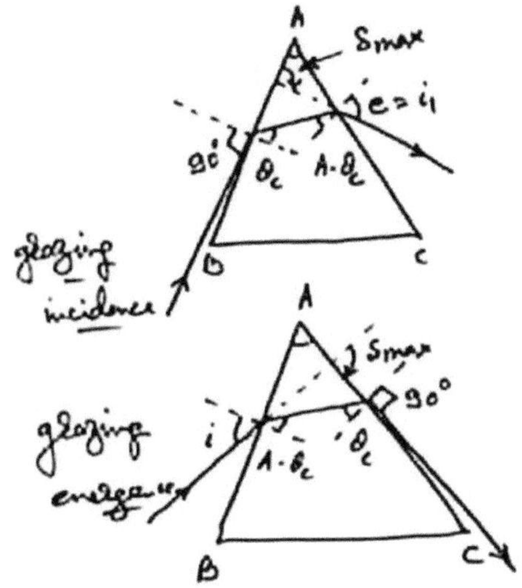
A
δmax
e = i₁
90°
θc
A-θc
B
C
glazing incidence
A
δmax
90°
i
θc
A-θc
glazing emergence
B
C

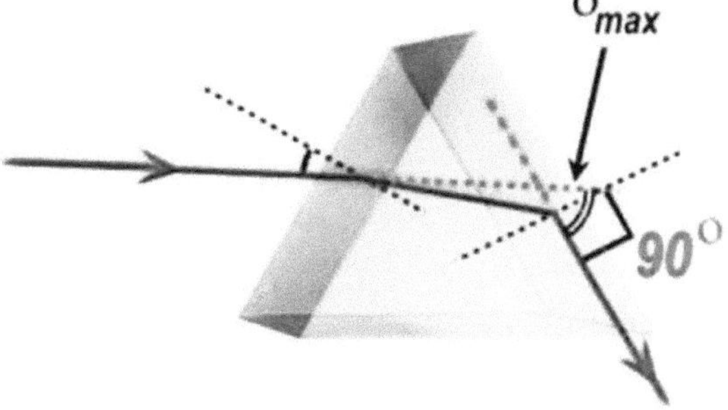
δmax
90°

Web Reference at www.physicsgalaxy.com | Scan for Video Explanation

Module-38 Condition for a Light to Pass Through a Prism

Condition for a light to pass through a Prism :

$$\theta_c = \sin^{-1}\left(\frac{1}{\mu}\right)$$

if $A \cdot \theta_c > \theta_c$

if $\underline{A > 2\theta_c} \Rightarrow r_2 > \theta_c$

& light ray will suffer TIR at the second nat surface of Prism.

NOTE: For any Prism if its Prism angle $A > 2\sin^{-1}\left(\frac{1}{\mu}\right)$, no light ray can pass through two adjoining faces of the Prism.

Module-39 Solved Example-19

Ex :   In figure shown find the angle of incidence of the light ray on face AB of the prism for which light will reach face AC at incidence angle 60°.

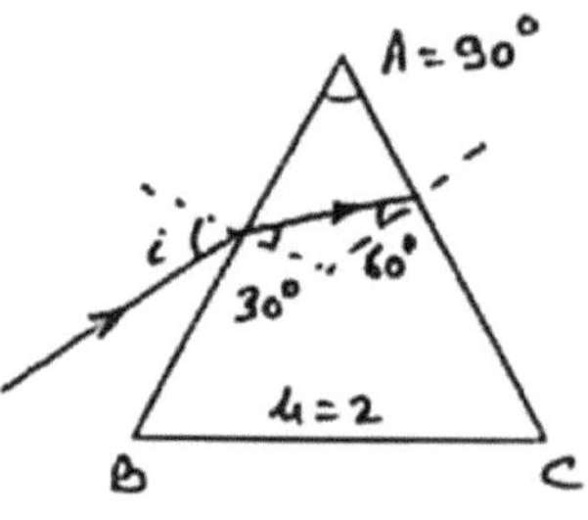

Sol^n: using Snell's law

$$r_1 + r_2 = A$$

$$\sin i = \mu \sin r_1$$

$$\sin i = 2 \times \sin 30° = 2 \times \frac{1}{2} = 1$$

$$\underline{i = 90°} \quad \text{grazing incidence} \quad \underline{Ans}$$

Module-40 Solved Example-20

Ex : On one face of an equilateral prism a light ray strikes normally. If its $\mu = \dfrac{3}{2}$, find the angle between incident ray and the ray that leaves the prism.

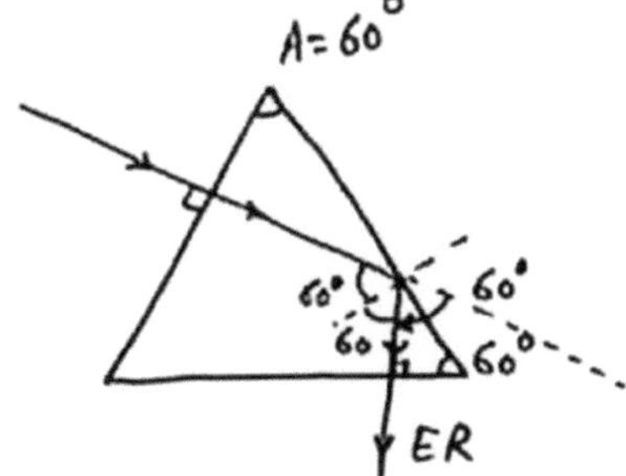

Sol :

for glass $\theta_c = \sin^{-1}\left(\dfrac{1}{\mu}\right)$

$= \sin^{-1}\left(\dfrac{2}{3}\right) \simeq 42°$

Angle between IR & ER

$\delta = 60°$ Ans.

 Scan for Video Explanation

Module-41 Solved Example-21

Ex : A prism has refracting angle 30° and $\mu = 2$. One of the mat surfaces of the prism is polished to make it reflecting. Find the incidence angle of a light ray on other mat surface of prism so that after reflection the ray will retrace the path of incident ray.

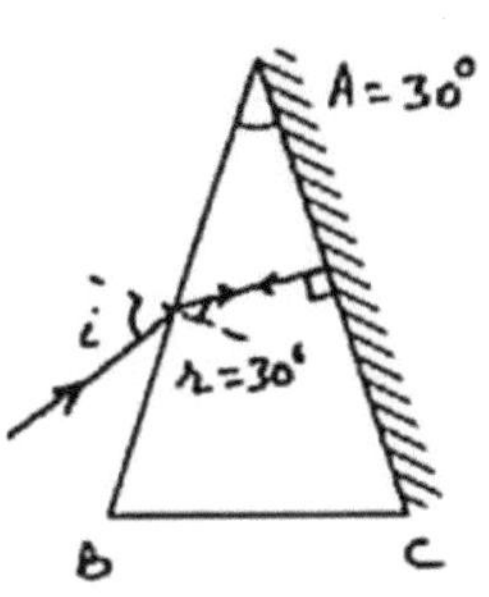

Sol : For retracing the path of light it should incident normally on face AC

By Snell's law

$\sin i = \mu \sin r$

$\sin i = 2 \times \frac{1}{2} = 1$

$i = 90°$ (grazing incidence)

Ans.

 Scan for Video Explanation

Module-42 Solved Example-22

Ex : Find the angle of incidence of a light ray on an equilateral prism of $\mu = \sqrt{2}$ for which light will suffer minimum deviation also find this minimum deviation angle.

Sol:

$\mu = \sqrt{2}$

$A = 60°$

min deviation produced by a prism can be calculated as

$$\sin\left(\frac{A+\delta_m}{2}\right) = \mu \sin(A/2)$$

$$\sin\left(\frac{60°+\delta_m}{2}\right) = \sqrt{2} \cdot \sin 30° = \frac{1}{\sqrt{2}}$$

$$\frac{60+\delta_m}{2} = 45° \Rightarrow \delta_m = 30° \text{ Ans.}$$

At min deviation $i = e$

& $\delta_m = 2i - A$

$$\Rightarrow i = \frac{\delta_m + A}{2} = \frac{30+60}{2} = 45° \text{ Ans.}$$

Module-43 Solved Example-23

Ex : An equilateral prism deviates a ray through 40° for two incidence angle which differ by 20°. Find the two incidence angles.

Sol: Deviation Angle

$\delta = i + e - A$

$i + e = \delta + A = 100°$ —(1)

$i - e = 20°$ —(2)

$2i = 120°$

$\left.\begin{array}{l} i = 60° \\ e = 40° \end{array}\right\}$ two possible incidence angles for which $\delta = 40°$

Ans.

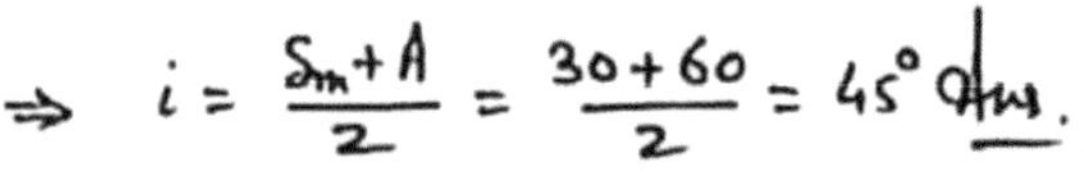

Module-44 Solved Example-24

Ex : Figure shows a small angled prism of prism angle 4° and $\mu = \dfrac{3}{2}$. A light ray almost normally incident on the prism is refracted and falls on a vertical mirror as shown. Find the total deviation of the ray after reflection from the mirror.

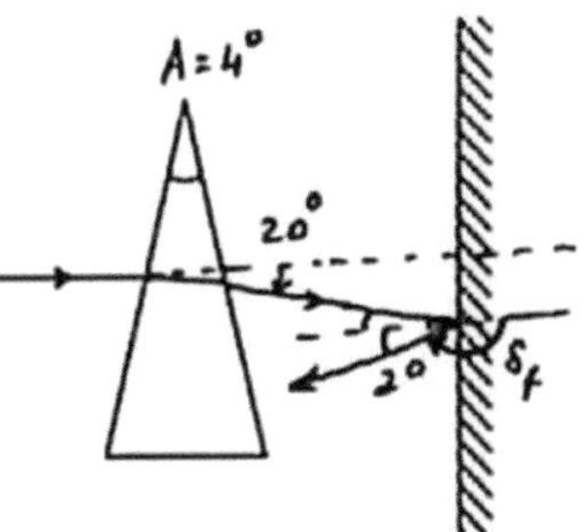

Sol^n: deviation angle $\delta = A(\mu - 1) = 4\left(\frac{3}{2} - 1\right) = 2°$

Total deviation of ray after reflection is

$$\delta_f = 180° - 2° = 178° \text{ clockwise}$$

Ans.

Scan for Video Explanation

Chapter 3

Geometrical Optics III - Thin Lenses

Lecture Notes Modules

\# Thin lenses: These are thin transparent regions bounded by two spherical surfaces. There are two types of lenses-

① Intersecting surface lenses [Convexo Lenses]

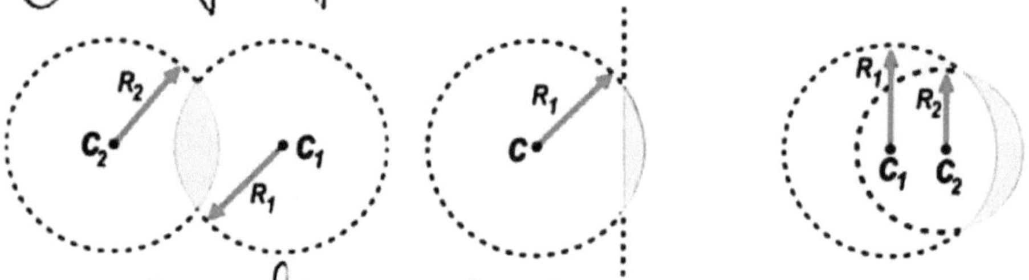

Biconvex lens.

Plano Convex.
$R_1 \smile$
$R_2 \to \infty$

Concavo Convex lens.

if $R_1 = R_2$ then it is termed as equiconvex lens.

② Non intersecting Surface lenses [Concave lenses]

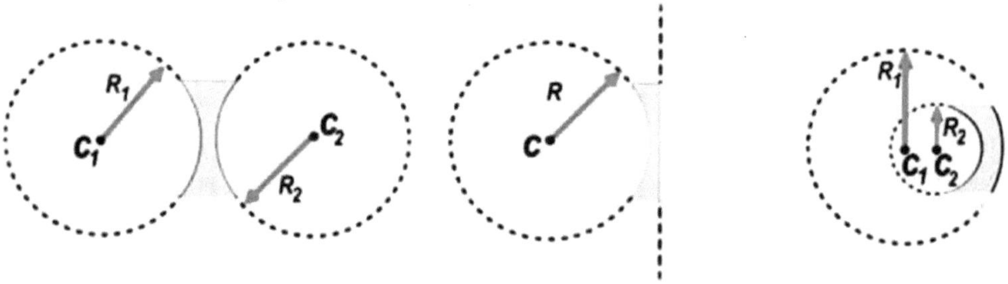

Biconcave lens.

Plano Concave lens.
$R_1 \smile$
$R_2 \to \infty$

Convexo Concave lens.

If $R_1 = R_2$ then it is called equiconcave lens.

Module-2 Converging & Diverging Behaviour of Convex Lenses

\# Converging & Diverging behaviour of Convex lenses:

If $\mu_L > \mu_s$ (Surr medium is rarer) then thin lens (Convex) behave as Converging lens;

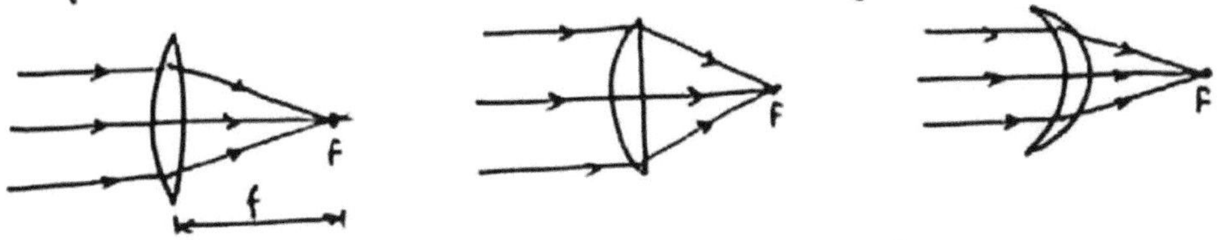

If $\mu_L < \mu_s$ behaviour of lens (Convex) changes to Diverging

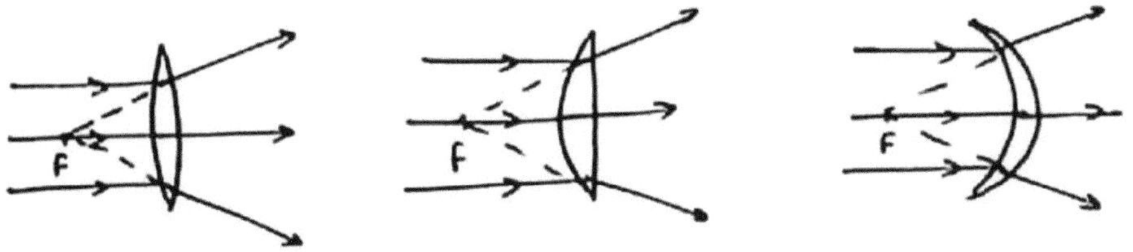

Scan for Video Explanation

Module-3 Converging & Diverging Behaviour of Concave Lenses

\# Converging & Diverging behaviour of Concave lenses:

If $\mu_L > \mu_s$ then lens (Concave) behave as diverging lens

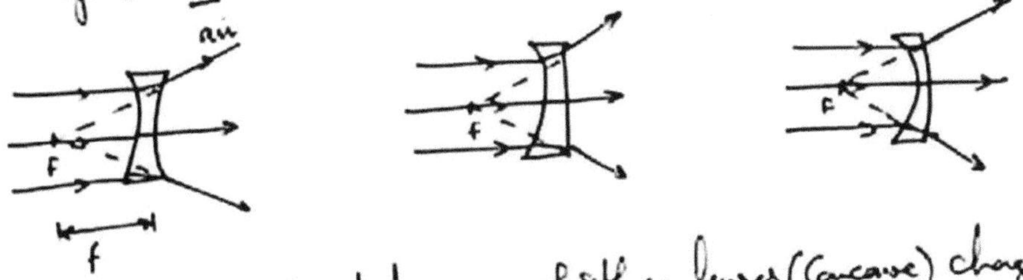

If $\mu_L < \mu_s$ then behaviour of these lenses (Concave) changes to Converging

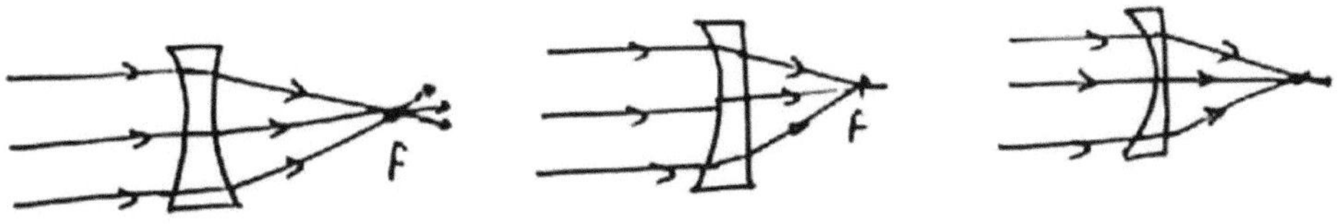

Scan for Video Explanation

Module-4 Focal Length of a Thin Lens

\# <u>Focal length of a thin lens:</u>

For a thin lens, its focal length can be given by Lens maker's formula for paraxial rays.

Lens maker's formula (LMF) –

$$\frac{1}{f} = (\mu - 1)\left[\frac{1}{R_1} - \frac{1}{R_2}\right]$$

here $\qquad \mu \longrightarrow \mu_2 = \frac{\mu_2}{\mu_1}$

$\qquad R_1 R_2 \longrightarrow$ Radii of curvature for the two surfaces.

Note: for a thin lens, focal length is independent of the dir of incident light.

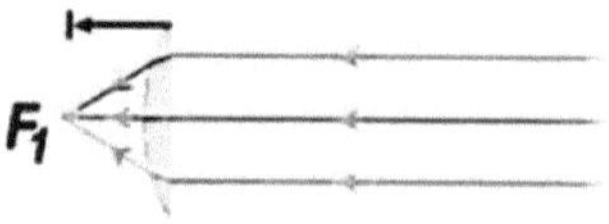

F_1

Plano - convex

Module-5 Magnitude of Focal Length of Different Lenses

\# <u>Magnitude of focal length of different lenses:</u>

<u>LMF</u> $\qquad \frac{1}{f} = (\mu - 1)\left[\frac{1}{R_1} - \frac{1}{R_2}\right]$

– <u>Biconvex</u> / <u>Bicarcave.</u>

$\qquad R_1 \,\&\, R_2 \longrightarrow$ opp sign. $\qquad \boxed{f = \dfrac{R_1 R_2}{(\mu - 1)(R_1 + R_2)}}$ ✓

for <u>Equiconvex</u> / <u>Equiconcave</u>

$\qquad R_1 = R_2 = R \qquad \boxed{f = \dfrac{R}{2(\mu - 1)}}$ ✓

– <u>Planoconvex</u> / <u>Planoconcave lens.</u>

$\qquad R_1 = R \,;\, R_2 \longrightarrow \infty \qquad \boxed{f = \dfrac{R}{(\mu - 1)}}$ ✓

– <u>Concavo Convex</u> / <u>Convexo Concave lens.</u>

$\qquad R_1 \,\&\, R_2 \longrightarrow$ same sign. $\qquad \boxed{f = \dfrac{R_1 R_2}{(\mu - 1)|R_1 - R_2|}}$

Module-6 Solved Example-1

Ex : Two symmetric double convex lenses A and B have same focal length but the radii of curvature differ so that $R_A = 0.9\, R_B$. If refractive index of A is 1.63 find that of B.

Sol^n. focal length of an equiconvex lens is given as

$$f = \frac{R}{2(\mu-1)}$$

for lenses A & B –

$$\frac{R_A}{2(\mu_A-1)} = \frac{R_B}{2(\mu_B-1)}$$

$$\frac{\mu_A-1}{0.9} = \mu_B-1$$

$$\frac{0.63}{0.9} = \mu_B-1 \quad \Rightarrow \quad \mu_B = 1+0.7 = 1.7 \;\text{Ans}.$$

Web Reference at www.physicsgalaxy.com | Scan for Video Explanation

Module-7 Solved Example-2

Ex : A biconvex lens has focal length 50 cm and the radius of curvature of one surface is double that of other. Find the radii of curvature if refractive index of lens material is 2.

Sol^n. For a biconvex lens focal length is

$$f = \frac{R_1 R_2}{(\mu-1)(R_1+R_2)} \qquad R_2 = 2R_1$$

$$f = \frac{2R_1^2}{(\mu-1)(3R_1)} = \frac{2R_1}{3(\mu-1)}$$

$$50 = \frac{2R_1}{3(2-1)} \quad \Rightarrow \quad \left.\begin{array}{l} R_1 = 75\,\text{cm.} \\ R_2 = 150\,\text{cm} \end{array}\right\}\text{Ans}.$$

Web Reference at www.physicsgalaxy.com | Scan for Video Explanation

\# Primary & Secondary focus of a thin lens:

Every thin lens has two focal pts on opp sides of the lens. These are called Pri and Sec focal pts.

Primary focus: If a pt object is located at primary focus of a thin lens, its image will be produced at ∞.

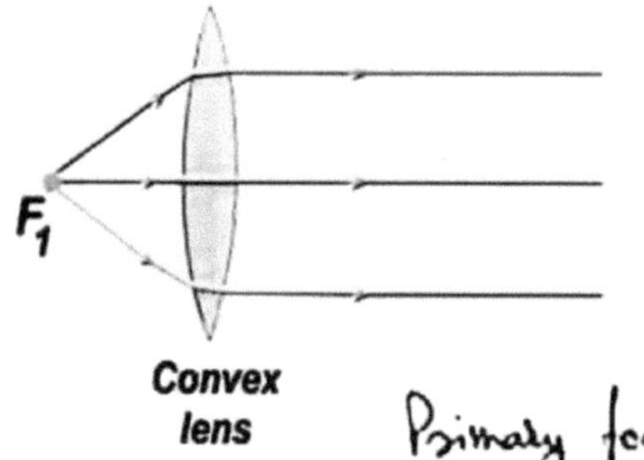

F_1

Convex lens

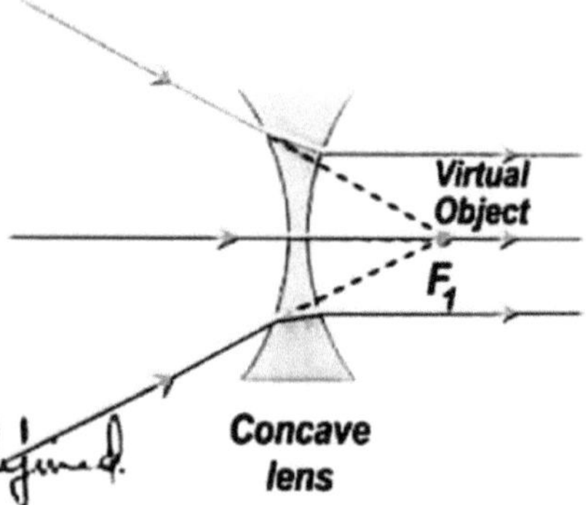

Virtual Object

F_1

Concave lens

Primary focus is defined for Convex & Concave lens.

\# Secondary focus: If an object is at ∞ then after refraction through a thin lens its image is produced at a point termed as Sec. focus of the lens.

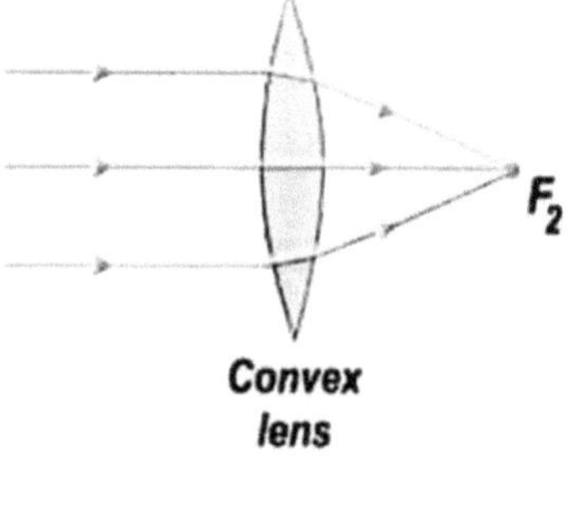

F_2

Convex lens

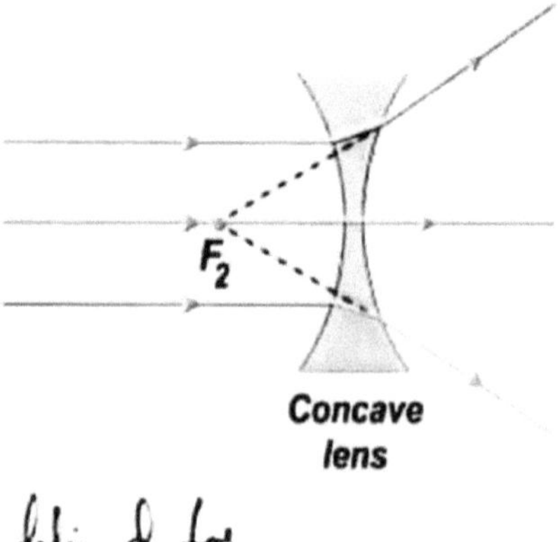

F_2

Concave lens

Sec focus is defined for Convex & Concave lenses

Module-9 Standard Paraxial Incident and Refracted Rays for Thin Lenses

\# Standard paraxial IRs and RRs for thin lenses:

Convex (Conv) lens.

Concave (Div) lenses

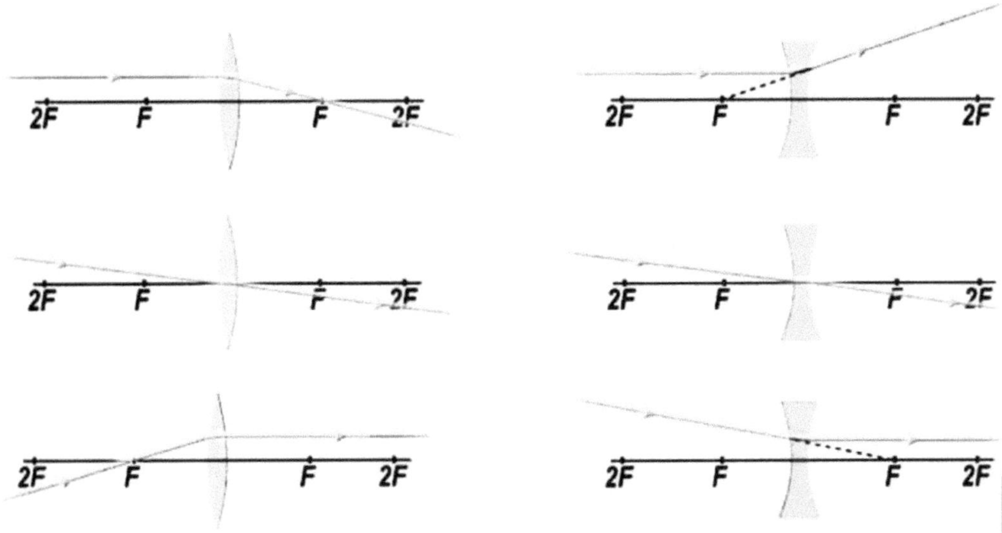

Module-10 Relative Position of Images Formed by a Convex Lens

\# Relative Position of Image formed by a Convex lens:

Case-I: When O is at ∞.

I is formed in f-plane.
Real and diminished.

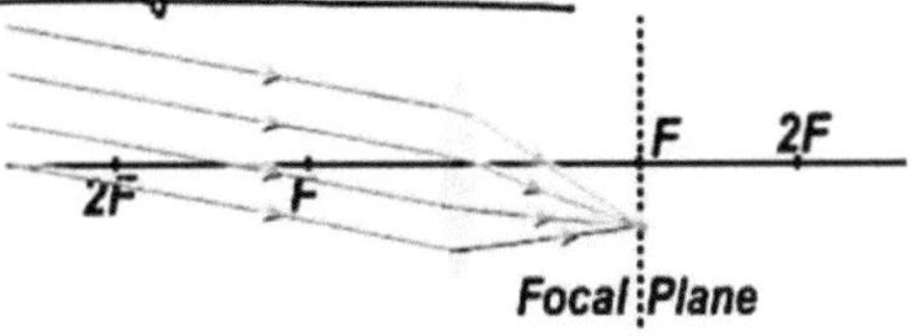

Focal Plane

Case-II: If O is placed beyond 2f point

I is formed betw^n F & 2f
Real, diminished, inverted

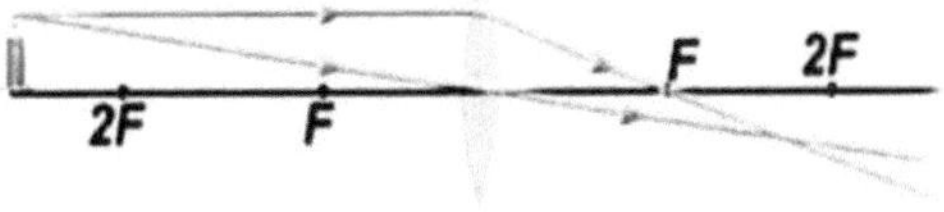

Case-III: If O is placed at 2F.

I is formed at 2f
Real, same size, inverted

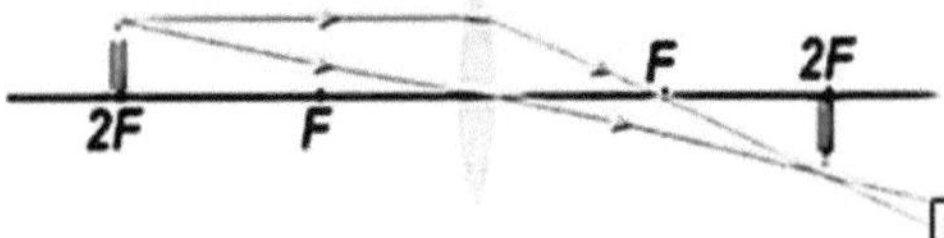

Module-10 Relative Position of Images Formed by a Convex Lens

Case-IV: If O is placed between F & 2F:

I is produced beyond 2F

Real, enlarged, inverted

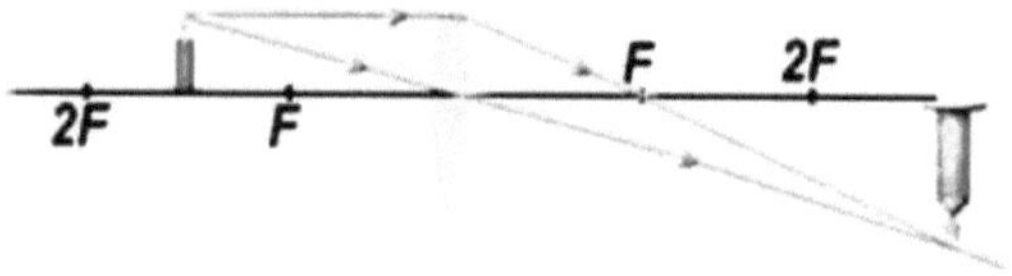

Case-V: If O is placed at F

I is formed at ∞

highly enlarged.

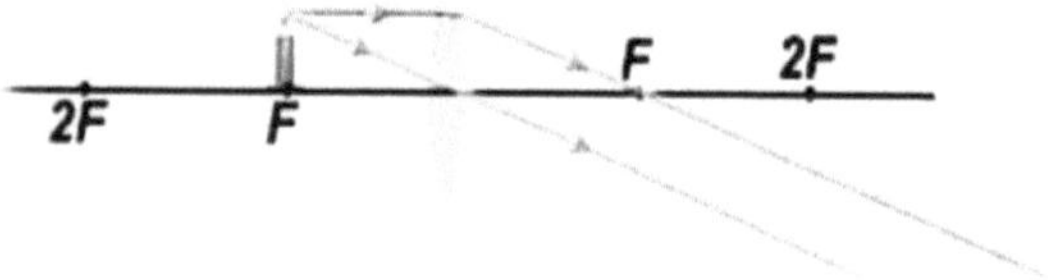

Case-VI: If O is placed between F & P.

I is produced on same side of object

Virtual, enlarged, ~~erected~~ erected.

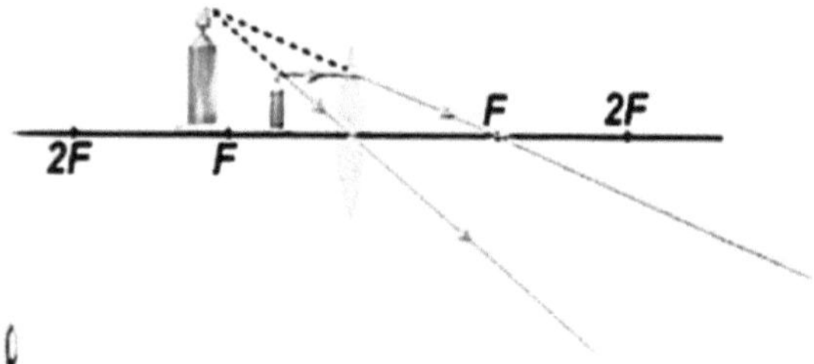

Scan for Video Explanation

Web Reference at www.physicsgalaxy.com

Module-11 Relative Position of Images Formed by a Concave Lens

Relative Position of Images formed by a Concave lens:

Case-I: If O is at ∞

I is formed in f-plane

Virtual, diminished

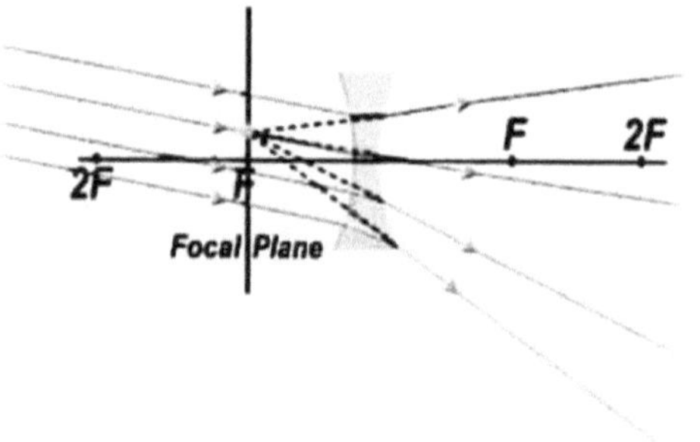

Case-II. If O is placed anywhere on PA of lens.

I is produced between F and O

Virtual, diminished, erected.

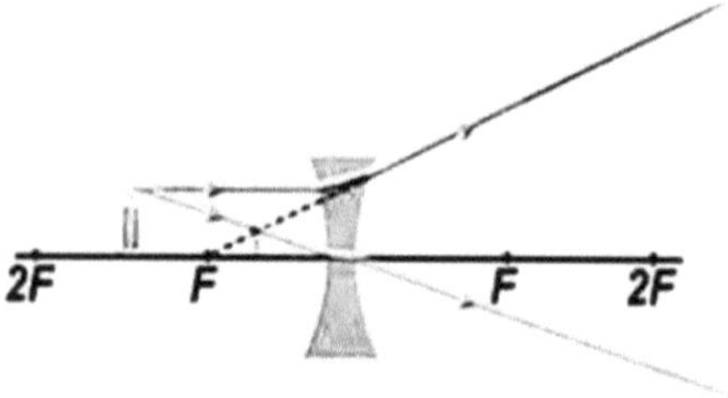

Scan for Video Explanation

Web Reference at www.physicsgalaxy.com

Module-12 Analysis of Image Formed by Thin Lenses

Analysis of Image formation by thin lenses:

For paraxial rays from an object on a thin lens, image parameters can be obtained by lens formula & mag formula.

Lens formula.

$$\frac{1}{v} - \frac{1}{u} = \frac{1}{f}$$

$u \rightarrow$ obj distance from lens
$v \rightarrow$ image distance from lens
$f \rightarrow$ focal length of lens.

Magnification formula.

mag $\quad m = \dfrac{v}{u}$

$$\begin{bmatrix} \text{Image height} \\ \text{abv PA of} \\ \text{lens} \end{bmatrix} = m \times \begin{bmatrix} \text{object} \\ \text{height abv} \\ \text{PA of lens} \end{bmatrix}$$

NOTE: u, v & f are substituted in lens formula with proper signs acc. to the sign Convention used.

Module-13 Longitudinal Magnification by Thin Lenses

Longitudinal magnification by thin lenses:

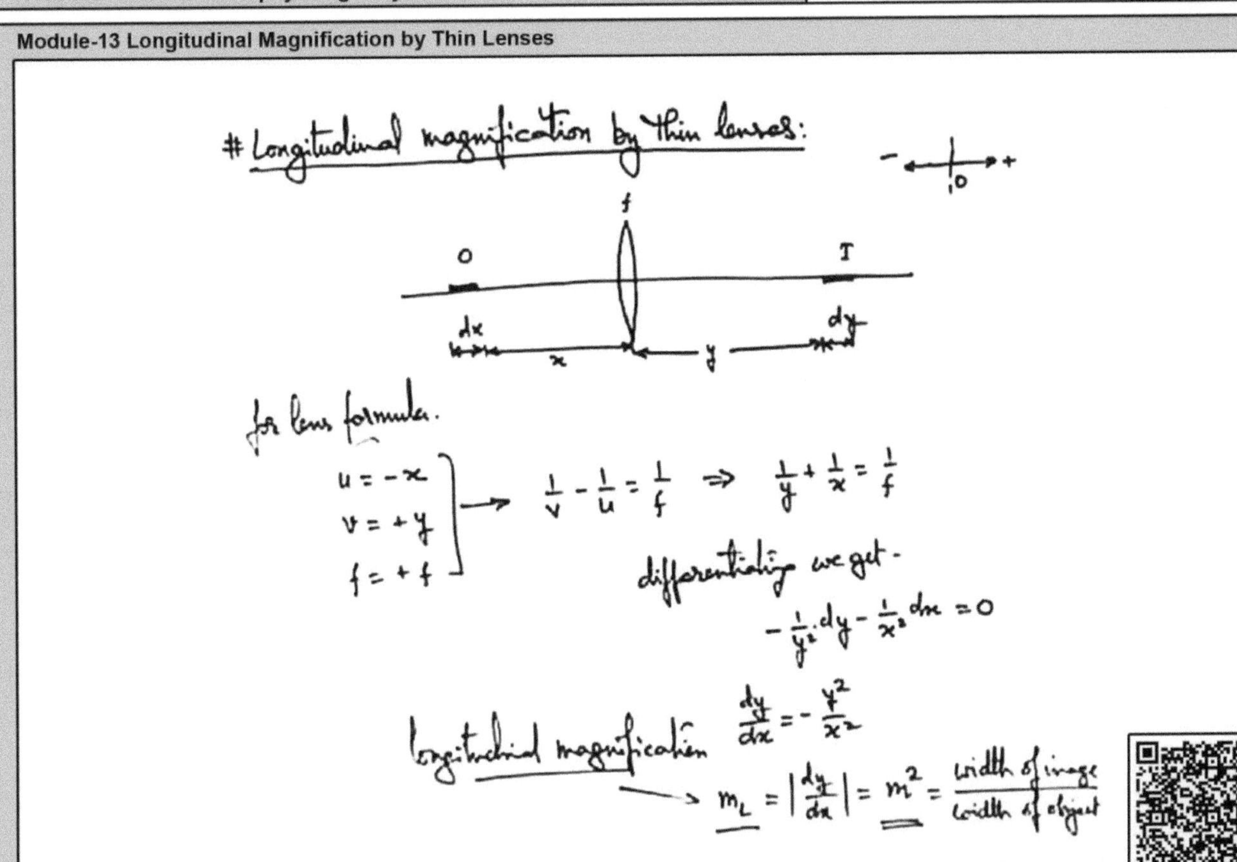

for lens formula.

$$\left. \begin{array}{l} u = -x \\ v = +y \\ f = +f \end{array} \right\} \rightarrow \quad \frac{1}{v} - \frac{1}{u} = \frac{1}{f} \quad \Rightarrow \quad \frac{1}{y} + \frac{1}{x} = \frac{1}{f}$$

differentiating we get -

$$-\frac{1}{y^2} \cdot dy - \frac{1}{x^2} \, dx = 0$$

longitudinal magnification $\dfrac{dy}{dx} = -\dfrac{y^2}{x^2}$

$$\longrightarrow \quad \underline{m_L} = \left| \frac{dy}{dx} \right| = \underline{m^2} = \frac{\text{width of image}}{\text{width of object}}$$

Module-14 Velocity Magnification by Thin Lenses

\# Velocity magnification by thin lenses:

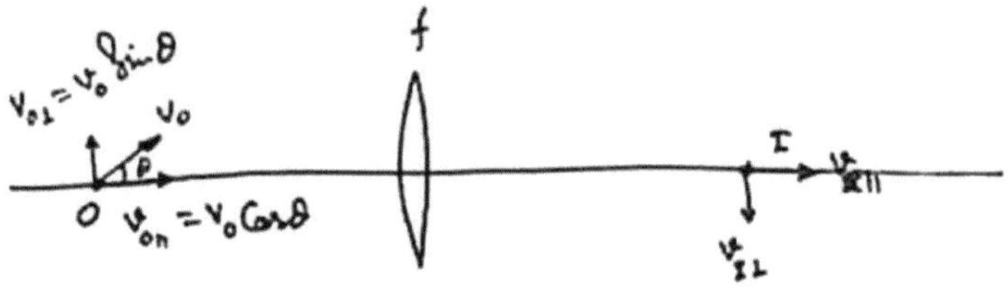

$$V_{o\perp} = V_o \sin\theta$$
$$V_{on} = V_o \cos\theta$$

Vel of Image $\perp$ to PA of lens $V_{I\perp} = m \times V_{o\perp}$ ✓

Vel of Image $\parallel$ to PA of lens $V_{I\parallel} = m^2 \times V_{I\parallel}$ ✓

here $\quad m = \left|\dfrac{v}{u}\right|$

Module-15 Power of an Optical Device

\# Power of an Optical Device: (Thin lenses & Sph. Mirrors)

For a lens or a mirror 'Power' gives an idea abt its capacity to Converge or diverge light rays falling on it.

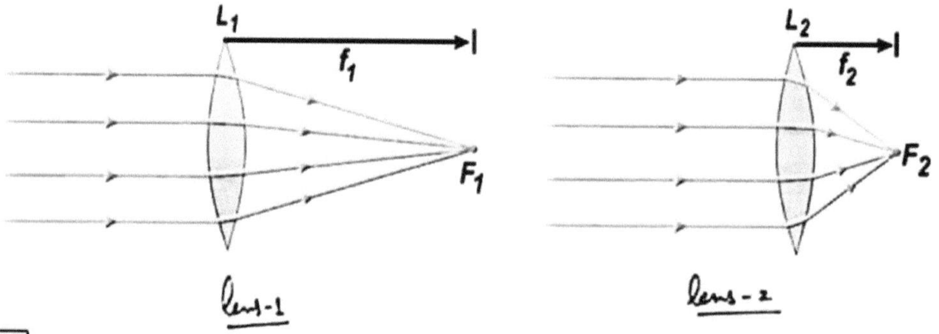

lens 2 is more powerful than lens-1

Module-15 Power of an Optical Device

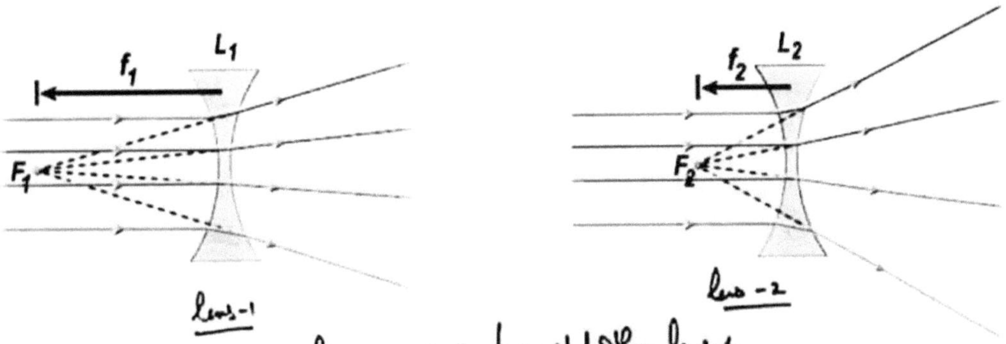

lens-1

lens - 2

lens 2 is more powerful than lens-1.

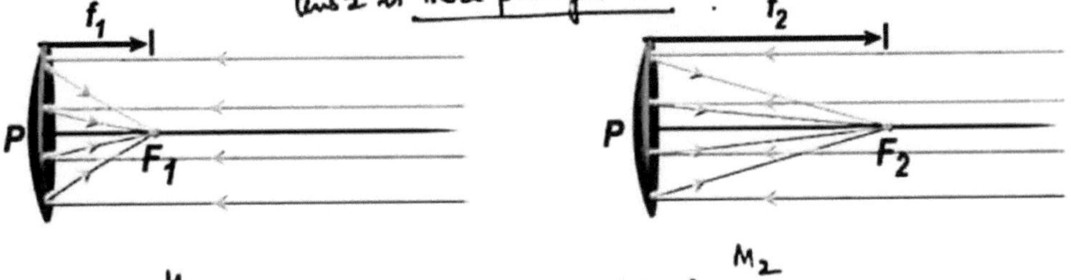

μ_1

M_2

mirror 2 is less powerful than mirror-1.

Power of a lens/mirror $\quad P = \dfrac{1}{f} \quad$ dioptre (D)

$\qquad\qquad\qquad\qquad\qquad\rightarrow$ means in m.

              Scan for Video Explanation

Module-16 Image Formed by a Converging Lens of Distant Objects

\# <u>Image formed by a Converging lens of distant objects:</u>

Lens

F

θ

O

Focal Plane

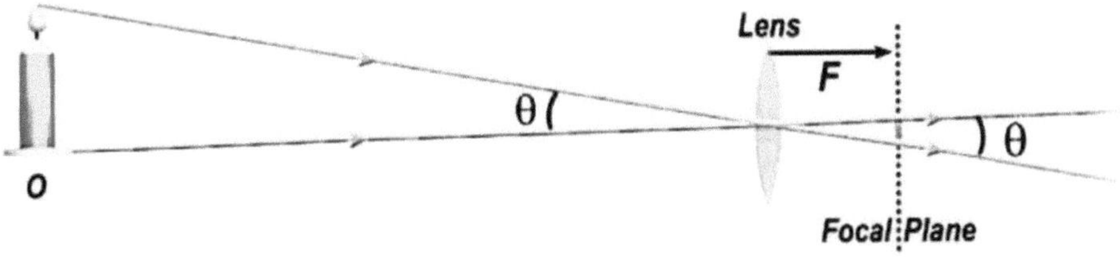

Size of image produced in focal plane is

$$\text{Size} = f\theta$$

              Scan for Video Explanation

Module-17 Solved Example-3

Ex : A convex lens of focal length 20 cm is placed at a distance 5 cm from a glass plate $\left(\mu = \dfrac{3}{2}\right)$ of thickness 3 cm. An object is placed at a distance 30 cm from lens on the other side of glass plate. Locate the image.

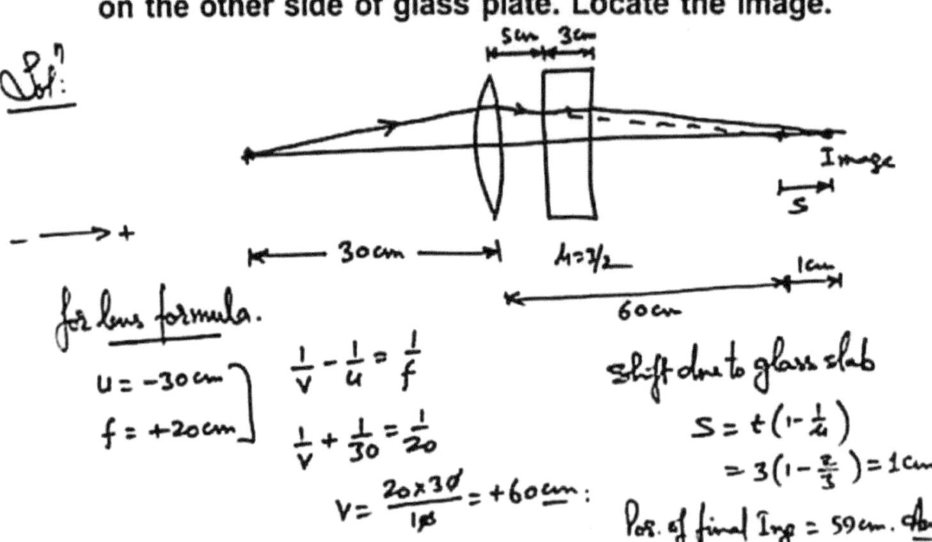

Solⁿ:

for lens formula.

$u = -30\,cm$
$f = +20\,cm$

$\dfrac{1}{v} - \dfrac{1}{u} = \dfrac{1}{f}$

$\dfrac{1}{v} + \dfrac{1}{30} = \dfrac{1}{20}$

$v = \dfrac{20 \times 30}{10} = +60\,cm$

shift due to glass slab

$S = t\left(1 - \dfrac{1}{\mu}\right)$

$= 3\left(1 - \dfrac{2}{3}\right) = 1\,cm.$

Pos. of final Img = 59 cm. Ans.

Module-18 Solved Example-4

Ex : A small pin of size 5 mm is placed along principal axis of a convex lens of focal length 6 cm at a distance 11 cm from the lens. Find the size of image of pin.

Solⁿ: for lens formula

$u = -11\,cm$
$f = +6\,cm$

by lens formula $\dfrac{1}{v} - \dfrac{1}{u} = \dfrac{1}{f}$

$\dfrac{1}{v} + \dfrac{1}{11} = \dfrac{1}{6}$

$\dfrac{1}{v} = \dfrac{1}{6} - \dfrac{1}{11} = \dfrac{5}{66} \Rightarrow v = \dfrac{66}{5}\,cm.$

magnification $m = \dfrac{v}{u} = \dfrac{66}{5 \times 11} = \dfrac{6}{5}$

longitudinal mag $m_L = m^2 = \dfrac{36}{25} \Rightarrow$ Image Size $= \dfrac{36}{25} \times 5\,mm$

$= \dfrac{36}{5}\,mm = 7.2\,mm$ Ans.

Module-19 Solved Example-5

Ex : A convex lens of focal length 20 cm and a concave lens of focal length 10 cm are placed 10 cm apart with their principle axis coinciding. A parallel beam of light of diameter 5 mm is incident on convex lens symmetrically. Prove that emerging beam will also be parallel & find its diameter.

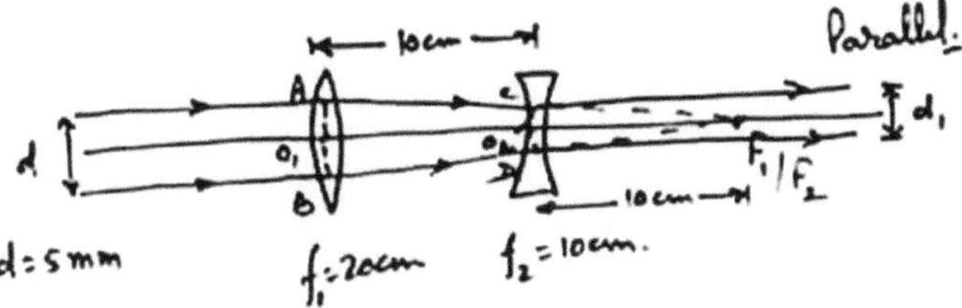

$$\frac{AB}{O_1 F_1} = \frac{CD}{O_2 F_1}$$

$$\frac{d}{20} = \frac{d_1}{10} \Rightarrow d_1 = \frac{d}{2} = 2.5 \text{ mm}. \quad \text{Ans.}$$

Scan for Video Explanation

Module-20 Solved Example-6

Ex : A diverging lens of focal length 20 cm is placed coaxially 5 cm toward left of a converging mirror of focal length 10 cm. Where would an object be placed toward left of the lens so that a real image is formed on object itself.

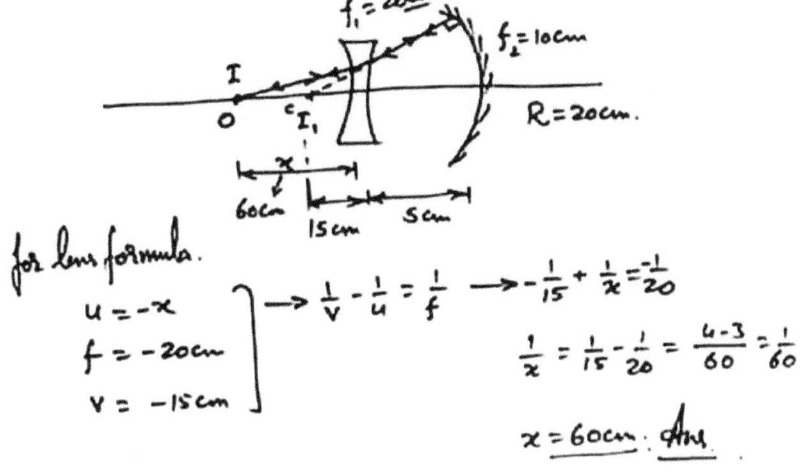

for lens formula.

$$u = -x$$
$$f = -20 \text{ cm}$$
$$v = -15 \text{ cm}$$

$$\frac{1}{v} - \frac{1}{u} = \frac{1}{f} \longrightarrow -\frac{1}{15} + \frac{1}{x} = \frac{-1}{20}$$

$$\frac{1}{x} = \frac{1}{15} - \frac{1}{20} = \frac{4-3}{60} = \frac{1}{60}$$

$$x = 60 \text{ cm}. \quad \text{Ans}$$

Scan for Video Explanation

Ex : A 5.0 diopter lens forms a virtual image which is <u>4</u> times the object placed perpendicularly on the principal axis of lens, find the distance of object from lens.

Sol:

$$P = 5D$$

$$\Rightarrow \text{focal length of lens} \quad f = \frac{1}{P} = \frac{1}{5} = 0.2\,m = 20\,cm.$$

given that $\quad v = 4u$.

As image is virtual $\Rightarrow$ $|u| < |f|$

here if we consider $\underline{u = -x} \Rightarrow v = -4x$

by lens formula - $\quad \dfrac{1}{v} - \dfrac{1}{u} = \dfrac{1}{f}$

$$-\frac{1}{4x} + \frac{1}{x} = \frac{1}{20} \quad\Rightarrow\quad \frac{3}{4x} = \frac{1}{20} \quad\Rightarrow\quad x = 15\,cm. \text{ Ans.}$$

\# <u>Combination of thin lenses and mirrors:</u>

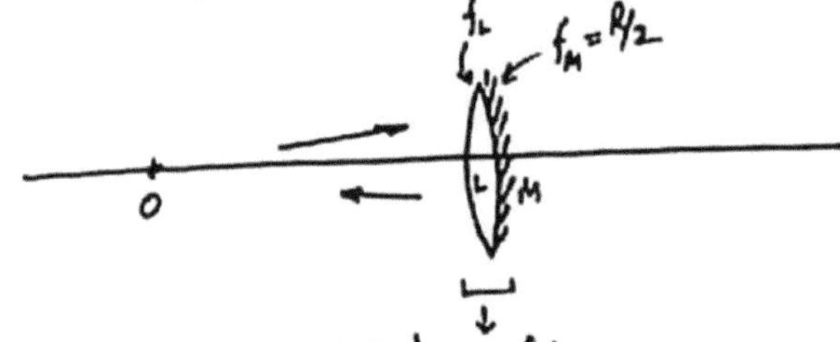

it behave like an eq. mirror,

When 2 or more thin lenses are kept in contact with a spherical mirror then overall power of such combinations is given by Sum of all individual power of independent lenses and mirrors with lenses to be used twice..

$$\underline{P_{eq} = P_L + P_M + P_L}$$

Commercial Sign Conv $\rightsquigarrow$ +ve powers $\rightarrow$ for Conv devices
$\qquad\qquad\qquad\qquad\quad$ −ve powers $\rightarrow$ for div devices.

Module-22 Combination of Thin Lenses and Mirrors

$$P_{eq} = P_L + P_M + P_L$$

$$\frac{1}{f_{eq}} = \frac{1}{f_L} + \frac{1}{f_M} + \frac{1}{f_L}$$

$$f_L, f_M \longrightarrow +ve \implies f_{eq} \longrightarrow +ve \ [\text{Conv device}]$$

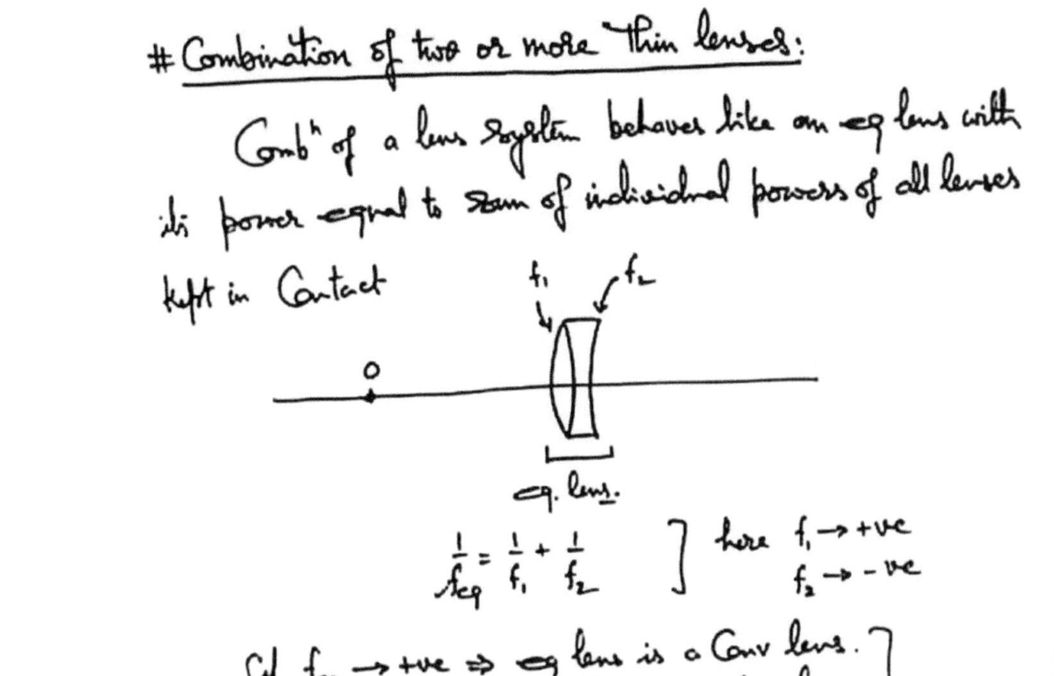

Scan for Video Explanation

Module-23 Combination of Two or More Thin Lenses

Combination of two or more Thin lenses:

Comb^n of a lens system behaves like an eq lens with its power equal to sum of individual powers of all lenses kept in Contact

$$\frac{1}{f_{eq}} = \frac{1}{f_1} + \frac{1}{f_2} \qquad \left] \begin{array}{l} \text{here } f_1 \longrightarrow +ve \\ f_2 \longrightarrow -ve \end{array} \right.$$

$$\left[\begin{array}{l} \text{if } f_{eq} \longrightarrow +ve \implies \text{eq lens is a Conv lens.} \\ f_{eq} \longrightarrow -ve \implies \text{eq lens is a div lens.} \end{array} \right]$$

Scan for Video Explanation

Module-24 Image Formation on a Screen by a Convex Lens

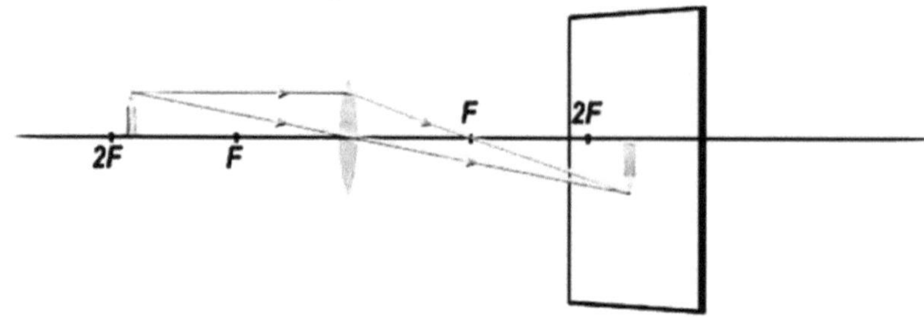

\# Image formation on a Screen by a Convex lens:

On a screen only real images can be obtained.

To obtain a sharp image on screen, it must be placed exactly at the location where image is formed.

Module-25 Solved Example-8

Ex : A point object is placed at a distance of 15 cm from a convex lens. The image is formed on the other side of lens at a distance 30 cm from lens. When a concave lens is placed in contact with convex lens, image is shifted away further by 30 cm. Calculate focal lengths of the two lenses.

Sol. for Convex lens.

$$u = -15\,cm,\quad v = +30\,cm \quad\to\quad \frac{1}{v} - \frac{1}{u} = \frac{1}{f_1} \Rightarrow \frac{1}{f_1} = \frac{1}{30} + \frac{1}{15} = \frac{3}{30}$$

$$\Rightarrow f_1 = 10\,cm \text{ Ans.}$$

for Comb^n of lenses.

$$u = -15\,cm,\quad v = +60\,cm \quad\to\quad \frac{1}{v} - \frac{1}{u} = \frac{1}{f_{eq}} \Rightarrow \frac{1}{f_{eq}} = \frac{1}{60} + \frac{1}{15} = \frac{5}{60} = \frac{1}{12}$$

$$f_{eq} = 12\,cm$$

for Combination of the two lenses in Contact

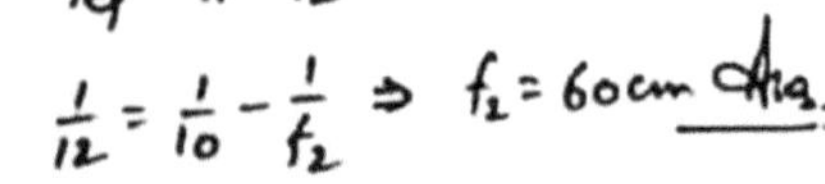

$$f_1 = +10\,cm \qquad f_2 = -ve. \quad\Rightarrow\quad \frac{1}{f_{eq}} = \frac{1}{f_1} - \frac{1}{f_2}$$

$$\frac{1}{12} = \frac{1}{10} - \frac{1}{f_2} \quad\Rightarrow\quad f_2 = 60\,cm \text{ Ans.}$$

Module-26 Solved Example-9

Ex : Two identical thin converging lenses are kept in contact at a distance 12.5 cm from an object. If image produced is 4 times enlarged what is the optical power of each lens.

Sol^n: If f_{eq} is the focal length of Comb^n $\dfrac{1}{v} - \dfrac{1}{u} = \dfrac{1}{f_{eq}}$

$u = -12.5\,cm$

for real image

$v = +50\,cm$.

$\dfrac{1}{50} + \dfrac{1}{12.5} = \dfrac{1}{f_{eq}}$

$\Rightarrow \dfrac{1}{f_{eq}} = \dfrac{1}{10} \Rightarrow f_{eq} = 10\,cm$.

Eq. Power of lens system $P_{eq} = \dfrac{1}{0.1} = 10\,D$

opt Power of each lens. is $P_{each} = 5\,D$ Ans.

Module-27 Solved Example-10

Ex : Convex surface of a plano convex lens of focal length 30 cm is silvered to make it reflecting. If lens material has refractive index $\dfrac{3}{2}$, find the image location for an object placed 40 cm from the lens on its principal axis.

Sol^n: for a plano Convex lens we use

$f = \dfrac{R}{\mu-1} \Rightarrow R = f(\mu-1)$

$= 30(3/2 - 1) = 15\,cm$.

If f_{eq} is the eq focal length of lens-mirror Com^n

then we use $\dfrac{1}{f_{eq}} = \dfrac{2}{f_L} + \dfrac{1}{f_M} = \dfrac{2}{30} + \dfrac{1}{7.5} = \dfrac{6}{30} = \dfrac{1}{5} \Rightarrow f_{eq} = 5\,cm$.

using mirror formula $V = \dfrac{u\,f_{eq}}{u - f_{eq}} = \dfrac{-40 \times -5}{-35 + 5} = -\dfrac{40}{7}\,cm$. Ans.

$u = -40\,cm$

$f_{eq} = -5\,cm$.

Module-28 Solved Example-11

Ex : A concavo convex lens is placed on a horizontal table with its convex surface polished to make it reflecting as shown. If radii of curvature of its two surfaces are 30 cm and 60 cm respectively find the position on its principal axis where a point object should be placed to obtain its image on itself. $\left(\mu_{lens} = \dfrac{3}{2} \right)$

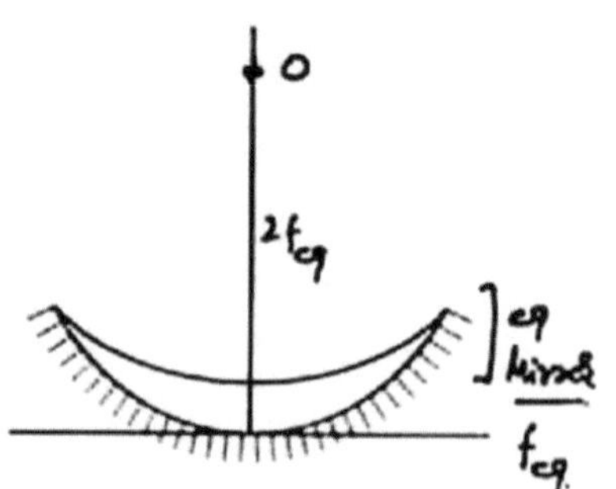

Sol.: focal length of thin lens $f_L = \dfrac{R_1 R_2}{(\mu-1)(R_1 - R_2)} = \dfrac{30 \times 60}{\frac{1}{2} \times 30} = 120 \, cm$

focal length of mirror is $f_M = \dfrac{30}{2} = 15 \, cm$

eq focal length of lens-mirror Comb^n is $\dfrac{1}{f_{eq}} = \dfrac{2}{f_L} + \dfrac{1}{f_M} = \dfrac{2}{120} + \dfrac{1}{15} = \dfrac{1}{12}$

$f_{eq} = 12 \, cm \Rightarrow$ object dist $= 2 f_{eq} = 24 \, cm$ Ans.

Module-29 Condition of Formation of Real Image of Real Object

\# <u>Condition of formation of a Real Image of Real object</u>

by a Convex lens :

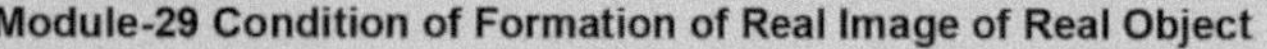

<u>NOTE:</u> If for an object using a Convex lens we produce an image on screen then for this always the sep betw^n O & Sc must be greater than or equal to $4 f_L$.

Module-30 Displacement Method to Obtain Focal Length of a Convex Lens

Displacement method to obtain focal length of a Convex lens:

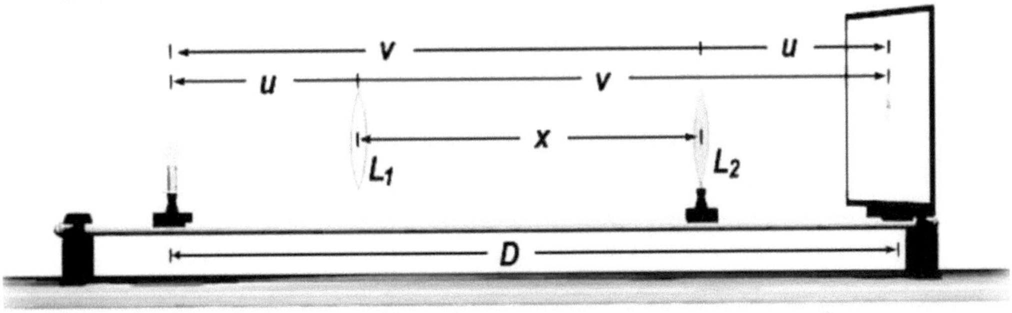

Sep between O & Sc is

$$D = u + v$$

$$m_1 = \frac{v}{u} \quad ; \quad m_2 = \frac{u}{v}$$

$$\boxed{m_1 m_2 = 1.}$$

Size of I_1 $S_{I_1} = m_1 S_0$

Size of I_2 $S_{I_2} = m_2 S_0$

$\longrightarrow S_0 = \sqrt{S_{I_1} S_{I_2}}$

here disp of lens between its two pos where sharp images are obtained

$$x = v - u$$

focal length of lens $f = \dfrac{uv}{u+v} = \dfrac{(u+v)^2 - (u-v)^2}{4(u+v)}$

$$\boxed{f = \frac{D^2 - x^2}{4D}}$$

$$D > 4f$$

Module-31 Solved Example-12

Ex : A lens placed between a candle and a fixed screen so that an image is produced on screen with magnification 3. When lens is moved away from candle by 80 cm again a sharp image is produced on screen. Determine the focal length of lens.

Sol: As disp method exp we can use $m_1 \cdot m_2 = 1$

Initially $\dfrac{v}{u} = 3$

$$v - u = 80 \text{ cm}.$$

$$2u = 80 \text{ cm} \implies u = 40 \text{ cm}$$

$$v = 120 \text{ cm}.$$

for a lens its focal length is $f = \dfrac{|u| \cdot |v|}{|u| + |v|} = \dfrac{40 \times 120}{160} = 30\ cm$ Ans.

Ex : A lens with a focal length <u>16 cm</u> produces a sharp image on a screen of a real object in two positions of lens which are <u>60 cm</u> apart. Find the distance between object and screen.

Sol.: In disp method exp we use $\qquad f = \dfrac{D^2 - x^2}{4D}$

$x \rightarrow$ disp of lens

$D \rightarrow$ dist betwⁿ O & Sc.

$$D^2 - 4Df - x^2 = 0$$

$$D = \frac{4f \pm \sqrt{16f^2 + 4x^2}}{2}$$

As D is +ve $\Rightarrow$ $D = \dfrac{4 \times 16 + \sqrt{16(16)^2 + 4(60)^2}}{2}$

$$D = 100\,cm = 1\,m \quad \text{Ans.}$$

Chapter 4
Dispersion of Light

Cauchy's Equation for Refractive Index:

For a transparent medium RI for a light depend on its wavelength and the relation is given by an empirical equation called Cauchy's eq^n –

$$\mu(\lambda) = A + \frac{B}{\lambda^2}$$

here A and B are constants which depend on medium characteristics.

for Red & Violet light $\lambda_R > \lambda_V \Rightarrow \mu_R < \mu_V$

<u>NOTE</u>: In a medium violet light travel slower than red light.

Dispersion of Light:

When White light is incident on a transparent medium all colours in WL are Refracted at different angles and light split into different Colours in other medium. This splitting of light into colours is called dispersion of light.

As $\mu_V > \mu_R$, violet colour bend more toward normal Compared to Red Colour.

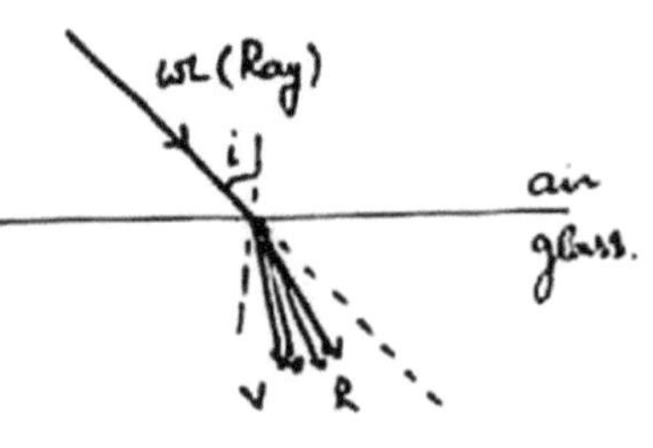

Module-3 Dispersion of White Light by a Prism

Dispersion of White light by a Prism :

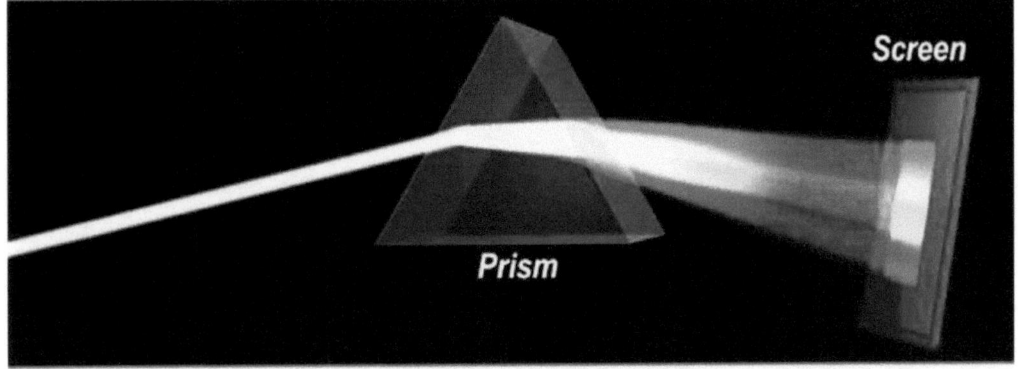

Due to refraction at two Surfaces of prism, with deviation emerging beam of light split into colours and it produces a spectrum of white light on screen as shown.

    Scan for Video Explanation

Module-4 Dispersion of White Light by a Glass Slab

Dispersion of white light by a glass slab:

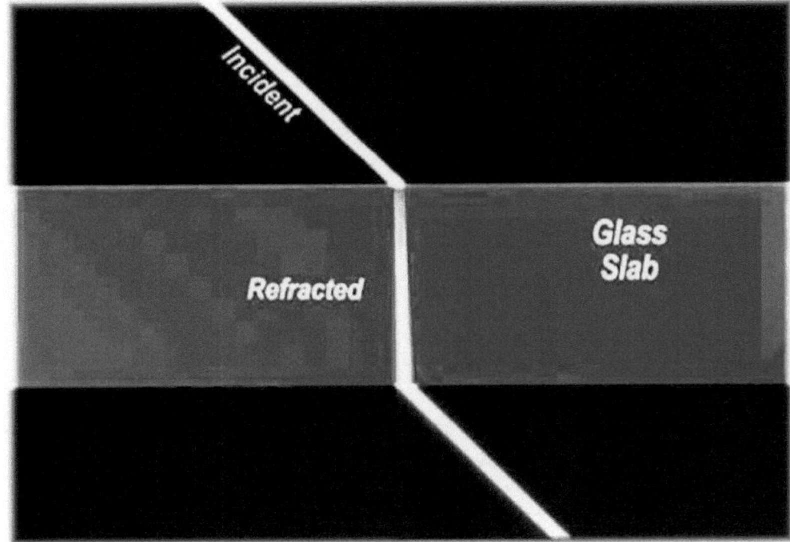

    Scan for Video Explanation

Module-5 Dispersive Power of a Prism Material

Dispersive Power of a Prism material :

DP of a mat is defined as relative deviation of light beam from its mean path as a function of $\underline{R.I}$. It is given as

$$\omega = \frac{d\theta}{\theta}$$

where θ is mean deviation of light & $d\theta$ is the change in deviation due to variation in RI $d\mu$ which is due to wavelength diff $d\lambda$.

for a small angled prism we use deviation $\theta = A(\mu-1)$

$$d\theta = A \cdot d\mu$$

$$d\theta = \left(\frac{\theta}{\mu-1}\right) d\mu$$

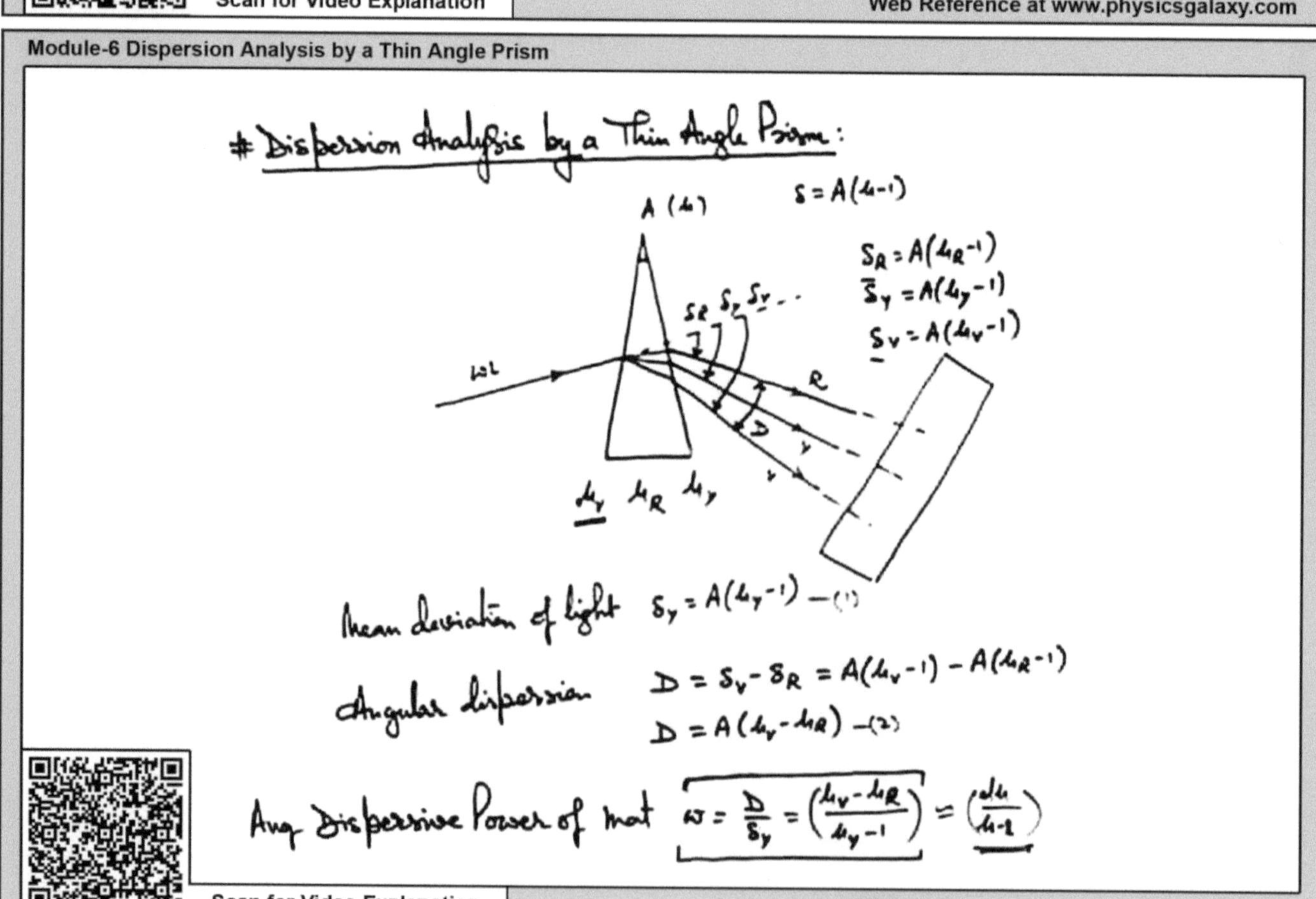

$$\boxed{\omega = \frac{d\theta}{\theta} = \frac{d\mu}{\mu-1}}$$

Module-6 Dispersion Analysis by a Thin Angle Prism

Dispersion Analysis by a Thin Angle Prism :

Mean deviation of light $S_y = A(\mu_y-1)$ —(1)

Angular dispersion $D = S_V - S_R = A(\mu_V-1) - A(\mu_R-1)$

$$D = A(\mu_V - \mu_R) \quad -(2)$$

Avg Dispersive Power of mat $\boxed{\omega = \frac{D}{S_y} = \left(\frac{\mu_V - \mu_R}{\mu_y - 1}\right) = \left(\frac{d\mu}{\mu-1}\right)}$

Module-7 Achromatic Prism Combination

Achromatic Prism Combination :

↓

'Deviation of w.l. without dispersion'

This is a Comb^n of two Prisms in which no dispersion take place

OR.

Dispersion produced by one Prism nullifies that produced by the other Prism.

$$D = D'$$

$$A(\mu_v - \mu_R) = A'(\mu_v' - \mu_R')$$

Condition of deviation without dispersion

Mean deviation of w.l.

$$\delta_m = \delta_y - \delta_y'$$

$$\delta_m = A(\mu_y - 1) - A'(\mu_y' - 1)$$

Scan for Video Explanation

Module-8 Direct Vision Prism Combination

Direct Vision Prism Combination :

↓

Dispersion of w.l. without deviation

This is a Comb^n of Prisms in which dispersion take place without any mean deviation of light

For this to happen.

$$\delta_y = \delta_y'$$

Condition of Dispersion without deviation.

$$\rightarrow \quad A(\mu_y - 1) = A'(\mu_y' - 1)$$

Total angular dispersion $\quad D_T = D - D' = A(\mu_v - \mu_R) - A'(\mu_v' - \mu_R')$

Scan for Video Explanation

Aberrations in lenses and mirrors:

Defects of images formed by lenses and mirrors are called Aberrations. These are classified in two main categories. These are-

① Chromatic Aberrations: These are defects due to dispersion of light by a lens. Mirrors are free from chromatic aberrations.

$$\frac{1}{f} = (\mu - 1)\left(\frac{1}{R_1} - \frac{1}{R_2}\right)$$

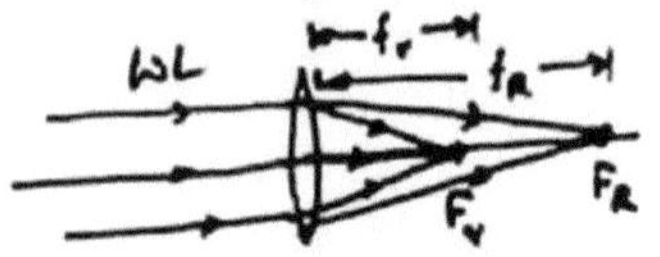

$\mu_V > \mu_R$

$f_V < f_R$

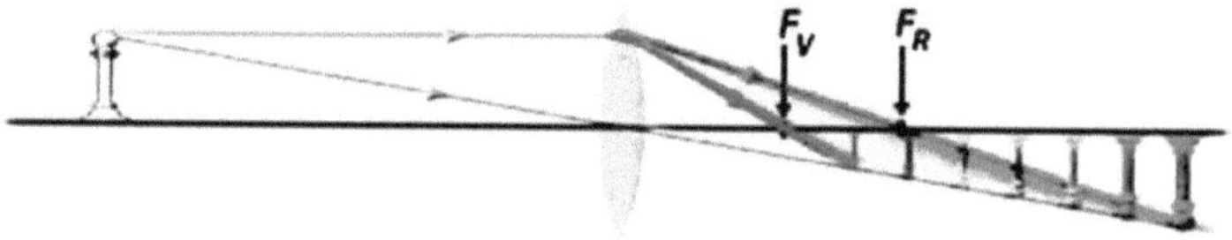

② Spherical Aberration:

These are defects in images due to large aperture of lenses or mirrors.

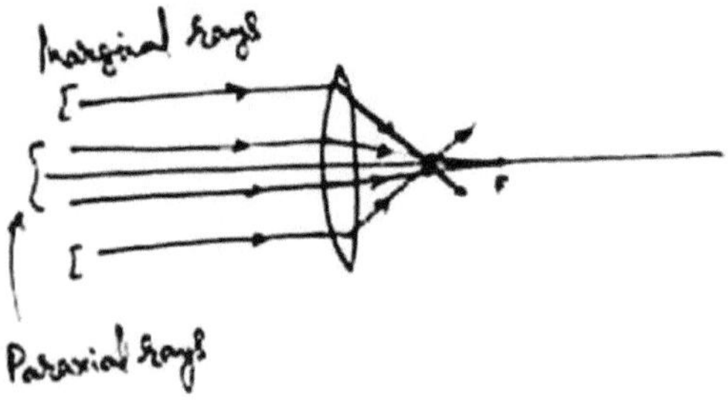

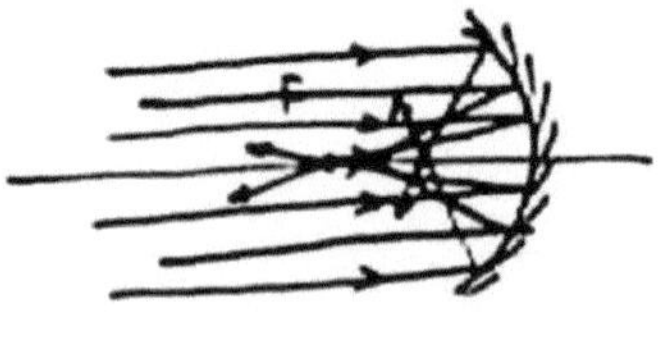

marginal rays

Paraxial rays

NOTE: Due to spherical aberrations a lens or a mirror of large aperture fails to produce sharp image of an object or point image of a pt. object due to marginal rays.

Module-10 Methods to Reduce Spherical Aberration

Methods to Reduce spherical Aberrations :

① By using stops

② By using two Convex lenses
   separated by some distance.

— When two convex lenses are separated by a distance
   equal to the diff in their focal lengths, by using
   this combination spherical aberration is minimized.

$$d = |f_1 - f_2|$$

Module-11 Longitudinal Chromatic Aberration in a Lens

longitudinal chromatic Aberration in a Lens :

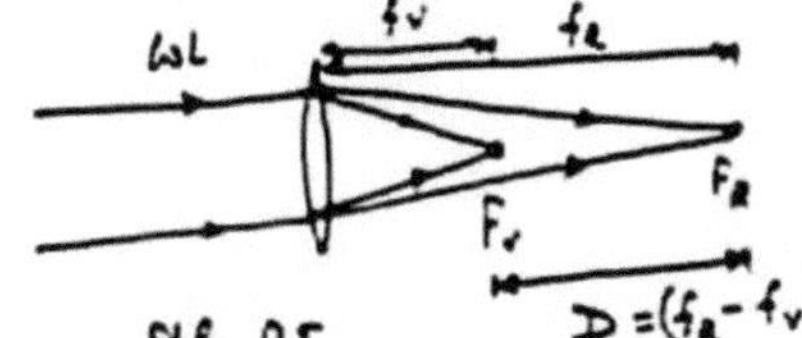

If μ_v and μ_R, μ_y are the RI
of lens matl for violet, Red & Yellow light

⇒ by LMF

$$\frac{1}{f_R} = (\mu_R - 1)\left[\frac{1}{R_1} - \frac{1}{R_2}\right] \; ; \; \frac{1}{f_v} = (\mu_v - 1)\left(\frac{1}{R_1} - \frac{1}{R_2}\right) \; ; \; \frac{1}{f_y} = (\mu_y - 1)\left[\frac{1}{R_1} - \frac{1}{R_2}\right]$$

$$\frac{1}{f_v} - \frac{1}{f_R} = (\mu_v - \mu_R)\left[\frac{1}{R_1} - \frac{1}{R_2}\right] \times \left(\frac{\mu_y - 1}{\mu_y - 1}\right)$$

$$\frac{f_R - f_v}{f_v f_R} = \frac{(\mu_v - \mu_R)}{(\mu_y - 1)} \cdot (\mu_y - 1)\left[\frac{1}{R_1} - \frac{1}{R_2}\right]$$

we can also use
$$f_v f_R = f_y^2$$

$$\boxed{f_R - f_v = \omega f_y}$$

Module-12 Achromatic Combination of Lenses

Achromatic Combination of Lenses:

When 2 or more lenses are combined in such a way that the comb^n is free from chromatic aberration than this comb^n is called achromatic comb^n.

by LMF

$$\frac{1}{f} = (\mu-1)\left[\frac{1}{R_1} - \frac{1}{R_2}\right] \xrightarrow{\text{diff}} -\frac{df}{f^2} = d\mu\left[\frac{1}{R_1} - \frac{1}{R_2}\right] \quad \overset{(2)}{\underset{(1)}{\Longrightarrow}} \quad -\frac{df}{f} = \frac{d\mu}{\mu-1} = \omega$$

for a lens comb^n of focal lengths f_1 and f_2 we use

$$\frac{1}{f_{eq}} = \frac{1}{f_1} + \frac{1}{f_2} \xrightarrow{\text{diff}} -\frac{df_{eq}}{f_{eq}^2} = -\frac{1}{f_1}\cdot\frac{df_1}{f_1} - \frac{1}{f_2}\cdot\frac{df_2}{f_2} = 0 \qquad \text{if comb}^n \text{ is free from ch. aberr.}$$

Condition of achromatic comb^n of two lenses, ← $\boxed{\dfrac{\omega_1}{f_1} + \dfrac{\omega_2}{f_2} = 0}$

f_1, f_2 must be of opp signs.

Chapter 5
Nature of Light and Interference

Lecture Notes Modules

Module-1 Nature of Light

Nature of Light:

Light is a form of energy which gives sensation of vision to eye. Some of the phenomenon associated with light are -

1. Rect prop of light
2. Reflection
3. Refraction
4. Dispersion
5. Interference
6. Diffraction
7. Polarization
8. Scattering
9. Photoelectric Effect.

To understand these phenomenon light energy was divided in two main categories based on which various theories were given to understand it -

1. Particle theory.
2. Wave theory.

Scan for Video Explanation

Web Reference at www.physicsgalaxy.com

Module-2 Newton's Corpuscular Theory

Newton's Corpuscular Theory:

(1675)

Light travels in form of stream of particles called 'corpuscles'.

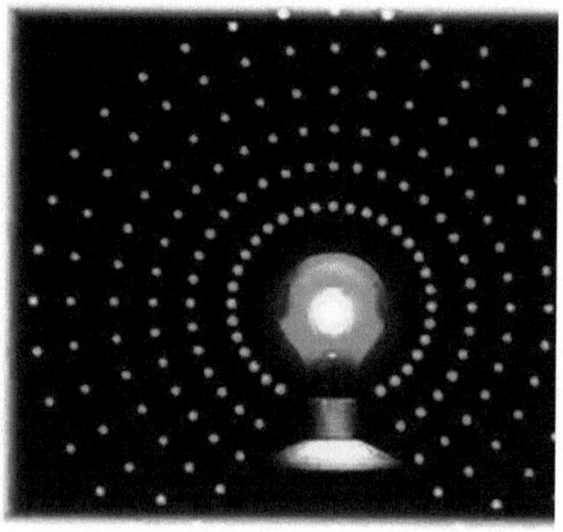

favr: Rect prop of light
Reflection
Refraction
Colours of light

against: interference
diffraction

Scan for Video Explanation

Web Reference at www.physicsgalaxy.com

Module-3 Huygen's Wave Theory

Huygen's Wave Theory:

Every light Source produces some disturbances in surr med which propagate at speed of light

Wavefront of a light beam:

It is the cross-sectional plane of a light beam in which all particles of med osc in same phase.

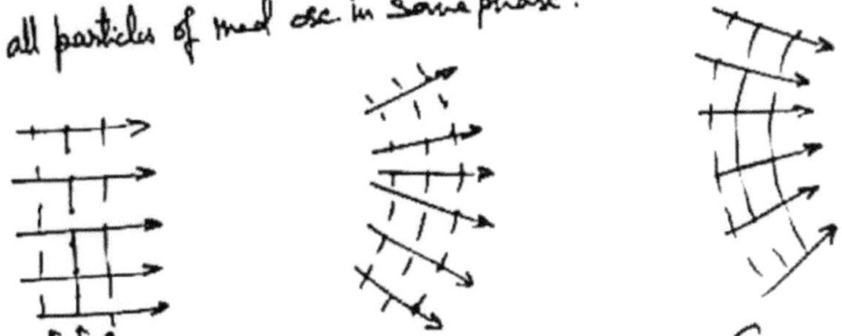

flat W/f of beam. Convex W/f. Concave W/f.

Web Reference at www.physicsgalaxy.com

Scan for Video Explanation

Module-4 Huygen's Theory of Wavefront Propagation of Light

Huygen's theory of Wavefront propagation:

Every pt of W/f in a light beam act as a source of new disturbances in surroundings which are called secondary wavelets. These sec wavelets produce their own spherical wavefronts and the common tangential plane of these W/f give the next position of prev W/f.

Parallel Beam Convex Beam Concave Beam

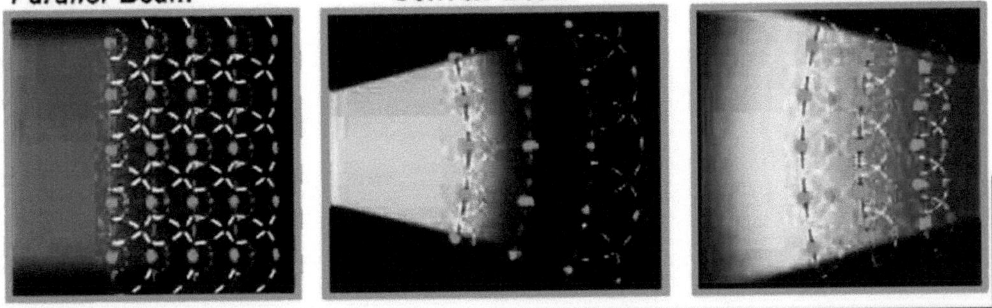

Web Reference at www.physicsgalaxy.com

Scan for Video Explanation

Maxwell's Electromagnetic Theory: 1873.

light energy is a wave which is EM in nature in which $\vec{E}$ & $\vec{B}$ oscillate simultaneously in planes $\perp$ to dir of prop of light.

here $\vec{E}$ & $\vec{B}$ are related as

$$E = cB$$

↑ Speed of light.

$\vec{E}$ ← light vector

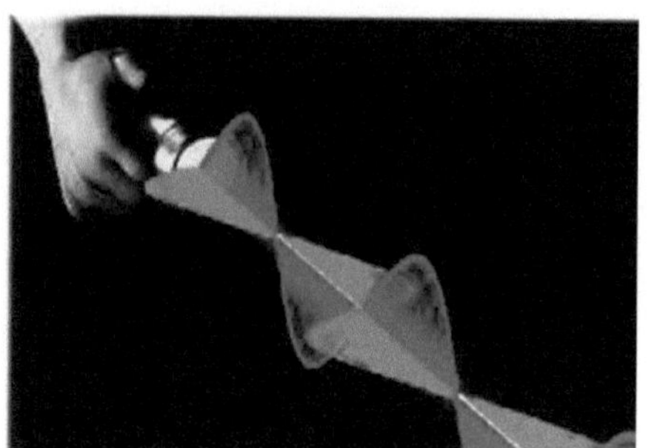

Interference of Light:

When two coherent light waves superpose at a point. the resultant intensity at that pt is diff from sum of the two int of ind waves. This modification in light int. at the pt of superposition of coherent waves is called "Interference of light".

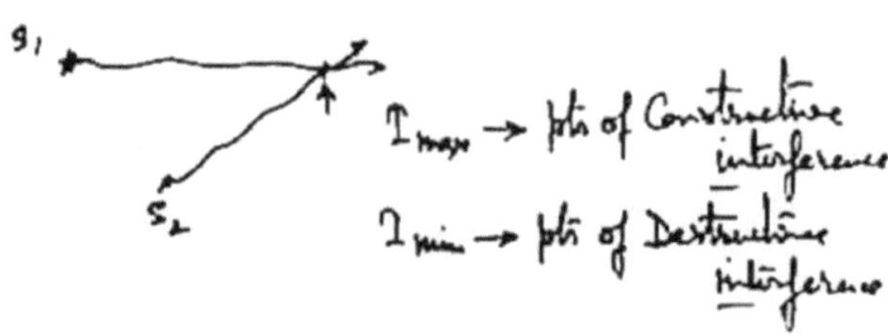

Module-7 Theory of Interference of Two Waves

Theory of Interference of Two Waves:

Let two coherent waves of freq ω & amp A_1 and A_2 sup at a pt with phase diff ϕ then ind disp of the two waves at the pt are given.

$$y_1 = A_1 \sin \omega t$$
$$y_2 = A_2 \sin(\omega t - \phi)$$

$y_1, y_2 \to \vec{E}$ in med for the two waves.

At the pt of sup res. disp is

$$y = y_1 + y_2$$
$$y = A_1 \sin \omega t + A_2 (\sin \omega t \cos \phi - \cos \omega t \sin \phi)$$
$$y = \underbrace{(A_1 + A_2 \cos \phi)}_{R \cos \theta} \sin \omega t - \underbrace{(A_2 \sin \phi)}_{R \sin \theta} \cos \omega t$$

$$y = R \sin(\omega t - \theta)$$

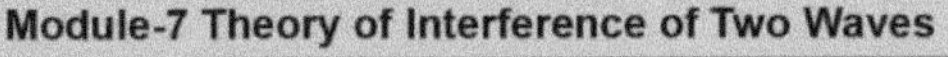

Module-7 Theory of Interference of Two Waves

$$\underset{\underset{\text{Res osc. amp at the pt of Sup.}}{\downarrow}}{y = R \sin(\omega t - \theta)}$$

where $R \cos \theta = A_1 + A_2 \cos \phi$ — (1)
$R \sin \theta = A_2 \sin \phi$ — (2)

$(1)^2 + (2)^2 \Rightarrow$

$$R = \sqrt{(A_1 + A_2 \cos \phi)^2 + (A_2 \sin \phi)^2}$$

$$R = \sqrt{A_1^2 + A_2^2 + 2A_1 A_2 \cos \phi}$$

$\dfrac{(2)}{(1)}$

$$\theta = \tan^{-1}\left(\frac{A_2 \sin \phi}{A_1 + A_2 \cos \phi}\right)$$

if $A_1 = A_2 = A$.

$$R = \sqrt{2A^2 + 2A^2 \cos \phi}$$

$$\boxed{R = 2A \cos \phi/2}$$

Here R is max when $\cos \phi = +1 \Rightarrow R_{max} = A_1 + A_2 = (2A)$ Constructive Interference
at $\phi = 2N\pi$ (Same phase)

Here R is min when $\cos \phi = -1 \Rightarrow R_{min} = |A_1 - A_2| = (0)$ ϕ part $|\vec{E}$ part$)$ $= 0$.   Destructive Interference
or $\phi = (2N+1)\pi$ (opp phase)

Module-8 Intensity of Light at the Point of Interference

\# <u>Intensity of light at the point of Interference:</u>

As we know   Intensity $\propto$ (Amp)^2

$$I = kA^2$$

At the pt of interference if res amp is R, intensity at the pt is given

$$I_R = kR^2$$

$$I_R = k\left[A_1^2 + A_2^2 + 2kA_1A_2\cos\phi\right]$$

$$I_R = kA_1^2 + kA_2^2 + 2kA_1A_2\cos\phi$$

$$\boxed{I_R = I_1 + I_2 + 2\sqrt{I_1 I_2}\cos\phi}$$

For Const int $[\cos\phi = +1] \Rightarrow I_{max} = I_1 + I_2 + 2\sqrt{I_1 I_2} = \left(\sqrt{I_1} + \sqrt{I_2}\right)^2$

For Dist int $[\cos\phi = -1] \Rightarrow I_{min} = I_1 + I_2 - 2\sqrt{I_1 I_2} = \left(\sqrt{I_2} - \sqrt{I_1}\right)^2$

Scan for Video Explanation   **Web Reference at www.physicsgalaxy.com**

Module-9 Interference of Equal Intensity Waves

\# <u>Interference of Equal intensity waves:</u>

$$I_R = I_1 + I_2 + 2\sqrt{I_1 I_2}\cos\phi$$

if $I_1 = I_2 = I_0$ $I_R = 2I_0 + 2I_0\cos\phi$

$$I_R = 2I_0(1 + \cos\phi)$$

$$1 + \cos\phi = 2\cos^2\phi/2$$

$$\boxed{I_R = 4I_0\cos^2\phi/2}$$

for Const int $I_{max} = \left(\sqrt{I_1} + \sqrt{I_2}\right)^2 = 4I_0$

for Dist int $I_{min} = \left(\sqrt{I_1} - \sqrt{I_2}\right)^2 = 0$

Contrast ratio $r = \dfrac{I_{max}}{I_{min}} = \left[\dfrac{\sqrt{I_1} + \sqrt{I_2}}{\sqrt{I_1} - \sqrt{I_2}}\right]^2 = \left[\dfrac{A_1 + A_2}{A_1 - A_2}\right]^2$

Scan for Video Explanation   **Web Reference at www.physicsgalaxy.com**

Module-10 Condition of Path Difference for Constructive and Destructive Interference

\# <u>Condition of path difference for Const & Dest Interference :</u>

As we know at the pt of interference $I = I_1 + I_2 + 2\sqrt{I_1 I_2}\cos\phi$

For Const int $\cos\phi = +1$ when $\underline{\phi = 2N\pi}$ (Same phase)

path diff betw" wave $\Delta = \dfrac{\lambda}{2\pi} \times \phi = \dfrac{\lambda}{2\pi} \times 2N\pi = N\lambda$

$\Rightarrow$ Two waves interfere constructively when $\Delta = \lambda, 2\lambda \ldots N\lambda$.

For Dest int $\cos\phi = -1$ when $\phi = (2N+1)\pi$ (opp phase)

path diff betw" waves $\Delta = \dfrac{\lambda}{2\pi} \times \phi$

$\qquad = \dfrac{\lambda}{2\pi} \times (2N+1)\pi = (2N+1)\,\lambda/2$

$\Rightarrow$ Two waves interfere destructively when $\Delta = \lambda/2, 3\lambda/2, \dfrac{5\lambda}{2} \ldots (2N+1)\lambda/2$

Scan for Video Explanation

Module-11 Solved Example-1

Ex : Determine the resulting intensity due to interference of the two waves at a point given below -

$$y_1 = 3 \sin(100\,\pi t)$$

$$y_2 = 4 \sin\left(100\pi t \cdot \frac{\pi}{3}\right)$$

Given that intensity due to first wave is I_0.

Sol^n: If int at point due to second wave is I'

$\Rightarrow \dfrac{I'}{I_0} = \left(\dfrac{A_2}{A_1}\right)^2 = \left(\dfrac{4}{3}\right)^2 \Rightarrow I' = \dfrac{16 I_0}{9}$

Resulting int after interference is $I_R = I_1 + I_2 + 2\sqrt{I_1 I_2}\cos\phi$

$\qquad = I_0 + \dfrac{16 I_0}{9} + 2\sqrt{I_0 \cdot \dfrac{16 I_0}{9}} \cdot \cos(\pi/3)$

$\qquad = I_0 + \dfrac{16}{9} I_0 + \dfrac{8}{3} I_0 \times \dfrac{1}{2}$

$\qquad = \dfrac{37}{9} I_0$ Ans.

Scan for Video Explanation

Module-12 Solved Example-2

Ex : Two coherent light beams of intensities I and 4I superpose in a region. Find the maximum and minimum possible intensities due to superposition in this region.

Sol^n: Due to interference of light beams.

max possible intensity is $I_{max} = \left(\sqrt{I_1} + \sqrt{I_2}\right)^2$

$$= \left(\sqrt{I} + \sqrt{4I}\right)^2$$

$$= 9I \text{ Ans}$$

min possible intensity is $I_{min} = \left(\sqrt{I_2} - \sqrt{I_1}\right)^2$

$$= \left(\sqrt{4I} - \sqrt{I}\right)^2$$

$$= I \text{ Ans}$$

Module-13 Solved Example-3

Ex : Figure shows a regular polygon with a point source of light placed at point P_1 if due to this source the intensity at point P_2 is I_0 find the intensity at point P_3.

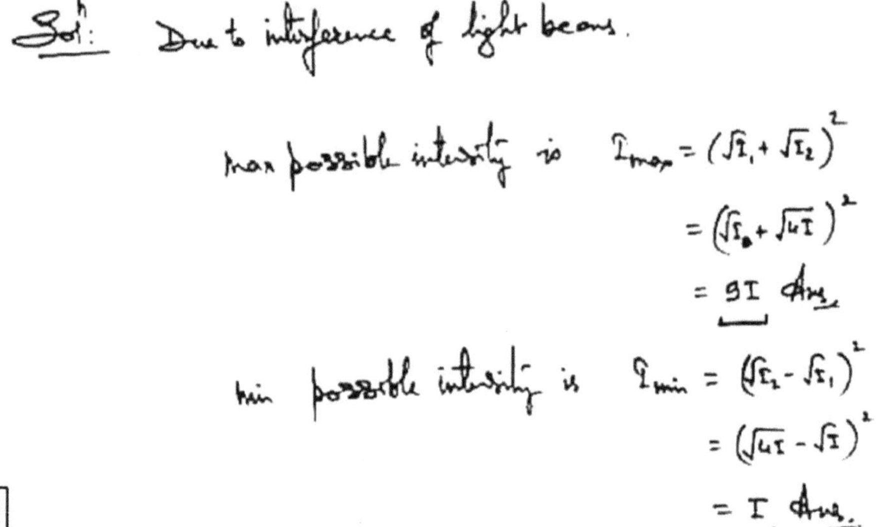

Sol^n: If power of light source placed at pt P_1 is P

$\Rightarrow$ light intensity at pt P_2 is

$$I_0 = \frac{P}{4\pi l^2} = \frac{P}{4\pi(\sqrt{3}a)^2} \quad -(1)$$

light intensity at pt P_3 is

$$I_{P_3} = \frac{P}{4\pi(2a)^2} \quad -(2)$$

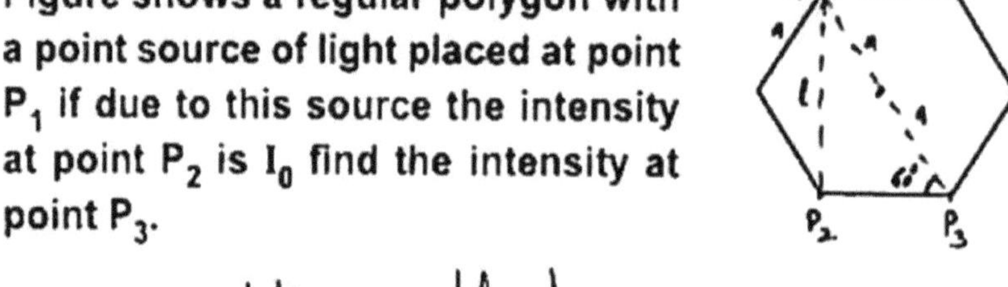

$l = 2a\sin 60°$

$l = \sqrt{3}a$

$$\frac{I_{P_3}}{I_0} = \left(\frac{\sqrt{3}}{2}\right)^2 = \frac{3}{4}$$

$$I_{P_3} = \frac{3}{4}I_0 \text{ Ans}$$

Module-14 Solved Example-4

Ex : There are two coherent sources S_1 and S_2 which produce waves in same phase placed on Y axis at points $(0, 2d)$ and $(0, d)$ as shown. A detector D is placed at origin which moves along X direction, find the number of maxima recorded by detector excluding points $x = 0$ and $x = \infty$. Given that wavelength of light produced is 6200A and separation between sources is 0.34 mm.

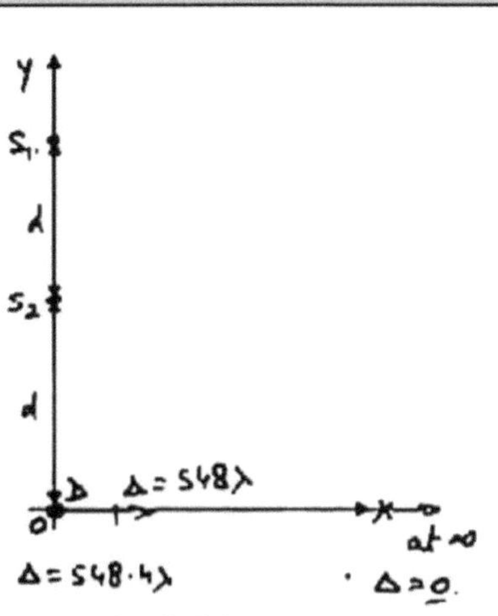

Sol^n: Path diff between waves from S_1 and S_2 at origin

$$\Delta = d = 3.4 \times 10^{-4} \, m \times \frac{\lambda}{\lambda}$$

$$\Delta = \frac{3.4 \times 10^{-4}}{6.2 \times 10^{-7}} \lambda = \underline{548.4\lambda}$$

Total No. of maxima on X axis Rec by D are $= 548$. Ans.

Module-15 Young's Double Slit Experiment

Young's Double Slit Experiment Setup :

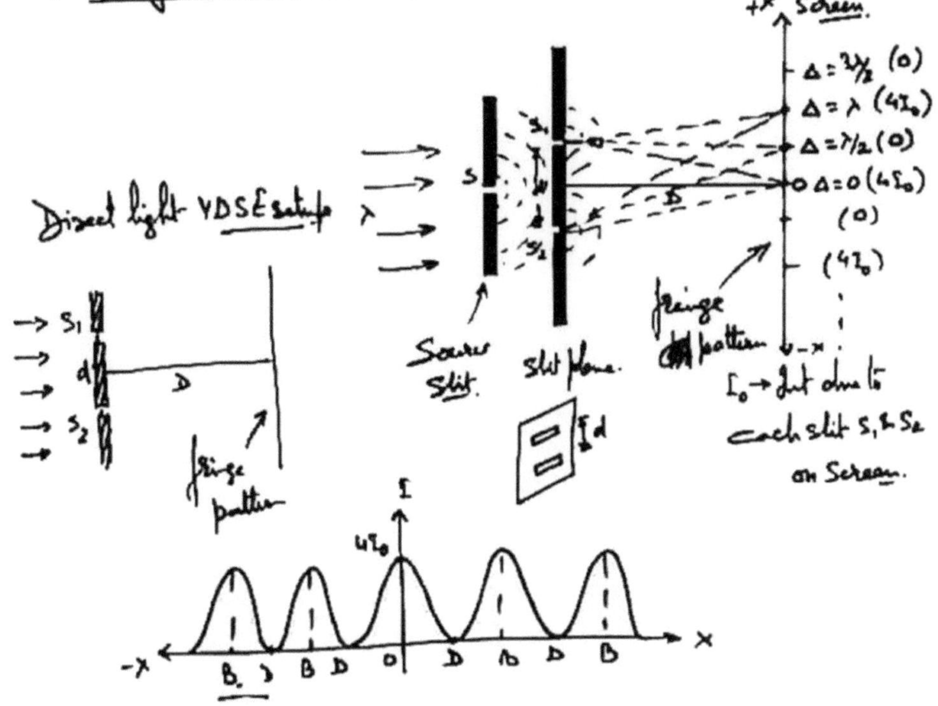

Direct light YDSE setup

Module-16 Light Intensity on Screen in YDSE

Light Intensity on Screen in YDSE:

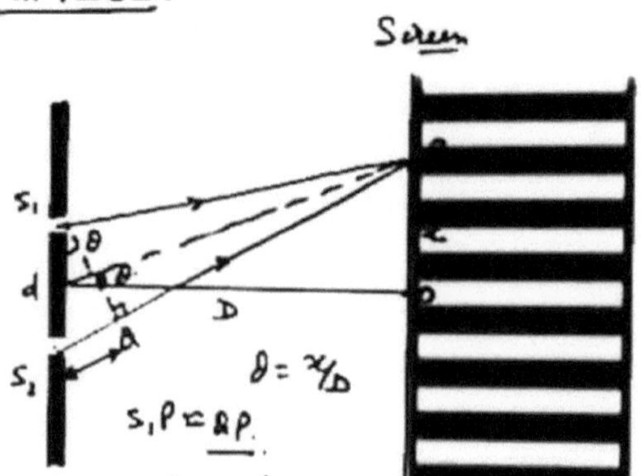

At pt P path diff in two waves from S_1 and S_2 is

$$\Delta = S_2P - S_1P = S_2Q$$

$$\Delta = d\sin\theta = d\theta$$

v.imp $\boxed{\Delta = \dfrac{dx}{D}}$ ✓

phase diff in the two waves at pt P is $\phi = \dfrac{2\pi}{\lambda}\left(\dfrac{dx}{D}\right) = \dfrac{2\pi dx}{\lambda D}$

Int at pt P is $I_P = 4I_0\cos^2(\phi/2)$

$$\boxed{I_P = 4I_0\cos^2\left(\dfrac{\pi dx}{\lambda D}\right)}$$ ✓

Screen

$\theta = x/D$

$S_1P = S_2P$

$\underline{D \gg d}$

θ is small

$I_0 \to$ int on screen du to each slit S_1 and $\underline{S_2}$

Module-17 Distance of Bright and Dark Fringes in YDSE

Distance of Bright and Dark fringes in YDSE:

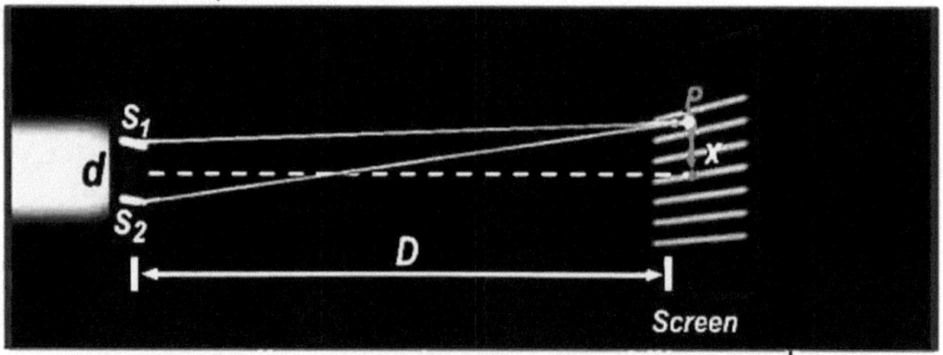

Path diff betwn waves from S_1 and S_2 at P is $\Delta = \dfrac{dx}{D}$

at pt P there is a bright fringe $(4I_0)$ if $\Delta = N\lambda$

$$\dfrac{dx}{D} = N\lambda$$

distance of Nth bright fringe from Central maxima.

$$\boxed{x_{NB} = \dfrac{N\lambda D}{d}}$$

Module-17 Distance of Bright and Dark Fringes in YDSE

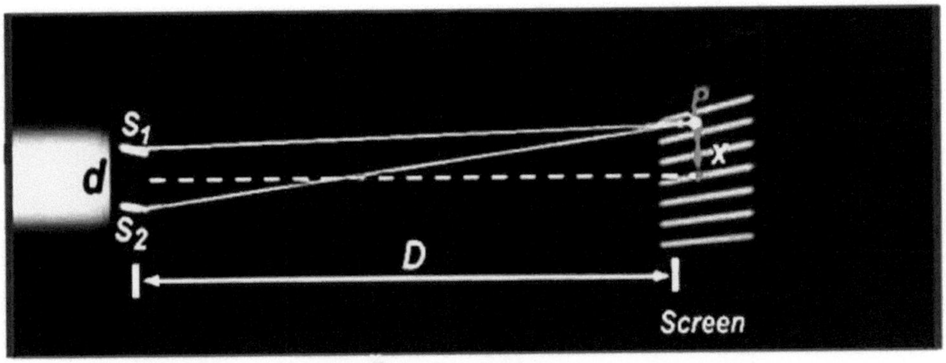

If there is a dark fringe at P if $\Delta = (2N-1)\lambda/2$ $N = 1, 2, 3 \ldots$

$$\frac{dx}{D} = (2N-1)\lambda/2$$

distance of Nth dark fringe from Central maxima ⟵ $$\boxed{x_{ND} = \frac{(2N-1)\lambda D}{2d}}$$

Web Reference at www.physicsgalaxy.com | Scan for Video Explanation

Module-18 Fringe Width in YDSE

Fringe width in YDSE:

↓ The sep betwn two consecutive Bright or Dark fringes.

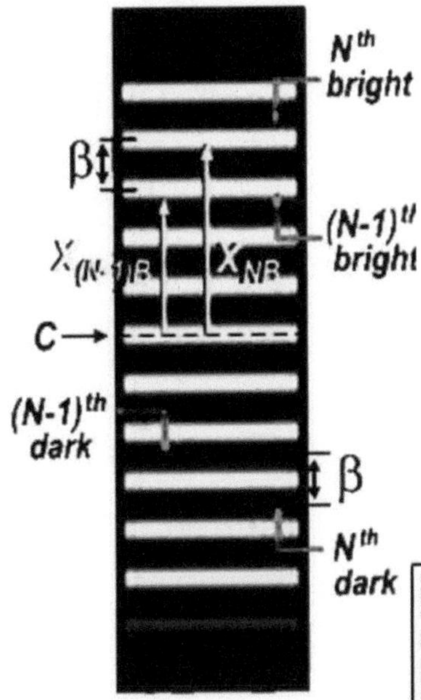

fringe width $\beta = x_{NB} - x_{(N-1)B}$

$$\beta = \frac{N\lambda D}{d} - \frac{(N-1)\lambda D}{d}$$

$$\boxed{\beta = \frac{\lambda D}{d}}$$ ✓

$\beta = x_{ND} - x_{(N-1)D}$

$$= \frac{(2N-1)\lambda D}{2d} - \frac{[2(N-1)-1]D\lambda}{2d}$$

$$\boxed{\beta = \frac{\lambda D}{d}}$$ ✓

Web Reference at www.physicsgalaxy.com | Scan for Video Explanation

Module-19 Solved Example-5

Ex : A YDSE setup is immersed in water ($\mu = 1.33$). If has slit
separation 1 mm and distance between slits and screen
is 1.33 m. Incident light on slits have wavelength 6300 Å.
Find the fringe width on screen.

W/L of light in water $\lambda_w = \dfrac{\lambda}{\mu} = \dfrac{6300}{1.33}$ Å

In YDSE fringe width is given as —

$$\beta = \dfrac{\lambda_w D}{d} = \dfrac{6300 \times 10^{-10} \times 1.33}{1.33 \times 10^{-3}}$$

$$= 6.3 \times 10^{-4}\ m$$

$$= 0.63\ mm.\ \text{Ans}$$

Module-20 Solved Example-6

Ex : In YDSE setup find the distance between two slits that
result in the third minimum for 4200Å violet light at an
angle 30°. Take d<<D.

At point P on Screen
path diff between waves
from S_1 and S_2 is

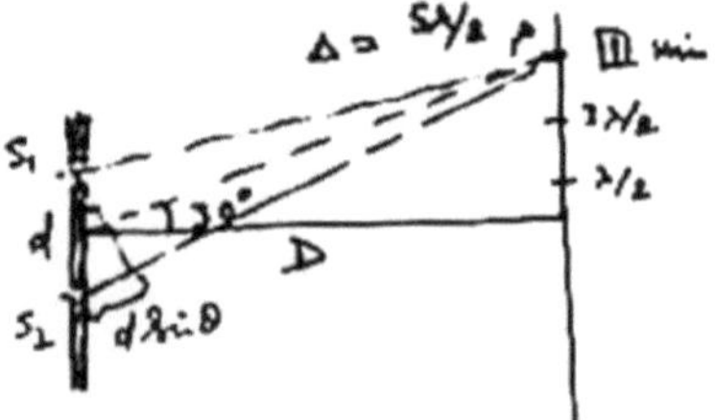

$$\Delta = d \sin 30° = \dfrac{d}{2} = \dfrac{5\lambda}{2} \quad (\text{for III min})$$

$$d = 5\lambda = 5 \times 4200 \times 10^{-10}\ m$$

$$= 2.1 \times 10^{-6}\ m\ \text{Ans}$$

Module-21 Solved Example-7

Ex : In YDSE setup a light of wavelength 6000Å is used. What should be the separation between the slits so that on screen in front of one of the slit there will be third bright fringe. Take D = 1 m.

Sol^n: at a dist x from screen course path diff betwⁿ the waves from S_1 and S_2 is

$$\Delta = \frac{dx}{D} = 3\lambda \quad \text{at } x = d/2$$

$$\frac{d^2}{2D} = 3\lambda \implies d = \sqrt{6\lambda D} = \sqrt{6 \times 6 \times 10^{-7} \times 1}$$

$$= \sqrt{36 \times 10^{-7}} \text{ m}$$

$$= 0.6\sqrt{10} \text{ mm. Ans}$$

Scan for Video Explanation

Module-22 Solved Example-8

Ex : In YDSE setup slits are illuminated by a light of wavelength 4000 Å and a light of unknown wavelength. It is observed that fourth dark fringe of known wavelength coincide with second bright fringe of unknown wavelength. Find the unknown wavelength.

Sol^n: For Nᵗʰ dark fringe from Centre $\quad x_{ND} = \frac{(2N-1)\lambda D}{2d}$

for N = 4, $\lambda = 4000$Å $\implies x_{4D} = \frac{7 \times 4 \times 10^{-7} \times D}{2d}$

For Nᵗʰ bright fringe from Centre $\quad x_{NB} = \frac{N\lambda D}{d}$

for N = 2, $\lambda = ?$ $\implies x_{2B} = \frac{2\lambda D}{d}$

Given that $\quad x_{4D} = x_{2B}$

$$\frac{7 \times 4 \times 10^{-7} \times D}{2d} = \frac{2\lambda D}{d} \implies \lambda = 7 \times 10^{-7} \text{ m} = 7000 \text{ Å Ans.}$$

Scan for Video Explanation

Module-23 Effect of Changing Direction on Incident Light in YDSE

\# Effect of changing direction of incident light in YDSE:

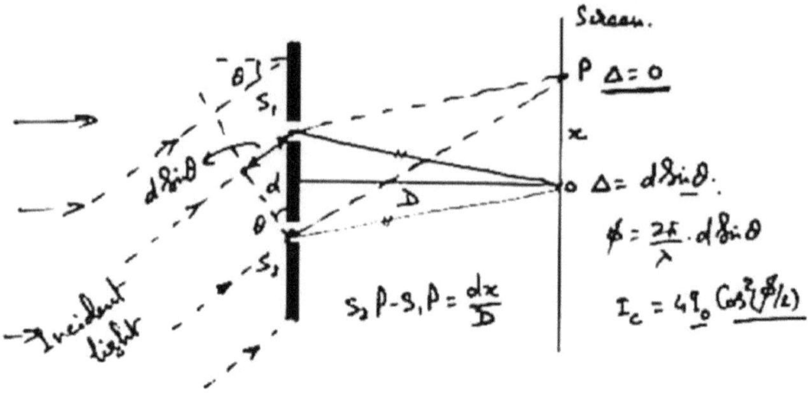

Screen.

P $\underline{\Delta = 0}$

$\Delta = d\sin\theta$.

$\phi = \frac{2\pi}{\lambda} \cdot d\sin\theta$

$I_c = 4I_0 \cos^2(\phi/2)$

$S_2P - S_1P = \frac{dx}{D}$

At pt P, $\Delta = 0$ if $\frac{dx}{D} = d\sin\theta$

$\Rightarrow \underline{x = D\sin\theta} \leftarrow$ position of central maxima on screen after changing the dir of incident light.

Module-23 Effect of Changing Direction on Incident Light in YDSE

\# Live shift of fringe pattern due to change in direction of incident light:

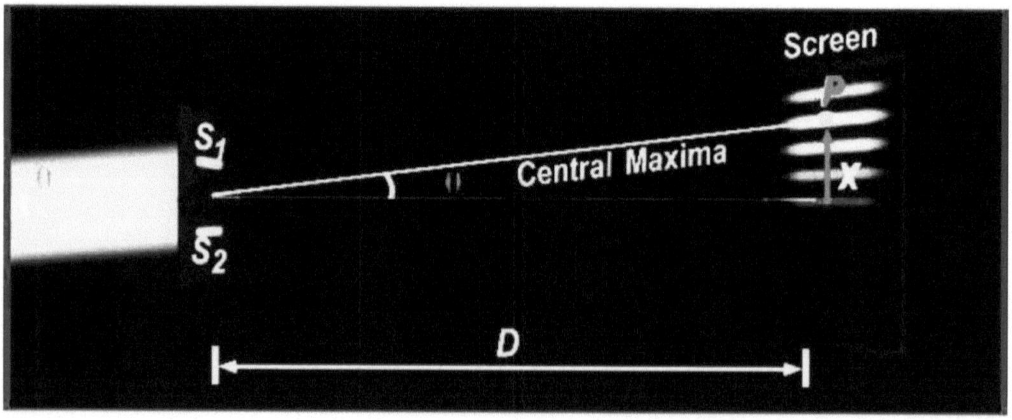

$$\frac{dx}{D} = d\sin\theta \Rightarrow \underline{x = D\sin\theta}.$$

Shift of Central maxima / fringe pattern

Module-24 Effect Submerging YDSE in a Transparent Media

\# <u>Effect of Submerging YDSE in a Transparent media</u> :

In a μ medium when a wave of wavelength λ enters, its wavelength changes to

$$\lambda' = \frac{\lambda}{\mu}$$

In interference pattern of YDSE fringe width also changes to

$$\beta = \frac{\lambda D}{d} \longrightarrow \beta' = \frac{\lambda D}{\mu d} = \frac{\beta}{\mu}$$

As $\beta' < \beta$.

$\Rightarrow$ fringe pattern shrinks on Submerging YDSE in a μ medium.

Module-25 Path Difference Between Two Parallel Waves due to a Denser Medium

\# <u>Path difference between two parallel waves due to a denser medium</u> :

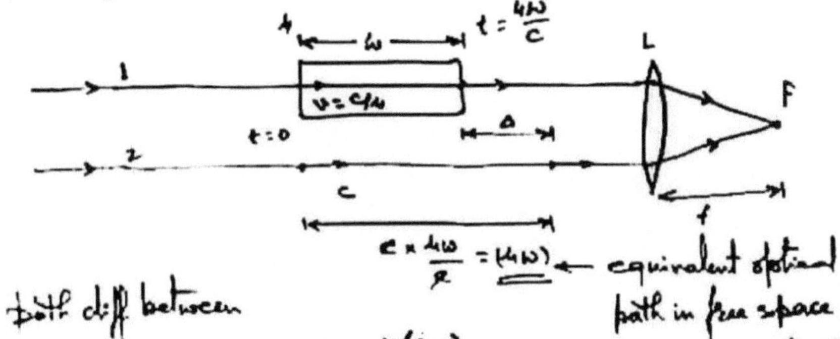

Path diff between waves 1 & 2 $\Delta = \mu w - w = \underline{w(\mu - 1)}$

If at pt F. each wave is having int I_0, resulting int at F Can be given as —

$$I_f = 4I_0 \cos^2(\phi/2) \qquad \text{where } \phi = \frac{2\pi}{\lambda} \times \Delta = \frac{2\pi}{\lambda} \times w(\mu - 1)$$

Module-26 Effect of Placing a Thin Transparent Film in YDSE

Effect of placing a Thin transparent film in YDSE:

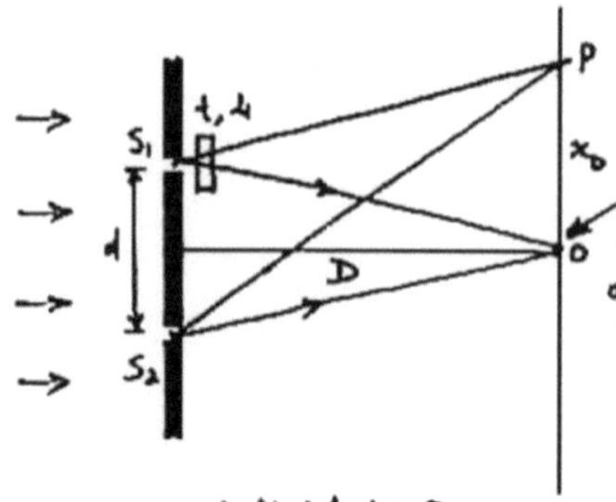

$\Delta_P = \frac{dx_0}{D} = t(\mu-1) \Rightarrow \Delta_P = 0$

Central bright fringe: $\Delta = 0$.

after placing the film

$\Delta_0 \neq 0$

$\Delta_0 = t(\mu-1)$

$\phi_0 = \frac{2\pi}{\lambda} \times t(\mu-1)$

$I_C = 4I_0 \cos^2(\phi_0/2)$

If Central max is shifted to pt P

$\Rightarrow \frac{dx_0}{D} = t(\mu-1)$

$$\boxed{x_0 = \frac{Dt(\mu-1)}{d}}$$ shift of fringe pattern.

Scan for Video Explanation

Web Reference at www.physicsgalaxy.com

Module-26 Effect of Placing a Thin Transparent Film in YDSE

Live shift of fringe pattern due to introduction of a thin film in YDSE:

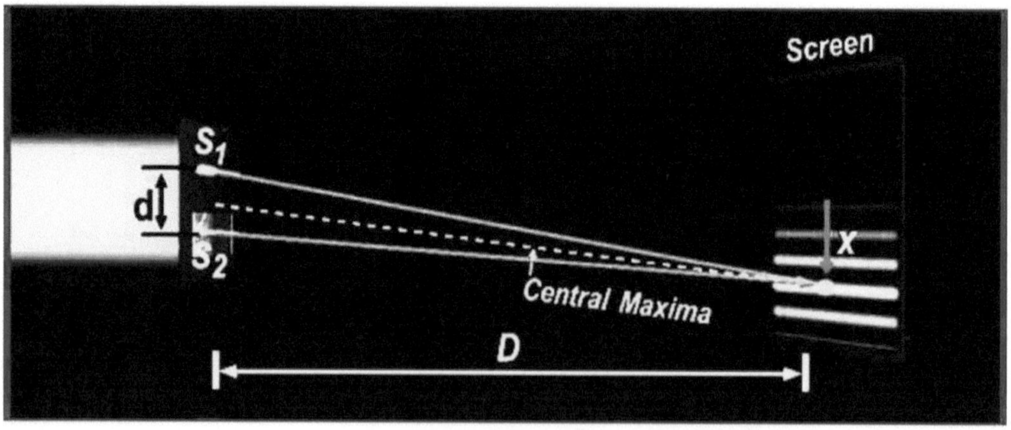

$t(\mu-1) = \frac{dx}{D} \longrightarrow x = \frac{Dt(\mu-1)}{d}$

Shift of fringe pattern

Scan for Video Explanation

Web Reference at www.physicsgalaxy.com

Module-27 Concept of z-value on YDSE Screen

Concept of z-value on YDSE Screen:

At any pt on YDSE Screen other then $\Delta = 0$ pt we can define a numeric parameter such that at that pt,

$$\Delta_p = z\lambda$$
$$\text{or } z_p = \frac{\Delta_p}{\lambda}$$

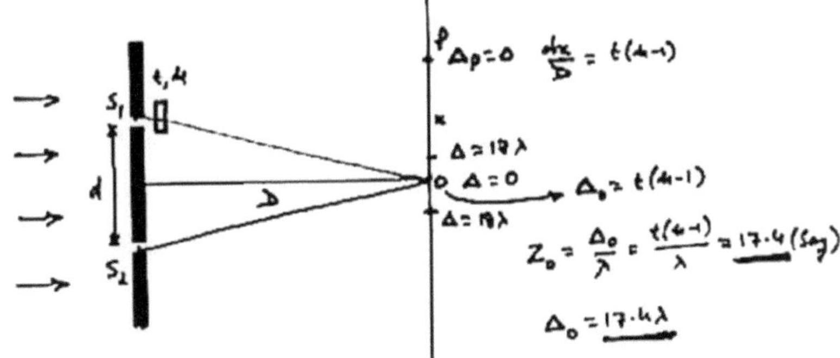

In this situation 17 bright fringes cross the screen Centre on introduction a thin film in front of Slit S_1.

Module-28 Use of White Light in YDSE

Use of White light in YDSE:

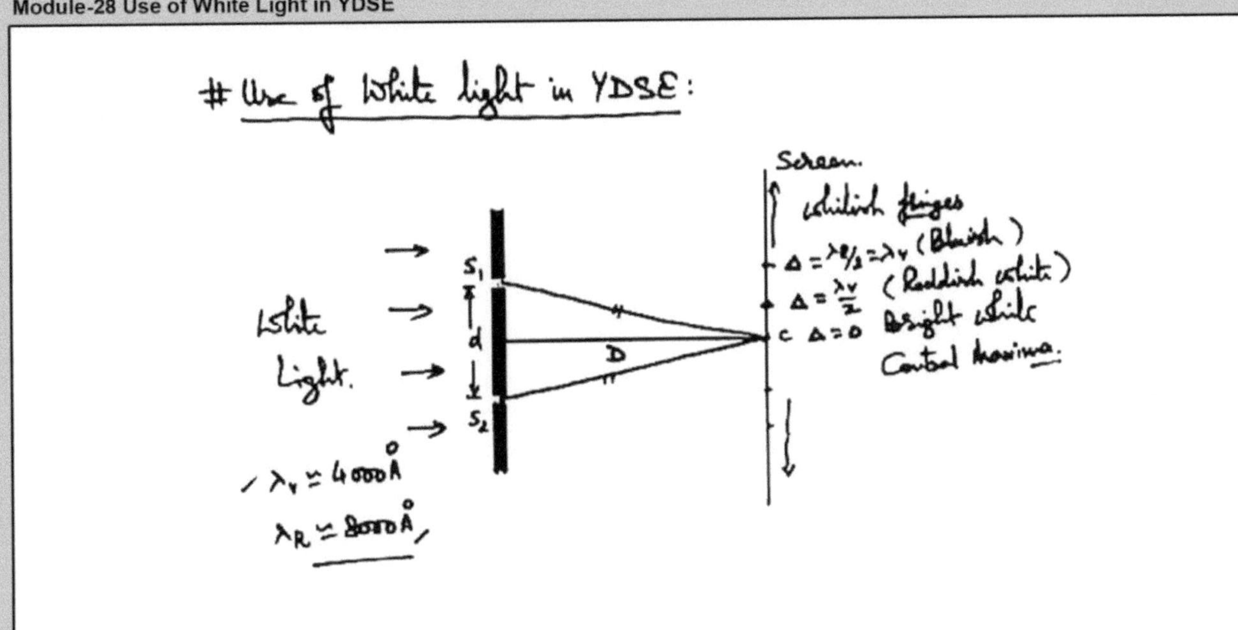

Module-29 Effect of Changing Slit Width in YDSE

Effect of changing slit width in YDSE:

If slit produces an intensity I on Screen then we have

$I \propto$ slit power

$I \propto w$ (Slit width)

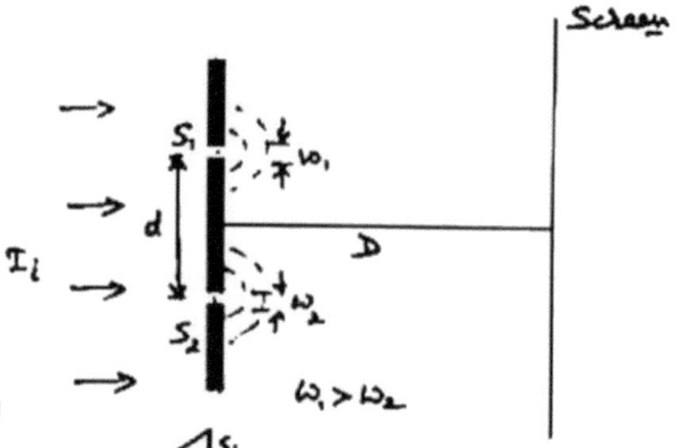

If both S_1 and S_2 are of equal width
$\Rightarrow$ on Screen $I_1 = I_2 = I_0$

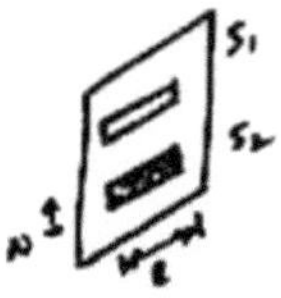

$$I_{Bright\,fr.} = 4I_0$$
$$I_{Dark\,fr} = 0$$
$\Rightarrow$ Int pattern is sharp.

$\omega_1 > \omega_2$

slit power $P = I_i \times w l$
$$= I_i\,w l.$$

If slits are of unequal widths
$$\Rightarrow I_1 \neq I_2$$
$$I_{Bright} = (\sqrt{I_1} + \sqrt{I_2})^2$$
$$I_{Dark} = (\sqrt{I_1} - \sqrt{I_2})^2 \neq 0.$$

Module-30 Fresnal's Biprism as a Limiting Case of YDSE

Fresnal's Biprism as a limiting case of YDSE:

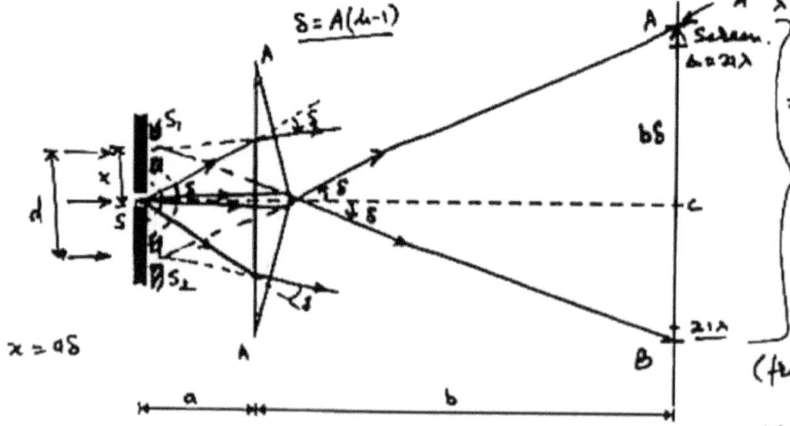

$$\delta = A(\mu - 1)$$

$$x = a\delta$$

$$z_A = \frac{\Delta}{\lambda} = \frac{d(bs)}{\lambda}$$
$$= 21 \cdot 3 (Say)$$
$$\Rightarrow \Delta_A = 21.3\lambda$$

Region of Interference

(fringe pattern)

Total bright fringes $= 43$

Sep between coherent sources $\underline{d = 2a\delta = 2aA(\mu-1)}$

Sep between slit plane & Screen $\underline{D = a+b}$

fringe width on screen. $\beta = \frac{\lambda D}{d} = \frac{\lambda(a+b)}{2aA(\mu-1)}$

Module-31 Lloyd's Mirror as a Limiting Case of YDSE

Lloyd's Mirror as a limiting case of YDSE:

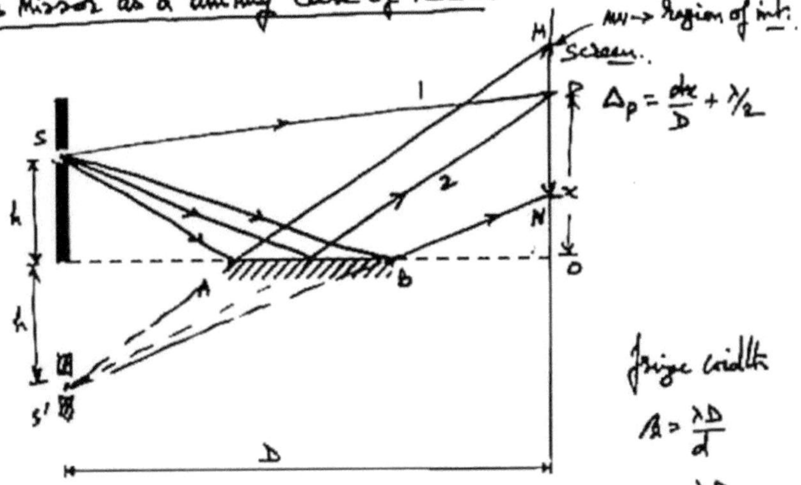
MN → Region of int.
Screen.
H
P
1
2
S
h
x
N
O
A
b
d = 2h.
h
S'
D

$\Delta_p = \frac{dx}{D} + \lambda/2$

fringe width

$\beta = \frac{\lambda D}{d}$

$\beta = \frac{\lambda D}{2h}$

for N^{th} bright fringe at P we use $\frac{dx}{D} + \frac{\lambda}{2} = N\lambda$

$$x_{NB} = \frac{(2N-1)\lambda D}{2d}$$

for N^{th} dark fringe at P we use $\frac{dx}{D} + \frac{\lambda}{2} = (2N+1)\lambda/2$

$$x_{ND} = \frac{N\lambda D}{d}$$

Web Reference at www.physicsgalaxy.com | Scan for Video Explanation

Module-32 Billet Split Lens as a Limiting Case of YDSE

Billet split lens as a limiting case of YDSE:

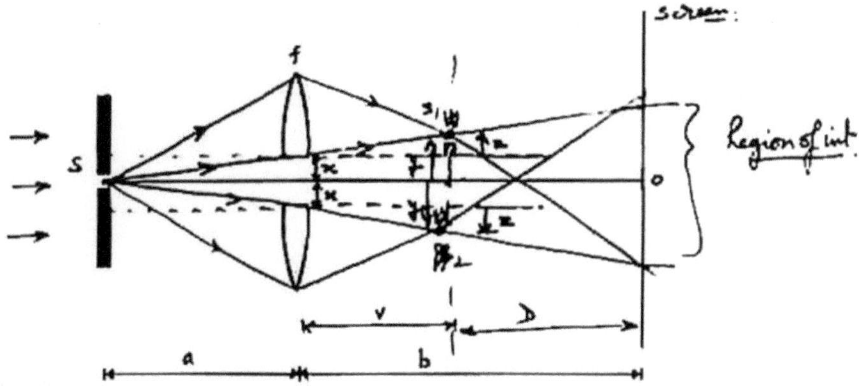
screen.
f
S
S_1
S_2
x
x
y
y
z
z
O
v
D
a
b
Region of int.

for lens formula.

$u = -a$

$f = +f$

$\frac{1}{v} + \frac{1}{a} = \frac{1}{f}$

$v = \frac{af}{a-f}$

$D = a + b - |v|$

$d = 2y = 2x + 2\frac{v}{u}|x$

$= 2x(1 + |\frac{v}{u}|)$

$z = \frac{v}{u} \cdot x$

$y = x + z$

fringe width $\beta = \frac{\lambda D}{d} = - - - -$

Web Reference at www.physicsgalaxy.com | Scan for Video Explanation

Module-33 Interference of Two Parallel Beams of monochromatic Light

Interference of two parallel beams of light:

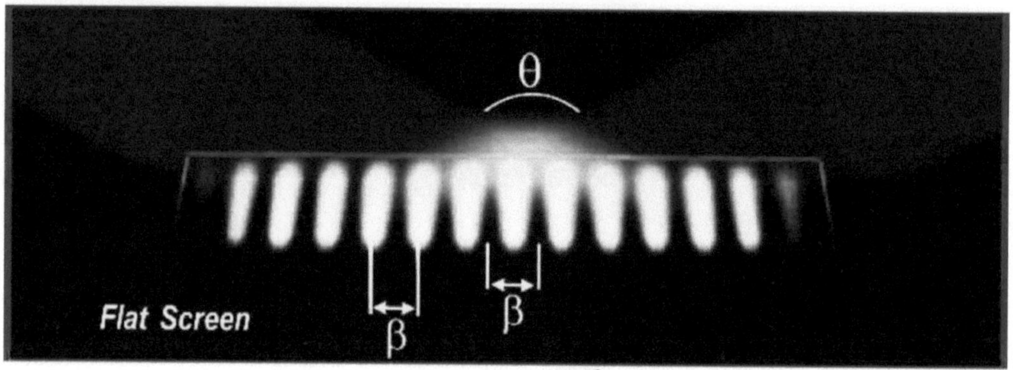

Fringe width $\beta = \frac{\lambda}{\theta}$

Scan for Video Explanation

Web Reference at www.physicsgalaxy.com

Module-34 Shapes of Fringes by Interference due to Difference Sources

Shape of fringes by interference due to different Sources:

Case-1 Int. due to two pt Sources in a line

(A) Screen is placed ∥ to the line joing the sources.

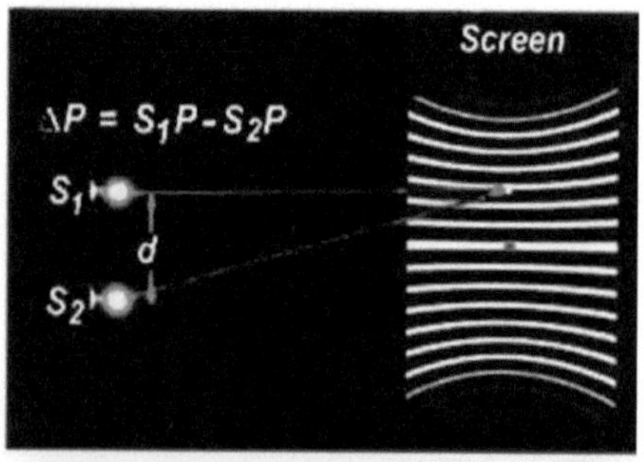

(B) Screen is placed ⊥ to the line joing the Sources.

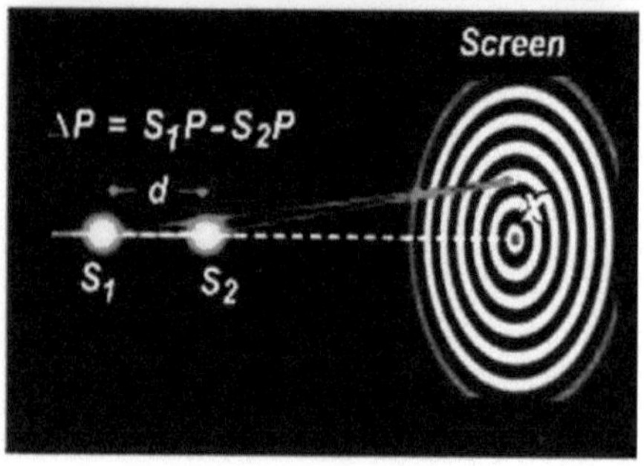

Scan for Video Explanation

Web Reference at www.physicsgalaxy.com

Module-34 Shapes of Fringes by Interference due to Difference Sources

Case-III: Two direct slit sources in same plane (YDSE)

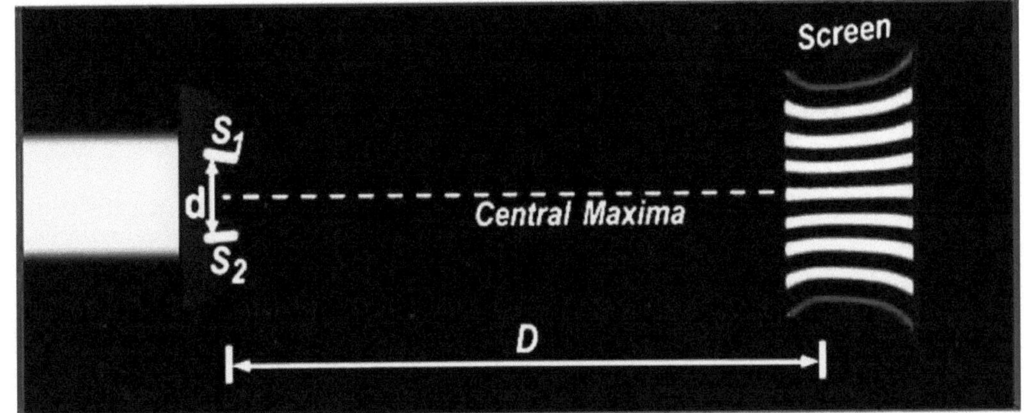

     Scan for Video Explanation

Module-35 Solved Example-9

Ex : **In YDSE experiment a uniform intensity light beam is incident on slit plane which has two slits having width ratio 9 : 4. Find the ratio of intensities of bright and dark fringes on screen.**

Solⁿ :   We know that intensities due to slits $\propto$ width of slit.

$$\frac{I_1}{I_2} = \frac{9}{4} = \frac{A_1^2}{A_2^2}$$

$$\Rightarrow \frac{A_1}{A_2} = \frac{3}{2} \quad \Rightarrow \begin{array}{l} A_1 = 3c \\ A_2 = 2c \end{array}$$

Ratio of max to min int on Screen. $\dfrac{I_{max}}{I_{min}} = \left(\dfrac{A_1 + A_2}{A_1 - A_2}\right)^2 = \left(\dfrac{3+2}{3-2}\right)^2$

$$\frac{I_{max}}{I_{min}} = 25 \quad \text{Ans.}$$

     Scan for Video Explanation

Module-36 Solved Example-10

Ex : A monochromatic light of wavelength 5000Å incident normally on slit plane of YDSE setup. If $d = 5 \times 10^{-4}$ m and $D = 1$ m and a thin film of thickness 1.5×10^{-6} m and $\mu = 1.5$ is place in front of one of the slits, find intensity of light at the centre of screen if each slit produces an intensity I_0 on screen.

Sol^n: Path diff at screen centre is

$$\Delta = t(\mu - 1)$$
$$= 1.5 \times 10^{-6} \times 0.5$$
$$= 7.5 \times 10^{-7} \, m.$$

phase diff in two waves at screen centre is $\phi = \dfrac{2\pi}{\lambda} \times \Delta$

$$= \frac{2\pi}{5 \times 10^{-7}} \times 7.5 \times 10^{-7}$$
$$= 3\pi.$$

Resulting intensity at C is

$$I_R = 4 I_0 \cos^2(\phi/2) = 0 \quad \text{Ans.}$$

Module-37 Solved Example-11

Ex : A Lloyd's mirror of length 5 cm is illuminated with monochromatic light of wavelength 6000 Å from a narrow slit 1 mm above the plane of mirror and 5 cm from one edge of mirror. Find fringe width on a screen at a distance 120 cm from slit and also find the width of interference pattern on screen.

Sol^n: In this eg setup of YDSE, we can use

$$d = 2 \, mm = 2 \times 10^{-3} \, m$$
$$D = 1.2 \, m$$

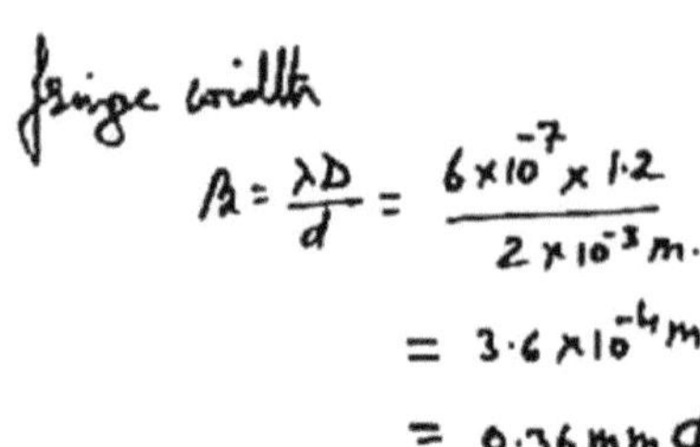

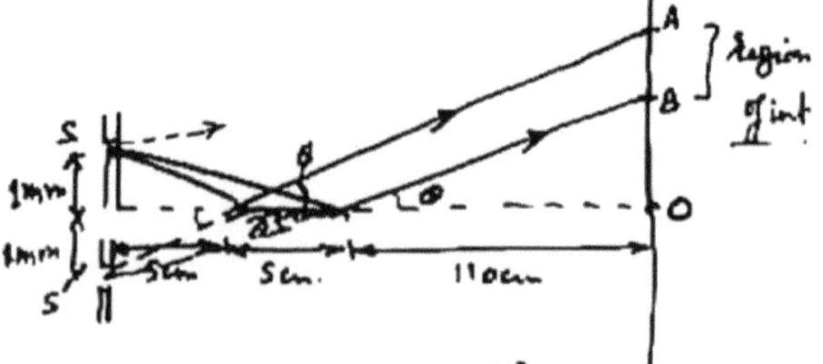

fringe width

$$\beta = \frac{\lambda D}{d} = \frac{6 \times 10^{-7} \times 1.2}{2 \times 10^{-3} \, m.}$$
$$= 3.6 \times 10^{-4} \, m$$
$$= 0.36 \, mm \quad \text{Ans.}$$

$$AB = OA - OB \qquad \frac{OB}{110} = \frac{0.1}{10}$$
$$AB = 2.3 - 1.1 \qquad \Rightarrow OB = 1.1 \, cm$$
$$= 1.2 \, cm \quad \text{Ans.} \qquad \frac{OA}{115} = \frac{0.1}{5}$$
$$OA = 2.3 \, cm.$$

Module-38 Solved Example-12

Ex : In a YDSE setup, light of wavelength 5000 Å is used and slit separation is 3×10^{-7} m. When a transparent sheet of thickness 1.5×10^{-7} m is placed over one of the slits which has $\mu = 1.17$, find the shift of fringe pattern. Take separation between slits and screen is 1 m.

Sol^n. At C path diff

$$\Delta = t(\mu - 1)$$

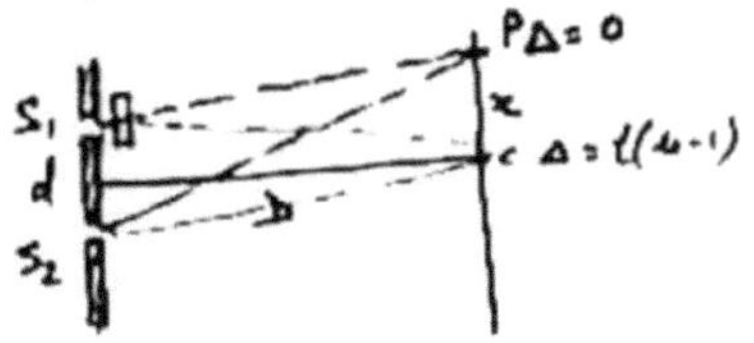

At pt P we have

$$\frac{dx}{D} = t(\mu - 1)$$

$$x = \frac{Dt(\mu - 1)}{d} = \frac{1 \times 1.5 \times 10^{-7} \times 0.17}{3 \times 10^{-7}}$$

$$x = 0.085 \, m = 8.5 \, cm \quad \text{Ans.}$$

Scan for Video Explanation

Module-39 Interference due to Thin Films in Reflected Light

\# Interference due to thin films in reflected light :

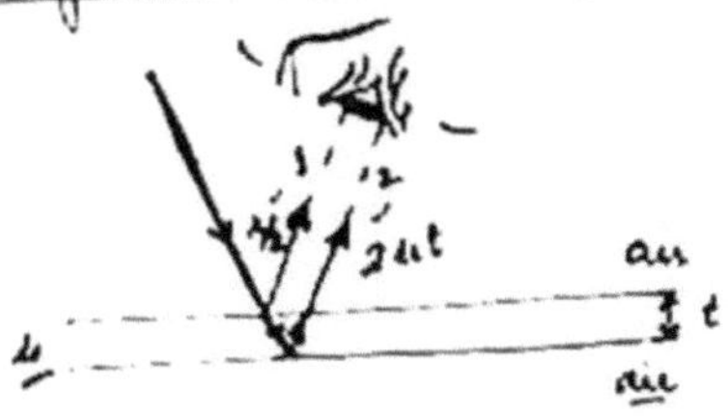

path diff in reflected beams 1 and 2 is

$$\Delta = 2\mu t - \lambda/2$$

Reflected beam will have high intensity when beams 1 and 2 will interfere constructively

$$\Rightarrow \boxed{2\mu t - \lambda/2 = N\lambda}$$

Reflected beam will have low intensity when beams 1 & 2 will interfere destructively

$$\Rightarrow \boxed{2\mu t - \lambda/2 = (2N+1)\lambda/2}$$

Scan for Video Explanation

Module-40 Interference due to Thin Films in Transmitted Light

Interference due to Thin films in Transmitted light:

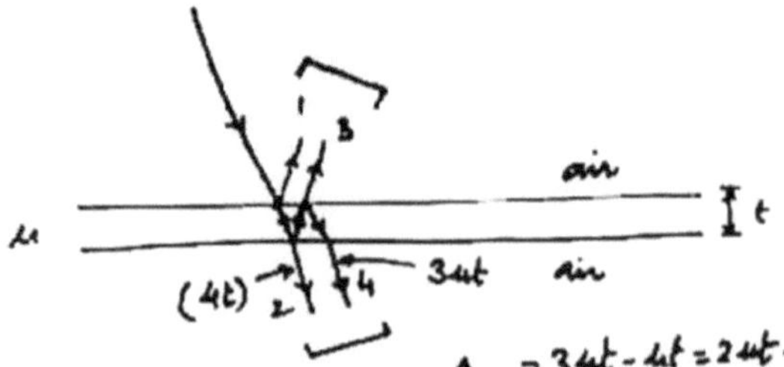

$\Delta_{24} = 3\mu t - \mu t = 2\mu t.$

Transmitted beam will have max intensity when.

$$\boxed{\Delta_{24} = 2\mu t = N\lambda} \rightarrow \text{Cont Int}$$

Transmitted beam will have min intensity when

$$\boxed{\Delta_{24} = 2\mu t = (2N+1)\lambda/2} \rightarrow \text{Dest Int.}$$

Scan for Video Explanation

Web Reference at www.physicsgalaxy.com

Module-41 Interference of Reflected Light by a Very Thin Film

Interference of reflected light by a very Thin film:

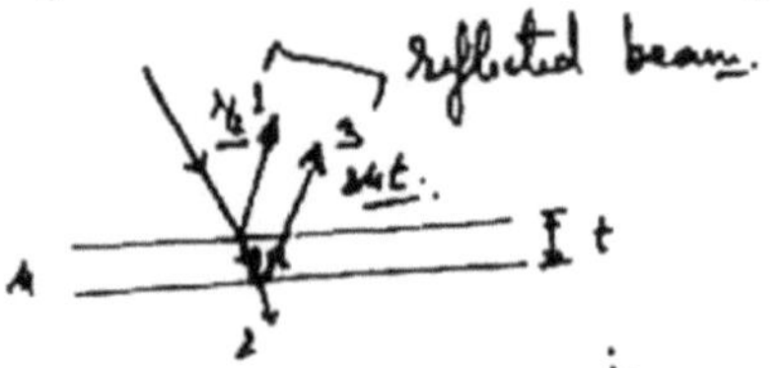

path diff in light waves in reflected beam is $\Delta_{13} = |2\mu t - \lambda/2|$

If film is very thin $t \rightarrow 0$

$\Rightarrow \Delta_{13} = \lambda/2$

$\Rightarrow$ the two waves will interfere destructively

In reflected light film will appear dark

OR

A very thin film does not reflect any light.

Scan for Video Explanation

Web Reference at www.physicsgalaxy.com

Module-42 Solved Example-13

Ex : **A soap film of thickness 0.0011 mm appears dark when seen by reflected light of wavelength 5800Å. What is the refractive index soap solution if it is between 1.2 and 1.5.**

Sol^n: Path diff in the two waves

Constituting the Reflected light is

$$\Delta = 2\mu t - \lambda/2 = (2N-1)\lambda/2 \quad \text{for dark int}$$

$$2\mu t = N\lambda$$

$$\mu = \frac{N\lambda}{2t} = \frac{N \times 5800 \times 10^{-10}}{2 \times 1.1 \times 10^{-6}}$$

$$1.2 < \mu < 1.5 \qquad \mu = 0.263N \qquad N = 1, 2, 3 \cdots$$

$$\text{for } N = 5 \qquad \mu = 1.318 \quad \text{Ans.}$$

Scan for Video Explanation

Module-43 Solved Example-14

Ex : **Find the minimum thickness of an oil film in air that gives an interference maxima in reflected light for wavelength 5360Å at normal incidence. Take μ_{oil} = 1.34.**

Sol^n:

path diff of two waves in Reflected beam is

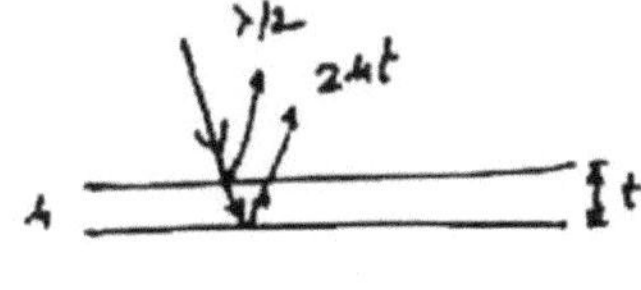

$$\Delta = 2\mu t - \lambda/2$$

for max Reflection $\quad 2\mu t - \lambda/2 = 0$

$$t = \frac{\lambda}{4\mu} = \frac{5360 \times 10^{-10}}{4 \times 1.34} = 10^{-7}\,m \quad \text{Ans.}$$

Scan for Video Explanation

Module-44 Solved Example-15

Ex :   A thin soap film of thickness 3×10^{-7} m and $\mu = 1.5$ is spreaded on a glass surface. When <u>white light</u> is normally incident on this sheet, find the colour which will be reflected maximum.

Sol :

For strong reflection

$$\Delta = 2\mu t = N\lambda$$

$$\lambda = \frac{2\mu t}{N} = \frac{2 \times 1.5 \times 3 \times 10^{-7}}{N} = \frac{9000 \,\overset{\circ}{A}}{N}$$

for $N = 1, 2, 3 \cdots$

$$\lambda = 9000\,\overset{\circ}{A}, \ \underline{4500\,\overset{\circ}{A}}, \ 3000\,\overset{\circ}{A}, \ - - -$$

Visible light (Blue/violet Colour)

Ans.

Module-45 Interference due to Thin Wedge Shaped Film

\# Interference due to Thin wedge shaped film:

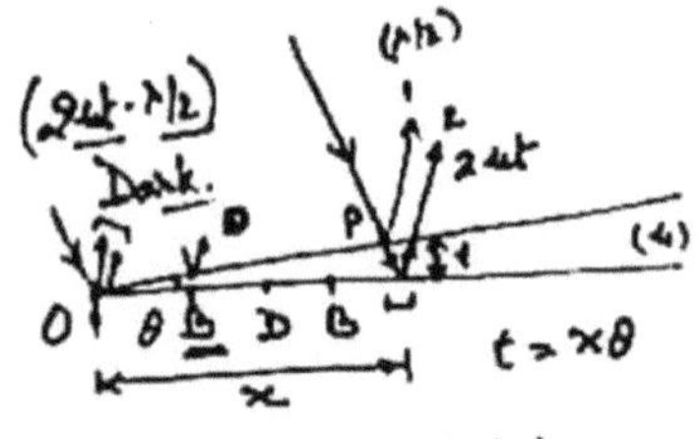

Path diff in reflected beam in waves 1 and 2 is $\Delta = 2\mu t - \lambda/2$

for a bright fringe at pt P $2\mu t - \lambda/2 = N\lambda$

$$x\theta = t = \frac{(2N+1)\lambda}{4\mu}$$

Distance of $(N+1)^{th}$ bright fringe from O.

$$x = \frac{(2N+1)\lambda}{4\mu\theta} \qquad N = 0, 1, 2, 3 \cdots$$

for a dark fringe at pt P $2\mu t - \lambda/2 = (2N-1)\lambda/2$

dist of Nth dark fringe from O.

$$x\theta = t = \frac{N\lambda}{2\mu}$$

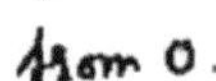

$$x = \frac{N\lambda}{2\mu\theta} ; \ N = 0, 1, 2.$$

Module-46 Interference by an Air Wedge

Interference by an air wedge:

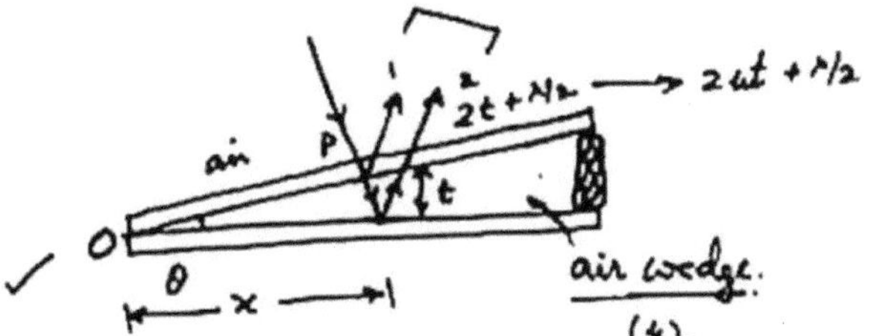

The reflected light at P is bright if $2\mu t + \lambda/2 = N\lambda$

$$x\theta = t = \frac{(2N-1)\lambda}{4\mu}$$

distance of Nth bright fringe from O. $\longleftarrow$ $x = \frac{(2N-1)\lambda}{4\mu\theta}$ $\quad N = 1,2,3,\cdots$

for No reflection at pt P $\quad 2\mu t + \lambda/2 = (2N+1)\lambda/2$

$$x\theta = t = \frac{N\lambda}{2\mu}$$

dist of Nth dark fringe from O. $\Longrightarrow$ $x = \frac{N\lambda}{2\mu\theta}$ $\quad$ where $N = 0, 1, 2, \cdots$

Scan for Video Explanation

Module-47 Shape of Interference Fringes in Reflected Light

Shape of Interference fringes in reflected light:

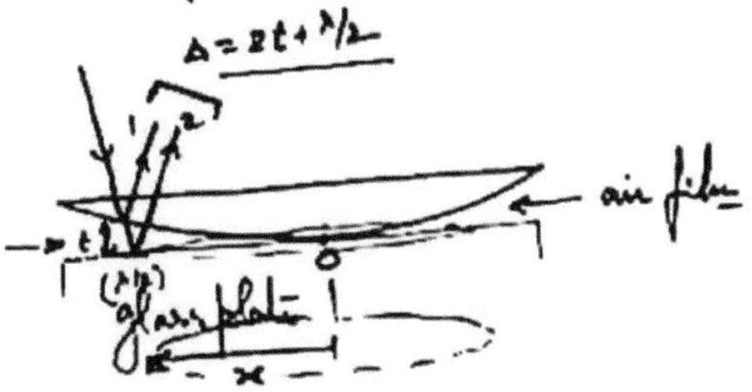

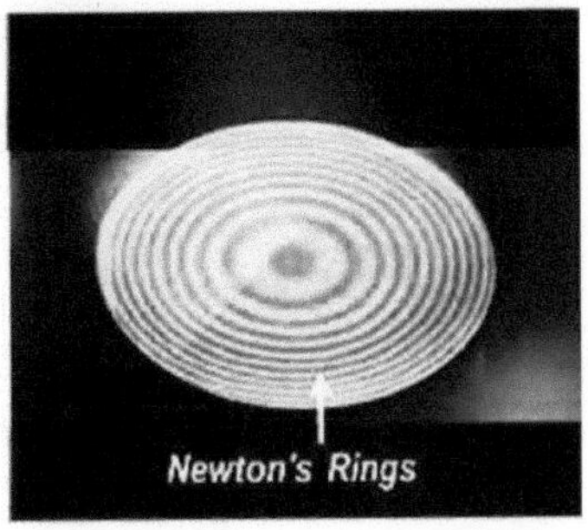

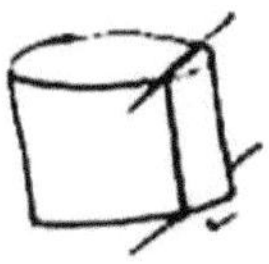

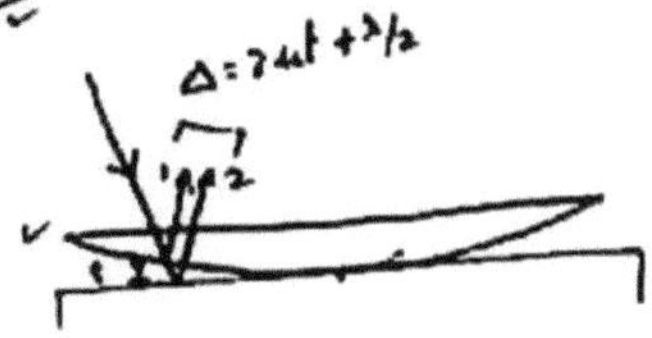

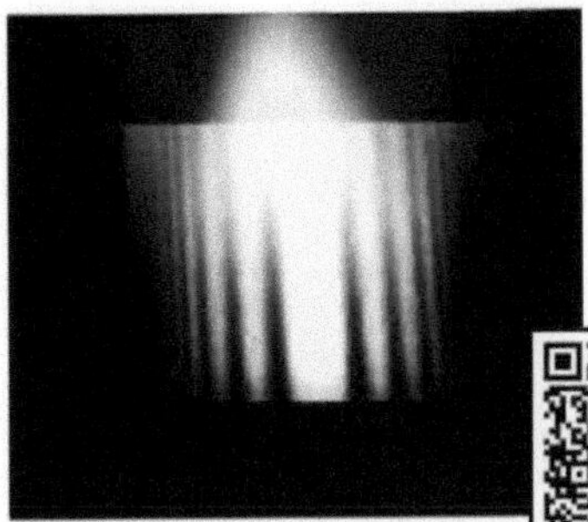

$\Delta = 2t + \lambda/2$

air film

glass plate

$\Delta = 2\mu t + \lambda/2$

Scan for Video Explanation

Chapter 6
Diffraction of Light

Module-1 Diffraction of Light

Diffraction of Light:

When the light passes through edges of an obstacle, it flares out in the shadow zone. This is called diffraction of light.

Scan for Video Explanation

Web Reference at www.physicsgalaxy.com

Module-2 Explanation of Diffraction by Huygen's Wave Theory

Explanation of Diffraction by Hygen's Wave Theory.

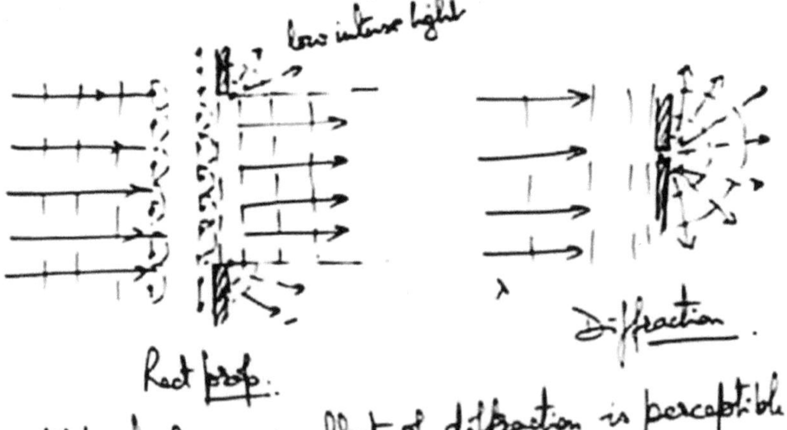

All kind of waves effect of diffraction is perceptible only if the wavelength of wave is comparable to the dimensions of diffracting device.

Scan for Video Explanation

Web Reference at www.physicsgalaxy.com

Module-3 Types of Diffraction

Types of Diffraction:

There are two ways in which diffraction analysis is done

(1) Fresnel Diffraction

When diff of light is analyzed from the diffracting device at a finite distance then it is studied as Fresnel's Diffraction.

(2) Fraunhofer Diffraction

When diff is analyzed at ∞/very large dist from diff device then it is called Fraunhofer diff.

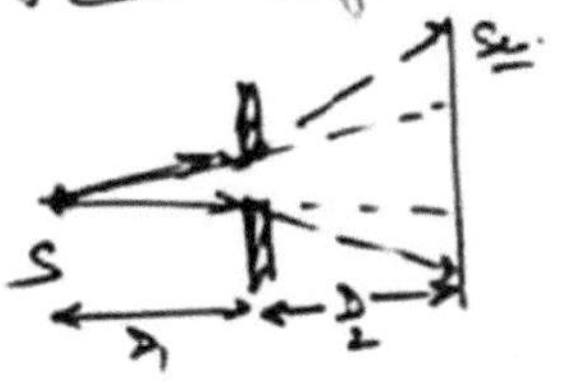

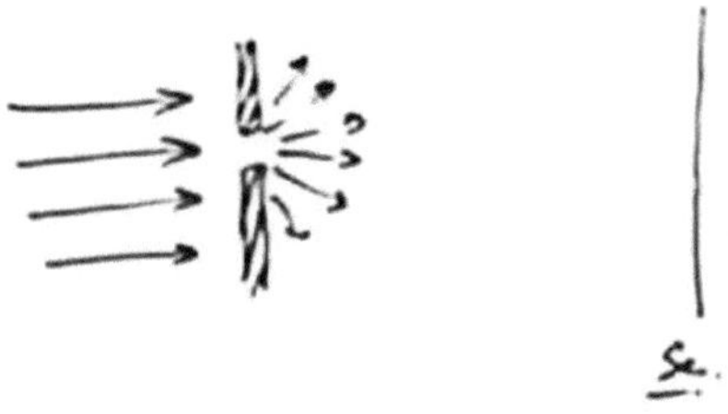

Module-4 Diffraction of Light by a Single Slit

Diffraction of light by a Single Slit:

$I_R = f(\theta)$

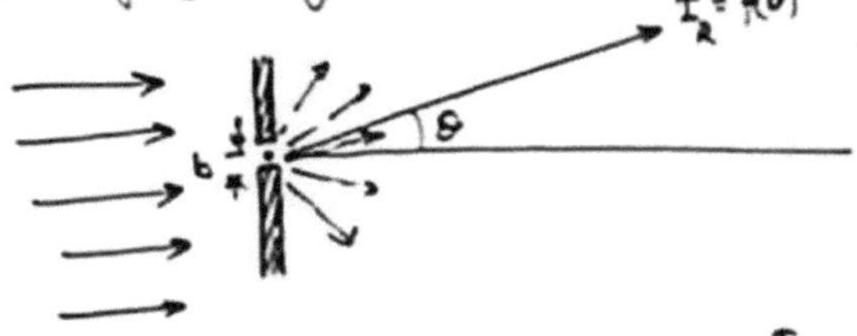

here $I = f(\theta)$ is analyzed by phenomenon of diffraction.

Magnified view of Slit

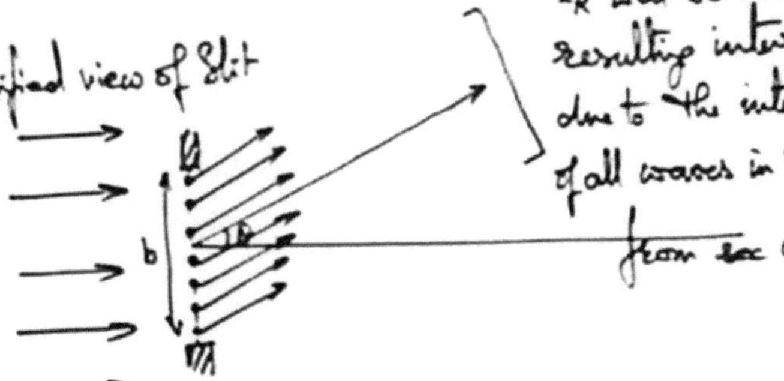

I_R will be the resulting intensity due to the interference of all waves in this dir from sec wavelets.

Module-5 Analysis of Diffraction of Light by a Single Slit

Analysis of Diffraction of light by a Single slit:

In dir θ, path diff between waves from wavelets 1 and 2 is

$\Delta_{12} = d\sin\theta \rightarrow \phi_{12} = \frac{2\pi}{\lambda} \cdot d\sin\theta = \phi$

$\Delta_{13} = 2d\sin\theta \rightarrow \phi_{12} = \frac{2\pi}{\lambda}(2d\sin\theta) = 2\phi$

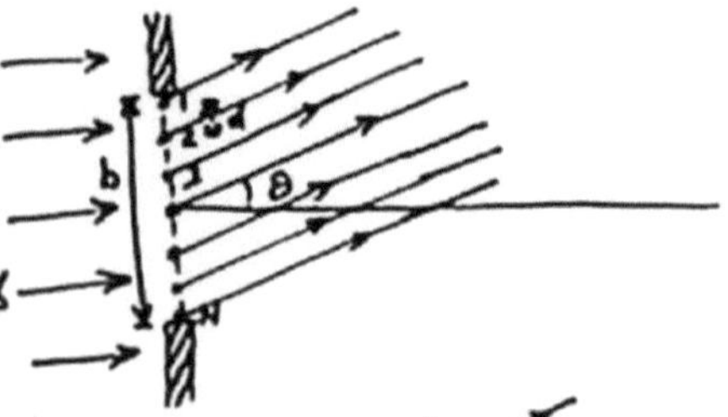

If disp produced by wavelets 1, 2, 3 ... N $(N-1)d = b$

at large dist are $y_1, y_2, y_3 \ldots y_N$ then we can write

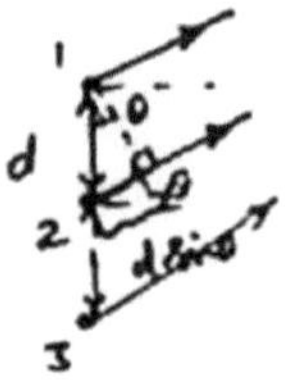

$y_1 = A\sin\omega t$

$y_2 = A\sin(\omega t - \phi)$

$y_3 = A\sin(\omega t - 2\phi)$

A → Amp due to each wavelet.

Scan for Video Explanation

Web Reference at www.physicsgalaxy.com

Module-5 Analysis of Diffraction of Light by a Single Slit

Resulting disp due to supp of all waves in dir θ is –

$y = y_1 + y_2 + \ldots y_N$

$y = A\sin\omega t + A\sin(\omega t - \phi) + A\sin(\omega t - 2\phi) + \ldots A\sin(\omega t + (N-1)\phi)$

Slit width $b = (N-1)d$

$N \gg 1$

$b \simeq Nd$

$y_R = A\frac{\sin(N\phi/2)}{\sin(\phi/2)} \cdot \sin\left(\omega t - \frac{(N-1)\phi}{2}\right)$

$y_R = R\sin(\omega t - \theta)$ [at very large dist from Slit]

Res. int is $I = kR^2 = k\left[A\frac{\sin(N\phi/2)}{\sin\phi/2}\right]^2 \times \frac{N^2}{N^2}$

$I = k\left[(NA)\frac{\sin(N\phi/2)}{(N\phi/2)}\right]^2$ $\phi = \frac{2\pi}{\lambda} \cdot d\sin\theta$

$$\boxed{I = I_0\frac{\sin^2\beta}{\beta^2}}$$

here $\beta = \frac{N}{2} \cdot \frac{2\pi}{\lambda} \cdot d\sin\theta$

$$\boxed{\beta = \frac{\pi b\sin\theta}{\lambda}}$$

$$\boxed{I = f(\theta)}$$

Scan for Video Explanation

Web Reference at www.physicsgalaxy.com

Module-6 Diffraction Minima due to Single Slit

Diffraction Minima due to Single Slit :

$$I_R = I_0 \frac{\sin^2\beta}{\beta^2} \quad ; \quad \beta = \frac{\pi b \sin\theta}{\lambda}$$

at $\theta = 0$, $\beta = 0$, $\underset{\beta \to 0}{Lt} \frac{\sin\beta}{\beta} \to 1 \Rightarrow I_R = I_0$ (max) $\begin{bmatrix} Central \\ Diffraction \end{bmatrix}$ Maxima

if $\beta = m\pi \Rightarrow I_R = 0$ (min)

$m \neq 0.$ $\quad m\pi = \frac{\pi b \sin\theta}{\lambda} \Rightarrow \sin\theta = \frac{m\lambda}{b} \qquad m = 1, 2, \cdots$ there will be a min

for $m = 1$ (first minima) $\sin\theta = \lambda/b$

$$\theta_1 = \sin^{-1}(\lambda/b)$$

$\left. \begin{array}{c} 1^{st} \ min \\ \theta_1 \\ \theta = 0 \\ 1^{st} \ min \end{array} \right\}$ Angular width of Central max

$$\theta_c = 2\theta_1 = 2\sin^{-1}(\lambda/b)$$

Module-7 Diffraction Maxima due to Single Slit

Diffraction Maxima due to Single Slit :

$$I_R = I_0 \frac{\sin^2\beta}{\beta^2} \qquad where \ \beta = \frac{\pi b \sin\theta}{\lambda}$$

at an angle θ if I_R is max $\Rightarrow \frac{dI}{d\beta} = 0$

$$\frac{\beta^2 [2\sin\beta\cos\beta] - (\sin^2\beta)(2\beta)}{} = 0$$

$$\boxed{\tan\beta = \beta}$$

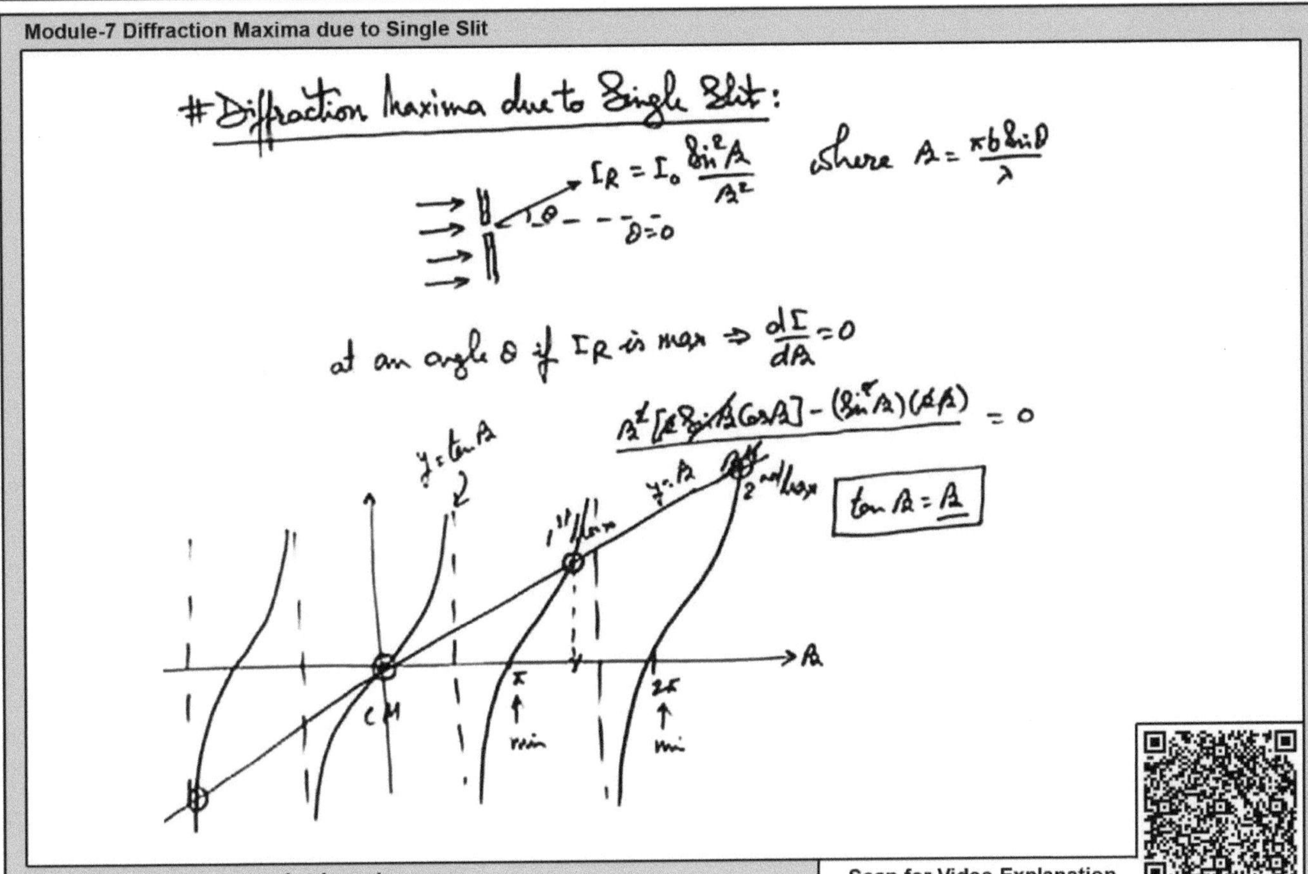

Observing Single Slit Diffraction Pattern on a Screen:

$$I_P = I_0 \frac{\sin^2 \beta}{\beta^2}$$

$$\beta = \frac{\pi b \sin\theta}{\lambda}$$

1st (min)

Central maxima

$\theta = 0$ I_0

1st (min)

$$\theta_1 = \sin^{-1}\left(\frac{\lambda}{b}\right)$$

$$\theta_1 \simeq \frac{\lambda}{b}$$

Screen

f

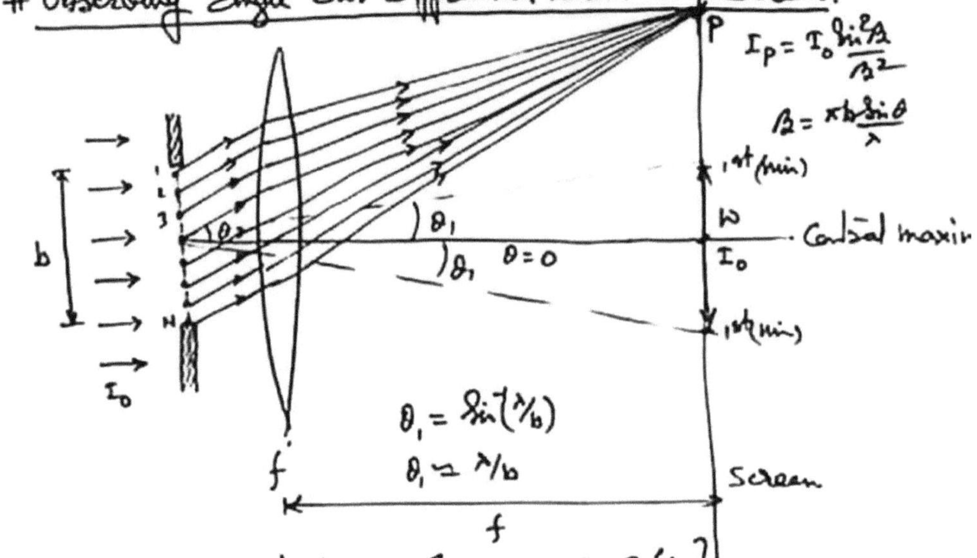

$$\text{width of Central max} \left\{ \omega = 2\theta_1 \cdot f = \frac{2 f \lambda}{b} \right\}$$

Dark fringe

angular pos. of diff minima $b\sin\theta = m\lambda \Rightarrow \theta_{min} = \sin^{-1}\left(\frac{m\lambda}{b}\right)$

Single slit diffraction pattern on a Screen:

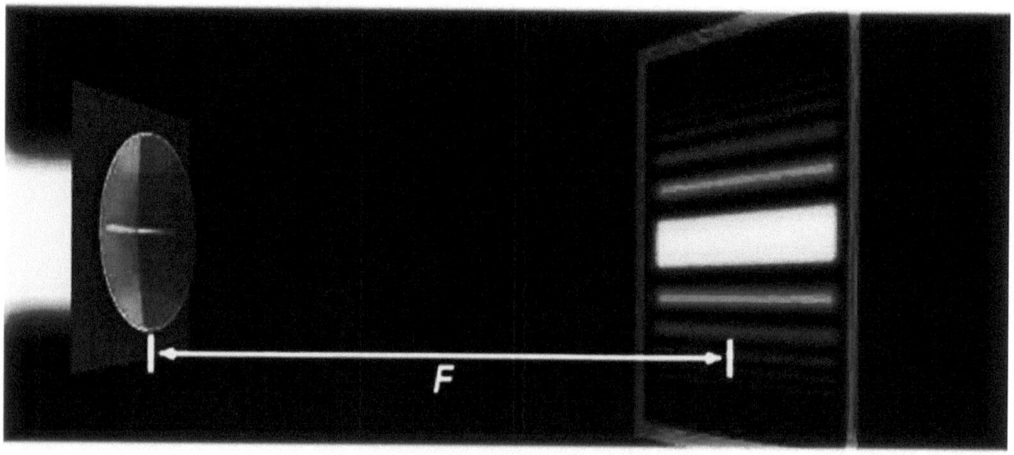

$$I_R = I_0 \frac{\sin^2 \beta}{\beta^2}$$

Module-10 Difference Between Interference and Diffraction Patterns

Difference between interference and diffraction pattern:

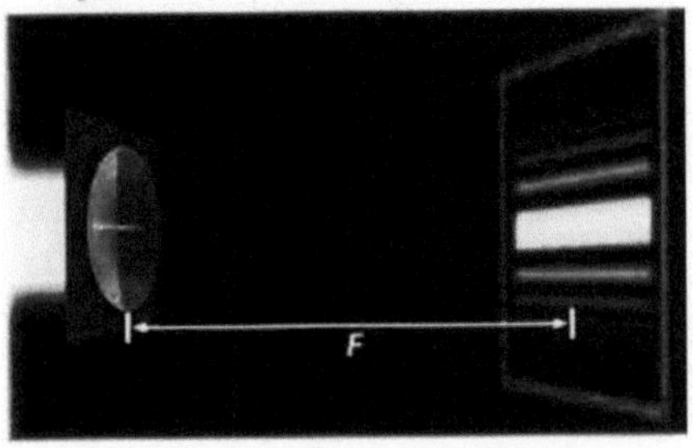
F

Differaction.

- All friges are of diff width.
- All friges have diff brightness
  ↓
  bright
- Due to interference of several monochromatic sources.
  ↓
  Coherent.

YDSE -

- All friges are of same width
- All friges have same brightness
  ↓
  bright
- Due to interference of two monochromatic coherent sources

S_1
S_2

Module-11 Illumination Pattern due to Diffraction by Single Slit

Illumination pattern due to diffraction by a single slit:

For a single slit first minima is located at $\theta = \sin^{-1}(\lambda/b)$

Case-I : If $b >> \lambda$

$\theta = \sin^{-1}\left(\frac{\lambda}{b}\right) \to 0$

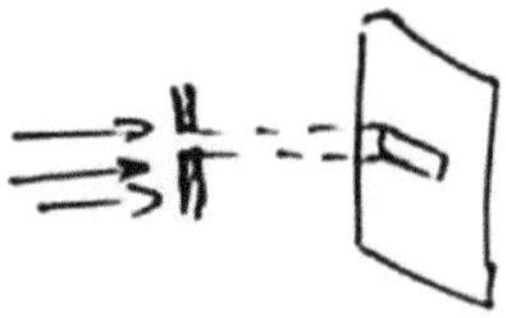

⇒ Rect prop of light.

Case-II : If $b > \lambda \Rightarrow \theta = \sin^{-1}(\lambda/b)$

⇒ diff pattern is seen

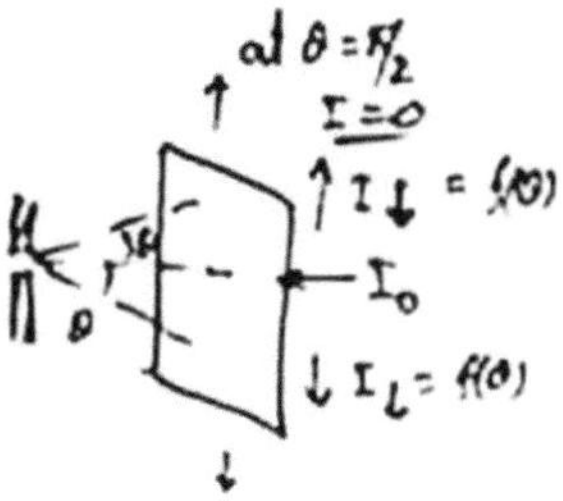
at $\theta = \pi/2$
$I = 0$
$I = f(\theta)$
I_0
$I_L = f(\theta)$
θ

Case-III : If $b = \lambda \Rightarrow \theta = \pi/2$ (1st min)

⇒ Central maxima will extend upto ∞.

Case-IV : If $b < \lambda \Rightarrow$ No minima

⇒ almost uniform illumination will be there on screen.

Diffraction by a Small Circular Aperture:

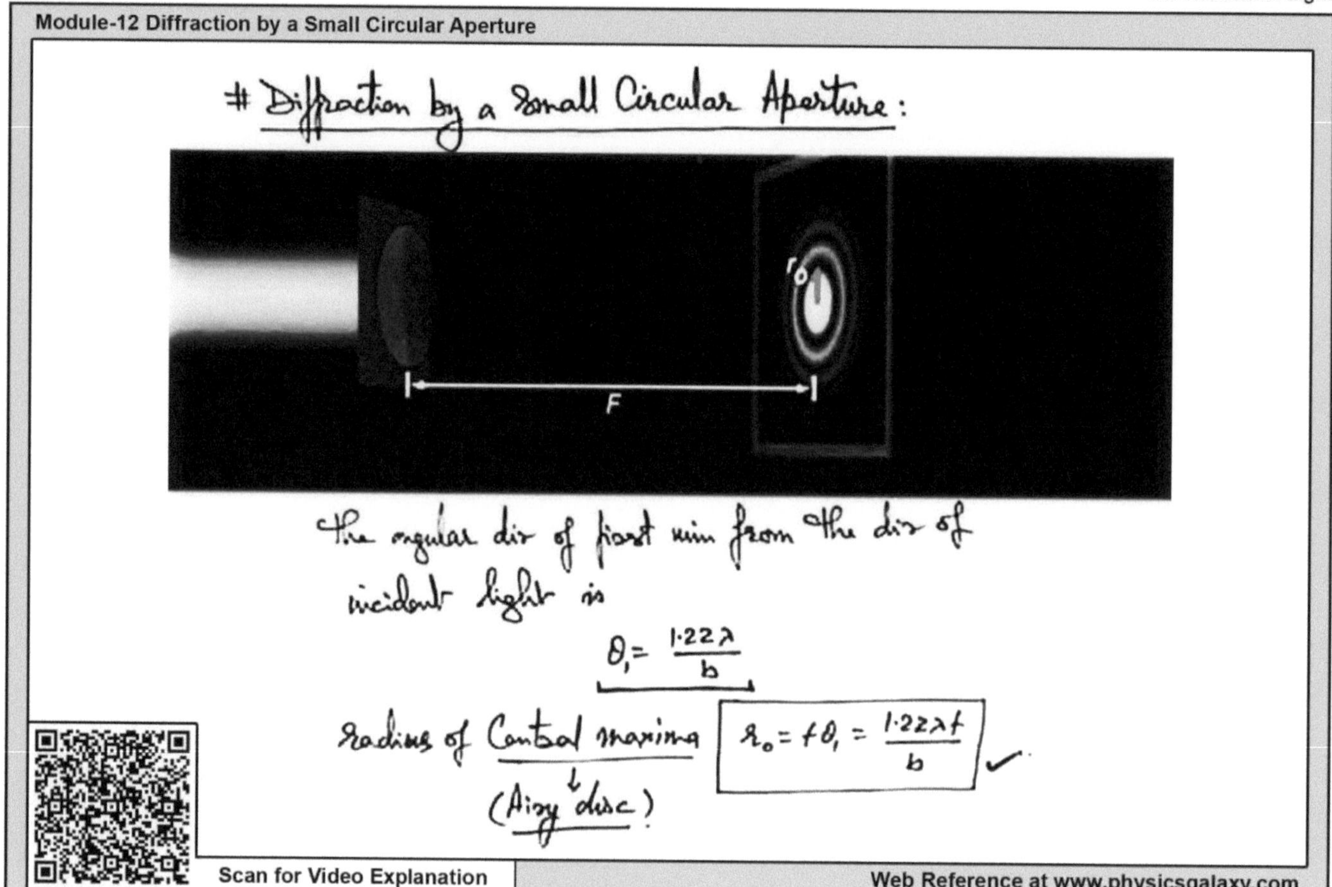

The angular dir of first min from the dir of incident light is

$$\theta_1 = \frac{1.22\lambda}{b}$$

Radius of Central maxima (Airy disc)

$$\boxed{r_0 = f\theta_1 = \frac{1.22\lambda f}{b}}$$ ✓

Chapter 7
Polarization of Light

Polarization of Light :

light is an EM wave and in ordinary light $\vec{E}$ osc in dir $\perp$ to prop dir of light in any plane.

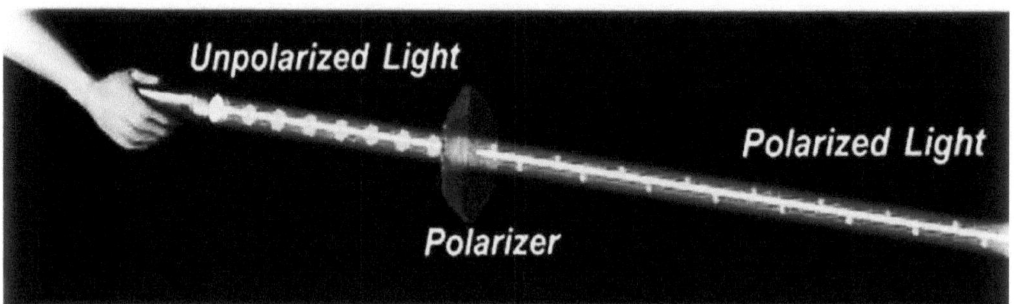

Restricting the osc of $\vec{E}$ in a light only in one plane is called Polarization and the plane is called plane of polarization.

Representation of unpolarized and polarized light :

Unpolarize light

Polarized light

Module-3 Circularly and Elliptically Polarized Light

Circularly and Elliptically Polarized Light:

In a cir polarized light $\vec{E}$ oscillates in a plane and the plane of vib rotates either ckwise or ackwise

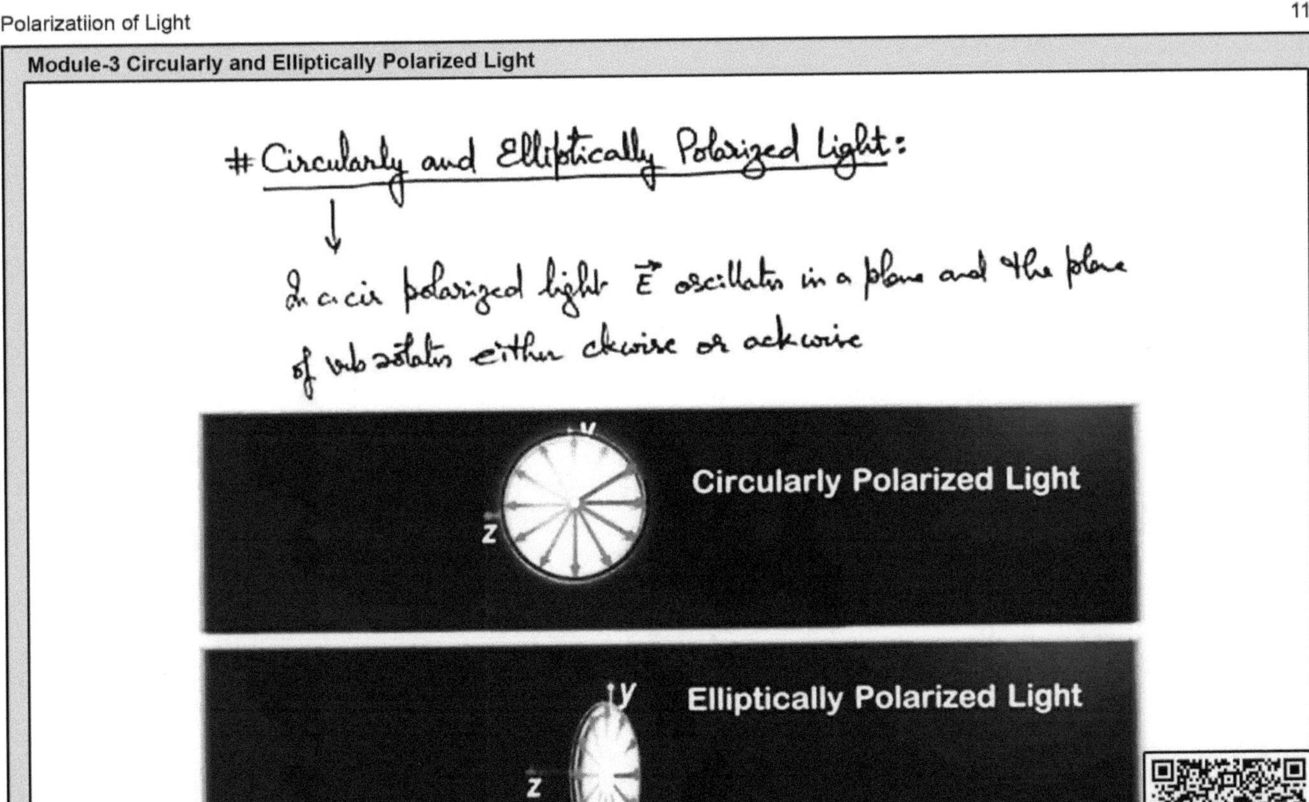

Scan for Video Explanation 

Module-4 Methods of Polarizing and Ordinary Light

Methods of Polarizing an Ordinary Light:

There are various ways by which a plane polarized light can be obtained from an unpolarized light.

Some of these method are —

① By Reflection

② By Refraction

③ By Double Refraction

④ By Dichroism

⑤ By Scattering

Scan for Video Explanation 

Module-5 Polarization by Reflection

Polarization by Reflection:

It was discovered that reflected light from a surface is plane pol when incident light is at an angle is such that from the surface Reflected and Refracted rays are ⊥ to each other ← Brewster's Law.

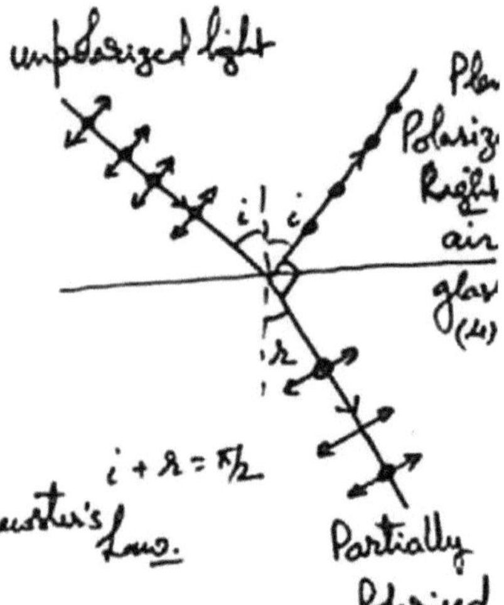

$i + r = \pi/2$

By using Snell's law-

$\mu \sin r = \sin i$

$\mu \sin(\pi/2 - i) = \sin i$

$\tan i = \mu$

(Brewster's Angle) ← $i_b = \tan^{-1}(\mu)$

NOTE: Reflected Polarized light has vib ⊥ to plane of incidence

Module-6 Polarization by Refraction

Polarization by Refraction:

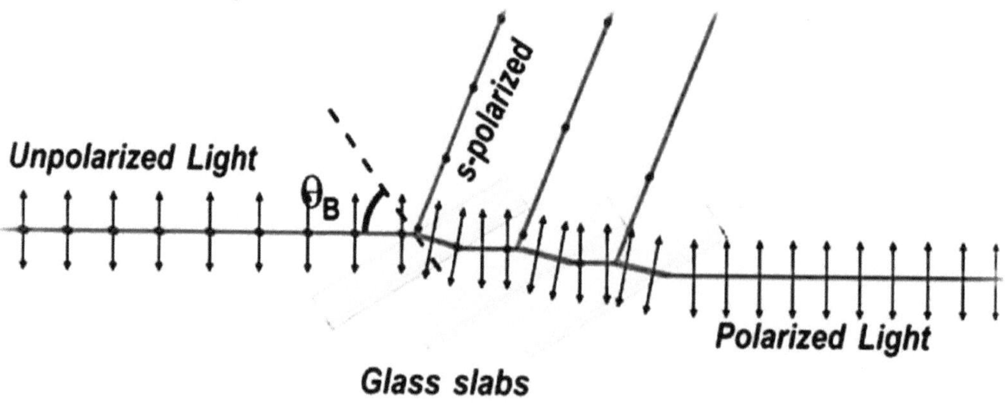

NOTE: Finally transmitted light has vib in the plane of incidence

#: <u>Polarization by double refraction</u>:

There are some s/p crystals like calcite, quartz, tourmaline etc. when a light is refracted th. these, it splits into two rays of equal intensities with ⊥ vib.

① <u>O-Ray</u>: It follows the laws of Refraction

② <u>E-Ray</u>: I does not obey laws of Refraction.

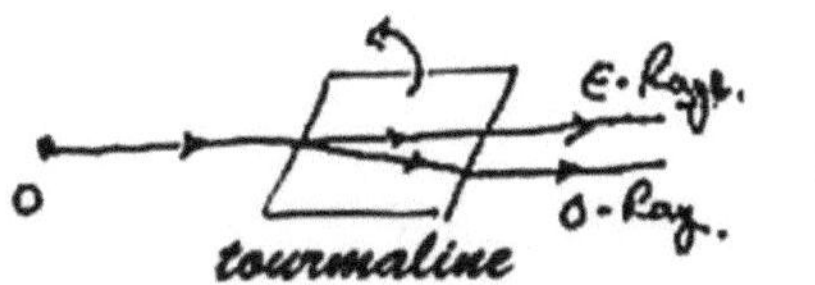

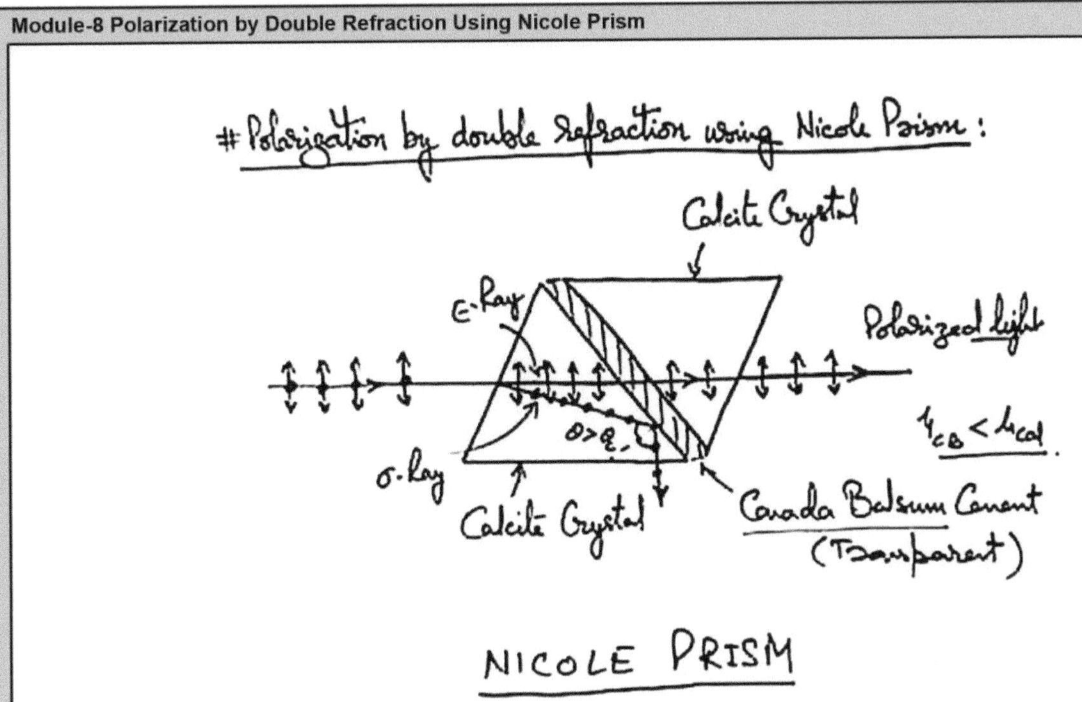

<u>Polarization by double Refraction using Nicole Prism</u>:

Module-9 Polarization by Dichroism

Polarization by 'Dichroism':

Some sp crystals have the prop of absorbing vibrations in perp dir with penetration and after some dist of penet the light will be plane polarized in dir $\perp$ to abs. vib.

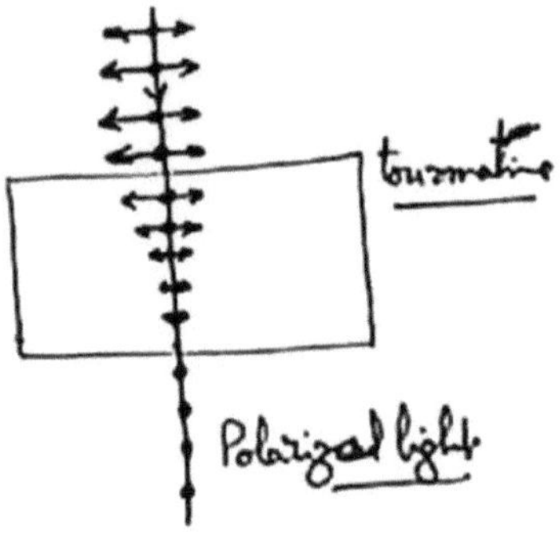

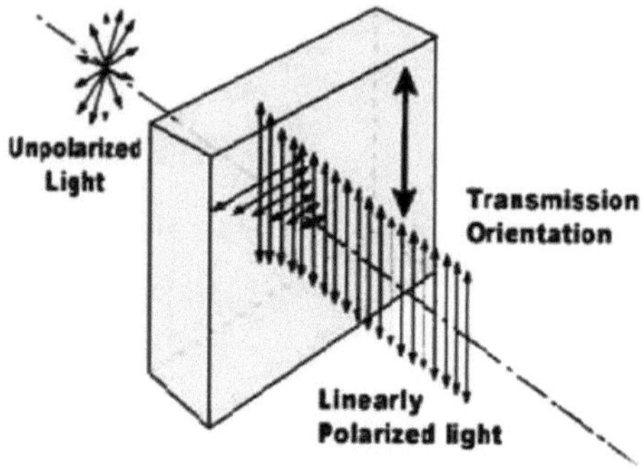

(Polaroids use dichroism prop for Pol of light)

Scan for Video Explanation

Web Reference at www.physicsgalaxy.com

Module-10 Polarization by Scattering

Polarization by Scattering:

Incident light is absorbed and re-radiated in diff direction.

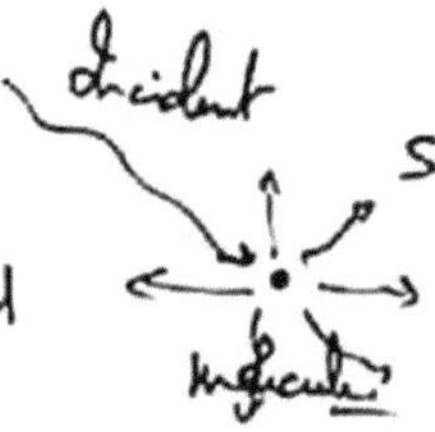

It is observed that scattered light in dir $\perp$ to incident dir is completely plane polarized and the transmitted light is partially polarized.

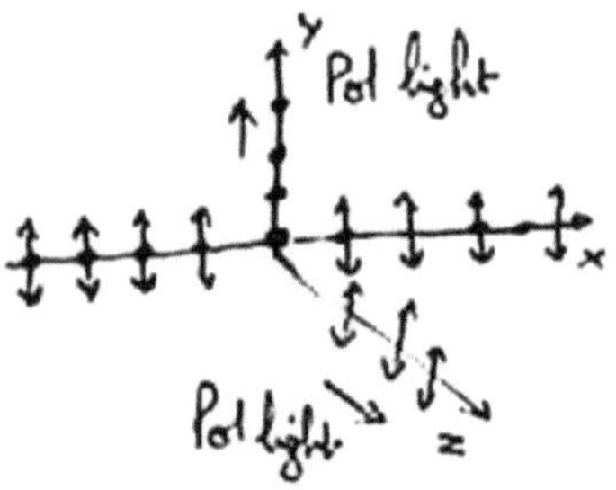

Scan for Video Explanation

Web Reference at www.physicsgalaxy.com

Malus Law:

A polaroid only allows those vib to pass th. it which have their vib plane along the transmission axis of polaroid..

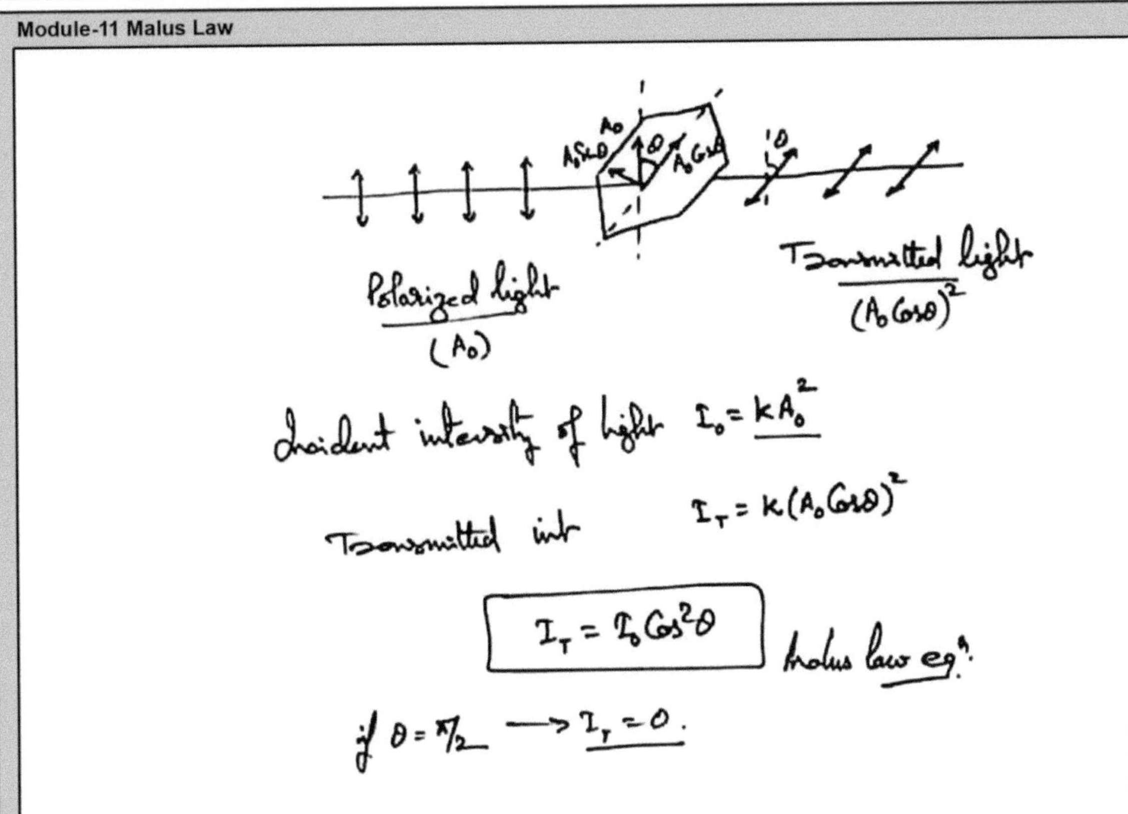

Malus law.

When a PPL with amp A_0 incident on a polaroid with the vib plane at angle θ to tr axis then the amp of vib in transmitted light will be $A_0\cos\theta$.

Scan for Video Explanation

Polarized light
(A_0)

Transmitted light
$(A_0\cos\theta)^2$

Incident intensity of light $I_0 = \underline{kA_0^2}$

Transmitted int $\qquad I_T = k(A_0\cos\theta)^2$

$$\boxed{I_T = I_0\cos^2\theta}$$ Malus law eq^n.

if $\theta = \pi/2 \longrightarrow \underline{I_T = 0}$.

Scan for Video Explanation

 # Light Intensity through a polaroid:

— An unpolarized light has vib in all dir $\perp$ to propagation dir

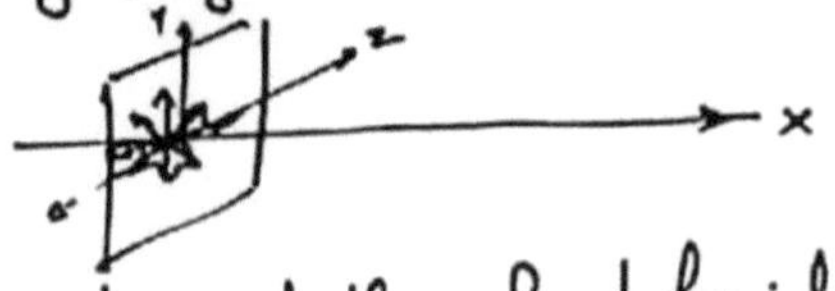

— When it is passed through a polaroid, component of each vib along the t_n axis will pass through it.

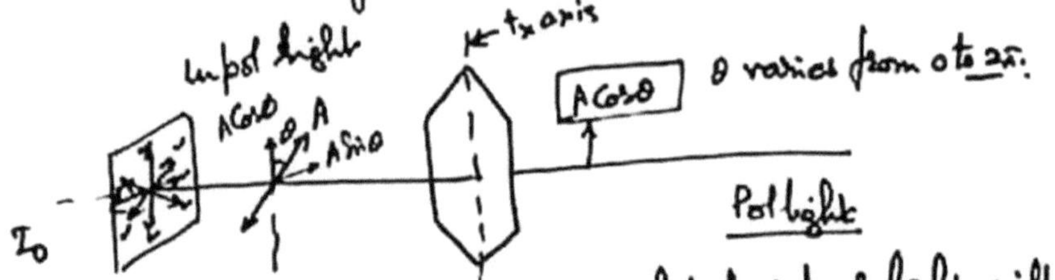

θ varies from 0 to 2π.

for all vib transmitted through pol, int of light will be

$$I_f = \left(I_0 \cos^2\theta\right)_{avg} = I_0 \left(\cos^2\theta\right)_{avg} = \frac{I_0}{2}$$

 # Optical Activity of Substances:

Some specific transparent Substances have prop to rotate the plane of polarization of a polarized light when it is passed th it. Such substances are called optically active Subst.

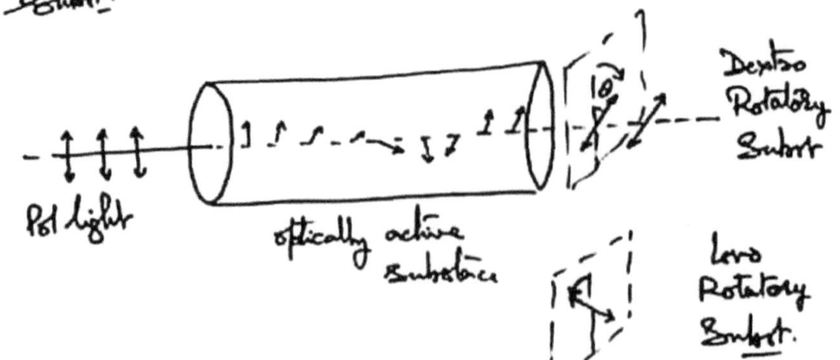

Chapter 8
Photometry

Photometry :

Study of meas of light energy & its illumination on a surface is called photometry.

Def of some imp terms used in Photometry :

① Radiant Flux (P): Total energy radiated by a light source (meas in watt) (J/sec).

② Luminous Flux (ϕ): This is the total light energy emitted by a light source. This is meas in units "lumen"

$\underline{1\ lumen} \longrightarrow$ light-energy rad by a source of $\underline{1/685\ watt}$ and in wavelength $\underline{5500\ \overset{\circ}{A}}$.

③ Luminous Efficiency (η): $\eta = \dfrac{\phi}{P}$ lumen/watt.

Luminous Intensity and Illuminance :

In a given direction it is the luminous flux per unit solid angle.

along dir $\hat{n}$ luminous intensity is given as $L = \dfrac{d\phi}{d\Omega}$ lumen/st

$\qquad\qquad\qquad\qquad\qquad\qquad\qquad\qquad = \dfrac{d\phi}{d\Omega}$ Cd

If source is isotropic $L = \dfrac{\phi}{4\pi}$ lumen/st or Cd.

in all dir

Illuminance : When light falls on a surface and illuminate it then Illuminance is defined as luminous flux/m² on the surface.

Module-3 Relation Between Luminous intensity & Illuminance

Relation between Luminous Intensity & Illuminance:

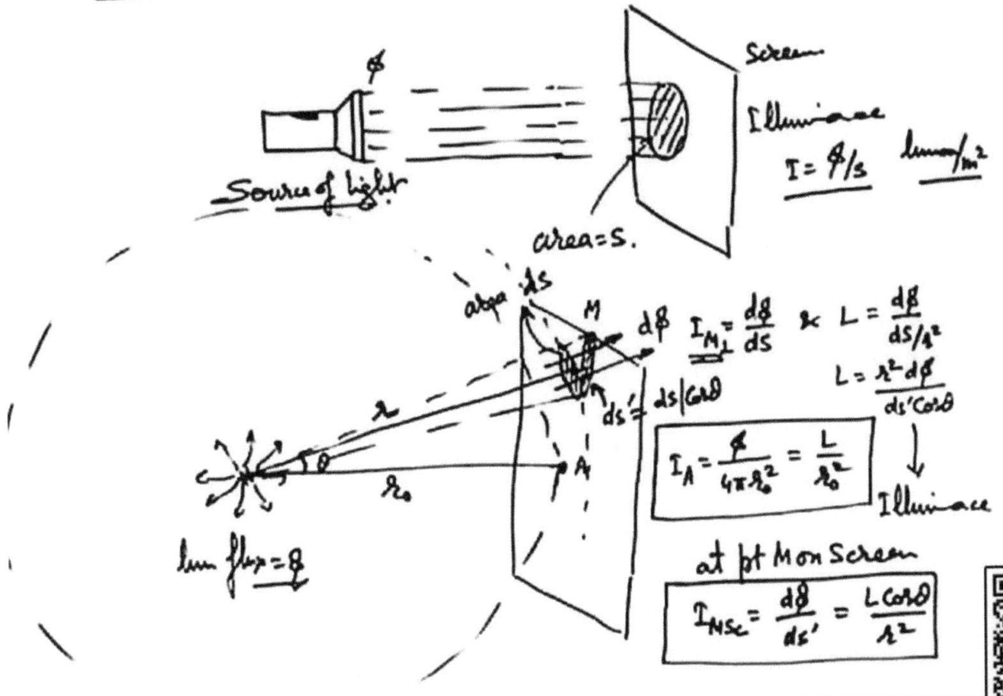
Screen
Illuminance
I = φ/s lumen/m²
Source of light
area = S.
area ds
M
dφ
$I_{M\perp} = \frac{d\phi}{ds}$ & $L = \frac{d\phi}{ds/r^2}$
$L = \frac{r^2 d\phi}{ds' \cos\theta}$
ds' = ds/Cosθ
$I_A = \frac{\phi}{4\pi r_0^2} = \frac{L}{r_0^2}$
Illuminance
r
θ
r₀
A
lum flux = φ
at pt M on Screen
$I_{MSc} = \frac{d\phi}{ds'} = \frac{L\cos\theta}{r^2}$

Web Reference at www.physicsgalaxy.com

Scan for Video Explanation

Module-4 Lambert Cosine Rule

Lambert Cosine Rule:

This rule gives the illuminance of light on a screen due to a pt source in any dir.

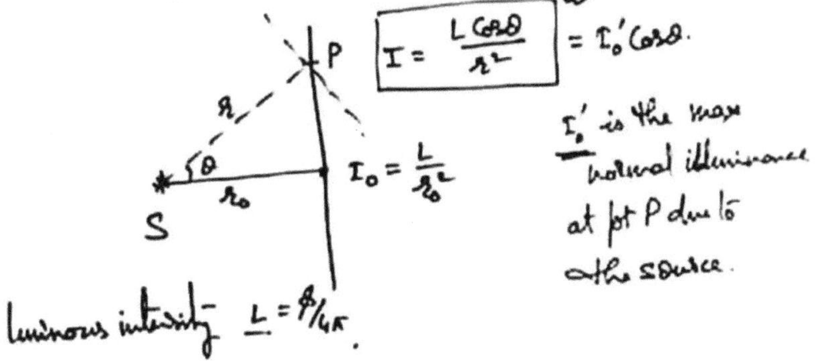
P
$I = \frac{L\cos\theta}{r^2} = I_0'\cos\theta.$
r
θ
S
r₀
$I_0 = \frac{L}{r_0^2}$
I_0' is the max normal illuminance at pt P due to the source.
luminous intensity $L = \phi/4\pi$.

Web Reference at www.physicsgalaxy.com

Scan for Video Explanation

Module-5 Photometer

\# <u>Photometer</u>: An exp setup use to Compare illuminance of two sources on a screen.

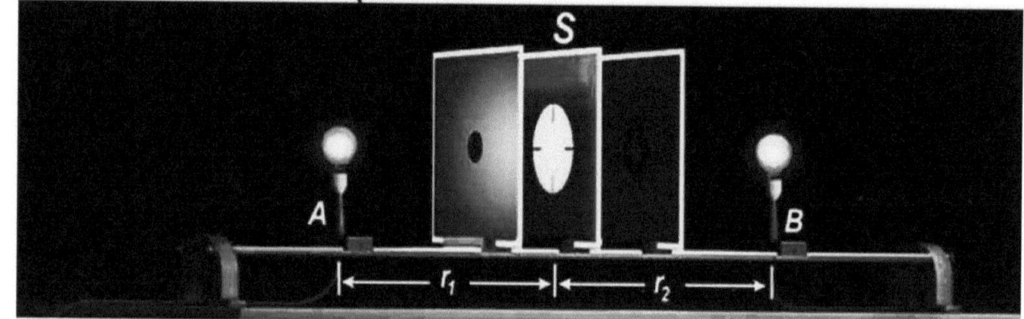

When illumination due to two Sources becomes equal on Screen $\Rightarrow$ we can use

$$\boxed{\frac{L_1}{r_1^2} = \frac{L_2}{r_2^2}} \quad -(1)$$

This is Called "Principle of Photometry".

Module-6 Solved Example-1

Ex : A 40W point isotropic light source has luminous efficiency 4π lumen/watt. Find the luminous flux and luminous intensity of the source and luminous intensity on a normal surface 2m from the source.

<u>Sol:</u>

luminous flux of source $\phi = \eta P = 4\pi \times 40 = 160\pi \;\frac{lumen}{}$. Ans

luminous intensity of a point Source $L = \frac{\phi}{4\pi} = \frac{160\pi}{4\pi} = 40\; Cd$. Ans

$$I = \frac{L}{r^2} = \frac{40}{(2)^2} = 10\; lux \quad Ans.$$

Module-7 Solved Example-2

Ex : A 100W bulb having luminous efficiency 10 lm/W is placed at a distance $\sqrt{3}\,m$ from a screen S as shown in figure. Find the luminous intensity on screen at a point P as shown in figure.

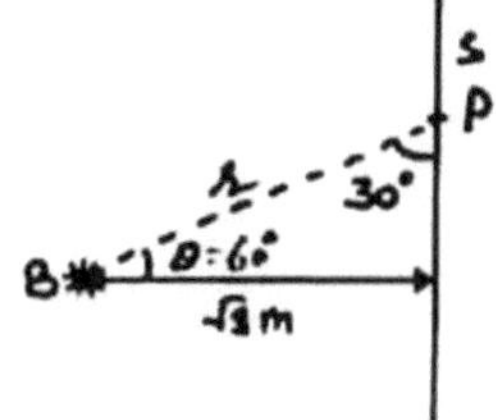

Sol^n: luminous flux of bulb. $\phi = \eta P = 10 \times 100 = 1000$ lumen.

luminous intensity of bulb $L = \dfrac{\phi}{4\pi} = \dfrac{1000}{4\pi} = \dfrac{250}{\pi}$ Cd.

Illuminance of bulb on screen at pt P as $\quad r = \dfrac{\sqrt{3}}{\cos 60°} = 2\sqrt{3}\,m$.

$$I = \frac{L\cos\theta}{r^2} = \frac{\overset{125}{\cancel{250}}}{\pi} \times \frac{\cancel{1/2}}{r^2}$$

$$I = \frac{125}{\pi(2\sqrt{3})^2} = 3.32 \text{ lux} \quad \underline{\text{Ans.}}$$

Scan for Video Explanation

Module-8 Solved Example-3

Ex : A point source of light is placed at a height h above the centre of a horizontal circular disc of radius R. What must be the value of $\underline{h}$ so that illumination is maximum on edge of disc.

Sol^n: If L be the luminous int of source the Illuminance at pt E will be-

$$I = \frac{L\cos\theta}{r^2} = \frac{L}{(R^2+h^2)} \times \frac{h}{\sqrt{R^2+h^2}}$$

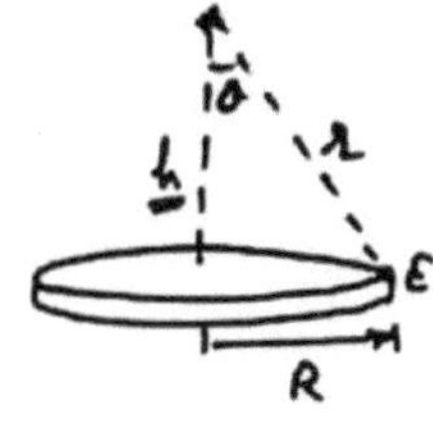

$r = \sqrt{R^2+h^2}$

$$I_E = \frac{Lh}{(R^2+h^2)^{3/2}}$$

for I_E to be max $\dfrac{dI_E}{dh} = 0$

$$\frac{(h^2+R^2)^{3/2} - \frac{3}{2}(R^2+h^2)^{1/2}\cdot 2h\cdot h}{(R^2+h^2)^3} = 0$$

$$h^2 + R^2 - 3h^2 = 0 \Rightarrow \underline{h = R/\sqrt{2}} \quad \underline{\text{Ans.}}$$

Scan for Video Explanation

Module-9 Solved Example-4

Ex : A point source of light is suspended at some height above the centre of a horizontal surface. Luminous intensity of source in different directions has different values such that the illuminance at all points on the table is same. In such situation if luminous intensity varies with angle 0 as $L = L_0 \cos^n 0$, find value of n.

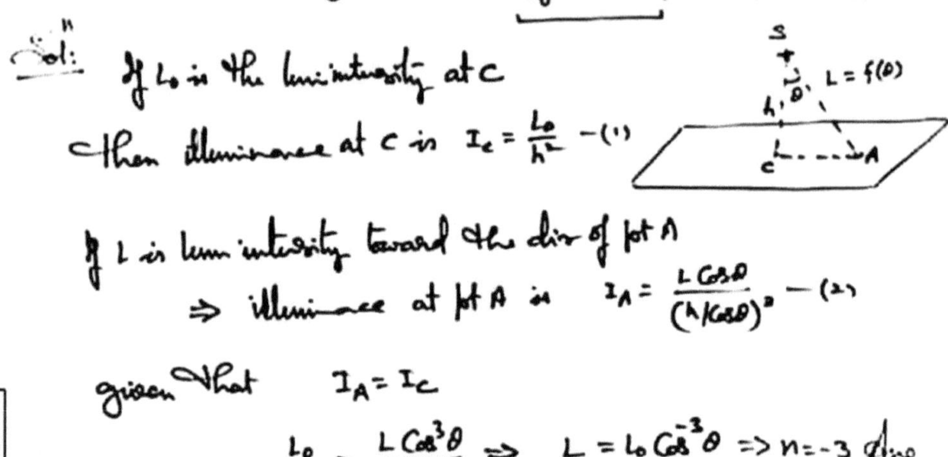

Sol: If L_0 is the lum. intensity at C

Then illuminance at C is $I_c = \dfrac{L_0}{h^2}$ —(1)

If L is lum. intensity toward the dir. of pt A

$\Rightarrow$ illuminance at pt A is $I_A = \dfrac{L \cos\theta}{(h/\cos\theta)^2}$ —(2)

given that $I_A = I_c$

$$\dfrac{L_0}{h^2} = \dfrac{L \cos^3\theta}{h^2} \Rightarrow L = L_0 \cos^{-3}\theta \Rightarrow n = -3 \text{ Ans.}$$

Module-10 Solved Example-5

Ex : In a photometer light from a bulb A is exactly balanced by that from another bulb B placed 30 cm from a screen. On placing a transparent glass sheet between the bulb A and screen, B has to be shifted by 10 cm to restore the balance. Find the fraction of light absorbed by the glass sheet.

Sol: If L_A and L_B are luminous intensities of bulbs A and B and let A is located at a dist x from the screen

$$\Rightarrow \dfrac{L_A}{x^2} = \dfrac{L_B}{(30)^2} \quad —(1)$$

after placing a glass sheet if a fraction x of light abs by it

$$\Rightarrow \dfrac{L_A(1-x)}{x^2} = \dfrac{L_B}{(40)^2} \quad —(2)$$

$$\left(\dfrac{(2)}{(1)}\right) \qquad 1-x = \left(\dfrac{3}{4}\right)^2 \Rightarrow x = 1-\dfrac{9}{16} = \dfrac{7}{16} = 0.44 = 44\% \text{ Ans.}$$

Chapter 9
Optical Instruments

Optical Instruments :

OI are devices which utilize the phenomenon of Reflection & Refraction for image formation of various object for their study in detail.

The most Common & imp OI we study are —

① Human Eye

② Simple Microscope

③ Compound Microscope

④ Refracting Telescope

⑤ Reflecting Telescope

⑥ Terrestrial Telescope

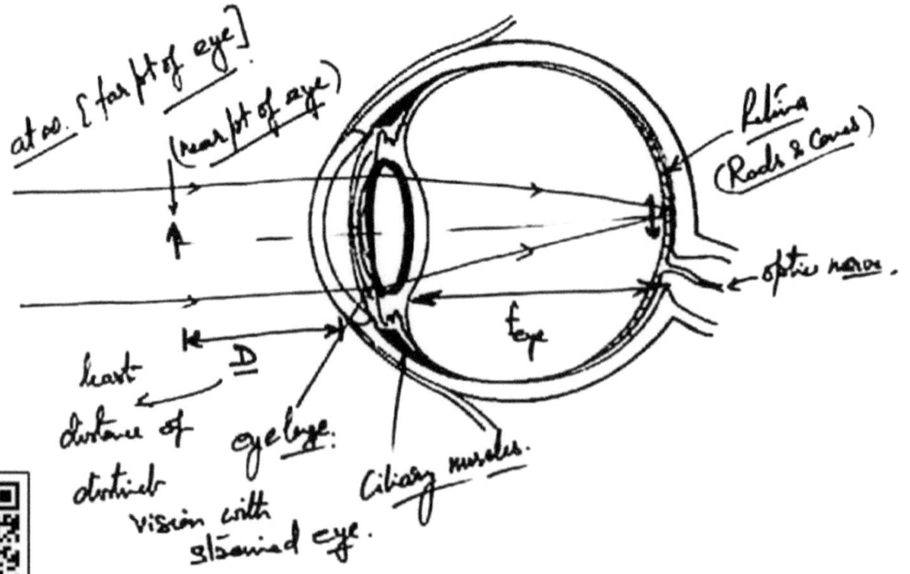

⑦ Galilean Telescope

Human Eye :

Module-3 Defects of Vision

\# Defects of vision:

① Short sightedness or Myopia:
dist object are not
clearly seen by eye.
Correction → by div lenses.

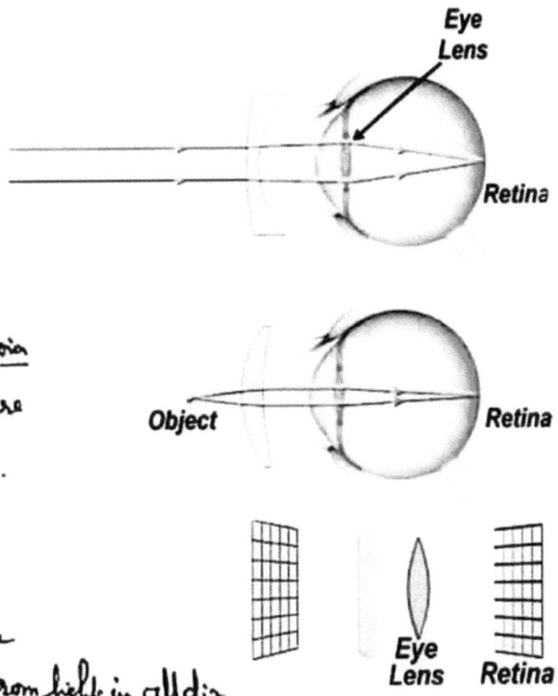

② Farsightedness or Hypermetropia
objects at near pt of eye are
not clearly seen by eye.
Correction → by Conv lenses

③ Astigmatism:
Eye lens fails to produce
sharp image on Retina from light in all dir.

Scan for Video Explanation

Module-4 Simple Microscope

\# Simple Microscope: (Magnifying glass)

- It is a Conv lens of small focal length
- In order to use a Simple microscope, it
  is held near the object and eye is
  placed on the other side.
- Image produced will be erect,
  virtual & magnified.

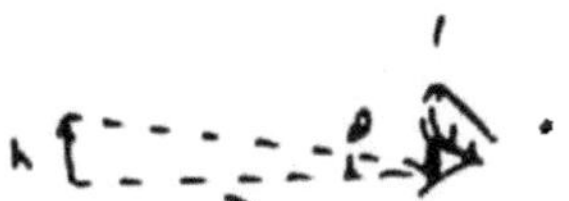

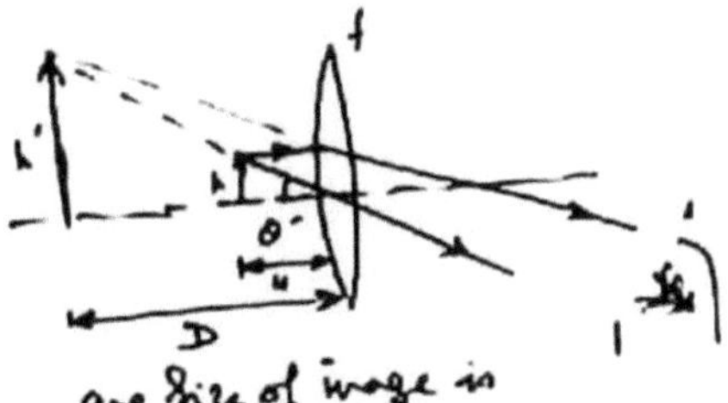

Magnification of a Simple microscope is

$$m = \frac{h'}{h} = \frac{\theta'}{\theta} = \frac{h/u}{h/D} = \frac{D}{u} = \frac{D}{\frac{Df}{D+f}}$$

$$\boxed{m_D = 1 + \frac{D}{f}}$$ when image is produced at near pt

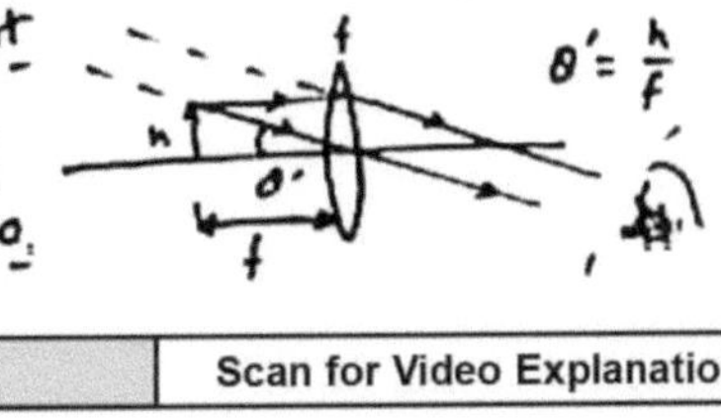

$$\boxed{m_\infty = \frac{h/f}{h/D} = \frac{D}{f}}$$ when image is prod at ∞.

Scan for Video Explanation

Module-5 Solved Example-1

Ex :   If focal length of a magnifying glass is 5 cm. Find the magnification of this magnifier for relaxed and strained eye.

Sol^n :   For relaxed eye image is prod at ∞.

$$MP = \frac{D}{f} = \frac{25\,cm}{5\,cm} = \underline{5} \quad Ans.$$

For strained eye image is prod at $D = 25\,cm$.

$$MP = 1 + \frac{D}{f} = 1 + \frac{25}{5} = 1 + 5 = 6 \;\underline{Ans.}$$

Scan for Video Explanation   **Web Reference at www.physicsgalaxy.com**

Module-6 Solved Example-2

Ex :   A man with normal near point (D = 25 cm) reads a book with small printing using a magnifying glass of f = 5 cm. What is the closet and farthest distance at which he can read the book using magnifying glass.

Sol^n :   for closest distance u is such that $v = -25\,cm$:

using lens formula

$$\frac{1}{v} - \frac{1}{u} = \frac{1}{f}$$

$$\frac{1}{-25} - \frac{1}{u} = \frac{1}{5} \Rightarrow \frac{1}{u} = -\frac{1}{25} - \frac{1}{5} = \frac{-6}{25}$$

$$u = -\frac{25}{6}\,cm = -\,4.17\,cm \;\underline{Ans}$$

for max value of u is such that $v \to \infty$.

$$u = f = \underline{5\,cm} \;Ans.$$

Scan for Video Explanation   **Web Reference at www.physicsgalaxy.com**

Module-7 Compound Microscope

Compound Microscope:

Single lens has limitations on its MP so for higher mag we use Compound mic. It uses two lenses called 'objective' and 'eyepiece'

closer to object — closer to eye
(small aperture)

If we use lens formula for 'Objective'

$$\frac{1}{v} - \frac{1}{u} = \frac{1}{f}$$ here $u = -u$, $v = +v$, $f = +f_o$ $\Rightarrow v = \frac{uf_o}{u-f_o}$

mag by objective $\quad m_o = -\frac{v}{u} = -\left(\frac{f_o}{u-f_o}\right)$

mag by eyepiece $\quad m_e = \left(1 + \frac{D}{f_e}\right) = \left(\frac{D}{f_e}\right)$

for image formed at near pt
for image formed at far pt.

$f_o < f_e$

Mag Power of Compound mic
$$MP_D = -\frac{v}{u}\left(1 + \frac{D}{f_e}\right)$$

$$MP_\infty = -\frac{v}{u}\left(\frac{D}{f_e}\right)$$

$u_e = f_e$

Scan for Video Explanation

Module-8 Tube Length of Compound Microscope

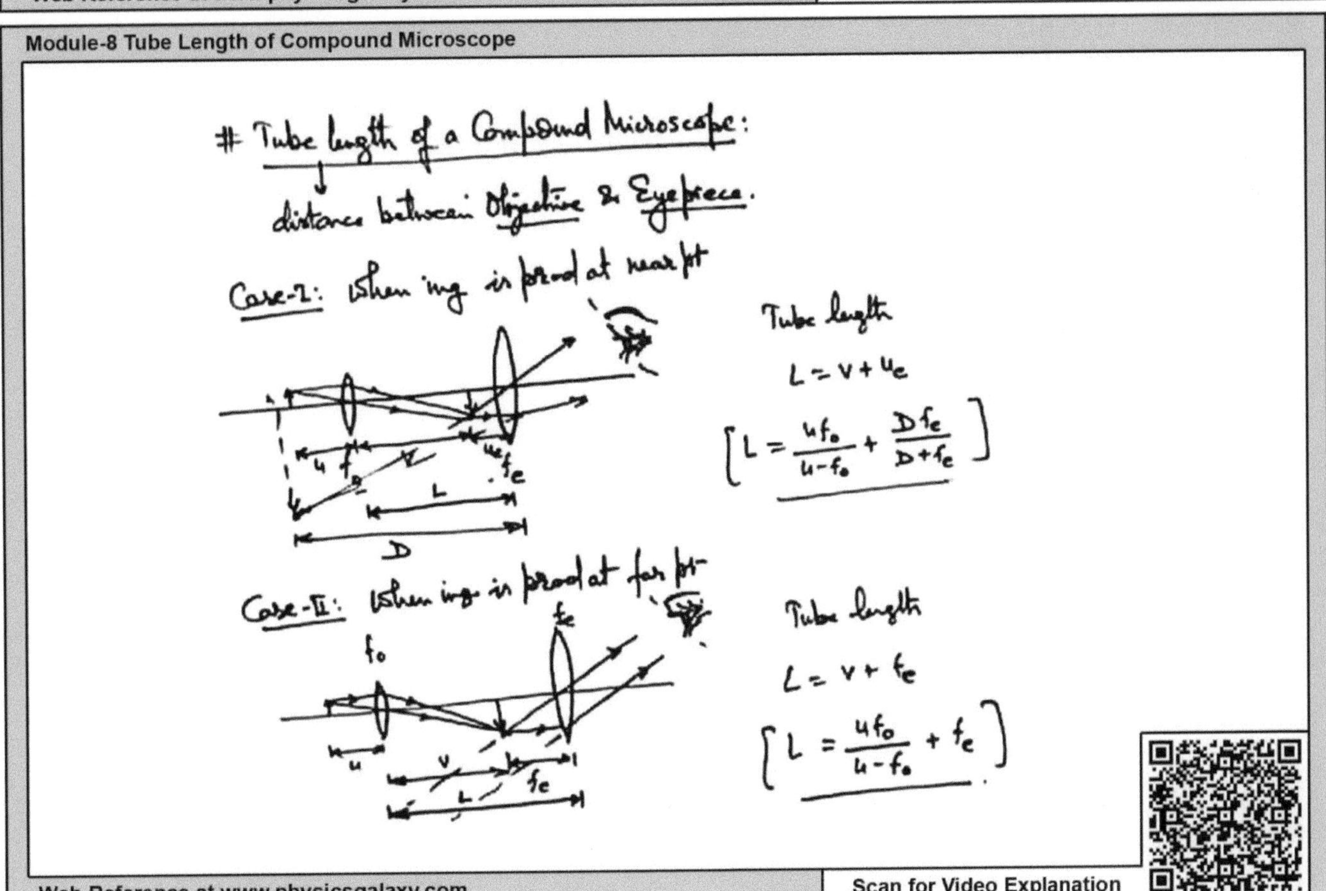

Tube length of a Compound Microscope:
distance between Objective & Eyepiece.

Case-I: When img is formed at near pt

Tube length
$$L = v + u_e$$
$$\left[L = \frac{uf_o}{u-f_o} + \frac{Df_e}{D+f_e} \right]$$

Case-II: When img is formed at far pt

Tube length
$$L = v + f_e$$
$$\left[L = \frac{uf_o}{u-f_o} + f_e \right]$$

Scan for Video Explanation

Ex : A compound microscope has magnifying power $\underline{30}$. If it is producing final image at near point of 25 cm, find the magnification of objective lens. (f_e = 5 cm)

Sol^n: for final image at near pt MP of eyepiece is

$$m_e = 1 + \frac{D}{f_e} = 1 + \frac{25}{5} = 1 + 5 = \underline{6}$$

$$\text{Total } MP = m_0 \cdot m_e$$

$$30 = m_0 \cdot 6$$

$$m_0 = \frac{30}{6} = 5 \text{ Ans.}$$

Ex : A compound microscope is used to enlarge an object kept at a distance $\underline{3 \text{ cm}}$ from its objective which is a combination of $\underline{3 \text{ convex lenses}}$ in contact has a focal length $\underline{2 \text{ cm}}$. If a convex lens of focal length 10 cm is removed from objective, find the distance by which eye-piece is to be shifted to refocus the image.

Sol^n: If image is prod by objective at a dist v

$\Rightarrow$ using lens formula $\underline{\dfrac{1}{v} - \dfrac{1}{u} = \dfrac{1}{f_0}}$ $\left.\begin{array}{l} u = -3 cm \\ f_0 = +2 cm \end{array}\right]$ $\Rightarrow \dfrac{1}{v} + \dfrac{1}{3} = \dfrac{1}{2}$

$$\Rightarrow v = \underline{6 cm}$$

A lens of 10 cm focal length is removed.

find f_0' of objective is given as - $\dfrac{1}{f_0'} = \dfrac{1}{f_0} - \dfrac{1}{10} = \dfrac{4}{10} \Rightarrow f_0' = \underline{2.5 cm}$

Now final image is prod by objective at v' s.t.

$$\dfrac{1}{v'} + \dfrac{1}{3} = \dfrac{1}{2.5} \Rightarrow v' = \underline{15 cm}$$

$$\text{displacement of eyepiece} = 15 - 6 = \underline{9 cm} \text{ Ans.}$$

Module-11 Solved Example-5

Ex : In a compound microscope has objective and eyepiece
of focal lengths 0.6 cm and 5 cm respectively and
separation between themis 12 cm. Find object distance
for final image to be produced at near point (25 cm).
Also find the magnifying power of microscope.

Sol: for eyepiece:
$$v = -25 \text{ cm} \\ f = +5 \text{ cm} \\ u = ?$$
$$\frac{1}{v} - \frac{1}{u} = \frac{1}{f} \Rightarrow -\frac{1}{25} - \frac{1}{u} = \frac{1}{5}$$
$$\frac{1}{u} = -\frac{1}{25} - \frac{1}{5} = -\frac{6}{25}$$
$$u = -\frac{25}{6} \text{ cm}$$

for objective:
$$v = 12 - \frac{25}{6} = +\frac{47}{6} \text{ cm} \\ f = 0.6 \text{ cm} \\ u = ?$$
$$\frac{1}{v} - \frac{1}{u} = \frac{1}{f} \Rightarrow \frac{6}{47} - \frac{1}{u} = \frac{10}{6}$$
$$\frac{1}{u} = \frac{6}{47} - \frac{10}{6} = -\frac{434}{6 \times 47}$$
$$u = -\frac{6 \times 47}{434} = 0.65 \text{ cm} \quad \text{Ans}$$

MP of microscope
$$MP = m_o . m_e = \frac{47/6}{0.65} \times \left(1 + \frac{25}{5}\right) = 72.3 \quad \text{Ans.}$$

Module-12 Refracting Telescope

Refracting Telescope : Astronomical telescope

– It provides ang mag for dist objects & uses two lenses

'objective' & 'eyepiece'

(large aperture)

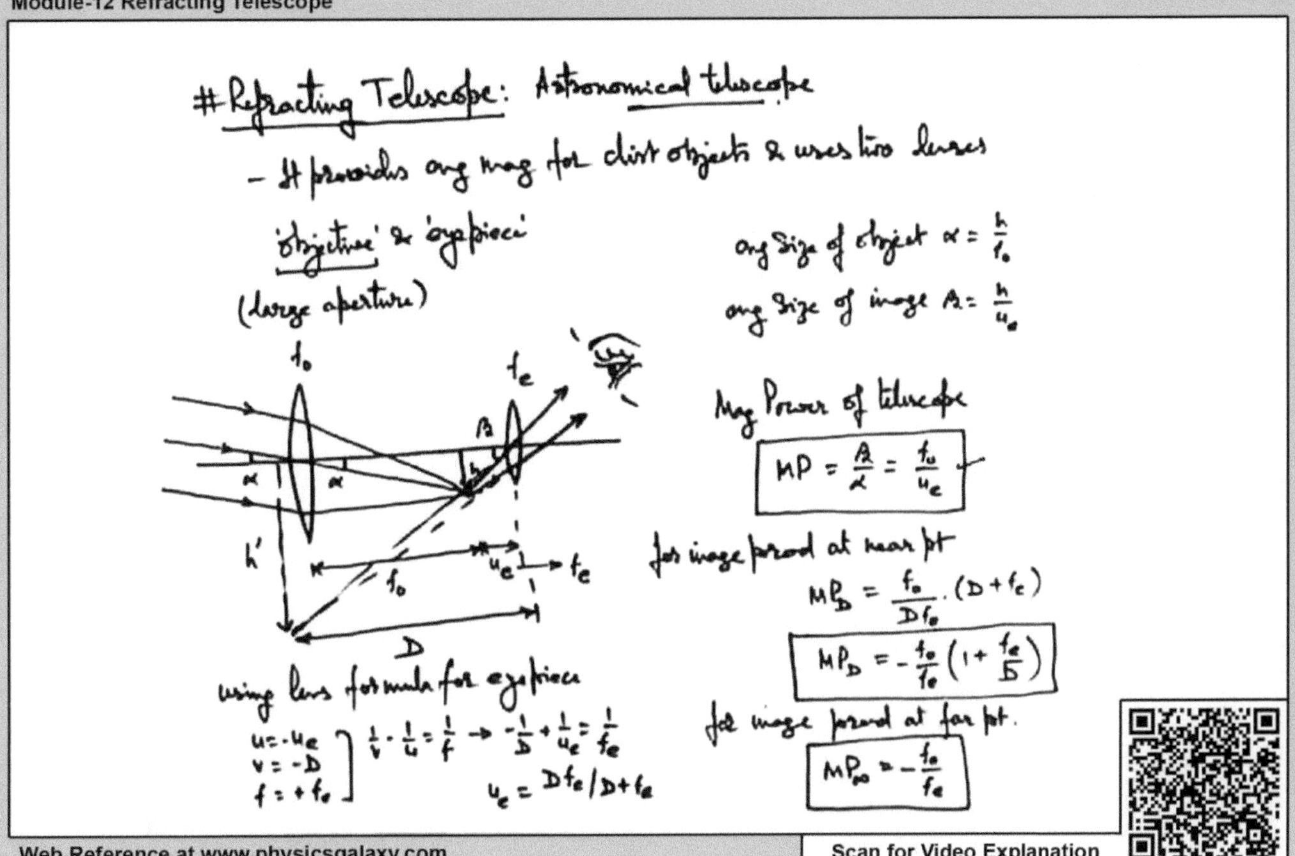

ang size of object $\alpha = \frac{h}{f_o}$

ang size of image $\beta = \frac{h}{u_e}$

Mag Power of telescope
$$MP = \frac{\beta}{\alpha} = \frac{f_o}{u_e}$$

for image formed at near pt
$$MP_D = \frac{f_o}{D f_e} . (D + f_e)$$
$$MP_D = -\frac{f_o}{f_e}\left(1 + \frac{f_e}{D}\right)$$

for image formed at far pt.
$$MP_\infty = -\frac{f_o}{f_e}$$

using lens formula for eyepiece
$$u = -u_e \\ v = -D \\ f = +f_e$$
$$\frac{1}{v} - \frac{1}{u} = \frac{1}{f} \rightarrow -\frac{1}{D} + \frac{1}{u_e} = \frac{1}{f_e}$$
$$u_e = D f_e / D + f_e$$

Module-13 Tube Length of a Refracting Telescope

Tube length of a Refracting Telescope:

Tube length → Sep between objective & eyepiece

Case-I: When img is at near pt.

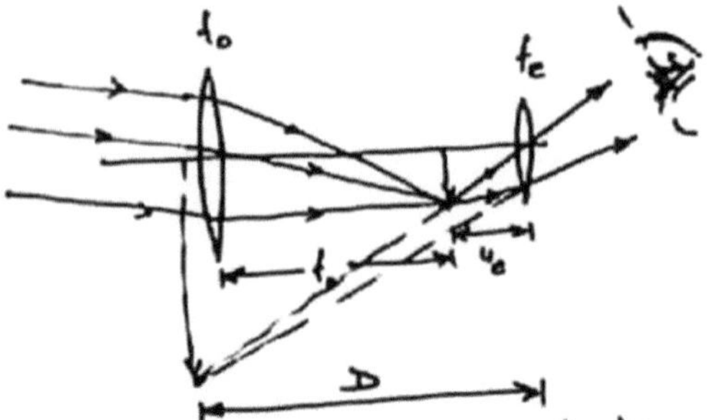

Tube length

$L = f_o + u_e$

$\left[L = f_o + \frac{Df_e}{D + f_e} \right]$

Case-II: When img is at far pt

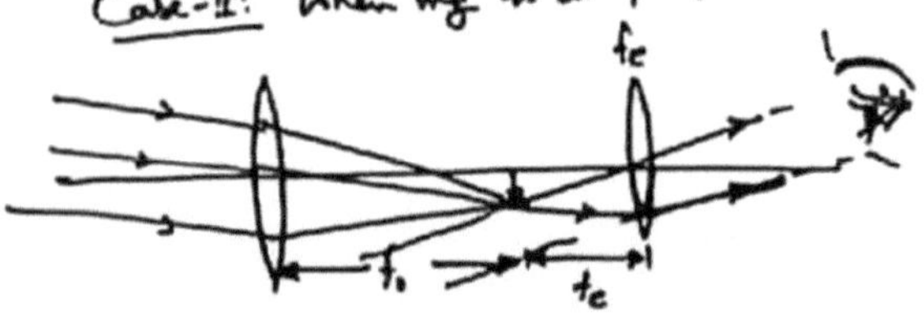

Tube length

$[L = f_o + f_e]$

Scan for Video Explanation

Web Reference at www.physicsgalaxy.com

Module-14 Reflecting Telescope

Reflecting Telescope: Astronomical telescope

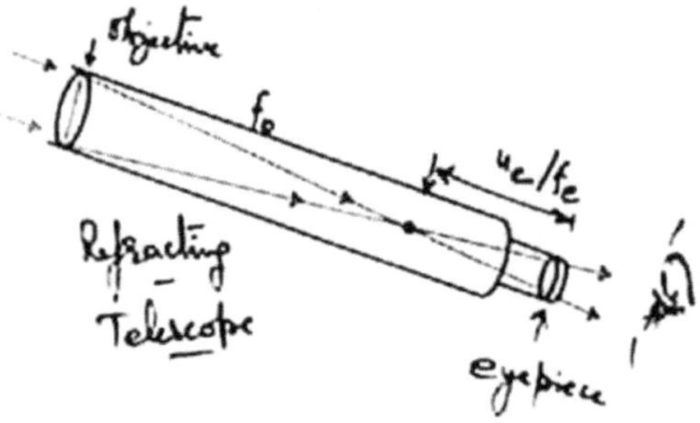

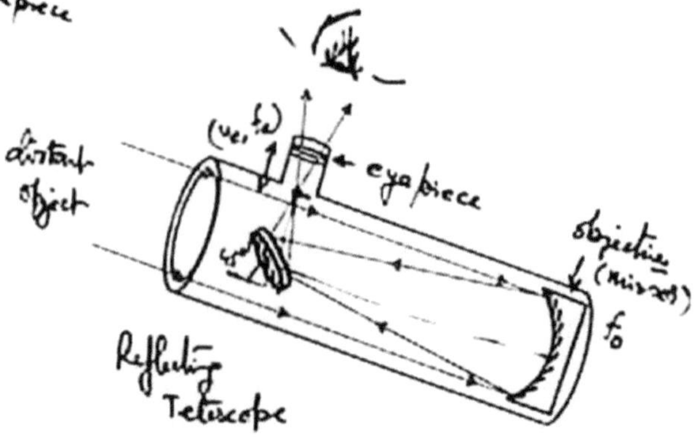

Scan for Video Explanation

Web Reference at www.physicsgalaxy.com

Module-15 Terrestrial Telescope

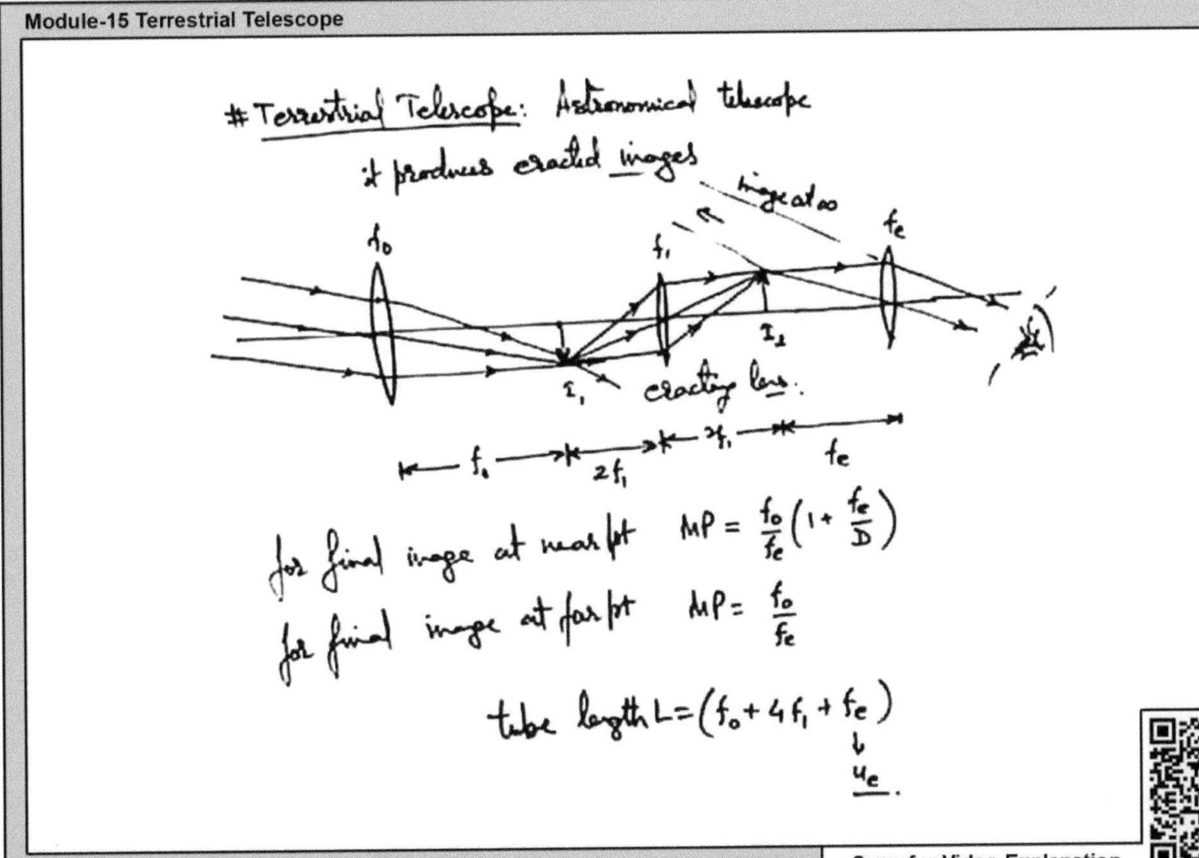

for final image at near pt $MP = \dfrac{f_0}{f_e}\left(1 + \dfrac{f_e}{D}\right)$

for final image at far pt $MP = \dfrac{f_0}{f_e}$

tube length $L = \left(f_0 + 4f_1 + f_e\right)$
                              $\downarrow$
                             u_e.

Module-16 Galilean Telescope

Galilean Telescope:
It also uses two lenses — (i) Convex (ii) Concave
                              $\downarrow$ $\downarrow$
                         objective   eyepiece.

– The advantage of Galilean telescope is shorter tube length and it gives erected image without using the erecting lens.

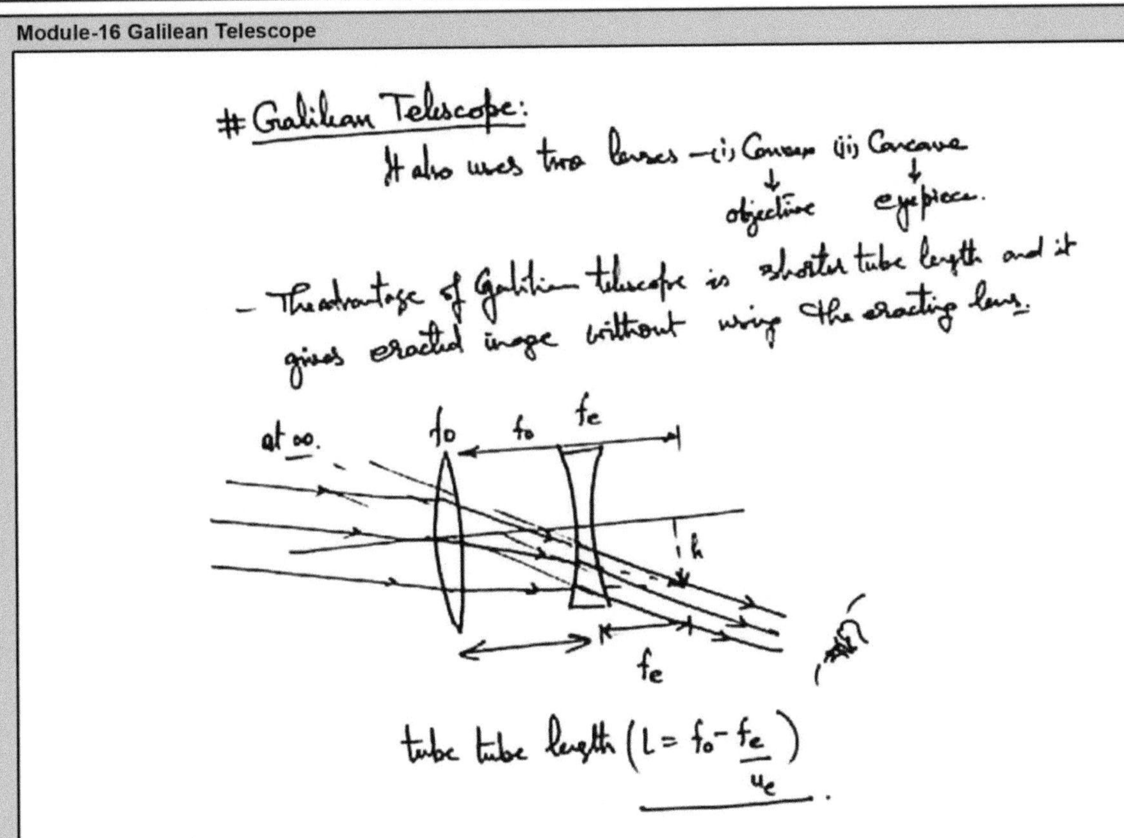

tube tube length $\left(L = \dfrac{f_0 - f_e}{u_e}\right)$.

Module-17 Solved Example-6

Ex : In a telescope focal lengths of objective and eye piece are 60 cm and 5 cm respectively. If is used to focus a distant object with final image at infinity. If object subtend and angle $2°$ on eye, find angular width of final image.

Sol^n: For relaxed state of eye

$$MP = \frac{f_o}{f_e} = \frac{\text{angular width of image}}{\text{ang width of object}} = \frac{\theta_i}{\theta_o}$$

$$\theta_i = \frac{f_o}{f_e} \times \theta_o$$

$$\theta_i = \frac{\cancel{60}^{12}}{\cancel{5}} \times 2° = \underline{24°}\ \text{Ans.}$$

Module-18 Solved Example-7

Ex : A telescope has objective and eye piece of focal lengths 50 cm and 5 cm respectively. The telescope is focussed on a scale placed 2 m from the objective for the final image at near point (25 cm). Calculate the magnification and separation between objective and eyepiece.

Sol^n: for eyepiece.

$$\left.\begin{array}{l} v = -25\,cm \\ f_e = 5\,cm \end{array}\right]\quad \frac{1}{v} - \frac{1}{u} = \frac{1}{f_e}$$

$$\frac{1}{u} = -\frac{1}{25} - \frac{1}{5} = -\frac{6}{25} \Rightarrow \underline{u = -\frac{25}{6}\,cm}$$

for objective.

$$\left.\begin{array}{l} u = -200\,cm \\ f_o = +50\,cm \end{array}\right]\quad \frac{1}{v} - \frac{1}{u} = \frac{1}{f_o}$$

$$\frac{1}{v} = \frac{1}{50} - \frac{1}{200} = \frac{3}{200} \Rightarrow \underline{v = \frac{200}{3}\,cm}$$

tube length $\rightarrow$ sep betw^n obj & eyepiece $= \frac{200}{3} + \frac{25}{6} = \frac{425}{6}\,cm$

$$= 70.8\,cm\ \text{Ans}$$

$$MP = m_o \cdot m_e = \frac{200/3}{200} \times \frac{25}{25/6} = \underline{-2}\ \text{Ans.}$$

Module-19 Solved Example-8

Ex : An astronomical telescope has an angular magnification 5 for distant objects. The separation between objective and eyepiece is 36 cm and final image is formed at infinity. Determine the focal length of objective and eye piece.

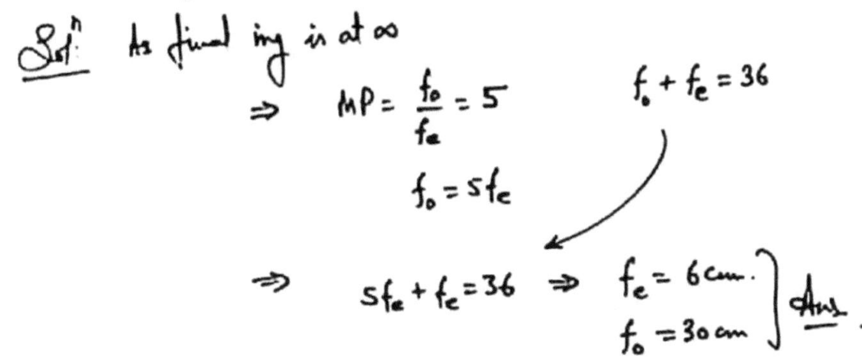

Sol^n As final img is at ∞

$$\Rightarrow \quad MP = \frac{f_0}{f_e} = 5 \qquad f_0 + f_e = 36$$

$$f_0 = 5 f_e$$

$$\Rightarrow \quad 5f_e + f_e = 36 \Rightarrow \left.\begin{array}{l} f_e = 6\,cm. \\ f_0 = 30\,cm \end{array}\right\} \underline{Ans}.$$

Scan for Video Explanation

Module-20 Solved Example-9

Ex : A Galilean telescope has objective of focal length 12 cm and eye piece of focal length 4 cm. What should be the separation between the two lenses so that for a distant object image is formed at least distance of distant vision 24 cm for observer. Also find the magnifying power of this telescope.

Sol^n for objective lens $u \to \infty$

$f_0 = 12\,cm$

for eyepiece lens:

$$\left.\begin{array}{l} v = -24\,cm \\ f_e = -4\,cm \end{array}\right] \quad \frac{1}{v} - \frac{1}{u} = \frac{1}{f_e}$$

$$\frac{1}{4} = -\frac{1}{24} + \frac{1}{4} = \frac{5}{24}$$

$$u = \frac{24}{5} = 4.8\,cm.$$

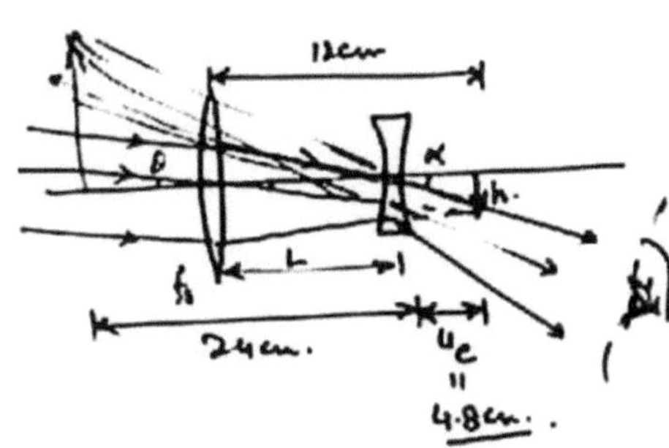

Sep between lenses.

$$L = 12 - 4.8 = 7.2\,cm \quad \underline{Ans}.$$

$$MP = \frac{\alpha}{\theta} = \frac{h/4.8}{h/12} = \frac{12}{4.8} = 2.5 \quad \underline{Ans}.$$

Scan for Video Explanation

Chapter 10
Atomic Structure

Lecture Notes Modules

Module-1 Bohr's Atomic Model-I Postulate

Bohr's Atomic Model:

- First successful exp for H-Spectrum
- This model was developed for <u>hydrogenic atom</u>
- This model was exp in 3 <u>steps</u>   one $\bar{e}$ system.
  Called postulates of Bohr model. $[\;\boxed{+Ze} \leftrightarrow \text{one } \bar{e}\;]$
       <u>$H,\ He^+,\ Li^{+2},\ Be^{+3}$</u>

'<u>I-Postulate</u> of Bohr model:

$$F_e = F_{cf.}$$

$$\frac{k.(ze)e}{\not{r}^2} = \frac{mv^2}{\not{r}}$$

$$\boxed{mv_n^2 = \frac{kze^2}{r_n}} \quad —(1)$$

Module-2 Bohr's Atomic Model-II Postulate

Bohr's Atomic Model – II Postulate:

Bohr observed that rev. $\bar{e}s$ around nucleus have some specific value of angular momentum.

$\bar{e}s$ revolve only in those specific orbits in which ang momentum of $\bar{e}$ is quantized.

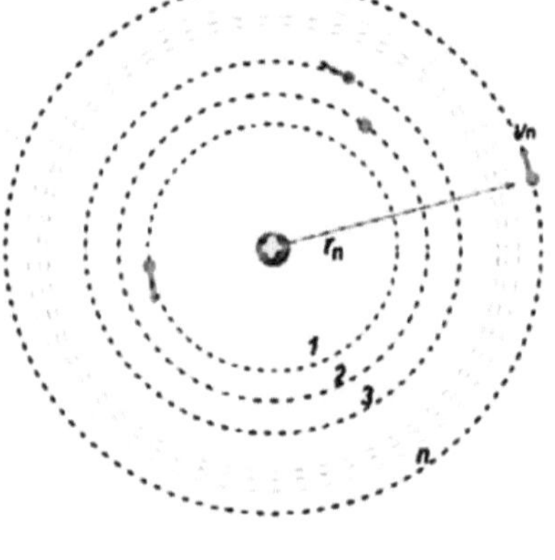

$$\boxed{L = mv_n r_n = n\left(\frac{h}{2\pi}\right)} \quad —②$$

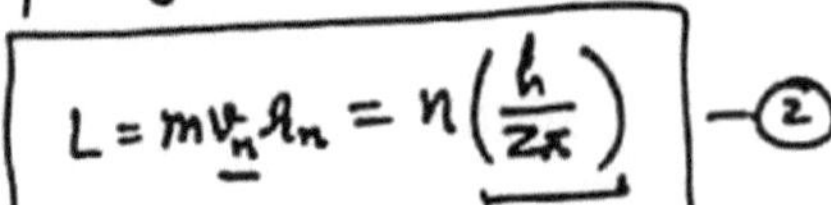

<u>NOTE</u>: A <u>stable</u> orbit around Nu is one for which both eq^n (1) & (2) are <u>satisfied</u>.

Module-3 Bohr's Atomic Model-III Postulate

Bohr's Atomic Model – III Postulate :

In a stable orbit $\bar{e}$ energy remains constant. $\bar{e}$ energy changes when it makes a transition from one <u>orbit</u> to another.

"energy level"

Such transitions are instantaneous and involve quantized energies in form of EM radiations photons.

$$\Delta E = E_{n_2} - E_{n_1} = h\nu = \frac{hc}{\lambda} \quad - \text{③}$$

Scan for Video Explanation

Module-4 Radius of nth Orbit in Bohr Model

Radius of nth Orbit in Bohr Model :

for n^{th} orbit acc to I-Postulate $\qquad m v_n^2 = \dfrac{kZe^2}{r_n} \quad ——— (1)$

$\qquad\qquad$ acc to II-Postulate $\qquad m v_n r_n = \dfrac{nh}{2\pi} \quad ——— (2)$

from eqn (1) $\qquad\qquad\qquad\qquad \hookrightarrow v_n = \dfrac{nh}{2\pi m r_n}$

$$r_n = \frac{kZe^2}{m\left(\dfrac{nh}{2\pi m r_n}\right)^2}$$

$$r_n = \frac{n^2 h^2}{4\pi^2 kZe^2 m} = \frac{h^2}{4\pi^2 k e^2 m} \times \frac{n^2}{Z}$$

$$r_n = 0.529 \times \frac{n^2}{Z} \, \overset{\circ}{A}$$

Scan for Video Explanation

Module-5 Velocity of Electron in nth Orbit in Bohr Model

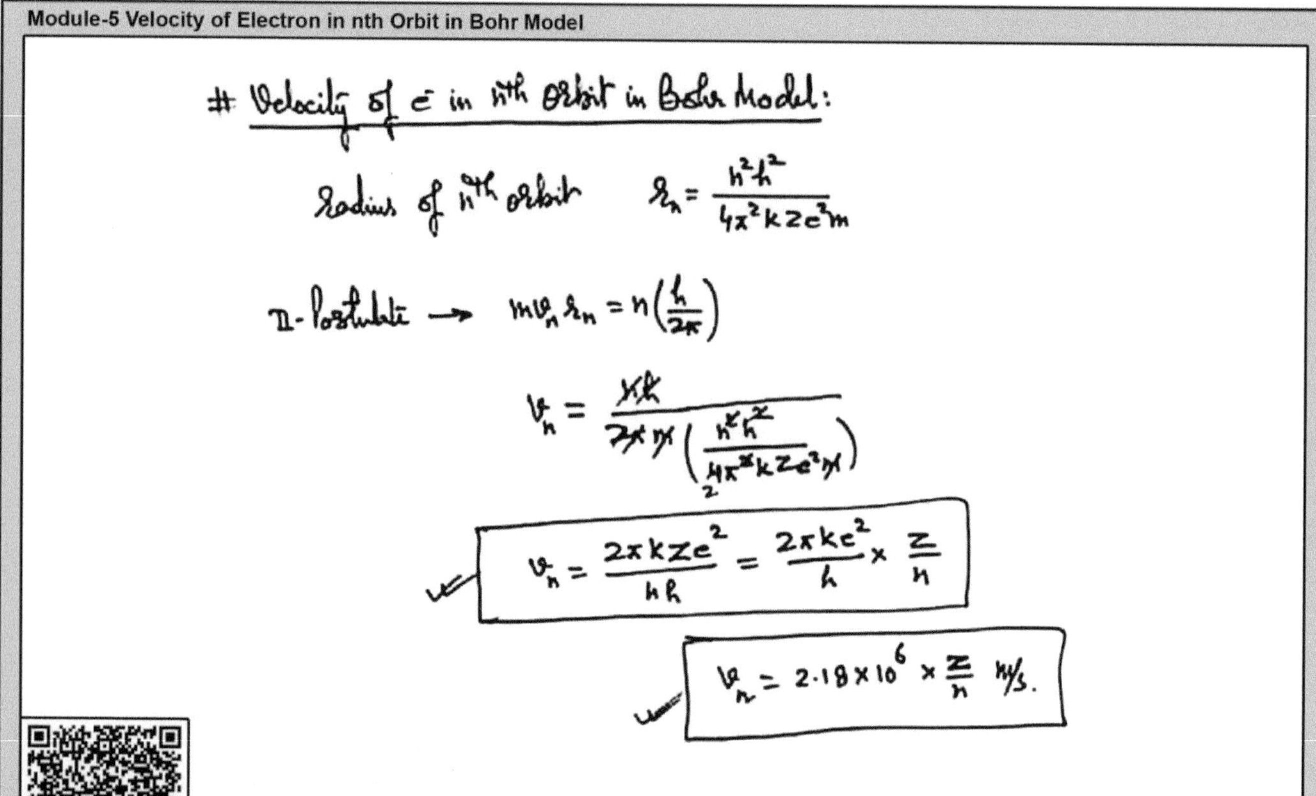

 # Velocity of e^- in nth Orbit in Bohr Model:

Radius of nth orbit
$$r_n = \frac{n^2 h^2}{4\pi^2 k Z e^2 m}$$

II-Postulate $\longrightarrow$ $m v_n r_n = n\left(\frac{h}{2\pi}\right)$

$$v_n = \frac{n h}{2\pi m \left(\frac{n^2 h^2}{4\pi^2 k Z e^2 m}\right)}$$

$$\boxed{v_n = \frac{2\pi k Z e^2}{n h} = \frac{2\pi k e^2}{h} \times \frac{Z}{n}}$$

$$\boxed{v_n = 2.18 \times 10^6 \times \frac{Z}{n} \ \text{m/s}}$$

Module-6 Angular Speed of Electron in nth Orbit in Bohr Model

 # Angular speed of e^- in nth Orbit in Bohr Model:

Angular speed of e^- in nth orbit

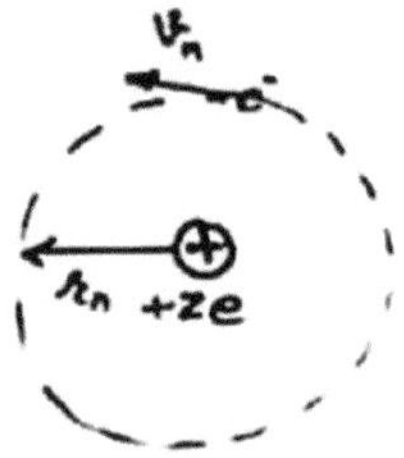

$$\omega_n = \frac{v_n}{r_n} = \frac{2\pi k Z e^2}{n h} \times \frac{4\pi^2 k Z e^2 m}{n^2 h^2}$$

$$\omega_n = \frac{8\pi^3 k^2 Z^2 e^4 m}{n^3 h^3}$$

$$\boxed{\omega_n = \frac{8\pi^3 k^2 e^4 m}{h^3} \times \frac{Z^2}{n^3}}$$

$$\left[\omega_n \propto \frac{Z^2}{n^3}\right]$$

$$v_n = \frac{2\pi k Z e^2}{n h}$$

$$r_n = \frac{n^2 h^2}{4\pi^2 k Z e^2 m}$$

Module-7 Revolution Frequency and Time Period of Electron in nth Orbit in Bohr Model

Revolution frequency & Time Period of e^- in n^{th} Orbit:

Rev freq$\qquad f_n = \dfrac{\omega_n}{2\pi}$

$$f_n = \frac{4\pi^2 k^2 e^4 m}{h^3} \times \frac{z^2}{n^3}$$

$$f_n \propto \frac{z^2}{n^3}$$

$$\omega_n = \frac{8\pi^3 k^2 e^4 m}{h^3} \times \frac{z^2}{n^3}$$

Time Period of rev of e^-

$$T_n = \frac{1}{f_n} = \frac{h^3}{4\pi^2 k^2 e^4 m} \times \frac{n^3}{z^2}$$

$$T_n \propto \frac{n^3}{z^2}$$

Scan for Video Explanation

Module-8 Current due to Revolution of Electron in nth Orbit in Bohr Model

Current due to rev of e^- in n^{th} Orbit:

Eq. current flowing in n^{th} orbit due to e^- rev is

$$I_n = \frac{e\omega_n}{2\pi} = e f_n$$

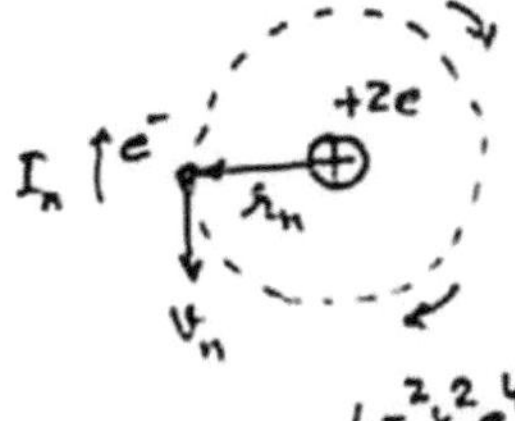

$$f_n = \frac{4\pi^2 k^2 e^4 m}{h^3} \times \frac{z^2}{n^3}$$

$$I_n = \frac{4\pi^2 k^2 e^5 m}{h^3} \times \frac{z^2}{n^3}$$

$$I_n \propto \frac{z^2}{n^3}$$

Scan for Video Explanation

Module-9 Magnetic Induction at Nucleus due to nth Orbit in Bohr Model

Magnetic Induction at Nucleus due to $\bar{e}$ rev in n^{th} Orbit:

Due to an eq. cir coil, MI
at the Centre is given as

$$B_n = \frac{\mu_0 I_n}{2 r_n}$$

$$B_n = \frac{8\pi^4 \mu_0 k^3 z^3 e^7 m^2}{n^5 h^5}$$

$$\boxed{B_n = \frac{8\pi^4 k^3 e^7 m^2 \mu_0}{h^5} \times \frac{z^3}{n^5}}$$

$$B_n \propto \frac{z^3}{n^5}$$

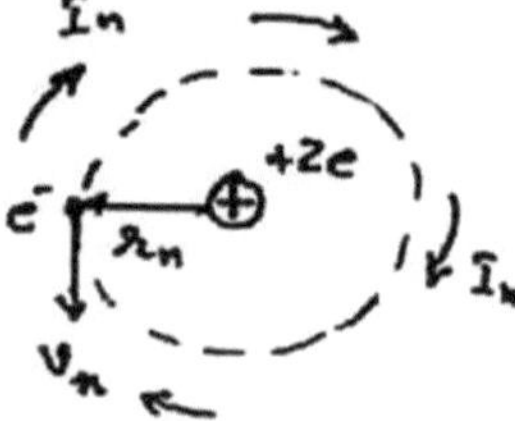

$$I_n = \frac{4\pi^2 k^2 z^2 e^5 m}{n^3 h^3}$$

$$r_n = \frac{n^2 h^2}{4\pi^2 k z e^2 m}$$

Module-10 Magnetic Moment of nth Orbit in Bohr Model

Magnetic Moment due to $\bar{e}$ rev in n^{th} Orbit:

Magnetic dipole moment
of the eq coil is

$$M_n = I_n \times \pi r_n^2$$

$$\boxed{M_n = \frac{enh}{4\pi m}}$$

for $n=1$ $\boxed{M_1 = \frac{eh}{4\pi m}}$ Bohr magneton.

$$I_n = \frac{4\pi^2 k^2 z^2 e^5 m}{n^3 h^3}$$

$$r_n = \frac{n^2 h^2}{4\pi^2 k z e^2 m}$$

Module-11 Energy of Electron in nth Orbit in Bohr Model

Energy of e^- in Bohr Energy Levels:

In an orbit total energy of e^- is given as —

$$E_n = K_n + U_n$$

$$E_n = \tfrac{1}{2} mv_n^2 + \left(-\frac{kze^2}{r_n}\right) \qquad \left[U = \frac{kq_1 q_2}{r}\right]$$

$$E_n = \frac{1}{2}\frac{kze^2}{r_n} - \frac{kze^2}{r_n} \qquad \left[\text{As } mv_n^2 = \frac{kze^2}{r_n}\right]$$

$$\boxed{E_n = -\frac{1}{2}\frac{kze^2}{r_n}}$$

here we can see $\quad |E_n| = |K_n| = \tfrac{1}{2}|U_n|$

— this is the rel when a particle rev under an inverse square force influence.

Scan for Video Explanation

Module-11 Energy of Electron in nth Orbit in Bohr Model

Energy of e^- in n^{th} Orbit:

$$E_n = -\frac{1}{2}\frac{kze^2}{r_n}$$

$$E_n = -\frac{1}{2}\frac{kze^2}{\left(\frac{n^2 h^2}{4\pi^2 kze^2 m}\right)} \qquad r_n = \frac{n^2 h^2}{4\pi^2 kze^2 m}$$

$$\boxed{E_n = -\frac{2\pi^2 k^2 z^2 e^4 m}{n^2 h^2}}$$

$$E_n = -\frac{2\pi^2 k^2 e^4 m}{h^2}\times\frac{z^2}{n^2}$$

$$\boxed{E_n = -13.6\times\frac{z^2}{n^2}\ eV}$$

$$1\,eV = 1.6\times10^{-19}\,J$$

Scan for Video Explanation

Module-12 Energy of Different Energy Levels in Hydrogenic Atoms

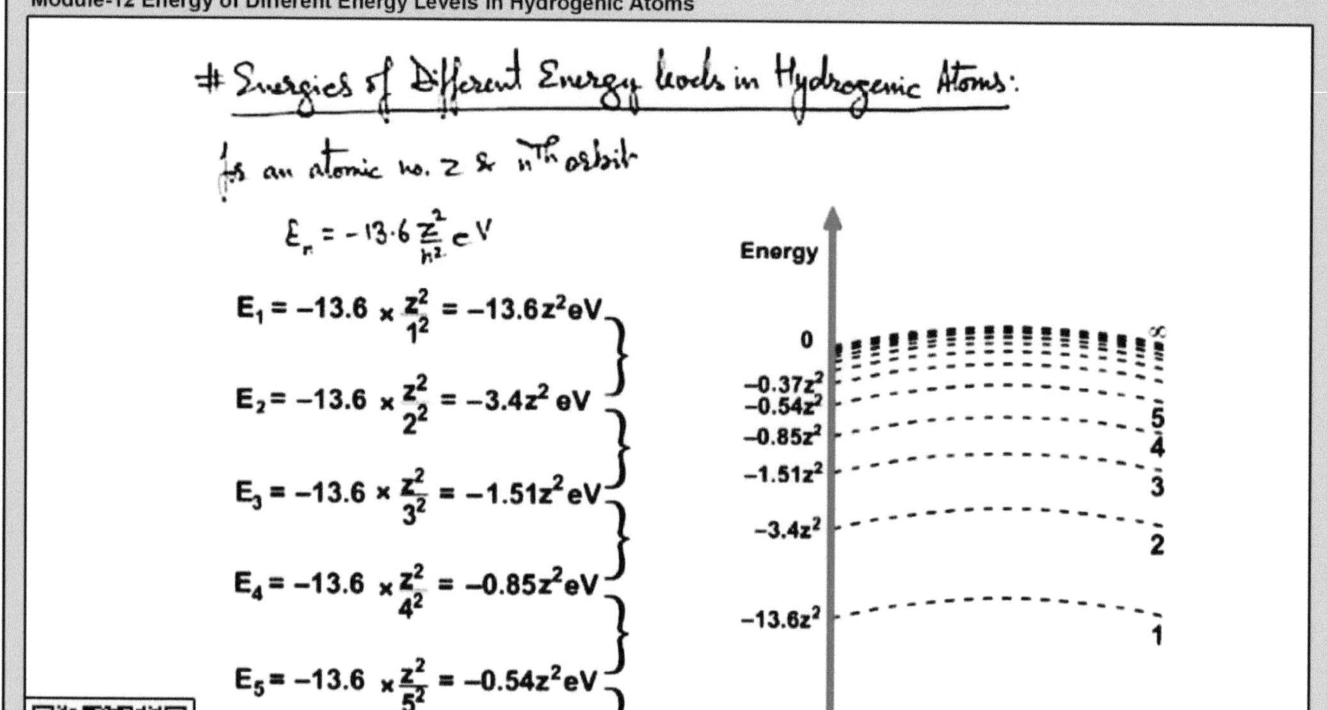

Energies of Different Energy levels in Hydrogenic Atoms:

For an atomic no. Z & n^{th} orbit

$$E_n = -13.6\,\frac{z^2}{n^2}\,eV$$

$$E_1 = -13.6 \times \frac{z^2}{1^2} = -13.6z^2\,eV$$

$$E_2 = -13.6 \times \frac{z^2}{2^2} = -3.4z^2\,eV$$

$$E_3 = -13.6 \times \frac{z^2}{3^2} = -1.51z^2\,eV$$

$$E_4 = -13.6 \times \frac{z^2}{4^2} = -0.85z^2\,eV$$

$$E_5 = -13.6 \times \frac{z^2}{5^2} = -0.54z^2\,eV$$

$$E_6 = -13.6 \times \frac{z^2}{6^2} = -0.37z^2\,eV$$

Module-13 Rydberg Scale of Energy

Rydberg Scale of Energy:

Energy of e^- in n^{th} level

$$E_n = -\frac{2\pi^2 k^2 e^4 m}{h^2} \times \frac{z^2}{n^2} \times \frac{ch}{ch}$$

$$E_n = -\left(\frac{2\pi^2 k^2 e^4 m}{ch^3}\right) ch \cdot \frac{z^2}{n^2}$$

$$\boxed{E_n = -Rch \times \frac{z^2}{n^2}}$$

here $R = \dfrac{2\pi^2 k^2 e^4 m}{ch^3}$ is called Rydberg's Constant

$$R = 10967800\ m^{-1} \simeq 10^7\ m^{-1}$$

for $z=1$, $n=1$

$$E_1 = -Rch = -13.6\,eV = 1\ \text{Rydberg Energy}$$

Module-14 Solved Example-1

Ex : Calculate the angular momentum of electron in a hydrogen atom which is having total energy − 3.4 eV.

Sol : for n^{th} orbit of a hydrogenic atom

$$E_n = -13.6 \times \frac{Z^2}{n^2} \, eV$$

for H-atom $\qquad E_n = -\frac{13.6}{n^2} = -3.4 \, eV$

$$n = \sqrt{\frac{13.6}{3.4}} = \sqrt{4} = \underline{2}$$

Angular momentum of $\bar{e}$ in $n=2$ is

$$L = \frac{nh}{2\pi} = \frac{2h}{2\pi}$$

$$L = \frac{h}{\pi} \quad \text{Ans.}$$

Scan for Video Explanation

Module-15 Solved Example-2

Ex : In H-atom an electron makes a transition $n_1 \rightarrow n_2$ where n_1 and n_2 are the principle quantum numbers of the two states. Assume Bohr model to be valid, the time period of the electron in the initial state is eight times that in the final state. What are the possible values of n_1 and n_2 ?

Sol : As we know $\qquad T_n \propto n^3$

$$\Rightarrow \quad \left(\frac{T_1}{T_2}\right) = \frac{n_1^3}{n_2^3}$$

$$T_1 = 8T_2 \quad \Rightarrow \quad \frac{n_1^3}{n_2^3} = 8 \quad \Rightarrow \quad \underline{n_1 = 2n_2}$$

$$\frac{T_1}{T_2} = 8$$

possible values of n_1 & n_2 are

n_1	n_2
2	1
4	2
6	3
:	:

Ans.

Scan for Video Explanation

Module-16 Solved Example-3

Ex :   Determine the wavelength that hydrogen atom will emit
if its electron makes a transition from $n_2 = 4$ to $n_1 = 2$.

Sol^n: Photon energy liberated $\Delta E = E_4 - E_2$

$$= (-0.85\,eV) - (-3.4\,eV)$$

$$= 2.55\,eV.$$

if λ is W/L of emitted photon

$$\Delta E = \frac{hc}{\lambda}$$

$$\lambda = \frac{hc}{\Delta E} = \frac{6.63 \times 10^{-34} \times 3 \times 10^{8}}{2.55 \times 1.6 \times 10^{-19}} \times \frac{1}{10^{-10}}\ \overset{o}{A}$$

$$\lambda = 4875\,\overset{o}{A}\quad \text{Ans}$$

Module-17 Solved Example-4

Ex :   Which energy level of triply ionized beryllium (Be^{+3}) has
the same electron orbital radius as that of <u>ground</u> state
of hydrogen.

Sol^n: orbital radii $\quad r_n = 0.529 \times \dfrac{n^2}{Z}\ \overset{o}{A}$

given that $\quad r_{1H} = r_{nBe^{+3}}$

$$[\text{As } Z = 4 \text{ for } Be]$$

$$0.529 = 0.529 \times \frac{n^2}{4}$$

$$n^2 = 4$$

$$n = 2\quad \text{Ans}.$$

Module-18 Solved Example-5

Ex : The orbital speed of the electron in the ground state of hydrogen is v. What will be its orbital speed when it is excited to the energy level having energy − 3.4 eV.

Sol^n: for n^{th} level $\quad E_n = -\dfrac{13.6}{n^2}\ eV = -3.4\,eV$

$$n = \sqrt{\dfrac{13.6}{3.4}} = \sqrt{4} = \underline{2}$$

Speed of e^- in n^{th} level

$$V_n = 2.18 \times 10^6 \times \dfrac{z}{n}\ m/s$$

$$V_2 = \dfrac{2.18 \times 10^6}{n}\ m/s.$$

$$\dfrac{V_1}{V_2} = \left(\dfrac{n_2}{n_1}\right)$$

$$V_2 = V_1 \times \dfrac{n_1}{n_2} = v \times \dfrac{1}{2} = \dfrac{v}{2}\ \underline{Ans}.$$

Module-19 Excitation and Ionization of an Atom

\# <u>Excitation and Ionization of an Atom:</u>   (lowest energy level

<u>Excitation:</u> Transition of an e^- in atom from ground state ($n=1$)

to <u>higher state</u> by absorption of energy by e^-.
          ↓
     excited state

<u>Ionization:</u> It is the transition of e^- from any level to

$n \to \infty$ (zero energy level) i.e. removal of e^- from that

atom by absorption of energy by e^-.

For Excitation & Ionization of an atom energy can be

supplied to an atom in two ways :-
          ① By EM Radiation photon
          ② By collisions with other
                    particles.

Module-20 Excitation of Atom by Electromagnetic Radiation

\# <u>Excitation of Atom by EM Radiation</u> :

Excitation will take place only if the photon energy is equal to the difference in energies of the two energy energy levels.

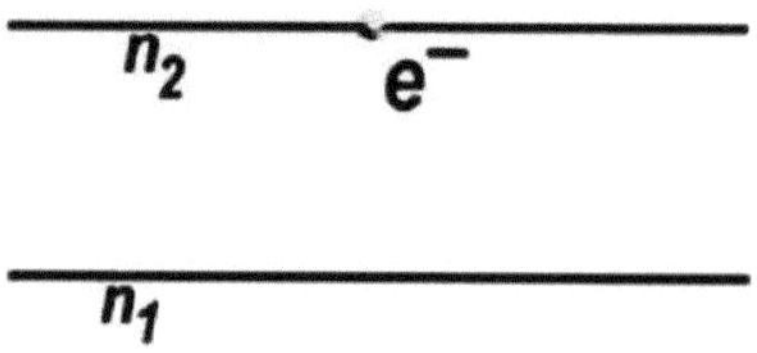

If $\quad E_{ph} = E_{n_2} - E_{n_1}$

then only excitation will occur.

$$\Delta E_{1-2} = (-3.4) - (-13.6) = 10.2\,eV$$
$$\Delta E_{1-3} = (-1.51) - (-13.6) = 12.09\,eV$$
$$\Delta E_{1-4} = (-0.85) - (-13.6) = 12.75\,eV$$
$$\Delta E_{ph} = \underline{11\,eV}$$

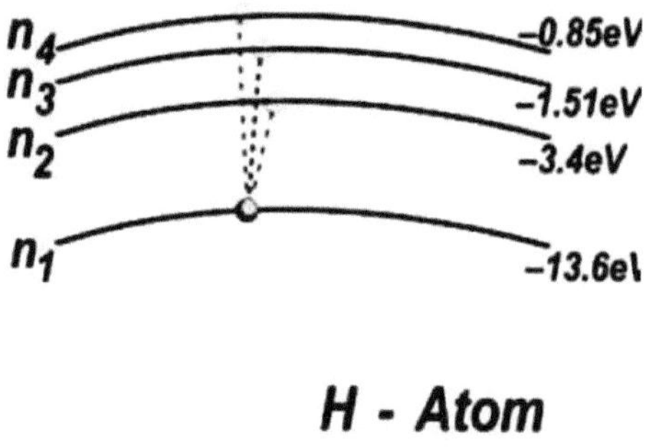

$n_2 \quad e^-$

n_1

$n_4 \quad\quad -0.85eV$
$n_3 \quad\quad -1.51eV$
$n_2 \quad\quad -3.4eV$
$n_1 \quad\quad -13.6eV$

H - Atom

Module-21 Ionization of Atom by Electromagnetic Radiation

\# <u>Ionization of Atom by EM Radiation</u> :

In an energy level, total energy of an e^- is $\underline{-ve}$ — Boundness.

When this energy becomes 0, e^- will be free from nuclear attraction.

for H-atom in $n=1$ $\quad \underline{E_1 = -13.6\,eV}$

If $\underline{13.6\,eV}$ energy (by photon) is supplied to H-atom, total e^- energy becomes $\underline{0}$, it will make e^- free from atom & the atom is ionized $\Rightarrow 13.6\,eV$ is called <u>Binding Energy</u> of e^- in $n=1$ of H-atom. For any orbit $|TE\,of\,e^-| \rightarrow$ Binding energy / Ionization energy

Module-22 Kinetic Energy of Electron After Ionization of an Atom

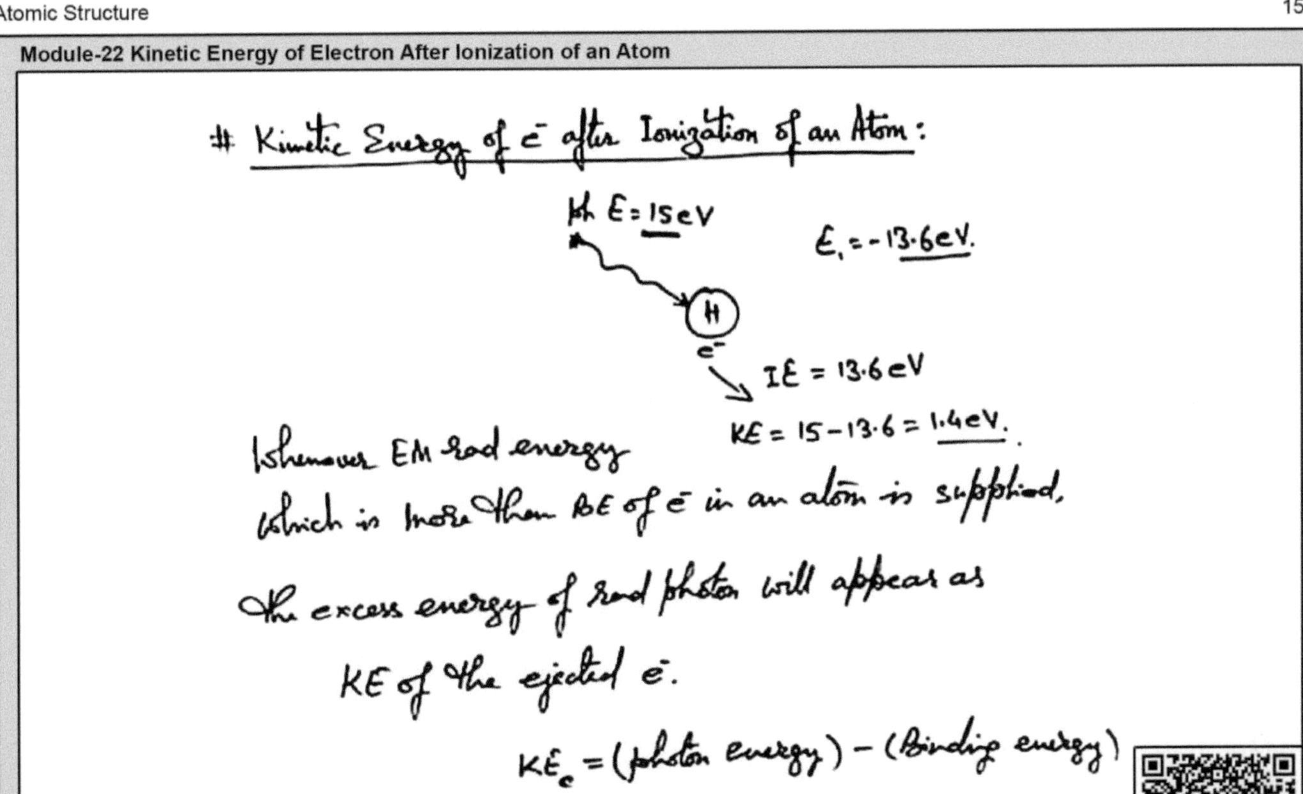

Whenever EM rad energy
which is more than BE of e^- in an atom is supplied,

the excess energy of rad photon will appear as

KE of the ejected e^-.

$$KE_e = (\text{photon energy}) - (\text{Binding energy})$$

Module-23 De-excitation of an Excited Atom

De-excitation of an excited atom :

photon
$\Delta E_{ph} = E_{n_2} - E_{n_1}$

Atom

$st \approx 10^{-8}$ sec (man).
(life time of excited state)

e^- n_2 n_1

lower energy levels are more stable
Compared to higher energy levels.

$\Delta E_{1-4} = 12.75$ eV

$\Delta E_{4\to 1} = 0.66$ eV
$\Delta E_{4\to 2} = 2.55$ eV
$\Delta E_{4\to 1} = 12.75$ eV

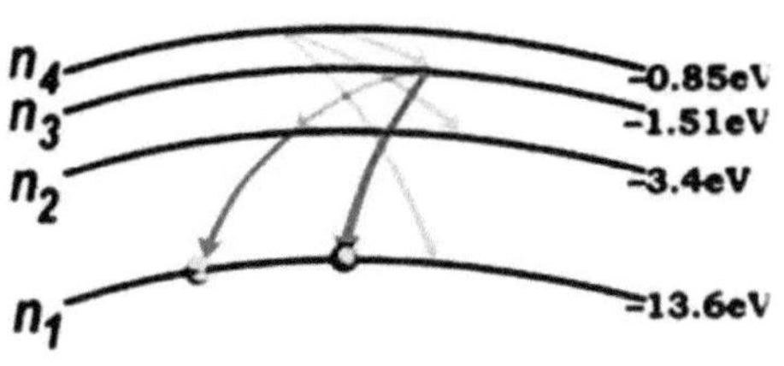

H - Nucleus

Module-24 Spectral Lines Emitted by H-Gas

Spectral lines emitted by a H-gas:

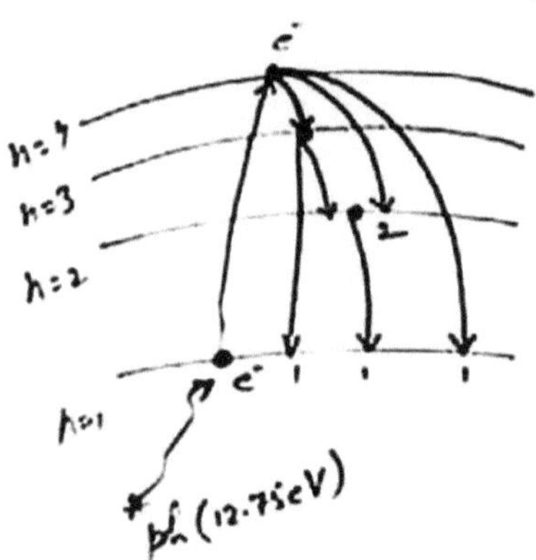

possible paths of
e^- for de-excitation

$4 \xrightarrow{} 3 \xrightarrow{} 2 \xrightarrow{} 1$ — Three ph.

$4 \xrightarrow{} 3 \xrightarrow{} 1$ — Two ph.

$4 \xrightarrow{} 2 \xrightarrow{} 1$ — Two ph.

$4 \xrightarrow{} 1$ — One ph.

If an e^- is excited to n^{th} energy level then total no. of possible spectral lines emitted during its de-excitation are

$$N = {}^nC_2 = \left(\frac{n(n-1)}{2}\right)$$

Module-25 Maximum Number of Photons Emitted by H-Atom During de-Excitation

Maximum No. of photons emitted by H-atom during de-excitation:

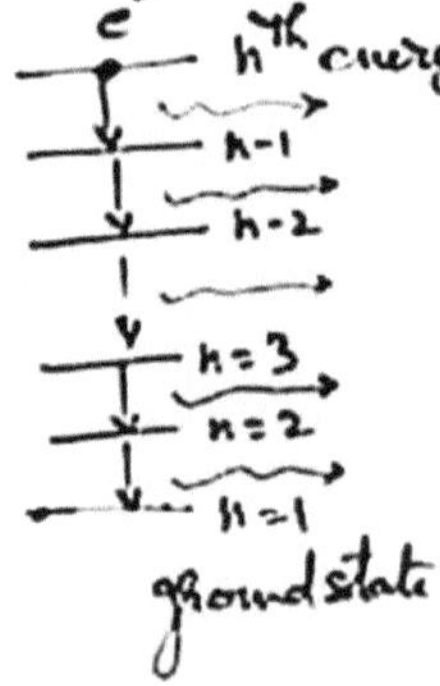

max no. of photons emitted by an e^- is equal to

$$\boxed{N = n-1} \text{ max.}$$

if e^- is in n^{th} energy level after excitation

Module-26 Energy and Wavelength of Emitted Radiation

Energy and Wavelength of emitted radiation :

$$\Delta E = E_{n_2} - E_{n_1} = \frac{hc}{\lambda} = h\nu$$

$$\Delta E = \left(-\frac{13.6\,z^2}{n_2^2}\right) - \left(-\frac{13.6\,z^2}{n_1^2}\right)\ eV$$

$$\boxed{\Delta E = \underline{13.6\,z^2}\left[\frac{1}{n_1^2} - \frac{1}{n_2^2}\right]}\ eV$$

For a hydrogenic atom $13.6\,z^2$ is its ionization energy (Ionization Potential) (IP)

$$\frac{hc}{\lambda} = \boxed{\Delta E = IP\left[\frac{1}{n_1^2} - \frac{1}{n_2^2}\right]}\ eV$$

$$\lambda = \frac{hc}{\Delta E} = \frac{(6.63\times10^{-34})\times(3\times10^8)}{(\Delta E\ in\ eV)\times(1.6\times10^{-19})}$$

$$\boxed{\lambda = \frac{12431}{\Delta E}\ \mathring{A}} \longrightarrow \boxed{\Delta E = \frac{12431}{\lambda(in\,\mathring{A})}\ eV}$$

Module-27 Rydberg's Formula for Wavelength of Emitted Radiation

Rydberg's Formula for radiation wavelength :

When an $\bar{e}$ makes a t, from $n_2 \longrightarrow n_1$

Photon energy $\Delta E = E_{n_2} - E_{n_1}$

$$\frac{hc}{\lambda} = \Delta E = 13.6\,z^2\left[\frac{1}{n_1^2} - \frac{1}{n_2^2}\right]$$

Rydberg's formula : $\quad \frac{1}{\lambda} = \left(\frac{13.6}{hc}\right)z^2\left[\frac{1}{n_1^2} - \frac{1}{n_2^2}\right]$

Wave no. : $\boxed{\bar{\nu} = \frac{1}{\lambda} = R\,z^2\left[\frac{1}{n_1^2} - \frac{1}{n_2^2}\right]}$

no. of waves, per unit length.
length.

where $R \to$ Rydberg's Const

$$R = \frac{13.6\,e}{hc} = \frac{2\pi^2 k^2 e^4 m}{c h^3}$$

$$\left\{\begin{array}{l} R = 10967800\ m^{-1} \\ R \simeq 10^7\ m^{-1} \end{array}\right\}$$

Module-28 The Hydrogen Spectrum

The Hydrogen Spectrum:

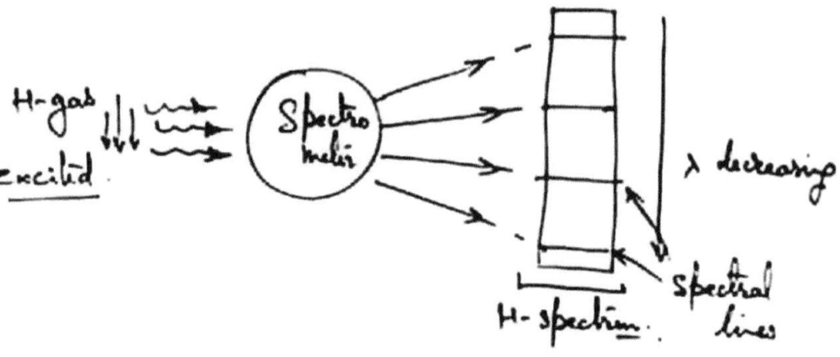

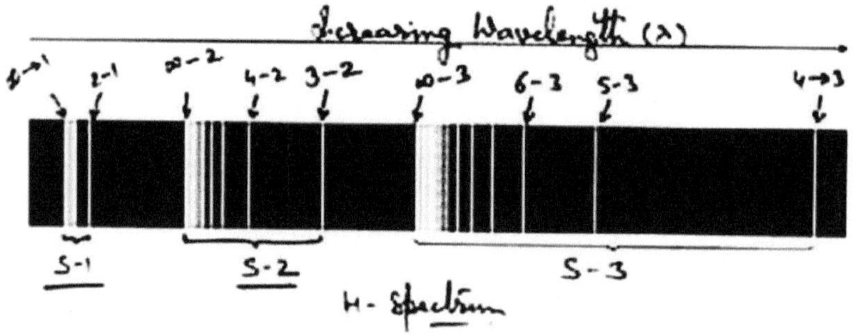

Scan for Video Explanation

Web Reference at www.physicsgalaxy.com

Module-29 Spectral Series of Hydrogen Atom

Spectral Series of Hydrogen Atom:

In H-spectrum each group of spectral lines corresponding to e^- transition to a particular state are called spectral series. These are divided in 6 categories.

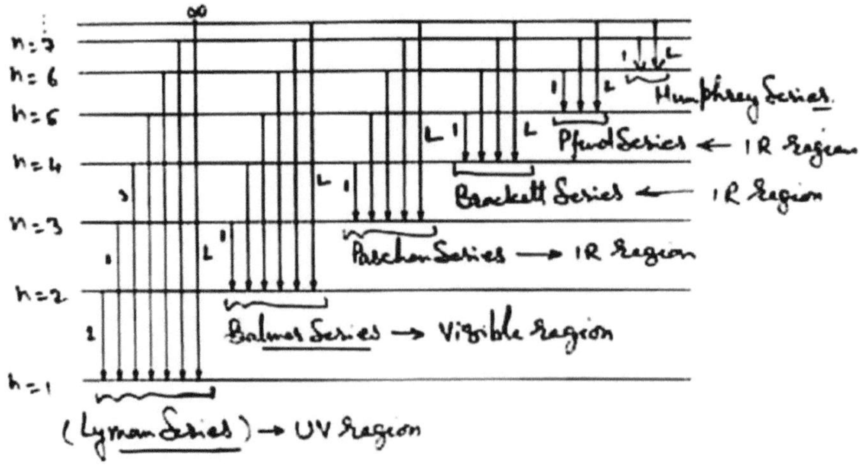

Scan for Video Explanation

Web Reference at www.physicsgalaxy.com

Module-29 Spectral Series of Hydrogen Atom

Different Spectral Series and their Series limits :

① **Lyman Series** n_2 ↓ $n_1 = 1$.   first line $2 \to 1$, last line $\infty \to 1$] $\lambda \to$ UV region

② **Balmer Series** n_2 ↓ $n_1 = 2$ first line $3 \to 2$, last line $\infty \to 2$] $\lambda \to$ Visible region

③ **Paschan Series** n_2 ↓ $n_1 = 3$ first line $4 \to 3$, last line $\infty \to 3$] $\lambda \to$ IR Region

④ **Brackett Series** n_2 ↓ $n_1 = 4$ first line $5 \to 4$, last line $\infty \to 4$] $\lambda \to$ IR Region

⑤ **Pfund Series** n_2 ↓ $n_1 = 5$ first line $6 \to 5$, last line $\infty \to 5$] $\lambda \to$ IR Region

⑥ **Humphrey Series.** n_2 ↓ $n_1 = 6$ first line $7 \to 6$, last line $\infty \to 6$] $\lambda \to$ IR Region → long wavelength Range.

    Scan for Video Explanation

Module-30 Solved Example-6

Ex : In <u>Hydrogen atom</u> an electron makes a transition from n = 4 to n = 2, find the wavelength of photon emitted.

Sol.   Photon energy liberated

$$\Delta E = 13.6 \left[\frac{1}{n_1^2} - \frac{1}{n_2^2} \right] eV \quad (Z = 1)$$

$n_2 = 4$ ↓ $n_1 = 2$

$$\Delta E = 13.6 \left[\frac{1}{2^2} - \frac{1}{4^2} \right] eV$$

$$= 13.6 \left(\frac{3}{16} \right) = \underline{2.55\,eV}$$

The wavelength of photon as $\lambda = \dfrac{12431}{\Delta E\,(\text{in eV})}\ \overset{\circ}{A}$

$$\lambda = \frac{12431}{2.55} = 4875\ \overset{\circ}{A}\ \text{Ans}.$$

    Scan for Video Explanation

Module-31 Solved Example-7

Ex : The wavelength of first line of Balmer series in hydrogen spectrum is <u>6563 Å</u>. Find the wavelength of first line of Lyman series in the same spectrum.

Sol^n:

for first line of Balmer Series $\quad \dfrac{1}{\lambda_1} = Rz^2\left[\dfrac{1}{2^2}-\dfrac{1}{3^2}\right] = \dfrac{5R}{36}$ —— (1)

$\qquad n_2 = 3 \longrightarrow n_1 = 2$

for first line of Lyman Series $\quad \dfrac{1}{\lambda_2} = Rz^2\left[\dfrac{1}{1^2}-\dfrac{1}{2^2}\right] = \dfrac{3R}{4}$ —— (2)

$\qquad n_2 = 2 \longrightarrow n_1 = 1$

$\dfrac{(1)}{(2)} \Rightarrow \quad \dfrac{\lambda_2}{\lambda_1} = \dfrac{5/36}{3/4} = \dfrac{5}{27}$

$$\lambda_2 = \dfrac{5}{27}\times\lambda_1 = \dfrac{5}{27}\times 6563 = 1215.37 \overset{\circ}{A} \quad \text{Ans.}$$

Module-32 Solved Example-8

Ex : Find the ratio of Binding energies of electron in n = 2 of Hydrogen atom and n = 3 of triply ionized Berelium atom.

Sol^n:

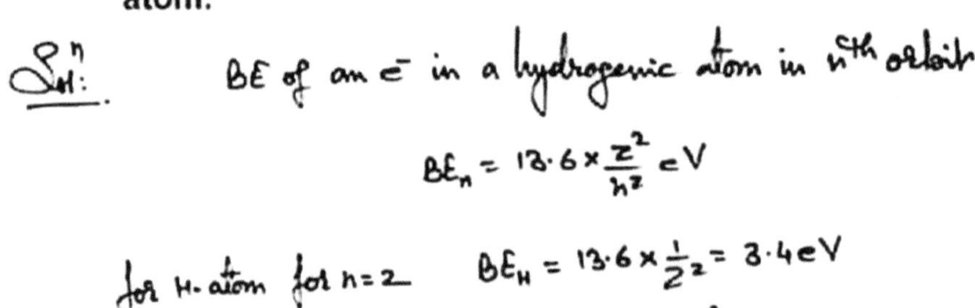

BE of an e^- in a hydrogenic atom in n^{th} orbit

$$BE_n = 13.6\times\dfrac{z^2}{n^2} \; eV$$

for H-atom for $n = 2 \qquad BE_H = 13.6\times\dfrac{1}{2^2} = 3.4 \, eV$

for Be^{+3} in $n = 3 \qquad BE_{Be^{+3}} = 13.6\times\dfrac{4^2}{3^2} = 24.18 \, eV.$

$$\dfrac{BE_H}{BE_{Be^{+3}}} = \dfrac{3.4}{24.18} = 0.14 \quad \text{Ans.}$$

Module-33 Solved Example-9

Ex : A **Hydrogen atom** is excited through electromagnetic radiation such that it emits **visible light** during de-excitation. Find the maximum wavelength of radiation by which it is possible.

Sol: → Transition to $\underline{n=2}$ in H-atom is corresponding to visible light

$n=3$ → I line of Balmer Series.

Energy of $\underline{EM\ rad}$ reqd is

$$\Delta E = 13.6\left[\frac{1}{1^2} - \frac{1}{3^2}\right] = 13.6 \times \frac{8}{9} = 12.09\ eV$$

W/L corresponding to this energy is (max)

$$\lambda = \frac{12431}{12.09} = 1028\ \overset{o}{A}\ \ Ans.$$

Module-34 Solved Example-10

Ex : **Hydrogen gas** with all its atoms are excited by means of a monochromatic radiation of wavelength <u>975A</u>. How many lines are possible in resulting spectrum. Calculate the longest wavelength amongest them.

Sol: photon energy of rad of $\underline{W/L\ 975\overset{o}{A}}$ is $\Delta E = \dfrac{12431}{975} = \underline{12.75\ eV}$

if after excitation e is excited to n^{th} energy level.

$$12.75 = 13.6\left[\frac{1}{1^2} - \frac{1}{n^2}\right] \Rightarrow n = \sqrt{\frac{13.6}{0.85}} = \sqrt{16}$$

or Simplifying $\underline{n = 4}$

No. of possible spectral lines in spectrum $= {}^nC_2 = \dfrac{4\times3}{2} = 6\ lines\ Ans.$

$$\Delta E_{43} = 13.6\left[\frac{1}{3^2} - \frac{1}{4^2}\right]$$
$$= 0.66\ eV$$

$$\lambda_{max} = \frac{12431}{0.66} = 18835\ \overset{o}{A}\ Ans.$$

Module-35 Solved Example-11

Ex : A hydrogen atom in a state with Binding energy 0.85 eV makes a transition to a state with excitation energy 10.2 eV. Find energy and wavelength of photon emitted.

Sol^n:

BE of e^- in H-atom $BE = \dfrac{13.6}{n_2^2} = 0.85\,eV$

$$n_2 = \sqrt{\dfrac{13.6}{0.85}} = \sqrt{16} = 4$$

Energy the state to which e^- makes a transition

$$E_{n_1} = (-13.6\,eV) + (10.2\,eV) = -3.4\,eV$$

Energy of e^- in state n_1 is $E_{n_1} = -\dfrac{13.6}{n_1^2} = -3.4\,eV$

$$n_1 = \sqrt{\dfrac{13.6}{3.4}} = \sqrt{4} = 2$$

$\left.\begin{array}{c} n_2 = 4 \\ \downarrow \\ n_1 = 2 \end{array}\right\}$ photon energy liberated

$$\Delta E = E_4 - E_2 = (-0.85) - (-3.4\,eV)$$
$$= 2.55\,eV \text{ Ans}$$

$$\lambda = \dfrac{12431}{2.55} = 4875\,\mathring{A} \text{ Ans}$$

Module-36 Solved Example-12

Ex : Ultraviolet light of wavelength 700 Å is incident on a hydrogen atom in ground state. Find the kinetic energy and speed of electron emitted.

Sol^n:

Energy of incident photon $\Delta E = \dfrac{12431}{700} = 17.75\,eV$

IE of H-atom for $n=1$ is $IE = 13.6\,eV$

KE of emitted e^- is

$$KE = 17.75 - 13.6 = 4.15\,eV \text{ Ans}$$

$$\tfrac{1}{2}mv^2 = 4.15 \times 1.6 \times 10^{-19}$$

$$v = \sqrt{\dfrac{2 \times 4.15 \times 1.6 \times 10^{-19}}{9.1 \times 10^{-31}}} = 1.2 \times 10^6 \, m/s \text{ Ans}$$

Module-37 Effect of Mass of Nucleus on Bohr's Atomic Model

Effect of Mass of Nucleus on Bohr Atomic Model:

As we consider $m_e << $ mass of Nu.

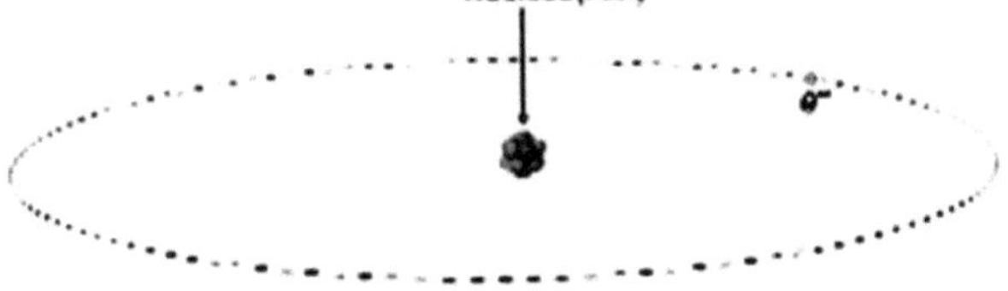

Practically mass of e^- is not zero so in absence of ext forces on a system its COM must be at rest.

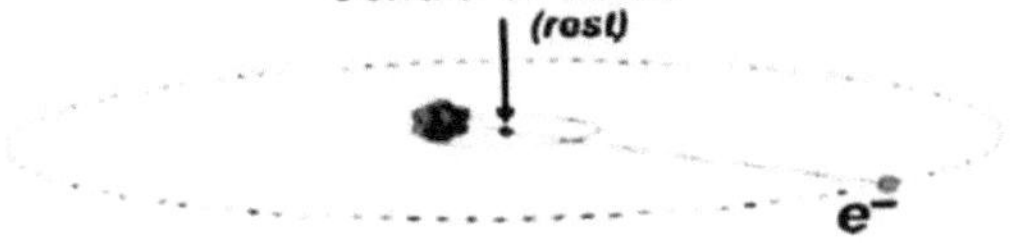

Module-37 Effect of Mass of Nucleus on Bohr's Atomic Model

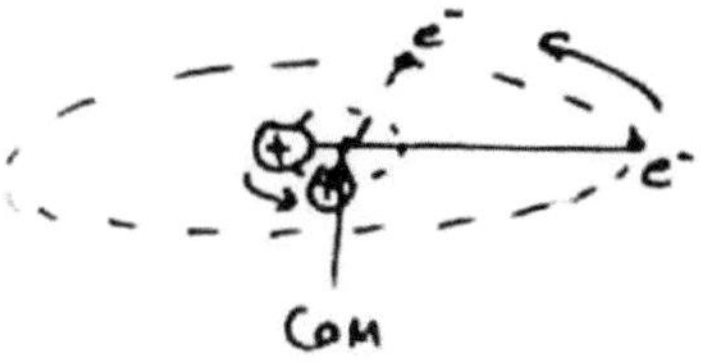

Concept of Reduced mass.

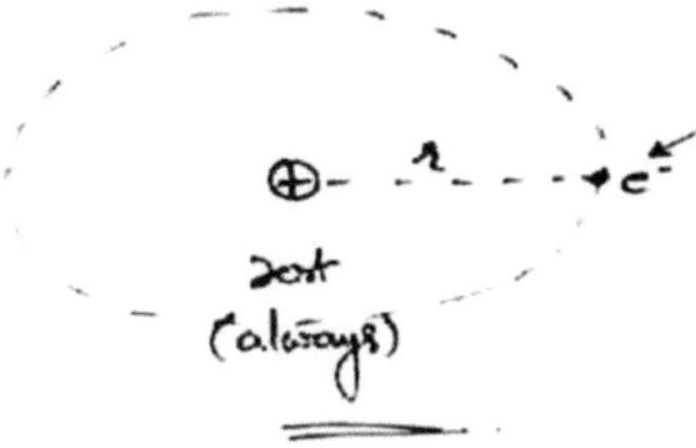

$$\mu = \frac{m_e \cdot m_N}{m_e + m_N}$$

Web Reference at www.physicsgalaxy.com
Scan for Video Explanation

Module-38 Effect of Nuclear Mass on Different Parameters of H-Atom

\# **Effect of Nuclear mass on different parameters of H-atom :**

For calculation of any parameter of H-atom in Bohr model we can replace the mass of $\bar{e}$ by reduced mass for accounting the mass of Nu.

Radius of nth orbit :
$$r_n = \frac{n^2 h^2}{4\pi^2 k z e^2 m_e}$$

If mass of Nu is accounted then we can replace $m_e \leftarrow \mu_e$

$$\mu_e = \frac{m_e \, m_N}{m_e + m_N}$$

$$r_n = \frac{n^2 h^2 (m_e + m_N)}{4\pi^2 k z e^2 (m_e \cdot m_N)} = 0.529 \left(\frac{m_e + m_N}{m_N} \right) \times \frac{h^2}{z} \, \overset{o}{A}$$

Module-39 Solved Example-13

Ex : Calculate the binding energy of electron in its ground state in a positronium consisting of an electron and positron revolving around their common centre of mass. Assume Bohr model to be valid.

Sol[n] : In positronium, reduced mass of $\bar{e}$ can be given as-

$$\mu = \frac{m_e \cdot m_e}{m_e + m_e} = \frac{m_e}{2}$$

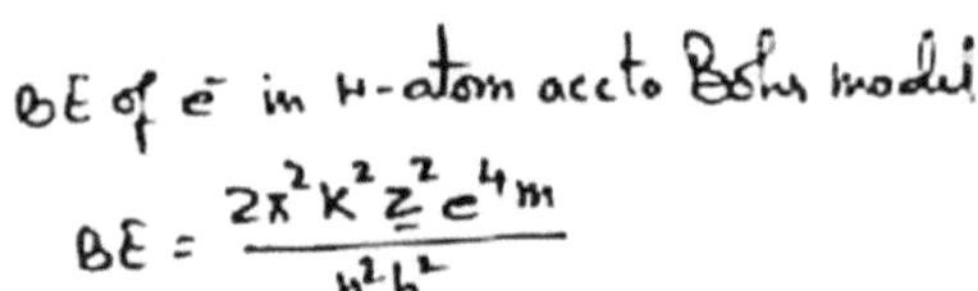

BE of $\bar{e}$ in H-atom acc to Bohr model

$$BE = \frac{2\pi^2 k^2 z^2 e^4 m}{n^2 h^2}$$

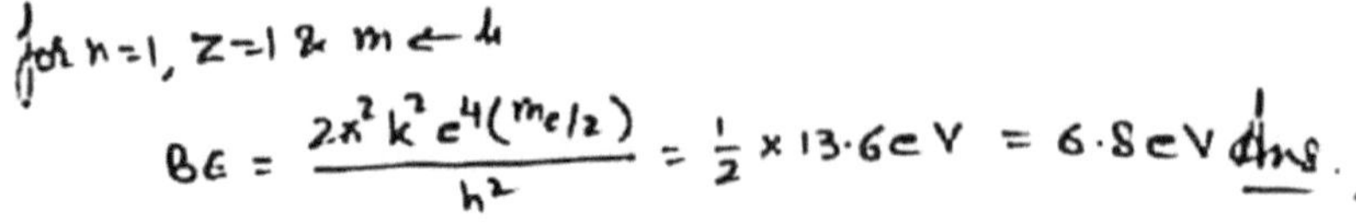

for $n=1$, $z=1$ & $m \leftarrow \mu$

$$BE = \frac{2\pi^2 k^2 e^4 (m_e/2)}{h^2} = \frac{1}{2} \times 13.6\,eV = 6.8\,eV \quad \text{Ans.}$$

Module-40 Solved Example-14

Ex : Calculate the difference between ionization potentials of atomic hydrogen and atomic deuterium. Given that $m_H = 1840\ m_e$ and $m_D = 3680\ m_e$.

Sol^n: BE of an e^- in hydrogenic atom $B\bar{E} = \dfrac{2\pi^2 k^2 z^2 e^4 m_e}{h^2}$

for both H & D atoms $z = 1$, accounting mass of Nu.-

IE of H atom is $\qquad IE_H = \dfrac{2\pi^2 k^2 e^4}{h^2}\left(\dfrac{m_e m_H}{m_e + m_H}\right)$

IE of D atom is $\qquad IE_D = \dfrac{2\pi^2 k^2 e^4}{h^2}\left(\dfrac{m_e m_D}{m_e + m_D}\right)$

$$\Delta E = IE_D - IE_H = \dfrac{2\pi^2 k^2 e^4 m_e}{h^2}\left[\dfrac{m_D}{m_e + m_D} - \dfrac{m_H}{m_e + m_H}\right]$$

$$\Delta E = 13.6\left[\dfrac{3680}{3681} - \dfrac{1840}{1841}\right] = 3.69 \times 10^{-3}\ eV$$

Ans.

Module-41 Use of Bohr Model to Define Hypothetical Energy Levels

\# <u>Use of Bohr Model to define hypothetical energy levels:</u>

In hydrogenic Atoms, Bohr's I & II Postulates are given as-

$$\left[\ \dfrac{k z e^2}{r_n^2} = \dfrac{m v_n^2}{r_n}\qquad —(1)\ \right.$$

$$\left.\ m v_n r_n = n\left(\dfrac{h}{2\pi}\right)\qquad —(2)\ \right]$$

If one e^- is rev around a <u>nucleus</u> in a hyp. atom in which the force field, the potential energy of e^- is given

$$\boxed{U = f(r)}$$

Bounding force on e^- is given as $\qquad \underline{F = \left|\dfrac{dU}{dr}\right|}$

Module-41 Use of Bohr Model to Define Hypothetical Energy Levels

$$U = f(r) \longrightarrow F = \left|\frac{dU}{dr}\right|$$

In such an atom Bohr's I Postulate can be modified as.

$$\left|\frac{dU}{dr}\right| = \frac{mv_n^2}{r_n} \quad \text{——(1)}$$

II Postulate $\qquad mv_n r_n = n\left(\frac{h}{2\pi}\right) \quad \text{——(2)}$

using abv eq^n (1) &(2) we can calculate all parameters for this hyp. atom.

Module-42 Solved Example-15

Ex : Suppose potential energy between electron and proton at a distance r is given by $-\dfrac{ke^2}{3r^3}$. Use Bohr's theory to find energy of electron in different energy levels in this atom.

Sol^n:
$$U = -\frac{ke^2}{3r^3}$$

Binding force betw^n e^- & p is $\quad F = \left|\frac{dU}{dr}\right| = \frac{ke^2}{r_n^4} \quad (\text{for } n^{th} \text{ orbit})$

from I Postulate $\quad \dfrac{mv_n^2}{r_n} = \dfrac{ke^2}{r_n^4} \implies mv_n^2 = \dfrac{ke^2}{r_n^3} \quad —(1)$

from II Postulate $\quad mv_n r_n = n\left(\frac{h}{2\pi}\right) \implies v_n = \dfrac{nh}{2\pi m r_n} \quad —(2)$

from (1) &(2) $\quad m\left(\dfrac{nh}{2\pi m r_n}\right)^2 = \dfrac{ke^2}{r_n^3}$

$$r_n = \frac{4\pi^2 ke^2 m}{n^2 h^2}$$

Module-42 Solved Example-15

$$r_n = \frac{4\pi^2 k e^2 m}{n^2 h^2}$$

Energy of e^- in n^{th} orbit of this atom —

$$E_n = K_n + U_n$$

$$= \frac{1}{2} m v_n^2 - \frac{k e^2}{3 r_n^3} \qquad \left[m v_n^2 = \frac{k e^2}{r_n^3} \right]$$

$$= \frac{1}{6} \frac{k e^2}{r_n^3}$$

$$= \frac{1}{6} k e^2 \left[\frac{n^2 h^2}{4\pi^2 k e^2 m} \right]^3$$

$$\boxed{E_n = \frac{n^6 h^6}{384 \pi^2 k^2 e^4 m^2}} \quad \underline{Ans.}$$

Scan for Video Explanation

Module-43 Solved Example-16

Ex : If in a hypothetical atom with z = 1, potential energy of electron at a distance r from Nucleus given as U = – ke ln(r). For such an atom calculate the radius of nth orbit assuming Bohr model to be valid for this atom.

Sol :

$$U = -ke \, \ln(r)$$

Binding force on e^- is $F = \left| \frac{dU}{dr} \right| = \frac{ke}{r}$

from I postulate $\quad \dfrac{ke}{r_n} = \dfrac{m v_n^2}{r_n} \implies v_n = \sqrt{\dfrac{ke}{m}} \quad$ (const)

from II postulate $\quad m v_n r_n = n\left(\dfrac{h}{2\pi} \right)$

$$r_n = \frac{n h}{2\pi m v_n} = \frac{n h}{2\pi m \left(\frac{ke}{m} \right)^{1/2}}$$

$$r_n = \frac{n h}{2\pi \sqrt{kme}} \quad \underline{Ans.}$$

Scan for Video Explanation

Module-44 Excitation of Hydrogenic Atoms by Collisions

Excitation of Hydrogenic Atoms by Collisions :

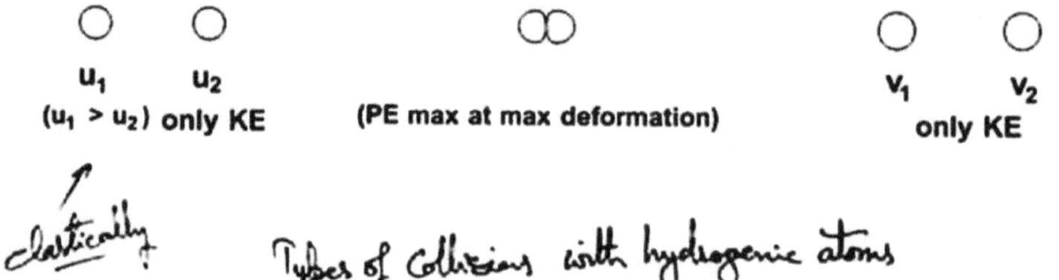
u_1
u_2
($u_1 > u_2$) only KE
(PE max at max deformation)
V_1
V_2
only KE
elastically

Types of Collisions with hydrogenic atoms

✓ (1) Collision with an $\bar{e}$

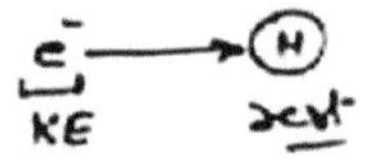
KE
excit

✓ (2) Collision with other atoms / particles

Scan for Video Explanation

Web Reference at www.physicsgalaxy.com

Module-45 Collision of a Hydrogenic Atoms by Collisions

Collision of a Hydrogenic Atom with an electron :

As $m_e << m_H$, we can always ignore the momentum of $\bar{e}$ colliding with atom, hence it is assumed that $\bar{e}$ can almost supply its full or any part of KE to the atom for its excitation.

for H-atom $\Delta E_{1-2} = 10.2\,eV$, $\Delta E_{1-3} = 12.09\,eV$

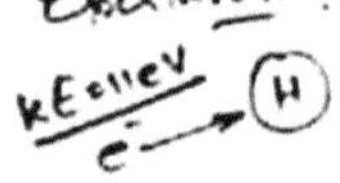
KE=11eV

Energy level of H-atom

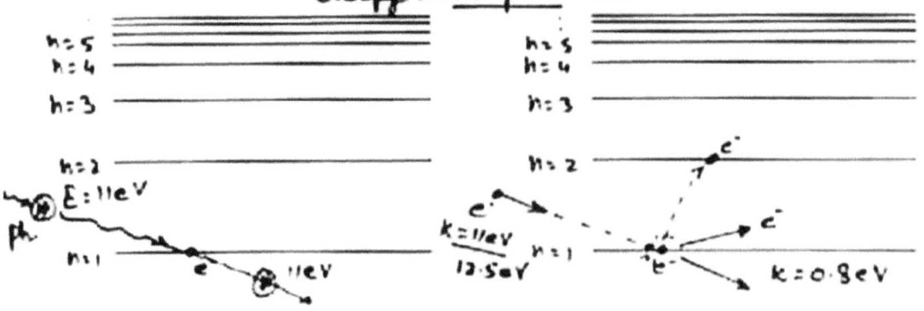
n=5
n=4
n=3
n=2
n=1
E=11eV
ph
e
11eV
k=11eV
13.5eV
k=0.8eV

Scan for Video Explanation

Web Reference at www.physicsgalaxy.com

Module-46 Collision of a Hydrogenic Atom with Another Atom Particles

Collision of a Hydrogenic Atom with another atom / particle :

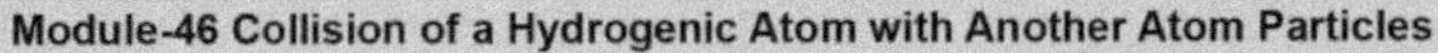

$$(H/n/p)$$

$$K_i = \frac{1}{2} m_1 v^2$$

$$1 \to 2 \; \checkmark$$
$$1 \to 3 \; \checkmark$$
$$1 \to 4 \; \checkmark$$
$$\vdots \quad \vdots$$

rest.

$$m_1 v = (m_1 + m_2) v_f$$

$$K_f = \frac{1}{2}(m_1 + m_2) v_f^2$$

max. KE loss $\underline{\Delta K = K_i - K_f}$

By Considering collision to be perfectly inelastic we can Calculate max loss in KE $\underline{\Delta K_{max}}$ and any fraction of this energy can be absorbed for excitation of e^-.

$$m_1 v = m_1 v_{1f} + m_2 v_{2f}$$
$$K_i - \Delta E_{exct} = \frac{1}{2} m_1 v_{1f}^2 + \frac{1}{2} m_2 v_{2f}^2 \qquad \begin{bmatrix} v_{1f} = - - - - \\ v_{2f} = - - - - \end{bmatrix}$$

Scan for Video Explanation

Module-47 Solved Example-17

Ex : An <u>electron</u> of kinetic energy 12.5 eV strikes a stationary hydrogen atom. State <u>all possible transitions</u> in H-atom.

 **Sol:**

Excitation energies of H-atom

$$\Delta E_{1 \to 2} = 10.2 \, eV \quad \checkmark$$

$$\Delta E_{1 \to 3} = 12.09 \, eV \quad \checkmark$$

$$\Delta E_{1 \to 4} = 12.75 \, eV \quad \times$$

Possible excitation transition are $\to 1 \to 2 , 1 \to 3$

Possible de-excitation transition are $\to 2 \to 1 , 3 \to 2, 3 \to 1$

$\underline{Ans.}$

Scan for Video Explanation

Module-48 Solved Example-18

Ex : A neutron with some initial kinetic energy strikes a stationary He$^+$ atom. Find the <u>minimum initial energy</u> of neutron for which inelastic collision may take place. Take $m_{He^+} = 4m_n$.

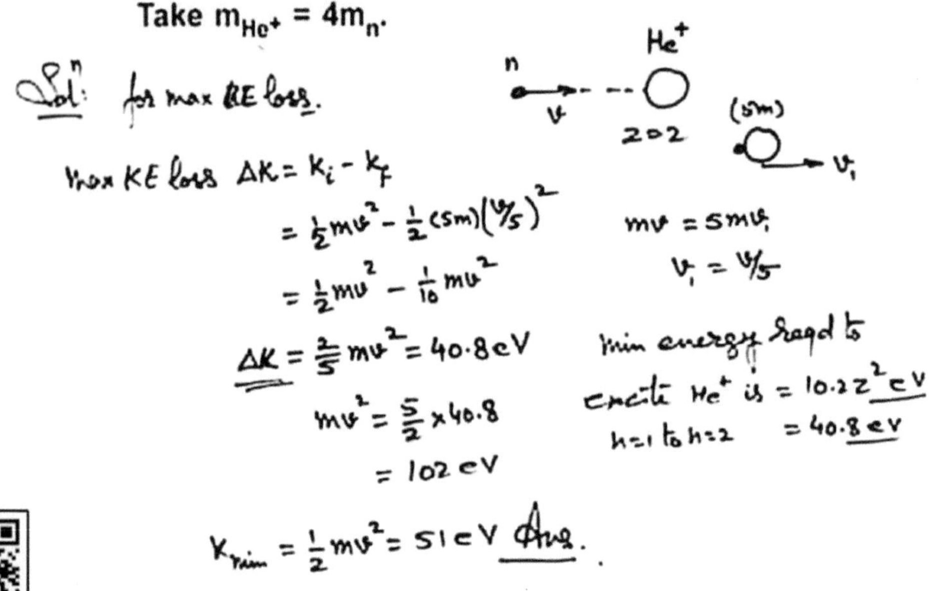

Sol: for max KE loss.

max KE loss $\Delta K = k_i - k_f$

$$= \tfrac{1}{2}mv^2 - \tfrac{1}{2}(5m)\left(\tfrac{v}{5}\right)^2$$

$$= \tfrac{1}{2}mv^2 - \tfrac{1}{10}mv^2$$

$$\Delta K = \tfrac{2}{5}mv^2 = 40.8\,eV$$

$$mv^2 = \tfrac{5}{2} \times 40.8$$

$$= 102\,eV$$

$mv = 5mv_i$

$v_i = \tfrac{v}{5}$

min energy reqd to excite He$^+$ is $= 10.2\,z^2\,eV$

$n=1$ to $n=2$ $\quad = 40.8\,eV$

$$K_{min} = \tfrac{1}{2}mv^2 = 51\,eV \quad \underline{Ans.}$$

Chapter 11
Photoelectric Effect

Module-1 Photoelectric Effect

\# *Photoelectric Effect*: Discovered by Albert Einstein in 1905

Emission of e^-s from metal surface by *light radiations* is called PEE.

\# *Electron emission from metals*:

'Work Function': (ϕ) min energy reqd to eject an e^- from a metal surface.

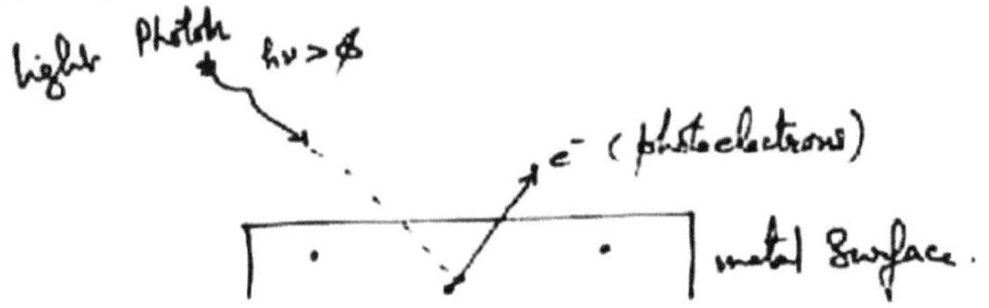

light Photon $\quad h\nu > \phi$

e^- (photoelectrons)

metal surface.

Module-1 Photoelectric Effect

\# *Working of a Photo Cell*:

which transform EM Rad energy to elect. energy

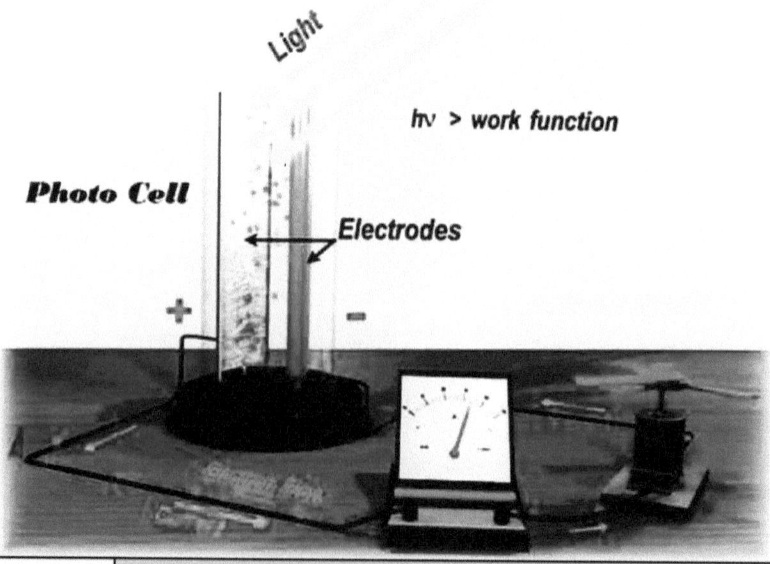

Module-2 Threshold Frequency

 # Threshold Frequency:

When a light incident on a metal, PEE will start only if the freq of incident radiation is more than a min fixed freq for that <u>metal</u> called 'threshold freq'. Denoted by (ν_{th})

Such that -

$$\boxed{h\nu_{th} = \phi}$$

W/F of metal

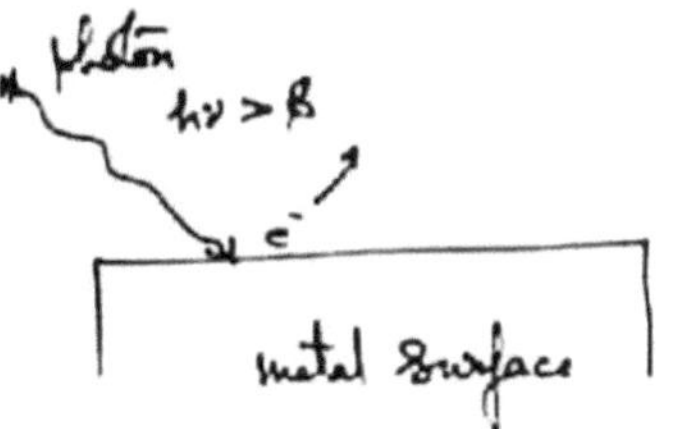

to start PEE from a metal $(\nu > \nu_{th})$

Module-3 Threshold Wavelength

 # Threshold Wavelength: Also called cutoff wavelength.

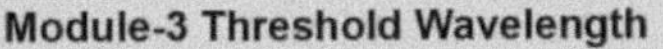

$$E_{ph} = h\nu = \frac{hc}{\lambda}$$

It is the max <u>wavelength</u> which is capable of ejecting photoelectrons from a metal. This implies -

$$\boxed{\frac{hc}{\lambda_{th}} = \phi}$$

to start PEE from a metal the W/L of incident rad $(\lambda < \lambda_{th})$

$$\lambda_{th} = \lambda_{green}$$

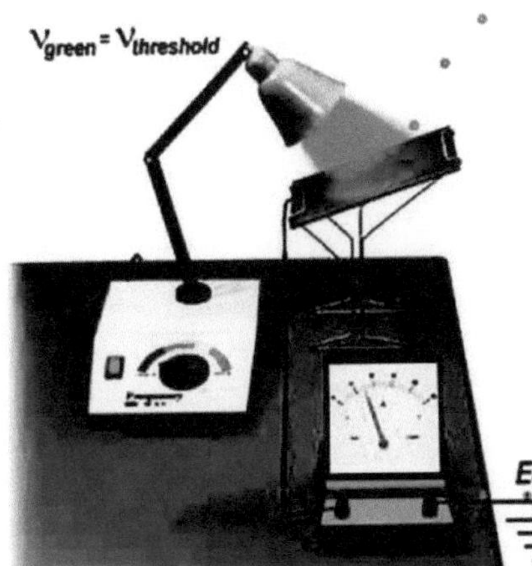

Module-4 Kinetic Energy of Photoelectrons

Kinetic Energy of Photoelectrons :

When energy of incident photon $(h\nu > \phi)$ is absorbed by a free e^-, it is used by e^- in two parts -

(1) A part of energy is used by e^- in doing work in ejection from the metal surface.

(2) Remaining part of energy is used by e^- as KE after ejection

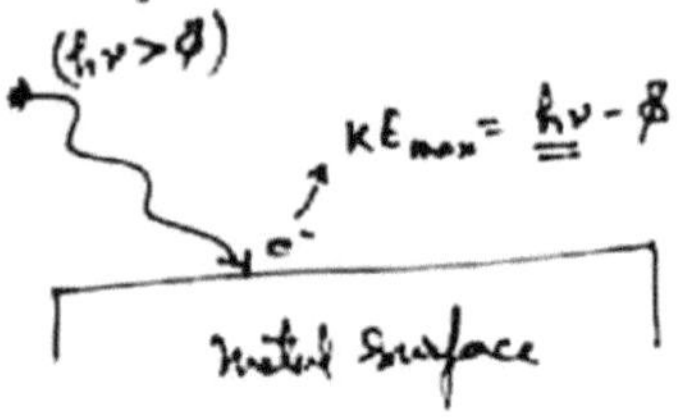

$$h\nu = \phi + \frac{1}{2}mv_{max}^2$$

↑ max possible KE of photo e^-s after ejection

$(h\nu > \phi)$

$KE_{max} = h\nu - \phi$

e^-

metal surface

Module-5 Distribution of Kinetic Energy of Photoelectrons

Distribution of Kinetic Energy of Photoelectrons :

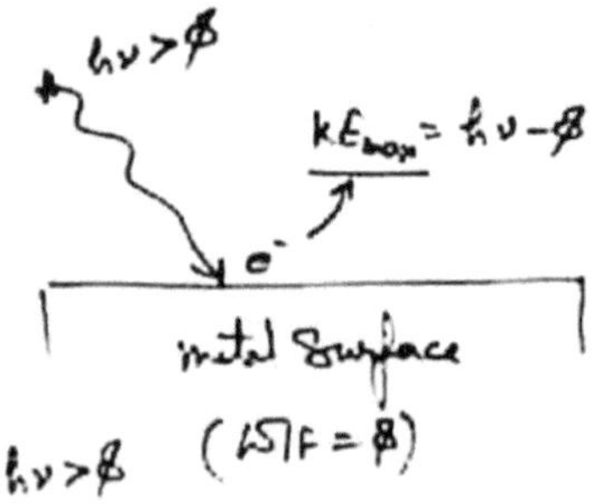

When a cont. rad. beam of freq ν $(h\nu > \phi)$ is incident on the metal surface, the ejected e^-s from surface have KE distributed between

0 to KE_{max}.

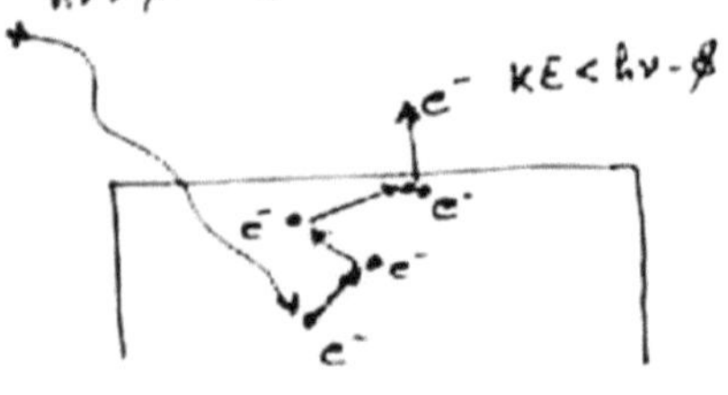

$$KE_{max} = h\nu - \phi$$

This dist is because e^- ejecting out may collide with some neighbouring e^- and loose some energy.

$h\nu > \phi$

$KE_{max} = h\nu - \phi$

e^-

metal surface

$(WF = \phi)$

$h\nu > \phi$

e^- $KE < h\nu - \phi$

Module-6 Quantum Efficiency of a Metal Surface

'Quantum Efficiency' of a metal Surface:

It may be possible that all photons in an incident rad beam ($h\nu > \phi$) will not eject e^-s from the surface.

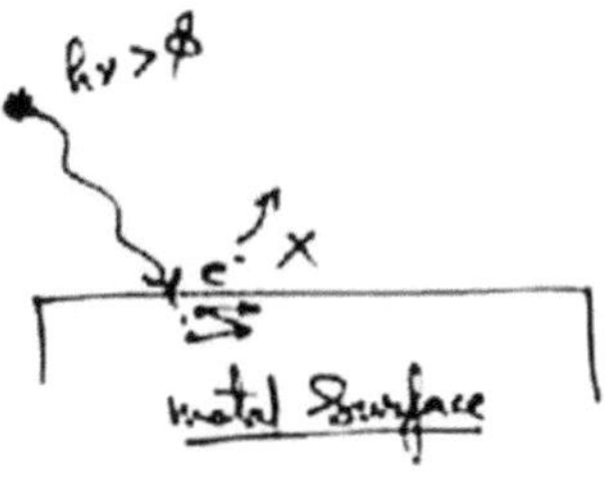

$\boxed{\text{In general no. of } e^-\text{s ejected will be } \underline{\text{less than}} \text{ the } \underline{\text{no. of photons}} \text{ incident on Surface.}}$

Quantum efficiency of metal Surface $\quad \eta = \dfrac{\text{no. of } e^- \text{ ejected}}{\text{no. of photons incident}} \times 100\ \%$

Module-7 Quantum Characteristics in Photoelectric Effect

Quantum Characteristics in Photoelectric Effect:

(1) No time lag exist in absorption of a photon and ejection of e^- from metal surface.

(2) If for incident rad $h\nu > \phi$ then each photon can at most eject one electron only.

(3) Two or more less energetic photon $\underline{h\nu < \phi}$ can never combine an eject an e^- from the metal Surface.

Module-8 Effect of Variation in Intensity of Light at Constant Frequency

Effect of variation in Intensity of light at Constant frequency:

for a light rad

Intensity $\propto$ no. of photon

at Constant freq.

$$E_{ph} = h\nu$$

$$h\nu = \phi + \frac{1}{2}mv_{max}^2$$

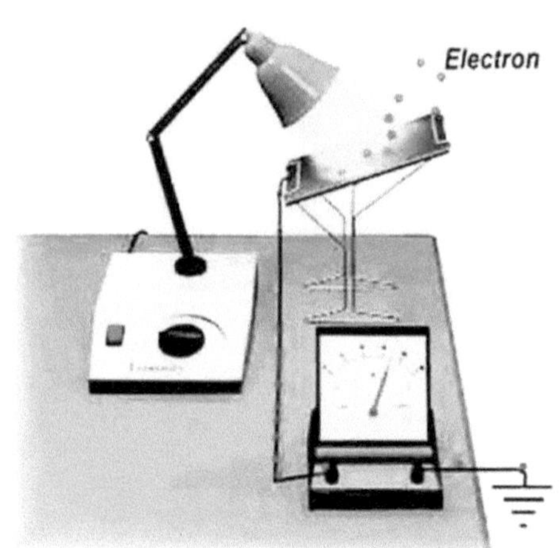

On inc intensity of incident beam, here no. of e's (ejected) will increase and hence photo current increases but kE_{max} of photoelectrons remains Constant.

Module-9 Effect of Variation in Frequency at Constant Photon Flux

Effect of variation in frequency at Constant 'photon flux':

Photon flux: In a rad beam it is the no. of photons passing through a unit normal/cross-section area of beam per unit time

As we know

$$h\nu = \phi + \frac{1}{2}mv_{max}^2$$

$$\nu > \nu_{th}.$$

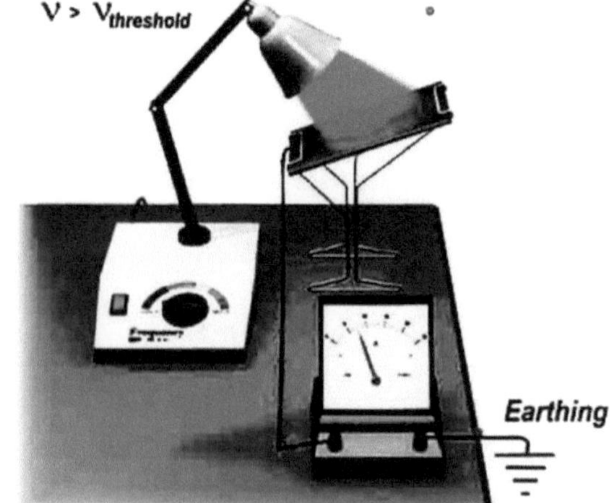

Module-10 Solved Example-1

Ex : For a given metal surface threshold wavelength is 2750 A. Find the work function of this metal and maximum kinetic energy of photoelectrons when surface is radiated by a radiation of wavelength 1800 A.

Sol^n: $\lambda_{th} = 2750\,\overset{\circ}{A}$

$\Rightarrow$ W/F of metal can be given as $\phi = \dfrac{hc}{\lambda_{th}} = \dfrac{12481}{2750}\,eV = 4.52\,eV$ Ans

Photon energy of incident rad. $E_{ph} = \dfrac{12431}{1800} = 6.9\,eV$

$E = 6.9\,eV$

$kE_{max} = E - \phi = 6.9 - 4.52 = 2.38\,eV$ Ans.

$\phi = 4.52\,eV$

Module-11 Solved Example-2

Ex : Light quanta with energy 4.9 eV eject photoelectrons from metal with work function 4.5 eV. Find the maximum impulse transmitted to the metal surface when electrons are ejected.

Sol^n: max KE of ejected e's $\quad kE_{max} = h\nu - \phi$

$$= 4.9 - 4.5 = 0.4\,eV$$

Impulse due to ejection of fastest electron is

$$P = \sqrt{2m(kE_{max})}$$

$$= \sqrt{2 \times 9.1 \times 10^{-31} \times 0.4 \times 1.6 \times 10^{-19}}$$

$$= 3.45 \times 10^{-25}\,kg\text{-}m/sec \quad \text{Ans.}$$

Module-12 Solved Example-3

Ex :   Lithium has work function 2.3 eV. It is exposed to light
of wavelength 4800 Å. Find the maximum kinetic energy
of emitted photoelectrons. Also find the longest
wavelength at which electron emission start from
Lithium surface.

Sol^n:

$$KE_{max} = h\nu - \phi$$

$$= \frac{hc}{\lambda} - \phi$$

$$= \frac{12431}{4800} - 2.3 = 2.59 - 2.3 = 0.29\,eV \quad Ans.$$

Threshold w/L.

$$\phi = \frac{hc}{\lambda_{th}}$$

$$\lambda_{th} = \frac{hc}{\phi} = \frac{12431}{2.3} = 5404\,\overset{\circ}{A} \quad Ans.$$

Module-13 Solved Example-4

Ex :   A beam of monochromatic light of wavelength λ ejects
photoelectrons from a cesium surface (ϕ = 1.9 eV).
These photoelectrons are made to collide with
hydrogen atoms in ground state. Find maximum value
of λ which can ionize hydrogen atoms.

Sol^n:

As we know

$$KE_{max} = \frac{hc}{\lambda} - \phi$$

$$\frac{hc}{\lambda} = KE_{max} + \phi$$

$$= 13.6 + 1.9 = 15.4\,eV$$

$$\Rightarrow \quad \lambda = \frac{hc}{15.4\,eV} = \frac{12431}{15.4} = 807\,\overset{\circ}{A} \quad Ans.$$

Module-14 Experimental Study of Photoelectric Effect

Experimental Study of Photoelectric Effect:

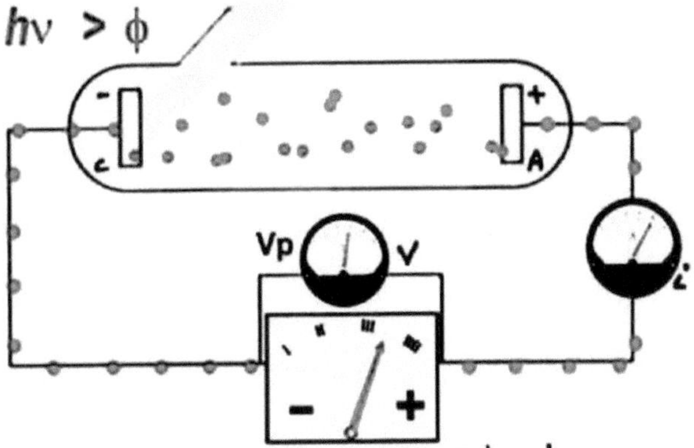

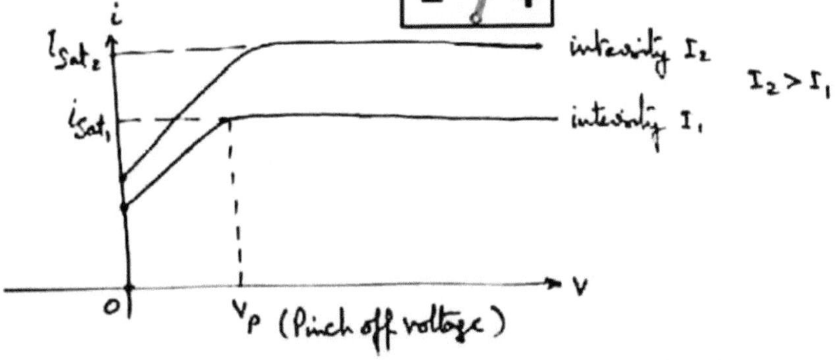

$$h\nu > \phi$$

Module-14 Experimental Study of Photoelectric Effect

Maximum and Minimum Energies of e^- reaching Anode:

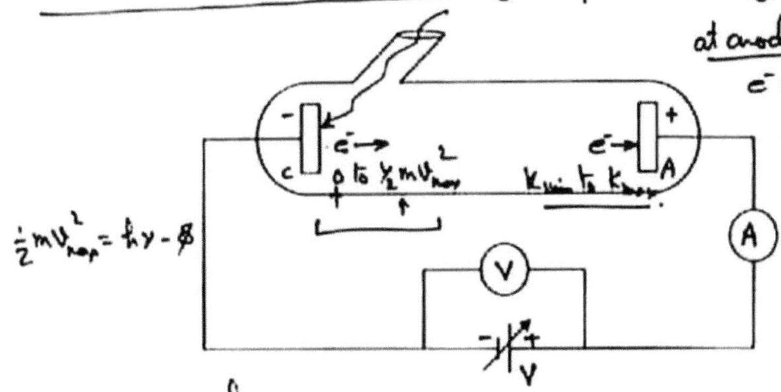

$$\frac{1}{2}mv_{max}^2 = h\nu - \phi$$

at anode.

$$\left[\begin{array}{l} K_{min} = 0 + eV \\ K_{max} = \frac{1}{2}mv_{max}^2 + eV \end{array} \right]$$

Module-14 Experimental Study of Photoelectric Effect

Experiment of PEE with reverse voltage:

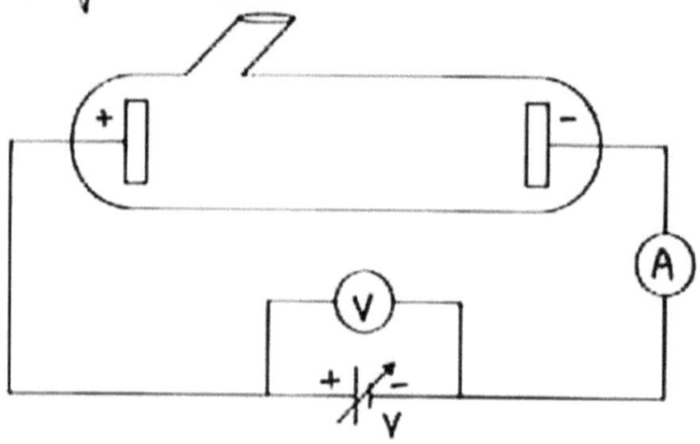

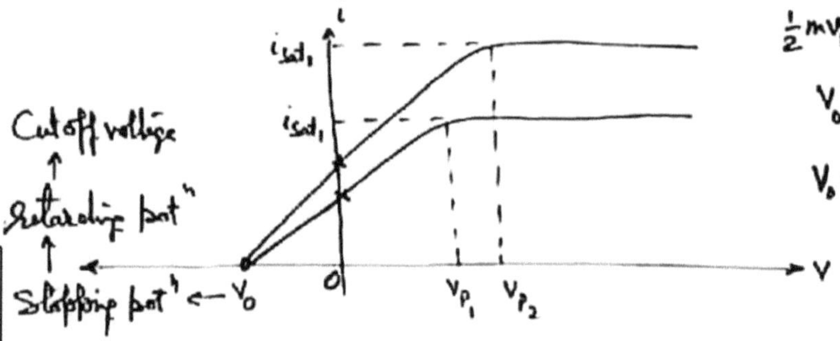

$$\frac{1}{2}mv_{max}^2 - eV_0 = 0$$

$$V_0 = \frac{KE_{max}}{e}$$

$$V_0 = \frac{h\nu - \phi}{e}$$

Scan for Video Explanation

Web Reference at www.physicsgalaxy.com

Module-15 Effect of Change in Frequency on Stopping Potential

Effect of change in frequency on Stopping Potential:

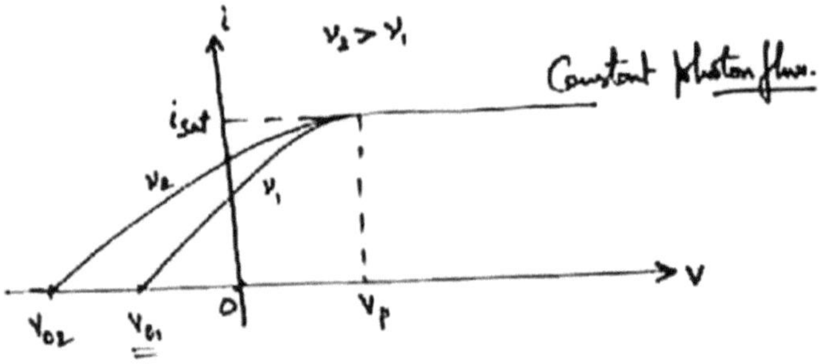

$KE_{max} = h\nu - \phi$

$$eV_0 = h\nu - h\nu_{th} \quad -(1)$$

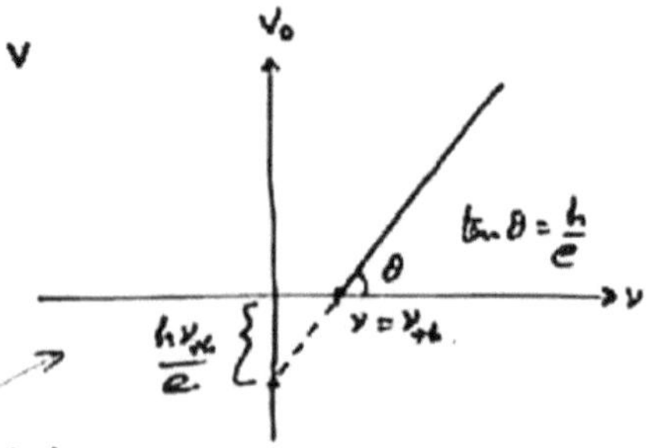

eq^n (1) is called Einstein eq^n of Photoelectric effect.

$$V_0 = \left(\frac{h}{e}\right)\nu - \left(\frac{h\nu_{th}}{e}\right)$$

$$y = mx + c$$

Scan for Video Explanation

Web Reference at www.physicsgalaxy.com

Module-16 Solved Example-5

Ex : In an experiment on photoelectric effect, the stopping potential is 3 volt and threshold frequency of metal used is 6×10^{14} Hz. Find the frequency of incident radiation.

Sol^n. As we know

$$h\nu = \phi + KE_{max}$$

$$\phi = h\nu_{th} = 6.63 \times 10^{-34} \times 6 \times 10^{14} = 3.88 \times 10^{-19}\, J$$

$$KE_{max} = eV_0 = 1.6 \times 10^{-19} \times 3 = 4.8 \times 10^{-19}\, J$$

$$\nu = \frac{\phi + KE_{max}}{h}$$

$$\nu = \frac{(3.88 + 4.8) \times 10^{-19}}{6.63 \times 10^{-34}} = 1.32 \times 10^{15}\ Hz\quad Ans.$$

Module-17 Solved Example-6

Ex : A light of wavelength 4360 Å is incident on a metal having work function 1.24 eV. Find the stopping potential for the ejected photoelectrons.

Sol^n

Energy of incident photon $E = \dfrac{12431}{4360} = 2.85\ eV$

max KE_{max} of ejected electrons $KE_{max} = E - \phi$

$$= 2.85 - 1.24\ eV$$

$$= 1.61\ eV$$

As we know

stopping pot^n $V_0 = \dfrac{KE_{max}}{e} = 1.61\ volt\quad Ans.$

Ex : Monochromatic light of wavelength 6402 Å is incident on calcium metal, the stopping potential for the ejected photoelectrons is measured to be 0.54 volt. What will be new stopping potential if wavelength is changed to 4272 Å.

Sol :

here we use $\quad \dfrac{hc}{\lambda} = \phi + eV_0$

$$\dfrac{12431}{6402} = \phi + 0.54\,eV \quad\text{——— (1)}$$

when λ is changed to 4272 Å if stopping pot^n becomes V_0'

$$\Rightarrow \qquad \dfrac{12431}{4272} = \phi + eV_0' \quad\text{——— (2)}$$

$(2) - (1) \Rightarrow \quad 12431\left[\dfrac{1}{4272} - \dfrac{1}{6402}\right] = e(V_0' - 0.54)$

$$(2.91 - 1.94)\,eV = e(V_0' - 0.54)$$

$$V_0' = 1.51 \text{ volt} \quad \underline{\text{Ans.}}$$

Chapter 12
Wave Particle Duality

Wave Particle Duality:

✓ W.P Duality for 'light':

$$
\begin{bmatrix}
\text{- Hygen} \rightarrow \text{light is a wave} & \text{Maxwell's theor of EM rad.} \\
\text{- Newton} \rightarrow \text{light is a stream} & \text{Einstein's Theory of P.E.E.} \\
\qquad\qquad\text{of particles} & \qquad\downarrow \\
& \text{Photon theory of light}
\end{bmatrix}
$$

✓ W-P Duality for matter:

De Broglie's Hypothesis of matter waves.

Momentum of a Photon:

Acc. to relativistic Theory, total energy E of a particle is related to its momentum as –

$$E^2 = p^2 c^2 + m_0^2 c^4$$

where $m_0 \rightarrow$ rest mass of the particle

for a photon $m_0 = 0$

$$\Rightarrow E = pc$$

$\Rightarrow$ momentum of a photon $p = \dfrac{E}{c}$

for a photon $E = \dfrac{hc}{\lambda} \Rightarrow \boxed{P = \dfrac{h}{\lambda}}$

Module-3 Rate of Photon Emission From a Light Source

Module-3 Rate of Photon Emission From a Light Source

\# Rate of Photon emission from a light Source :

$\lambda_L = \lambda$

P watt

Energy of each photon emitted is $\underline{E = \dfrac{hc}{\lambda} = h\nu}$

If N photons are emitted by the Source in $\underline{1\ sec}$.

$$N = \frac{P}{(hc/\lambda)} = \frac{P\lambda}{hc}\quad ph/sec$$

P watt.

for isotropic Source.

Module-4 Photon Flux in a Light Beam

\# <u>Photon Flux in a light beam</u> :

It is the total no. of photons crossing a given section of the light beam per unit area per unit time. It is denoted by 'ϕ_P'.

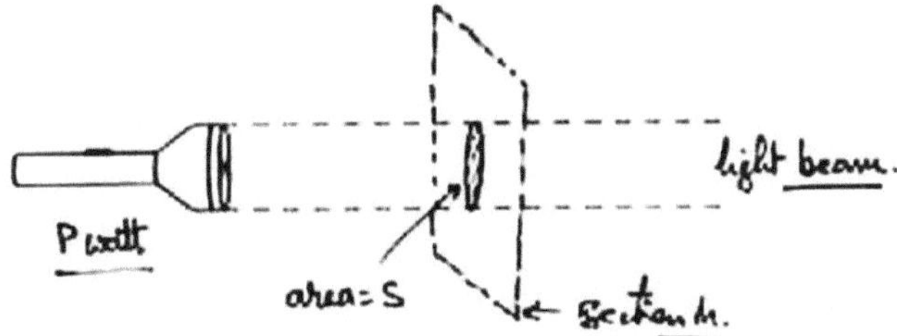

No. of photons emitted/sec $= \dfrac{P\lambda}{hc}$

photon flux $\quad \phi_P = \dfrac{P\lambda/hc}{S} = \dfrac{P\lambda}{Shc} = \dfrac{I\lambda}{hc}$

where $I = \dfrac{P}{S}$ watt/m² is the intensity of light beam.

Module-5 Photon Flux Due to a Point Source of Light

Photon Flux due to a point Source of light :

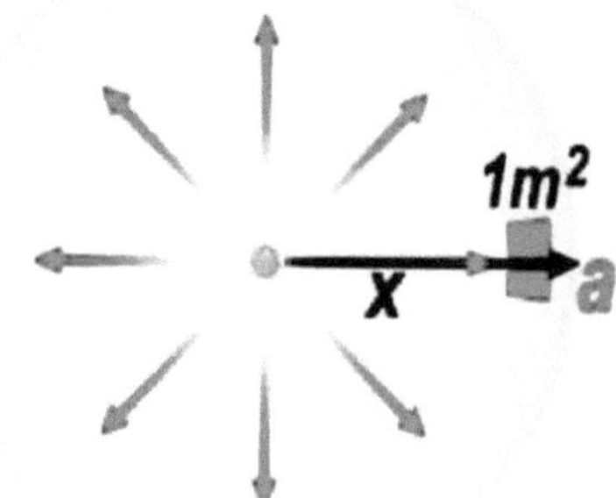

Total photons emitted/sec $= \dfrac{P\lambda}{hc}$

photon flux.

$$\phi_P = \dfrac{P\lambda/hc}{4\pi x^2}$$

$$\phi_P = \dfrac{I_A \lambda}{hc} = \dfrac{P\lambda}{4\pi hc\, x^2}$$

$$I_A = \dfrac{P}{4\pi x^2}$$

Module-6 Photon Density in a Light Beam

Photon Density in a light beam :

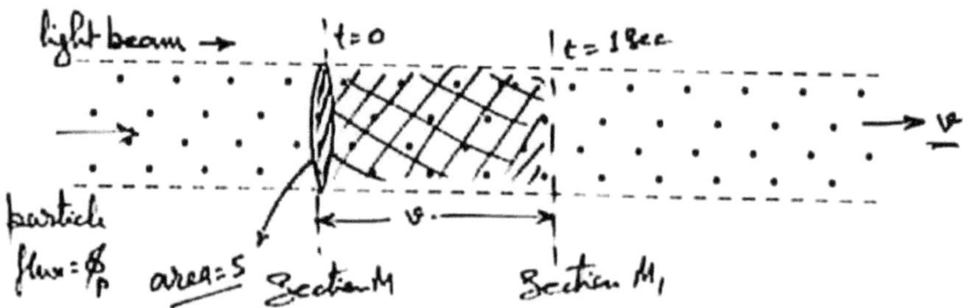

no. of particles incident on Section M in 1 sec. $= \phi_P S$

Density of particles (photons) in beam $\rho_P = \dfrac{\phi_P S}{S v}$

$$\boxed{\rho_P = \dfrac{\phi_P}{v}}$$

$$\left[\; \text{photon density} = \dfrac{\text{Photon flux}}{\text{Speed of light}} \;\right]$$

Module-7 Solved Example-1

Ex : Calculate the number of photons emitted by a 60W sodium lamp in 10 hrs. Take wavelength of sodium light is 5893 Å.

Sol^n:

$$\text{Rate of photon emission} = \frac{P\lambda}{hc} \ \text{ph/sec}$$

$$\text{total no. of photons emitted in time } t = \frac{P\lambda}{hc} \times t$$

$$= \frac{60 \times 5893 \times 10^{-10}}{6.63 \times 10^{-34} \times 3 \times 10^{8}} \times 10 \times 3600$$

$$= 6.4 \times 10^{24} \text{ photons} \quad \text{Ans.}$$

Scan for Video Explanation

Module-8 Solved Example-2

Ex : A light of power 1mW and wavelength 4560 A incident on a metal with work function 2eV. If quantum efficiency of surface is 0.5% find the photocurrent emitted from the surface.

Sol^n: Energy of photons incident on surface is $E = \frac{12431}{4560} = 2.72eV$

No. of photons incident on Surface/sec $N = \frac{P\lambda}{hc}$

$$= \frac{10^{-3} \times 4560 \times 10^{-10}}{6.63 \times 10^{-34} \times 3 \times 10^{8}}$$

$$= 2.29 \times 10^{15} \ \text{ph/sec.}$$

No. of electrons ejected from Surface/sec are

$$n = 2.29 \times 10^{15} \times \frac{0.5}{100} = 1.14 \times 10^{13} \ \text{e}^-\text{s/sec}$$

photocurrent $I = ne = 1.14 \times 10^{13} \times 1.6 \times 10^{-19} \ \text{Coul/sec}$

$$= 1.824 \times 10^{-6} = 1.824 \mu A \quad \text{Ans.}$$

Scan for Video Explanation

Module-9 Solved Example-3

Ex : A beam of light has three wavelengths 4144A, 4972A and 6216A with a total intensity of 3.6×10^{-3} W/m^2 equally distributed among the three wavelengths is incident on a metal surface of work function 2.3 eV. If each capable photon ejects one electron, calculate the number of photoelectrons ejected in two seconds from 1 m^2 surface.

Sol^n: Threshold W/L of metal $\lambda_{th} = \dfrac{12431}{2.3} = 5405 \, \overset{o}{A}$

No. of photons incident on metal $\quad N = \dfrac{P\lambda_1}{hc} + \dfrac{P\lambda_2}{hc} = \dfrac{P}{hc}(\lambda_1 + \lambda_2)$

$P = 10^{-3} \times 1.2 \text{ W/m}^2 \quad$ of $\lambda_1 \& \lambda_3$

$$N = \dfrac{1.2 \times 10^{-3}}{6.63 \times 10^{-24} \times 3 \times 10^{8}}(4144 + 4972) \times 10^{-10}$$

$$N = 5.5 \times 10^{15} \text{ ph/sec}$$

e^-s emitted in 2 sec also $= 5.5 \times 10^{15} \times 2 = 1.1 \times 10^{16}$ electrons **Ans.**

Module-10 Solved Example-4

Ex : A small metal plate is placed normally at a distance 2m from a point source of light and a photo current of 18 mA is measured from the metal plate. If the plate shifted away from the source at a distance of 6m find the new photocurrent.

Sol^n:

Photo current $\propto$ no of ph/sec
$\propto$ Intensity of light

$I = \dfrac{P}{4\pi x^2} \Rightarrow I \propto \dfrac{1}{x^2}$

photocurrent $\propto \dfrac{1}{x^2}$ ...(i)

$\dfrac{i_1}{i_2} = \dfrac{x_2^2}{x_1^2} \Rightarrow i_2 = i_1 \times \dfrac{x_1^2}{x_2^2} = 18 \times \left(\dfrac{2}{6}\right)^2 \text{ mA}$

$$= 2 \text{ mA} \text{ Ans.}$$

Module-11 Solved Example-5

Ex : A monochromatic light source of power 5 mW emits 8×10^{15} photons/sec. This light ejects photoelectrons from a metal surface. The stopping potential for these electrons is 2V. Calculate the work function of the metal surface.

Sol^n. Rate of photon emission from a Source $N = \dfrac{P\lambda}{hc}$ ph/sec

$$\lambda = \dfrac{Nhc}{P} = \dfrac{8\times10^{15} \times 6.63\times10^{-34} \times 3\times10^{8}}{5\times10^{-3}}$$

$$= 3182 \,\overset{\circ}{A}$$

Energy of each photon

$$E = \dfrac{12431}{3182} = 3.9\,eV$$

Max. KE of photoelectron $kE_{max} = eV_0 = 2eV$

$$\Rightarrow \quad E = \phi + kE_{max}$$

$$\phi = E - kE_{max} = 3.9 - 2 = 1.9\,eV \quad Ans.$$

Module-12 Force Exerted by a Light Beam on a Surface

Force exerted by a light beam on a Surface:

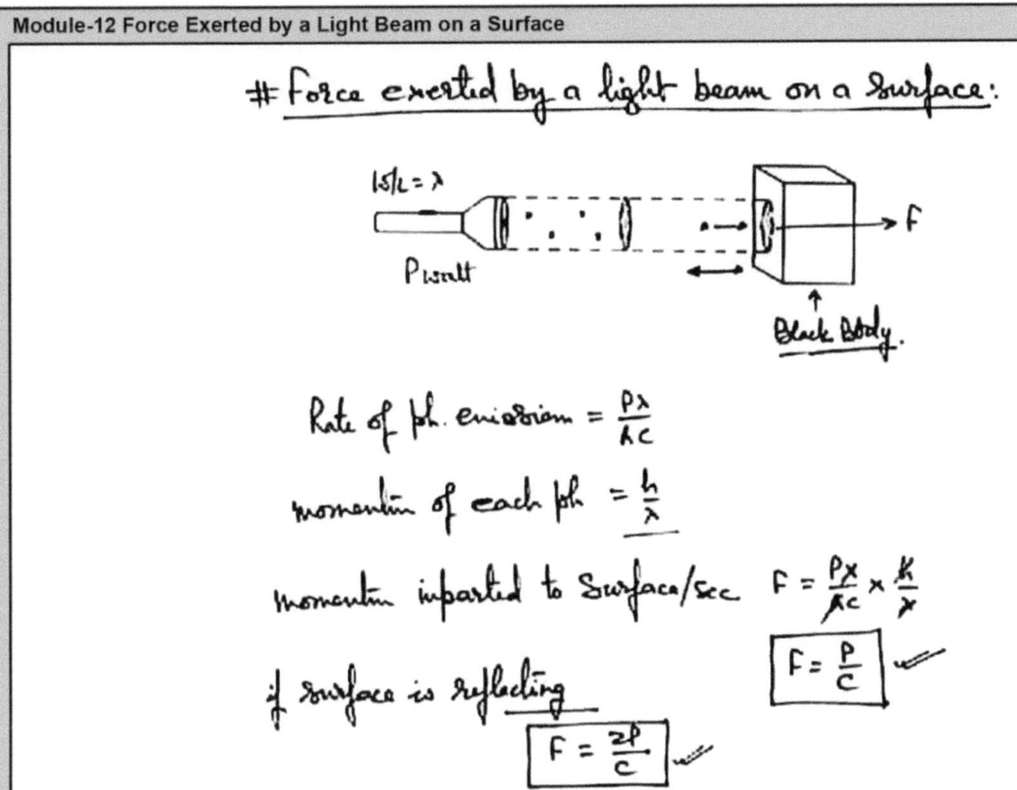

Rate of ph. emission $= \dfrac{P\lambda}{hc}$

momentum of each ph $= \dfrac{h}{\lambda}$

momentum imparted to Surface/sec $\quad F = \dfrac{P\lambda}{hc} \times \dfrac{h}{\lambda}$

$$\boxed{F = \dfrac{P}{c}}$$

if surface is reflecting

$$\boxed{F = \dfrac{2P}{c}}$$

Module-12 Force Exerted by a Light Beam on a Surface

If Surface is partially _reflecting_, it reflects 30% of light and absorbs 70% of light.

$$f = 0.3 \times \frac{2P}{c} + 0.7 \times \frac{P}{c}$$

$$f = \frac{1.3P}{c}$$

Web Reference at www.physicsgalaxy.com

Module-13 Force Exerted on a Black Body in Path of a Light Beam

force exerted on a black body in path of a light beam:

light beam ($I\ W/m^2$)

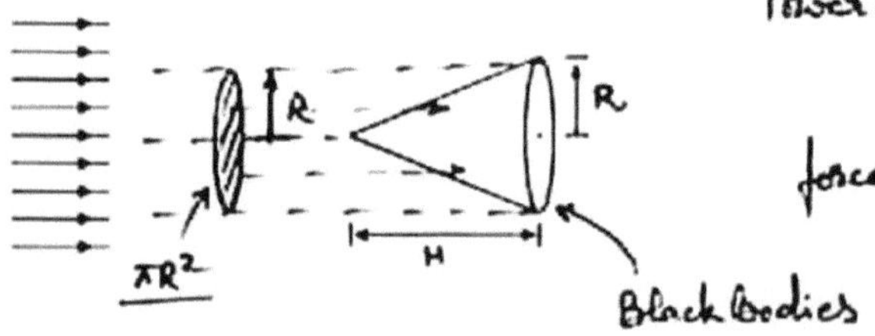

Power incident on Cone
$$P = I \pi R^2$$
force on Cone $f = \frac{P}{c} = \frac{I \pi R^2}{c}$

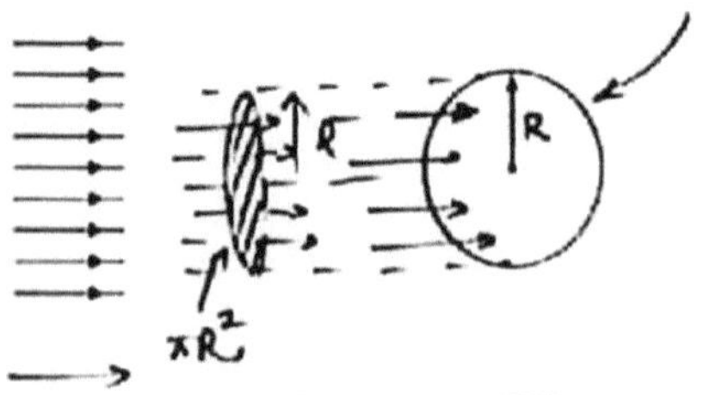

Black bodies

Power incident on sphere
$$P = I \pi R^2$$
force on sphere $f = \frac{P}{c} = \frac{I \pi R^2}{c}$

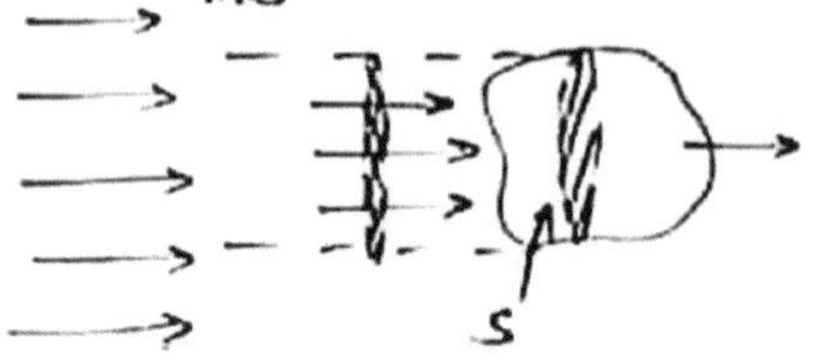

$$f = \frac{IS}{c}$$

Web Reference at www.physicsgalaxy.com

Module-14 Force Exerted by a Light Beam on a Mirror

Force exerted by a light beam on a mirror:

Total momentum of all photons in light beam per unit time.

$$\Delta p = \frac{P}{c}$$

Total change in momentum/sec of light beam along N

$$F = 2\Delta P \cos\theta$$

$$\boxed{F = \frac{2P}{c}\cos\theta}$$

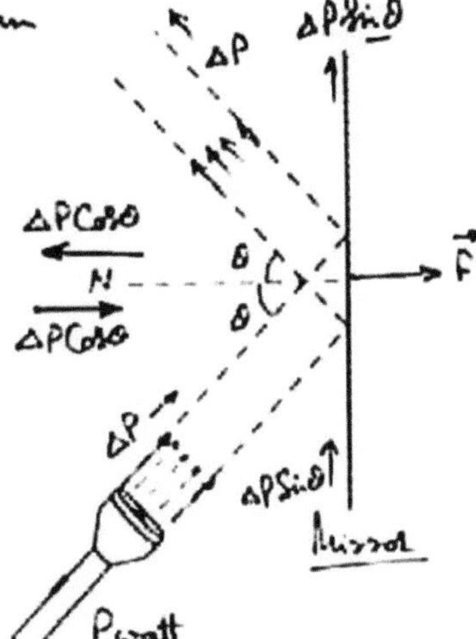

Module-15 Recoiling of an Atom During de-excitation

Recoiling of an atom during de-excitation:

momentum of a photon $P = \frac{h}{\lambda}$

by Cons of momentum $\Rightarrow$ $m_H V_R = \frac{h}{\lambda}$ $\Rightarrow$ $V_R = \frac{h}{m_H \lambda}$

by Rydberg's formula $\quad \frac{1}{\lambda} = Rz^2\left[\frac{1}{n_1^2} - \frac{1}{n_2^2}\right]$

recoil speed $\boxed{V_R = \frac{hRz^2}{m_H}\left[\frac{1}{n_1^2} - \frac{1}{n_2^2}\right]}$ approx. ✓

Module-15 Recoiling of an Atom During de-excitation

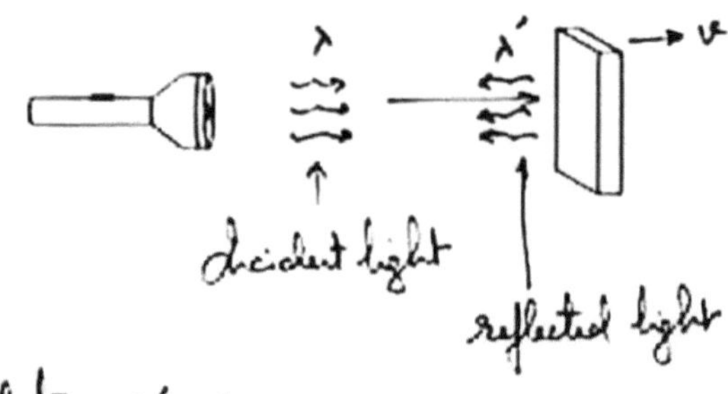

$$hcRZ^2\left[\frac{1}{n_1^2} - \frac{1}{n_2^2}\right] = \frac{hc}{\lambda'} + \frac{1}{2}m_H v_R^2 \quad - (1)$$

also by Cons. of momentum

$$m_H v_R = \frac{h}{\lambda'} \quad - (2)$$

using (1) & (2) after solving we'll get

$$\left[\begin{array}{l} \lambda' = - - - \\ v_R = - - - \end{array}\right]$$

Module-16 Variation in Wavelength of Light Due to Reflection

\# <u>Variation in wavelength of light due to Reflection:</u>

On Reflection $\lambda' > \lambda$

As incident light impart some energy to the reflecting Surface always the reflected light will have Slightly greater wavelength.

Module-17 De Broglie's Hypothesis

\# **De Broglie's Hypothesis:**

It was established for a photon

momentum of a photon $\left[P = \dfrac{h}{\lambda} \quad \text{or} \quad \lambda = \dfrac{h}{P} \right]$

De Broglie assumed that as an EM wave can possess momentum and behave like a particle, a moving particle must also behave like an EM wave of which wavelength can be given as -

$$\lambda = \frac{h}{P_{particle}} = \frac{h}{mv}$$

Module-18 Solved Example-6

Ex : With what speed an electron must travel so that its momentum is equal to that of a photon of light wavelength 5200 A.

Sol[n]:

momentum of a photon $\quad P = \dfrac{h}{\lambda} = \dfrac{6.63 \times 10^{-34}}{5200 \times 10^{-10}}$

for electron $\quad P_e = mv$

$$v = \frac{P_e}{m} = \frac{h}{m\lambda} = \frac{6.63 \times 10^{-34}}{9.1 \times 10^{-31} \times 5200 \times 10^{-10}}$$

$$v = 1401 \text{ m/s} \quad \underline{Ans.}$$

Module-19 Solved Example-7

Ex : Find the ratio of De Broglie wavelength of a proton and an α-particle which are accelerated through same potential difference.

Sol^n: for a p.d = V, KE gained by a charge q is $E = qV$

momentum of this charge $P = \sqrt{2mE}$

De Broglie W.L of this particle $\lambda = \dfrac{h}{P} = \dfrac{h}{\sqrt{2mE}} = \dfrac{h}{\sqrt{2mqV}}$

for a proton $\quad \lambda_p = \dfrac{h}{\sqrt{2m_p q_p V}}$

for an α-part $\quad \lambda_\alpha = \dfrac{h}{\sqrt{2m_\alpha q_\alpha V}}$

$$\dfrac{\lambda_P}{\lambda_\alpha} = \sqrt{\dfrac{m_\alpha q_\alpha}{m_p q_p}}$$

$$\dfrac{\lambda_P}{\lambda_\alpha} = \sqrt{\dfrac{4}{1} \times \dfrac{2}{1}} = 2\sqrt{2}$$

$$\underline{Ans.}$$

Module-20 Solved Example-8

Ex : Hydrogen gas is excited to state where potential energy of electrons is –1.7 eV. Now a metal plate with work function 2.3 eV is exposed to the emission spectrum of this gas. Find the minimum De Broglie wavelength of the ejected photoelectrons.

Sol^n: KE of e's $= \dfrac{1}{2}|PE| = 0.85\,eV$

$\quad TE = -1.7 + 0.85 = -0.85\,eV \;[n = 4]$

max energy photon is emitted for $n_2 = 4 \longrightarrow n_1 = 1$.

$\quad \Delta E_{max} = E_4 - E_1 = (-0.85) - (-13.6\,eV) = \underline{12.75\,eV}$

the KE$_{max}$ for photoelectrons $\underline{KE_{max}} = 12.75 - 2.3 = 10.45\,eV$

$\quad P_{max} = \sqrt{2m(KE_{max})}$

De Broglie W.L of these e's $\lambda_{min} = \dfrac{h}{P_{max}} = \dfrac{6.63 \times 10^{-34}}{\sqrt{2 \times 9.1 \times 10^{-31} \times 10.45 \times 1.6 \times 10^{-19}}}$

$$= 3.8\,\overset{\circ}{A}\ \underline{Ans.}$$

Module-21 Solved Example-9

Ex : If a light beam from a source of power 100 watt is incident on a black body of mass 50 kg in space at rest, find the acceleration of body.

Sol^n :

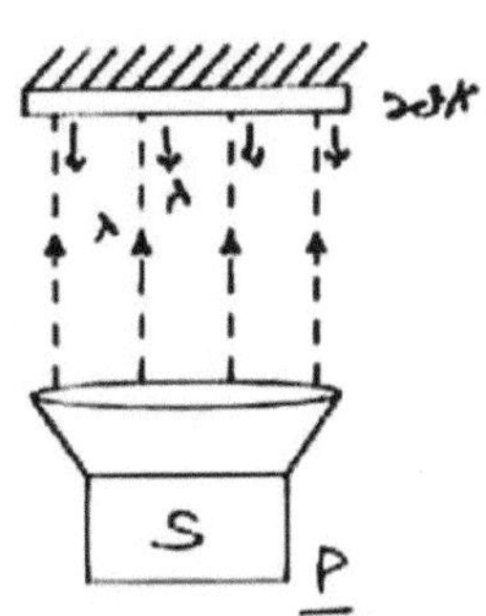

acc^n of body $\quad a = \dfrac{F}{m} = \dfrac{P}{mc} = \dfrac{100}{50 \times 3 \times 10^8}$

$$= \dfrac{2}{3} \times 10^{-8}$$

$$= 6.66 \times 10^{-9} \ m/s^2 \ \text{Ans.}$$

Scan for Video Explanation

Module-22 Solved Example-10

Ex : Figure shows a mirror of mass 20 gm held at rest horizontally in space by a light beam from a source S. Assume 30% of rated power of source is produced in form of light find the rated power of source.

Sol^n : the light power produced by this source will be 0.3P

Force exerted by light beam on mirror is

$$F = \dfrac{2(0.3P)}{c} = mg$$

$$P = \dfrac{mgc}{0.6} = \dfrac{20 \times 10^{-3} \times 10 \times 3 \times 10^8}{0.6}$$

$$= 10^8 \ W = 100 \ MW \ \text{Ans.}$$

Scan for Video Explanation

Chapter 13
X-Rays

Module-1 Introduction to X-Rays

X-Rays:

→ These are high freq EM rad with wavelengths ranging from $0.01 Å$ to $100 Å$.

$$E = h\nu$$

→ Due to high energy, X-Rays have higher penetration depth. for physical substances compared to other EM rad like UV, IR & vis. rad.

→ X-Rays are produced by breaking of high energy e^- of cathode Rays.

fast moving e^-

Module-2 Types of X-Rays

 # Types of X-Rays:

Based on Energy and penetration depth, X-rays are divided in two groups -

① **Soft X-Rays.** : $\lambda > 10 Å$, rel. low energy

② **Hard X-Rays:** $\lambda < 1 Å$, rel. high energy.

Module-3 Production of X-Rays

Production of X-Rays:

X-Rays are produced in a disch. tube called Coolidge tube which is operated at high p.d.

In the tube –

    <u>Cathode</u> – Source of Cathode Rays (fast moving e^-)

    <u>Anode</u> – Source of X-rays.

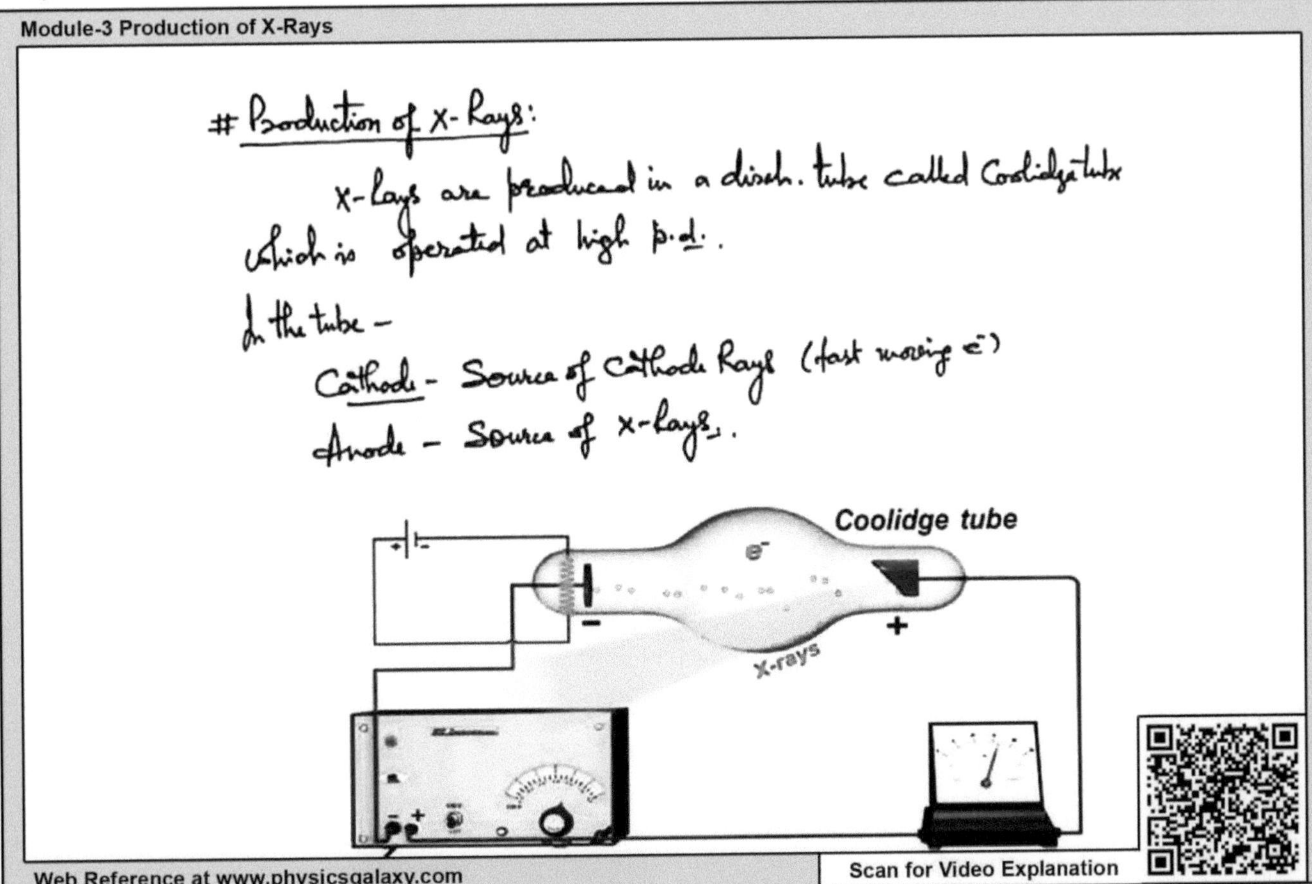

Module-4 Production Mechanism and Classification of X-Rays

Production of X-Rays –

On the basis of production mechanism, X-Rays are classified in two broad categories. –

(1) <u>Continuous</u> X-Rays: When acc. e^- in vacc. tube strike the anode and it is further accelerated due to the strong EF of Nu in the Anode then the KE of e^- is radiated as Cont. X-Rays.

(2) <u>Characteristic</u> X-Rays: When high energy e^- strike any of the orbiting e^-'s of the anode atom and it knocks out these electron and it result in emission of a line spectrum of the element.

Module-5 Production of Continuous X-Rays

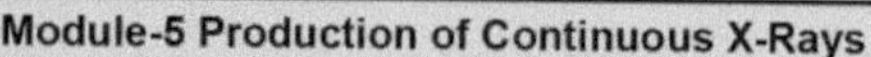

Production of Continuous X-Rays: (white x-Rays)

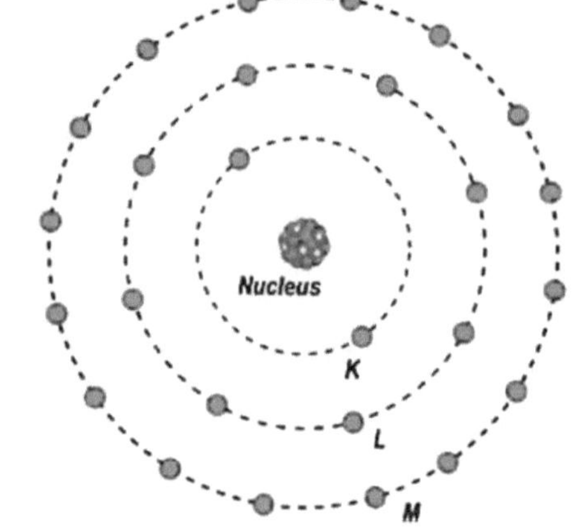

$$KE \text{ of } CR\, e^- = eV$$

$$eV = \frac{hc}{\lambda} \ (max)$$

$$\lambda_{min} = \frac{hc}{eV}$$

$$\lambda_{min} = \frac{12431}{V} \ \overset{\circ}{A}$$

Cutoff w/L
of Cont. X-Rays.

Module-5 Production of Continuous X-Rays

- from x-ray tube, x-Rays are emitted in range from

λ_c to ∞ and-

$$\lambda_c = \left(\frac{12431}{V}\right) \overset{\circ}{A}$$

Continuous
w/L distribution.

(White X-Rays)

Module-5 Production of Continuous X-Rays

Spectrum of Continuous X-Rays:

Variation of spectral intensity with wavelength

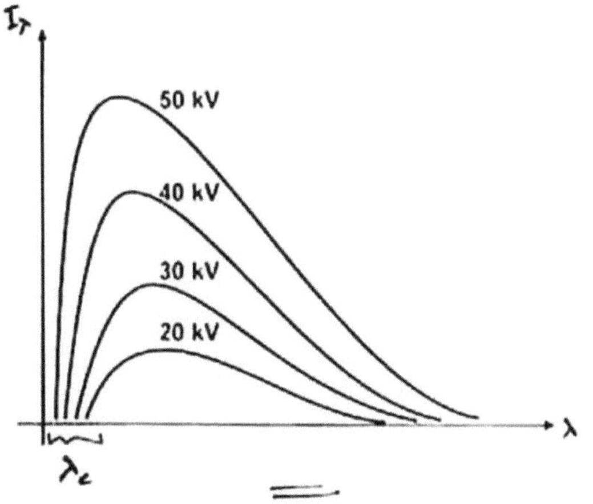

Web Reference at www.physicsgalaxy.com

Scan for Video Explanation

Module-6 Production of Characteristic X-Rays

Production of Characteristic X-Rays:

These x-Rays are produced when CR e^- strikes with an orbiting e^- of anode atom.

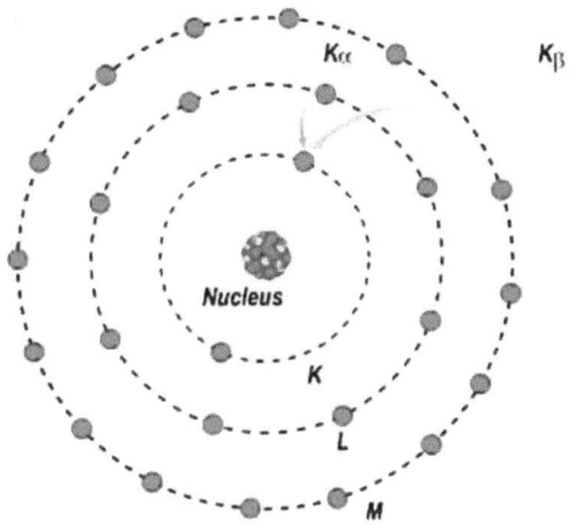

$eV > E_{BK}$

L → K $\rightsquigarrow K_\alpha$

M → K $\rightsquigarrow K_\beta$

↓

characteristic X-rays.

Web Reference at www.physicsgalaxy.com

Scan for Video Explanation

Module-6 Production of Characteristic X-Rays

Spectral Series of Characteristic X-Rays:

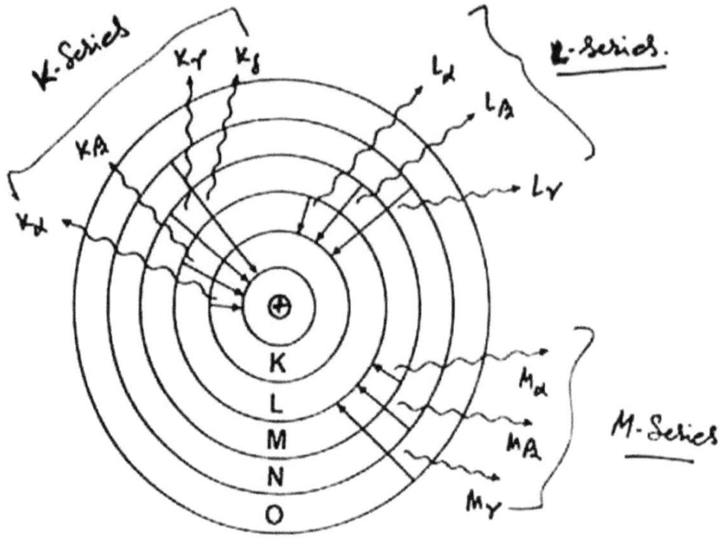

Scan for Video Explanation

Web Reference at www.physicsgalaxy.com

Module-6 Production of Characteristic X-Rays

Wavelength Spectrum of characteristic X-Rays:

Variation of I_λ with λ.

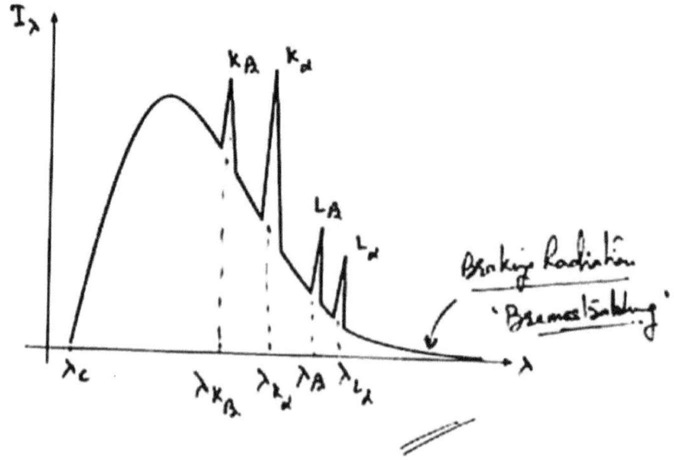

Scan for Video Explanation

Web Reference at www.physicsgalaxy.com

Module-7 Moseley's Law

\# __Moseley's Law__ :

The wavelength of ch. X-Rays can be obtained by modified Rydberg's formula.

$$\frac{1}{\lambda} = R(z-\sigma)^2 \left[\frac{1}{n_1^2} - \frac{1}{n_2^2} \right]$$

here $\underline{\sigma} \longrightarrow$ Screening Constant

$z - \sigma = z_{eff}$ effective atomic no. of element.

if ν is the freq of emitted x Rays then we can use

$$\nu = \frac{c}{\lambda} = \underline{Rc}\,(z-\sigma)^2 \left[\frac{1}{n_1^2} - \frac{1}{n_2^2} \right]$$

$$\boxed{\sqrt{\nu} = a\,(z-\sigma)} \leftarrow \text{Moseley's } \underline{Law.}$$

here $a = \sqrt{Rc \left(\frac{1}{n_1^2} - \frac{1}{n_2^2} \right)}$ is a Const for a given transition.

 | Scan for Video Explanation

Module-8 Solved Example-1

Ex : An X-Ray tube operates at 20kV. Find the maximum speed of the electron striking the anticathode. Also find the minimum wavelength of X-Rays generated. Take charge of electron = 1.6×10^{-19} C and mass of electron = 9×10^{-31} Kg.

 Sol:

$$K_i = eV = \frac{1}{2}mv^2$$

$$v_{max} = \sqrt{\frac{2eV}{m}} = \sqrt{\frac{2 \times 1.6 \times 10^{-19} \times 20000}{9 \times 10^{-31}}}$$

$$= 8.4 \times 10^7 \text{ m/s} \quad \underline{Ans.}$$

Cut off w/l of X-Rays.

$$\lambda_c = \frac{12431}{V} \overset{\circ}{A}$$

$$= \frac{12431}{20000} = 0.6215 \overset{\circ}{A} \quad \underline{Ans.}$$

 | Scan for Video Explanation

Module-9 Solved Example-2

Ex : Calculate the wavelength of the emitted characteristic X-Ray from tungsten (Z = 74) target when an electron drops from M shell to a vacancy in K shell.

Sol.

for K shell $\sigma = 1$.

$$Z_{eff} = Z - 1 = 73.$$

for $M \longrightarrow K$, ($n_2 = 3$, $n_1 = 1$) the wavelength for k_β X-Ray is given as

$$\frac{1}{\lambda_{k_\beta}} = R\,(z-1)^2\left[\frac{1}{n_1^2} - \frac{1}{n_2^2}\right]$$

$$\frac{1}{\lambda_{k_\beta}} = 10967800 \times (73)^2\left[1 - \frac{1}{9}\right]$$

$$\lambda_{k_\beta} = 0.192\ \overset{\circ}{A}\quad \text{Ans.}$$

Module-10 Solved Example-3

Ex : A free atom of iron emits K_α X-Ray of energy 6.4 keV. Calculate the recoil kinetic energy of the atom. Mass of iron atom = 9.3×10^{-20} kg.

Sol.

W/L of emitted photon $\lambda = \dfrac{12431}{6400}\ \overset{\circ}{A} = 1.942\,\overset{\circ}{A}$

$$P = \frac{h}{\lambda}$$

for cons of momentum $P = MV_R = \dfrac{h}{\lambda}$

K.E of recoiled atom $k = \dfrac{P^2}{2m} = \dfrac{(h/\lambda)^2}{2m}$

$$k = \frac{\left(6.63 \times 10^{-34} / 1.942 \times 10^{-10}\right)^2}{2 \times 9.3 \times 10^{-20} \times 1.6 \times 10^{-19}}\ eV$$

$$K = 3.9 \times 10^{-10}\ eV\quad \text{Ans.}$$

Module-11 Solved Example-4

Ex : The wavelength of K_α X-Ray emitted from Zinc (Z = 30) is 1.415 Å. Find the wavelength of K_α line emitted from molybdenum (Z = 42).

Sol^n: for k-Series X-Rays we can use

$$\nu \propto (Z-1)^2$$

$$\frac{1}{\lambda} \propto (Z-1)^2$$

for two elements the w/l are λ_1 and λ_2 then

$$\frac{\lambda_1}{\lambda_2} = \frac{(Z_2-1)^2}{(Z_1-1)^2}$$

$$\lambda_2 = \lambda_1 \left[\frac{Z_1-1}{Z_2-1}\right]^2 = 1.415 \times \left[\frac{29}{41}\right]^2 \text{Å}$$

$$= 0.708 \text{ Å } \underline{Ans}.$$

Scan for Video Explanation

Module-12 Solved Example-5

Ex : Find the frequency of K_α X-Ray of La (Z = 57) if frequency of K_α X-Ray of Cu (Z = 29) is 1.88×10^{18} Hz.

Sol^n: using Moseley's law -

$$\sqrt{\nu} \propto (Z-\sigma)$$

$\sigma = 1$ for K_α X-Ray

for La & Cu.

$$\sqrt{\frac{\nu_2}{\nu_1}} = \left[\frac{Z_2-1}{Z_1-1}\right]$$

$$\nu_2 = \nu_1 \left[\frac{Z_2-1}{Z_1-1}\right]^2$$

$$= 1.88 \times 10^{18} \times \left[\frac{56}{28}\right]^2$$

$$= 7.52 \times 10^{18} \text{ Hz } \underline{Ans}.$$

Scan for Video Explanation

Module-13 Solved Example-6

Ex : The wavelength of K_α and L_α X-Rays of a material are 21.3 pm and 141 pm respectively. Find the wavelength of K_β X-Ray of the material.

Sol: As we know:

K_α line correspond to $2 \rightarrow 1$

K_β "   " $3 \rightarrow 1$

L_α "   " $3 \rightarrow 2$

$$E_{K\beta} = E_{K_\alpha} + E_{L_\alpha}$$

$$\frac{hc}{\lambda_{K\beta}} = \frac{hc}{\lambda_{K_\alpha}} + \frac{hc}{\lambda_{L_\alpha}}$$

$$\lambda_{K\beta} = \frac{\lambda_{K_\alpha} \cdot \lambda_{L_\alpha}}{\lambda_{K_\alpha} + \lambda_{L_\alpha}} = \frac{21.3 \times 141}{21.3 + 141} = 18.5 \text{ pm } Ans.$$

Chapter 14
Nuclear Structure & Radioactivity

Lecture Notes Modules

Module-1 Composition and Structure of Nucleus

\# Composition and Structure of Nucleus:

In 1911 → Ruth's α-scattering exp → Disc of Nu

In 1932 → Exp by James Chadwick → Disc of neutrons in Nu.

Structure of Nu.  $p \to$ +ve charge
  $n \to$ neutral

In a nucleus   no. of proton → Atomic number of element (z)

Total nucleons ($p + n$) → Mass number of element (A)

Notation used for an element X was $^A_z X$ or $_z X^A$ mass no. ↗ ↖ charge no.

$$\begin{bmatrix} \text{protons} \longrightarrow {}^1_1 p \\ \text{neutrons} \longrightarrow {}^1_0 n \\ \text{electrons} \longrightarrow {}^0_{-1} e \end{bmatrix}$$

Module-2 Nuclear Groups

\# Nuclear Groups:

Based on similarity in nu structure diff elements are devided in some groups called Nu groups-

① Isotopes: These are elements which have <u>same z</u> but <u>diff A</u>.

② Isobars: These are elements with <u>same A</u> and <u>diff z</u>.

③ Isotones: These are elements which have same no. of <u>neutrons ($A-z$)</u>.

④ Isodiaphers: These are elements which have same difference in <u>neutrons & protons</u>.

$$\underline{(A - 2z) = \text{Constant}}$$

Module-3 Size of a Nucleus

Size of a Nucleus:

Based on several exp it was found that all nuclei are made up of a highly dense mat called nuclear matter, the density of interior of every Nu is almost constant. So volume of a Nu is directly propto no. of nucleons in it.

$$\text{Volume of a Nu} \propto A \ (\text{mass no. of elements})$$

$$\frac{4}{3}\pi R^3 \propto A$$

$$\text{Nuclear Radius} \quad R \propto A^{1/3}$$

$$\boxed{R = R_0 A^{1/3}} \leftarrow \text{exp of fermi radius}$$

fermi Constant

$$R_0 \equiv 1.2 \times 10^{-15}\ m = 1.2\ \text{fermi}.$$

Scan for Video Explanation

Module-4 Nuclear Force and Stability of Nucleus

Nuclear Force and Stability of Nucleus:

Nucleus → nucleons are bounded in a very small volume.

There are two types of forces exist inside a Nu.

① Electrostatic force → A strong repulsive force between protons.

② Nuclear force → A relatively weak force and it is independent of charge and it exist as attractive force between nucleons (n–n, n–p, p–p)

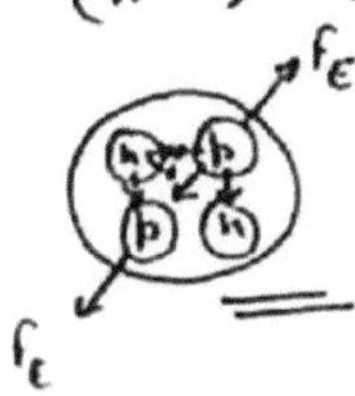

Scan for Video Explanation

Module-4 Nuclear Force and Stability of Nucleus

\# <u>Some facts about Nuclear Forces</u>:

- Nu force is independent of charge on particles.

- Nu force is a very short range force i.e. it appears between two particles at very close sep of the order of $\simeq 10^{-15}$ m.

<u>Imp</u>: For a <u>nucleus</u> to be stable Electrostatic force between protons must be balanced by the all Nu forces between nucleons due to the <u>Strong Nu. force</u>.

Module-5 Effect of Nuclear Size on its Stability

\# <u>Effect of Nuclear Size on its stability</u>:

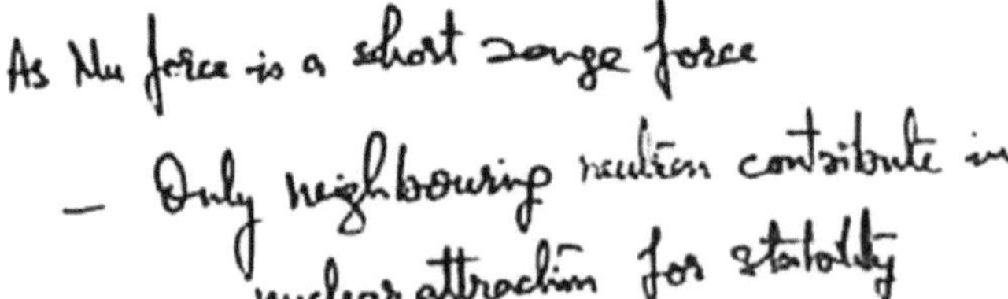

As electrostatic force is a long range force

- all proton in Nu repell each other

As Nu force is a short range force

- Only neighbouring nucleon contribute in nuclear attraction for stability

$\Rightarrow$ In almost all stable Nuclei (if size is large / heavy Nu)

no of <u>neutrons</u> > no. of <u>protons</u>

Module-6 Very Heavy Nucleus are Unstable

Very Heavy Nucleus are unstable:

In heavy Nuclei, due to large size balancing of forces can not be achieved even by extra neutron due to size.

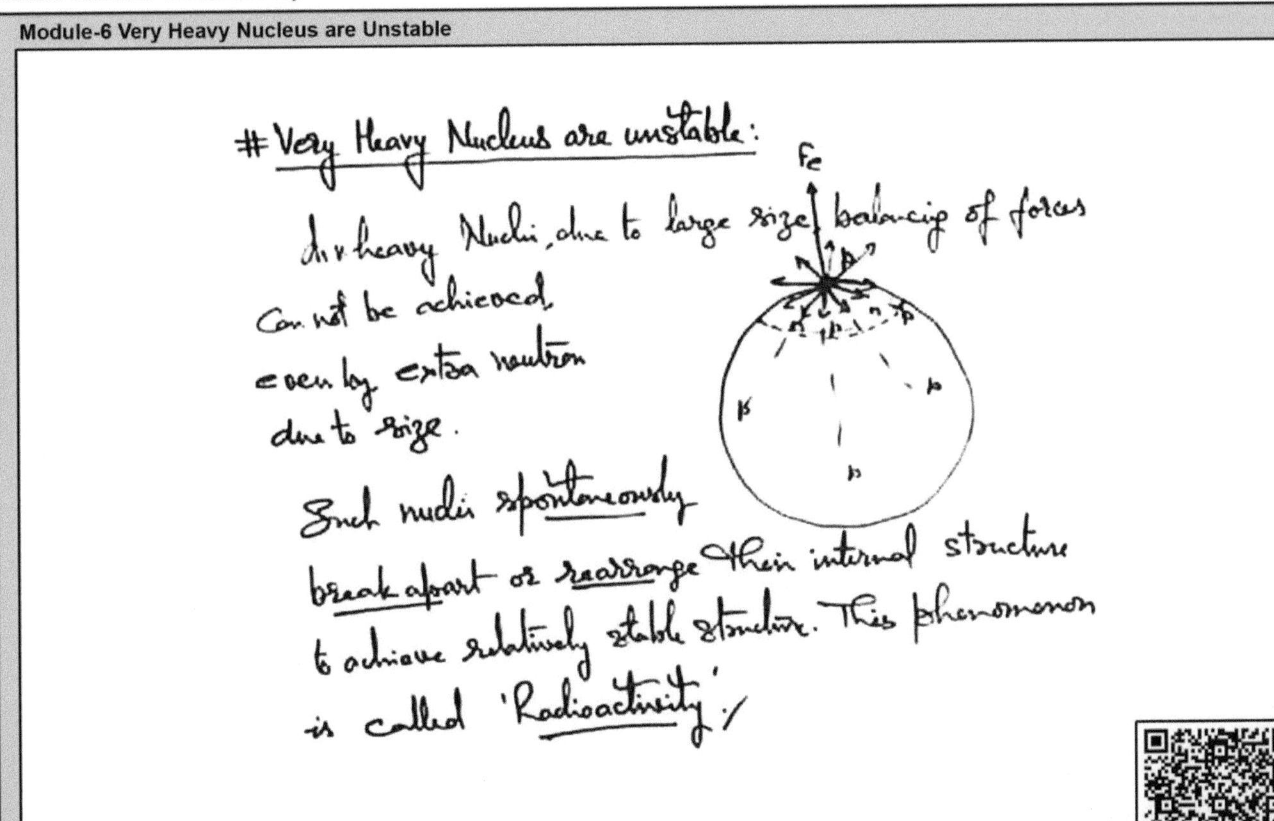

Such nuclei spontaneously break apart or rearrange their internal structure to achieve relatively stable structure. This phenomenon is called 'Radioactivity'.

Scan for Video Explanation

Module-7 Nuclear Binding Energy

Nuclear Binding Energy:

A Nu is stable because strong Nu forces bond all nucleons in the very small vol of a nucleus.

Due to <u>attractive</u> Nu forces the system PE is negative.

The total energy reqd to be supp to a Nu to break it apart into its free nucleons is called '<u>Binding Energy</u> of the Nu.'

$$^A_Z X + (BE) \longrightarrow Z \text{ protons} + (A-z) \text{ neutrons}$$

Binding Energy
of Nu X

Higher the <u>BE</u> of a Nucleus, more <u>stable</u> the Nu will be.

Scan for Video Explanation

Formation of a Nucleus:

An element $^A_Z X$, its nucleus consist of
Z protons & $(A-z)$ neutrons

$$Z(p) + (A-z)n \longrightarrow {}^A_Z X \uparrow^{M_x} + Energy$$

(more stable)

$$Z m_p + (A-z) m_n \longrightarrow \underline{M_x} + Energy$$

BE of Nu X

$\downarrow m_p \qquad \downarrow m_n$

Nuclear reaction for formation of Nu of element x.

Mass defect of a Nuclear Reaction:

Nuclear Reaction for formation of a Nu $^A_Z X$

$$Z m_p + (A-z) m_n \longrightarrow M_x + Energy$$

Here it is observed that

$$M_x < [Z m_p + (A-z) m_n]$$

mass defect. $\quad \Delta m = Z m_p + (A-z) m_n - M_x$

mass that is transformed into
energy during reaction.

B.E. of Nu X is $\boxed{\Delta E = \Delta m c^2}$

Module-10 Mass Energy Equivalence

Mass-Energy Equivalence:

Generally atomic & Nu masses are measured in Atomic Mass Unit (AMU or amu), it is given as

$$1\,amu \text{ or } 1u = 1.656 \times 10^{-27}\,kg$$

In a nuclear reaction if $1u$ is mass defect then amount of energy released due to this —

$$\Delta E = \Delta mc^2 = \frac{(1.656 \times 10^{-27})(3 \times 10^8)^2}{1.6 \times 10^{-19}}\,eV$$

$$\Delta E = 931.5 \times 10^6\,eV$$

$$\boxed{\Delta E = 931.5\,MeV}$$

Scan for Video Explanation

Module-11 Binding Energy Per Nucleon

'Binding Energy' per Nucleon:

To compare stability of diff nuclei we use Binding Energy per nucleon. This is given as —

$$(BE)_N = \frac{BE \text{ of an element}}{\text{mass number}} = \frac{B.E.}{A}$$

if Δm is the mass defect for formation of an element x

$$\boxed{(BE_x)_N = \frac{\Delta mc^2}{A}}$$

The energy reqd to remove one nucleon from the Nucleus.

Scan for Video Explanation

Module-12 Binding Energy Per Nucleon as a Stability Criterion

\# Binding Energy per nucleon as a stability criterion:

If we consider two Nuclei ^{56}Fe & ^{209}Bi, BE of these nuclei are —

$$\begin{bmatrix} BE_{Fe} = 492.8\, MeV \\ BE_{Bi} = 1640\, MeV \end{bmatrix}$$

BE per nucleon —

$$(BE_{Fe})_N = \frac{492.8}{56} = 8.8\, MeV$$

$$(BE_{Bi})_N = \frac{1640}{209} = 7.84\, MeV$$

Removal of one nucleon from Fe nu requires more energy than Bi so Fe is more stable.

Module-13 Variation of Binding Energy Per Nucleon with Mass Number of Element

\# Variation of BE per nucleon with mass no:

Module-14 Solved Example-1

Ex : Find Binding Energy an α-particle from the data given below-

Mass of He nucleus = 4.001265 amu
Mass of proton = 1.007277 amu
Mass of neutron = 1.008665 amu

Sol. Nuclear Reaction for formation of He Nu (α-particle) is –

$$2p + 2n \longrightarrow {}^{4}_{2}He + Energy \longrightarrow BE \ of \ \underline{He}.$$

mass defect $\Delta m = 2m_p + 2m_n - M_{He}$

$$= 2 \times 1.007277 + 2 \times 1.008665 - 4.001265 \ amu.$$

$$= 0.030621 \ amu.$$

Binding Energy $\Delta E = \Delta m \wedge 931.5 \ MeV$

$$= 0.030621 \times 931.5 = \underline{28.52 \ MeV} \ Ans$$

Module-15 Solved Example-2

Ex : The Binding Energy of ${}^{35}_{17}Cl$ is 298 MeV. Find its atomic mass. Given, mass of proton m_p = 1.007825 amu and mass of a neutron m_n = 1.008665 amu.

Sol. mass defect for formation of ${}^{35}_{17}Cl$ is $\Delta m = \dfrac{BE}{931.5} = 0.32 \ amu$

Nu. Reaction is

$$17p + 18n \longrightarrow {}^{35}_{17}Cl + Energy.$$

mass defect $\Delta m = 17m_p + 18m_n - M_{cl}$

$$0.32 = 17 \times 1.007825 + 18 \times 1.008665 - M_{cl}.$$

$$M_{cl} = 34.969 \ amu \ Ans.$$

Module-16 Solved Example-3

Ex : Calculate the electric potential energy due to electric repulsion between two $^{12}_{6}C$ nuclei when they touch each other.

Sol^n: Rad of $^{12}_{6}C$ Nucleus is given as —

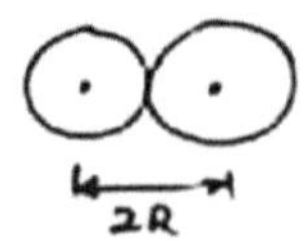

$$R = R_0 A^{1/3}$$

$$R = 1.2 \times 10^{-15} \times (12)^{1/3} \text{ m}$$

$$= 2.75 \times 10^{-15} \text{ m}$$

Elet pot^n energy of the two Nu of $^{12}_{6}C$ is —

$$U = \frac{kq^2}{2R} = \frac{K(6e)^2}{2R} = \frac{36 ke^2}{2R} \text{ J}$$

$$U = \frac{36 \times 9 \times 10^9 \times 1.6 \times 10^{-19}}{2 \times 2.75 \times 10^{-15}} \text{ eV}$$

$$U = 9.425 \text{ MeV} \quad \underline{Ans}$$

Module-17 Radioactivity

Radioactivity :

Due to imbalance of forces inside the Nu or due to limited range of Nu forces, nuclides spontaneously disintegrates into other nuclide.

This phenomenon is called Radioactivity.

A RA substance achieves stability by disintegrating into a lighter nuclei and excess energy is emitted in form of RA Radiations.

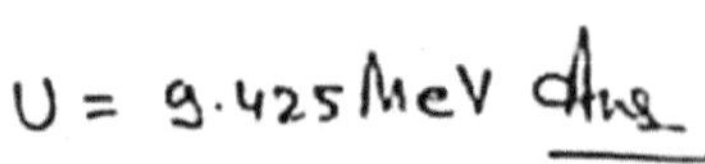

$$[\; x \longrightarrow y + RA \, Rad \,(Energy) \;]$$

Module-18 Measurement of Radioactivity

Measurement of Radioactivity :

$$RA \rightarrow \text{spontaneous disintegration of Nu.}$$

RA of an element is measured in terms of 'dps', the rate at which RA nuclei disintegrate.

This rate is called 'Activity' of the RA sample.

If at an instant in the 'dt' no of nuclei disintegrate are 'dN'

Then activity of that element is given as -

$$A_c = \left| \frac{dN}{dt} \right| \qquad \text{or} \qquad A_c = -\frac{dN}{dt}$$

unit used for RA is Bequeral (Bq)

other units for RA meas are Curie & Rutherford.

$$\left. \begin{array}{l} \underline{1 Bq = 1 dps} \\ 1 Ci = 3.7 \times 10^{10} \underline{dps} \\ 1 Ru = 10^{6} \underline{dps}. \end{array} \right]$$

Scan for Video Explanation

Module-19 Fundamental Laws of Radioactivity

Fundamental laws of Radioactivity :

Some laws to understand RA developed on the basis of exp performed by Rutherford & Soddy.

(1) RA is purely a Nuclear phenomenon, it is not Concerned with the extra nuclear part of an atom.

(2) RA is independent of electronic Config of an element. In diff isotopes the chemical prop of RA & NRA isotopes remain same.

(3) RA is a random process i.e. out of several Nuclei in a Sample which will disintegrate first is just a matter of chance

(4) In a RA Sample due to randomness, disintegration density (dps/vol) remain Constant.

Scan for Video Explanation

Module-20 Radioactive Decay Law

Radioactive Decay Law:

→ This law relates Activity to the no. of Parent Nu at an instant.

It is stated as-

"At any instant activity of a RA Substance is <u>dir prop</u> to the no. of <u>undecayed nuclei</u> (Parent Nu) in the substance at <u>that instant</u>".

If at $t=0$, there were N_0 nuclei & at time <u>t</u>, N are left undecayed.

from time <u>t</u> to <u>$t+dt$</u> if $d\underline{N}$ nuclei will more decay

→ Activity of substance at time t is $A_c = \left|\dfrac{dN}{dt}\right|$

Acc to RA decay law $\left|\dfrac{dN}{dt}\right| \propto \underline{N}.$

Module-20 Radioactive Decay Law

$$\left|\frac{dN}{dt}\right| \propto N$$

$$\frac{dN}{dt} = -\lambda N$$

$$\left[\begin{array}{l}\text{here } \lambda \text{ is a prop Const} \\ \text{for an element called} \\ \text{its Decay Constant}\end{array}\right]$$

$$\int_{N_0}^{N} \frac{dN}{N} = -\int_0^t \lambda\, dt$$

$$\left[\ln N\right]_{N_0}^{N} = -\lambda t$$

$$\ln \frac{N}{N_0} = -\lambda t$$

$$\boxed{N = N_0 e^{-\lambda t}} \longrightarrow \boxed{m = m_0 e^{-\lambda t}}$$

$$\boxed{A_c = A_{c_0} e^{-\lambda t}}$$

$$\underline{\underset{=}{\text{RA decay}} \atop \underline{\text{Eq}^n}}$$

Module-21 Decay Constant of a Radioactive Element

 # Decay Constant of a RA element:

At an instant activity (dps) of a RA element —

$$A_c = \left|\frac{dN}{dt}\right| = \lambda N \qquad \longrightarrow \text{decay Constant}$$

$$\lambda = \frac{|dN/dt|}{N} = \frac{\text{Activity of Sample}}{\text{no. of active Nu.}}$$

Constant —$(\to \lambda = $ Activity per Nu of RA element$)$

$\lambda \leftarrow$ it is a measure of stability of a RA element

RA element:
$\left[\begin{array}{l} \text{high value of } \lambda \Rightarrow \text{less stable element \& high activity} \\ \text{low value of } \lambda \Rightarrow \text{more stable element \& low } \underline{\text{activity}} \end{array}\right.$

Module-22 Half Life of a Radioactive Substance

 # Half life of a Radioactive Substance:

It is the time in which half of total Nu in a Sample will decay.

for a RA element if at $t=0$, $N=N_0$

& at $\underline{t=T} \longrightarrow \underline{N = N_0/2}$.

half life

from RA decay eq^n

$$N = N_0 e^{-\lambda t}$$

$$\frac{N_0}{2} = N_0 e^{-\lambda T}$$

$$\lambda T = \ln(2)$$

Constant for each element $\longleftarrow$
$$\boxed{T = \frac{\ln(2)}{\lambda} = \frac{0.693}{\lambda}}$$

Module-23 Alternative Forms of Radioactive Decay Equations

Alternative forms of RA Decay Equations:

If a RA element x decays to Y with a decay Constant λ.

$$X \xrightarrow{\lambda} Y$$

Decay eqn is written as $N = N_0 e^{-\lambda t}$

$$\ln\left(\frac{N}{N_0}\right) = -\lambda t \qquad \lambda = \left(\frac{\ln 2}{T}\right)$$

$$\ln\left(\frac{N}{N_0}\right) = \left(-\frac{t}{T}\right)\ln(2)$$

$$\frac{N}{N_0} = (2)^{-t/T}$$

$$N = N_0 (2)^{-t/T} \rightarrow m = m_0 (2)^{-t/T} \rightarrow A_c = A_{c_0} (2)^{-t/T}$$

Scan for Video Explanation

Web Reference at www.physicsgalaxy.com

Module-24 Mean Life of a Radioactive Element

Mean Life of a Radioactive element:

As RA is a random process some Nu decay in begining (short life time)

& some decay after a long time.

(have long life time)

Mean life of a RA element $T_m = \left(\frac{\text{Sum of lives of all Nu in a Sample}}{\text{Total No of Nu in that Sample}}\right)$

$$T_m = \frac{1}{\lambda}$$ → Constant for every element.

imp.

Scan for Video Explanation

Web Reference at www.physicsgalaxy.com

Module-25 Calculation of Mean Life of a Radioactive Element

\# Calculation of Mean Life of a RA element :

If at $t = 0$, there were N_0 Nu of an element & after time $t = t$, N are left. If in further time t to $t + dt$, dN nu will decay.

$\Rightarrow$ total life of these dN nuclii will be t.

$\Rightarrow$ Sum of lives of these dN nuclii will be $dT_L = t\,dN$

Sum of lives of all Nuclii in Sample will be $T_L = \int t\,dN$

acc. to decay law $dN = \lambda N\,dt \Rightarrow T_L = \int_0^\infty t\,\lambda N_0 e^{-\lambda t}\,dt$

$$T_L = \lambda N_0 \left[-\frac{t}{\lambda} e^{-\lambda t} + \frac{e^{-\lambda t}}{\lambda^2} \right]_0^\infty = \frac{N_0}{\lambda}$$

Mean life of RA element $\boxed{T_m = \dfrac{T_L}{N_0} = \dfrac{1}{\lambda}}$.

Module-26 Solved Example-4

Ex : Half life of Radon is 3.8 days. Find after how many days only one twentieth of a Radon sample will be left over ?

Sol. Decay eq^n as $N = N_0 (2)^{-t/T}$

$N = \dfrac{N_0}{20}$ at time $t = t$

$T = 3.8$ day

$$\frac{N_0}{20} = N_0 (2)^{-t/3.8}$$

$$(2)^{t/3.8} = 20$$

$$\frac{t}{3.8} = \frac{\log 20}{\log 2}$$

$$t = 3.8 \times \frac{\log 20}{\log 2} = 16.42 \text{ days } Ans.$$

Module-27 Solved Example-5

Ex : One gram of a radioactive substance takes 50 sec to loose 1 centigram. Find its half life period.

Sol: By decay eqⁿ
$$m = m_0 (2)^{-t/T}$$

$$\left.\begin{array}{l} m = 0.99 \text{ gm} \\ m_0 = 1 \text{ gm} \\ t = 50 \text{ sec} \end{array}\right\} \rightarrow \quad 0.99 = (2)^{-50/T}$$

$$T = \frac{50 \log(2)}{\log(100/99)} = \frac{50 \log(2)}{\log(100) - \log(99)}$$

$$T = \frac{50 \times 0.301}{2 - 1.9956} = 3420 \text{ sec}$$
$$= 57 \text{ min} \quad Ans.$$

Module-28 Solved Example-6

Ex : In an ore of uranium, the ratio of ^{238}U to ^{206}Pb nuclei is 3. Calculate the age of ore, assuming that all the lead present in ore is the final stable product of ^{238}U. Take the half life of ^{238}U to be 4.5×10^9 years.

Solⁿ. Given that $\dfrac{N_U}{N_{Pb}} = 3$

if we take $N_{Pb} = N_1 \Rightarrow N_U = 3N_1$ at time $t = t$ (at present)

at $t = 0$ all Nu were of U $\Rightarrow N_0 = 4N_1$

using decay eqⁿ $\quad N = N_0 (2)^{-t/T}$

$$t = T \frac{\log(N_0/N)}{\log(2)} = 4.5 \times 10^9 \times \frac{\log(4/3)}{\log 2}$$

$$= 4.5 \times 10^9 \times \frac{0.125}{0.301} \text{ yrs}$$

$$= 1.87 \times 10^9 \text{ yrs} \quad Ans.$$

Module-29 Solved Example-7

Ex : The disintegration rate of a certain radioactive sample at any instant is <u>4750</u> dis/min. Five minutes later the rate becomes <u>2700</u> dis/min. Calculate the half life of the sample.

Sol^n: using decay eq^n $\quad A_c = A_0 (2)^{-t/T}$

Half life $\quad T = t \times \dfrac{\log(2)}{\log(A_{c0}/A_c)}$

$\qquad = 5 \times \dfrac{\log(2)}{\log\left(\dfrac{4750}{2700}\right)}$

$\qquad = 5 \times \dfrac{0.301}{0.245} = 6.14 \text{ min}$ Ans.

Scan for Video Explanation

Module-30 Solved Example-8

Ex : A radioactive sample contains equal mass of each of two substances A and B with half lives 4 sec and 8 sec respectively. Their atomic weights are in the ratio of 1 : 2. Find the ratio of nucleus A and B nuclei after an internal of 16 seconds.

Sol^n: Initial ratio of No of A and B is $\dfrac{N_{0A}}{N_{0B}} = \dfrac{m \times A_B}{m \times A_A} = \dfrac{2}{1}$

after time $t = 16$ sec ratio No of A and B is

$\dfrac{N_A}{N_B} = \dfrac{N_{0A}(2)^{-16/4}}{N_{0B}(2)^{-16/8}} = 2 \times \dfrac{2^{-4}}{2^{-2}}$

$\qquad = 2 \times 2^{-2} = \dfrac{1}{2}$ Ans.

Scan for Video Explanation

Radioactive Series :

When a RA Nucleus decays into another and when resulting daughter Nu is also unstable or RA, it subsequently decays to another sub-daughter Nu and the process continues until a stable end product appear.

$$\left[A_1 \xrightarrow{\lambda_1} A_2 \xrightarrow{\lambda_2} A_3 \xrightarrow{\lambda_3} A_4 \to \cdots \cdots \xrightarrow{\lambda_{n-1}} A_N \atop \text{stable end product.} \right]$$

Radioactive Series

In general

$$\lambda_1 > \lambda_2 > \lambda_3 - - - > \lambda_{n-1}$$

There are 4 RA Series discovered and most of RA elements can be considered to be members of one of these series.

These 4 RA Series have their elements with their mass nos in the form 4n, 4n+1, 4n+2 and 4n+3 with $n \in I$.

Mass Numbers	Series	Parent	Half-life, y	Stable End Product
4n	Thorium	$^{232}_{90}\text{Th}$	1.39×10^{10}	$^{208}_{82}\text{Pb}$
4n + 1	Neptunium	$^{237}_{93}\text{Np}$	2.25×10^{6}	$^{209}_{83}\text{Bi}$
4n + 2	Uranium	$^{238}_{92}\text{U}$	4.51×10^{9}	$^{206}_{82}\text{Pb}$
4n + 3	Actinium	$^{235}_{92}\text{U}$	7.07×10^{8}	$^{207}_{82}\text{Pb}$

Np Series is an artificial lab disc series due to very short life time of its elements & other 3 RA Series are found in Nature.

Module-32 Radioactive Equilibrium

 # Radioactive Equilibrium :

In a RA Series.

$$A_1 \xrightarrow{\lambda_1} A_2 \xrightarrow{\lambda_2} A_3 \longrightarrow \ \text{----} \ A_N.$$

at time(t) N_1 N_2 N_3

Production rate of A_2 = Dis rate of A_1 = $\lambda_1 N_1$
(Activity of A_1)

Dis rate of A_2 = $\lambda_2 N_2$
(Act of A_2)

Element A_2 will be in RA eq^m when. $\boxed{\lambda_1 N_1 = \lambda_2 N_2}$

<u>NOTE</u>: In RA eq^m the no. of nuclei of element will be maximum.

Scan for Video Explanation

Module-33 Simultaneous Decay Modes of a Radioactive Element

 # 'Simultaneous Decay Modes' of a RA element :

$$X \longrightarrow Y$$
$$X \searrow Z$$

$$x \xrightarrow{\lambda_1} Y$$
$$x \xrightarrow{\lambda_2} z$$

if half life of x is T
$\Rightarrow \lambda_{eff} = \dfrac{\ln 2}{T}$

When a RA element has prob of more than one decay then its effective decay constant can be given as

$$\lambda_{eff} = \lambda_1 + \lambda_2$$

If prob of disintegration of x to Y or Z are P_1 and P_2 then we can use

$$\lambda_1 = P_1 \lambda_{eff} \quad \& \quad \lambda_2 = P_2 \lambda_{eff}.$$

Scan for Video Explanation

Module-33 Simultaneous Decay Modes of a Radioactive Element

If at $t=0$, there are N_0 Nu of X then after time $\underline{t}$ no of Nu left are -

$$N = N_0 e^{-(\lambda_1 + \lambda_2)t}$$

at time t:

rate of production of Nu of Y is $R_y = \lambda_1 N$

rate of production of Nu of Z is $R_z = \lambda_2 N$.

Module-34 Accumulation of a Radioactive Element in a Radioactive Series

\# __Accumulation of a RA element in a RA Series:__

$$A_1 \xrightarrow{\lambda_1} A_2 \xrightarrow{\lambda_2} A_3 \longrightarrow$$

let at $t=0$ N_0 0 0

$t=t$ N_1 N_2 N_3 $N_1 = N_0 e^{-\lambda_1 t}$

At time t if dN_2 Nu of A_2 are accumulated in time $\underline{dt}$

$$\Rightarrow \quad dN_2 = \lambda_1 N_1 dt - \lambda_2 N_2 dt$$

$$\left[\frac{dN_2}{dt} = \lambda_1 N_1 - \lambda_2 N_2\right] \quad \text{rate of acc. of } \underline{A_2}.$$

$$\left[\frac{dN_2}{dt} + \lambda_2 N_2 = \lambda_1 N_0 e^{-\lambda_1 t}\right] \quad \text{linear diff eq}^n \text{ of form}$$

$$\left[\frac{dy}{dx} + Py = Q\right]$$

after solving this eq^n we get $\boxed{N_2 = \dfrac{\lambda_1 N_0}{(\lambda_1 - \lambda_2)}\left[e^{-\lambda_1 t} - e^{-\lambda_2 t}\right]}$

Module-35 Solved Example-9

Ex : A radioactive substance decay in two ways simultaneously for α-emission and β-emission with mean lives 1620 yrs & 405 yrs respectively. Find the time during which three fourth of a sample will decay.

Sol: for simultaneous decay modes we use

$$\lambda_{eff} = \lambda_1 + \lambda_2 \qquad \lambda = \frac{1}{T_m}$$

$$\lambda_{eff} = \frac{1}{1620} + \frac{1}{405} = \frac{1}{324} \text{ yr}^{-1}$$

using decay law $\quad N = N_0 e^{-\lambda t}$

we use $N = \dfrac{N_0}{4} \Rightarrow \dfrac{N_0}{4} = N_0 e^{-\lambda t}$

$$t = \frac{\ln(4)}{\lambda_{eff}} = 1.386 \times 324 = 449 \text{ yrs} \underline{\text{ Ans}}.$$

Scan for Video Explanation

Module-36 Solved Example-10

Ex : Find half life of ^{238}U, given that 3.32×10^{-7} gm of ^{226}Ra is found per gm of ^{238}U in old minerals. Given that half life of ^{226}Ra is 1600 yrs.

Sol: As in old minerals of U, amt of Ra is Constant

$\Rightarrow$ Ra is in RA eq^n.

$$\Rightarrow \quad \lambda_U N_U = \lambda_{Ra} N_{Ra}$$

$$\frac{N_U}{T_U} = \frac{N_{Ra}}{T_{Ra}}$$

$$T_U = \frac{N_U}{N_{Ra}} \cdot T_{Ra} = \frac{m_U A_{Ra}}{m_{Ra} A_U} \cdot T_{Ra}$$

$$= \frac{1 \times 226}{3.32 \times 10^{-7} \times 238} \times 1600$$

$$= 4.7 \times 10^{9} \text{ yrs} \underline{\text{ Ans}}.$$

Scan for Video Explanation

Ex : A radionuclide ^{32}P with half life 14.3 days is produced in a reactor at a rate of $q = 2.7 \times 10^9$ per second. How soon after the beginning of production of radionuclide its activity will be 10^9 dis/sec.

Sol^n: after time t, if no. of nuclei of ^{32}P are N

$\Rightarrow$ its accumulation rate will be $\dfrac{dN}{dt} = q - \lambda N$

$$\int_0^N \frac{dN}{q - \lambda N} = \int_0^t dt$$

$$-\frac{1}{\lambda}\Big[\ln(q - \lambda N)\Big]_0^N = t \quad \Rightarrow \quad t = \frac{1}{\lambda} \ln\left(\frac{q}{q - \lambda N}\right)$$

$$t = \frac{14.3}{0.693} \times \ln\left(\frac{2.7 \times 10^9}{1.7 \times 10^9}\right)$$

$$\lambda = \frac{\ln 2}{T} = \frac{0.693}{14.3} \text{ day}^{-1}$$

$$t = 9.55 \text{ days} \quad Ans.$$

Chapter 15
Nuclear Reactions

Lecture Notes Modules

Nuclear Reactions:

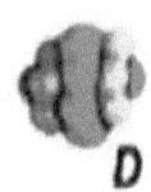

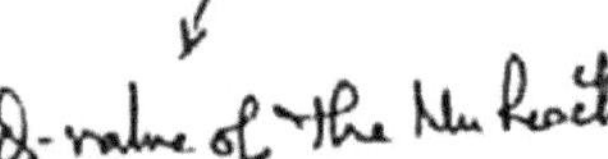

The reaction of this process $A + B \longrightarrow I^{*} \longrightarrow \underline{C} + \underline{D} + energy$

mass defect of this Nu reaction $\underline{\Delta m} = (m_A + m_B) - (m_C + m_D)$

<u>Released energy</u> $\Delta E = \Delta mc^2 = \Delta m \times 931.5 \, MeV$

(in amu)

Q-value of the Nu reaction

Q-Value of a Nuclear Reaction:

It is defined as the diff in rest mass energies of all particles and nuclei before reaction and those of products formed after reaction.

Module-2 Types of Nuclear Reactions

\# __Types of Nuclear Reactions:__

In general Nu reactions can be broadly categorized as

① Fission Reaction

② Fusion Reaction

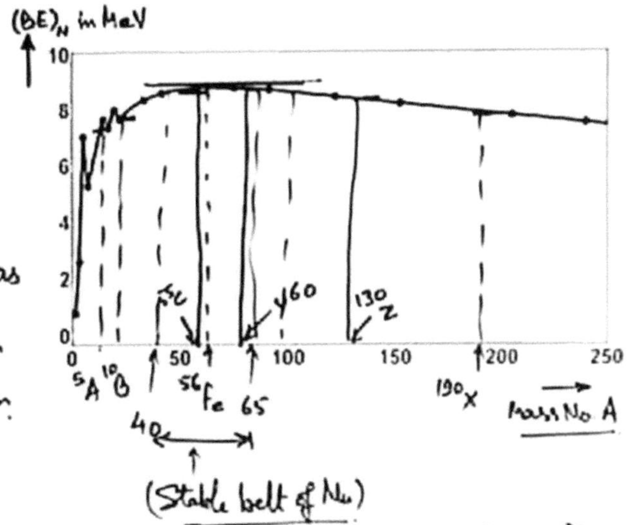

$$3\,^{5}A + 4\,^{10}B \longrightarrow\, ^{55}C + \Delta E.$$
$$\underline{\text{Fusion Reaction}}$$

$$^{190}X \longrightarrow\, ^{60}Y + ^{130}Z + \Delta E$$
$$\underline{\text{Fission Reaction}}$$

Module-3 Nuclear Fission Reaction

\# __Nuclear Fission:__

Consider a Reaction

$$^{150}X \longrightarrow\, ^{60}Y + ^{90}Z + \underline{\Delta E}$$
$$①$$

Fission energy.

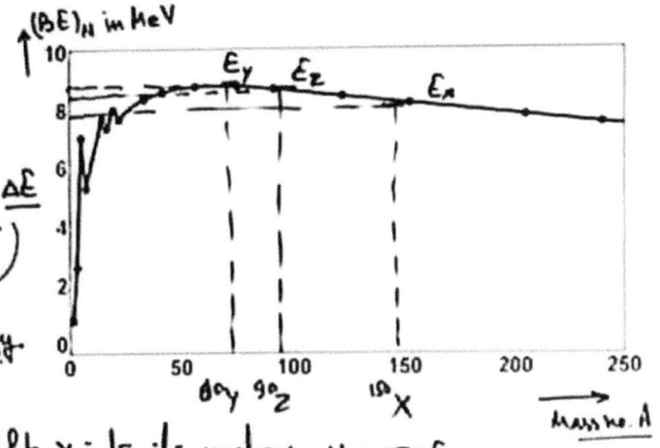

Energy reqd to split X into its nucleons $U_1 = \underline{150E_x}$

Energy released when Y and Z are produced $U_2 = \underline{60E_y + 90E_z}$

Total energy released in react (1) is $\Delta E = U_2 - U_1$

$$= 60E_y + 90E_z - 150E_x$$

This energy can also be cal as — $\Delta E = (M_x - M_y - M_z) \times c^2$

Nuclear Fission is always an Induced Reaction :

Nuclear Fission is not a spontaneous Phenomenon. To split a heavy Nu we need to externally induce the reaction by injecting a particle into it.

Fission of Uranium Isotopes :

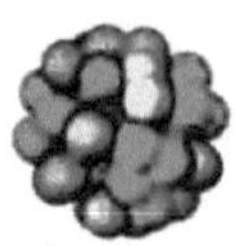

$$ {}_{0}^{1}n + {}_{92}^{235}U \longrightarrow {}_{92}^{236}U^{*} \longrightarrow {}_{56}^{141}Ba + {}_{36}^{92}kr + 3\,{}_{0}^{1}n \quad -(1) $$

another possibility of disintegration of ${}^{236}U$ is —

$$ {}_{0}^{1}n + {}_{92}^{235}U \longrightarrow {}_{92}^{236}U^{*} \longrightarrow {}_{54}^{140}Xe + {}_{38}^{94}Sr + 2\,{}_{0}^{1}n \quad -(2) $$

Out of many possibilities max yield is in eq^{n} (1) even in some cases as many as 5 neutrons are also produced but on avg no. of neutrons in diff app^{n} in fission of ${}^{235}U$ are taken 2.5. (avg).

Module-6 Chain Reactions

Chain Reactions :

In a fission total energy released is distributed in following forms.

(1) KE of the fragments ~ 80 to 85%.

(2) KE of neutrons ~ 3 to 5%.

(3) γ-rays emission ~ 2 to 4%.

(4) Excitation of fragment Nu ~ 8-10%. [This energy is emitted as β-part or γ-rays by these fragment Nu after fission]

– In a fission if initial amt of Nuclei are taken properly then it is possible that emitted neutron further continue fission in the available amt & it can start a self sustained fission reaction continuously → "Chain Reaction"

Web Reference at www.physicsgalaxy.com | Scan for Video Explanation

Module-6 Chain Reactions

Chain Reaction:

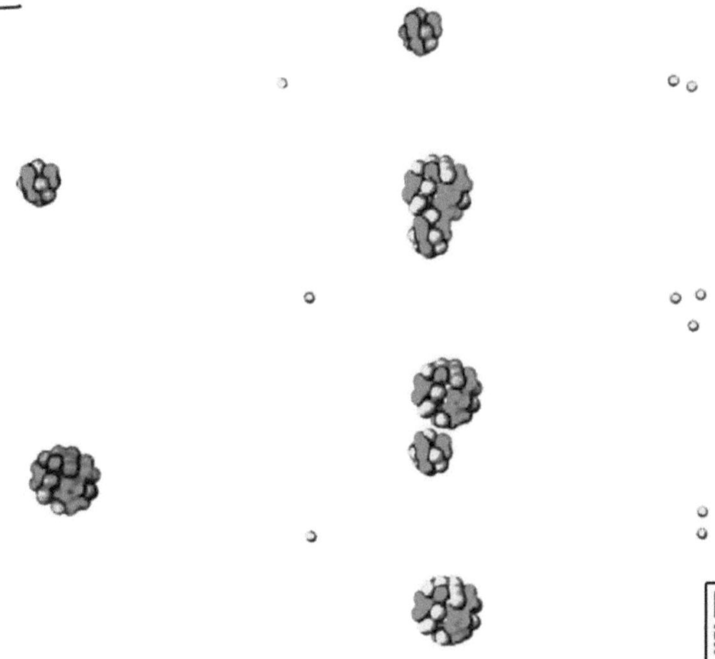

Web Reference at www.physicsgalaxy.com | Scan for Video Explanation

Module-7 Nuclear Fusion

Nuclear Fusion :

Consider a reaction

$2\,{}^{5}A + 3\,{}^{6}B \rightarrow {}^{28}C + \Delta E$

Fusion energy

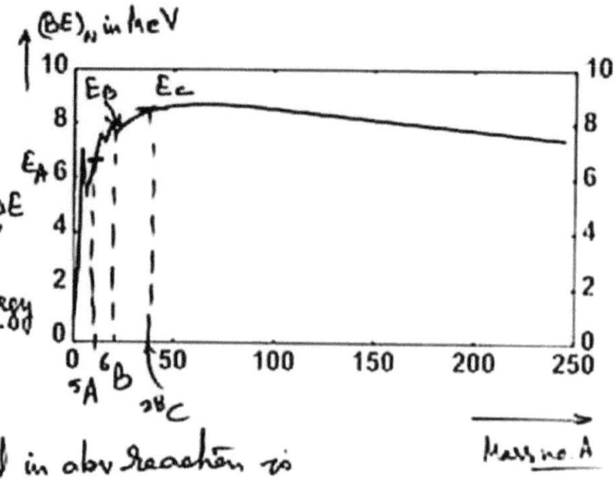

energy released in above reaction is

$\Delta E = 28E_c - [10\,E_A + 18\,E_B]$

$\Delta E = [2M_A + 3M_B - M_c] \times 931.5\ MeV$

NOTE: Fusion Reactions start when nuclei are brought v. close to each other at sep $\simeq 10^{-14}$ m or less. This happens only when sample temp is very high $\simeq 10^6$ to 10^7 K. That's why these reactions are called "Thermonuclear Reactions".

Scan for Video Explanation

Web Reference at www.physicsgalaxy.com

Module-8 Solved Example-1

Ex : In a nuclear reactor of 200 MW rating, following fusion reaction is used to produce power

$${}^{2}_{1}H + {}^{2}_{1}H \longrightarrow {}^{4}_{2}He$$

If energy from this equation is used at 25% efficiency in reactor, calculate how many gram of ${}^{2}_{1}H$ will be needed per day. Take masses of ${}^{2}_{1}H$ and ${}^{4}_{2}He$ are 2.0141 amu and 4.0026 amu respectively.

Sol^n. One fusion reaction releases energy $\Delta E = (2M_D - M_{He}) \times 931.5\ MeV$

$= 0.0256 \times 931.5 = 23.846$

$= 23.847\ MeV$.

No. of reactions reqd./sec

$$N = \frac{200 \times 10^6}{23.847 \times 10^6 \times 1.6 \times 10^{-19} \times 0.25} = 2.1 \times 10^{20}\ react/sec.$$

No. of ${}^{2}_{1}H$ reqd/sec $= 4.2 \times 10^{20}$ nu/sec

Amt of ${}^{2}_{1}H$ reqd/day $= \dfrac{4.2 \times 10^{20} \times 86400}{6.023 \times 10^{23}} \times 2 = 120.5$ gms Ans.

Scan for Video Explanation

Web Reference at www.physicsgalaxy.com

Module-9 Solved Example-2

Ex : The binding energy per nucleon for $_1^2H$ and $_2^4He$ are 1.1 MeV and 7.0 MeV respectively. Calculate the energy released when two deuteron fuse to form one helium nucleus.

Sol^n:　　The reaction

$$_1^2H + _1^2H \longrightarrow _2^4He + Energy.$$

Energy released in this reaction is

$$\Delta E = 4(BE_{He})_N - 4(BH_D)_N$$

$$= 4 \times 7.0 - 4 \times 1.1$$

$$= 28.0 - 4.4 = 23.6\, MeV\ \underline{Ans}.$$

Module-10 Radioactive Radiations and Their Properties

Radioactive Radiations and their properties :

$$X \xrightarrow{\ \lambda\ } Y + \underset{\substack{\downarrow \\ \text{in form of } RA\ rad.}}{Energy}$$

there are 3 kinds of RA radiations, which are

① α - emission
② β - emission
③ γ - emission

in a RA reaction any one or more of these can be emitted.

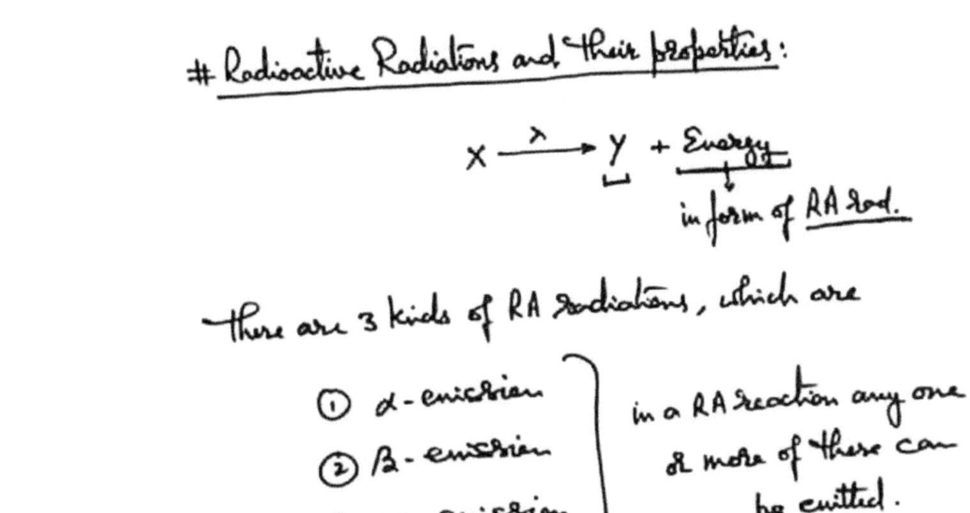

Module-11 Characteristics of Alpha Emission

Alpha Emission :

Due to short range of Nu forces in large sized Nu, repulsive force are not balanced by Nu forces.

In such nuclei alpha decay occurs for increasing stability by reducing its size.

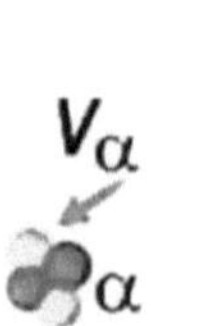

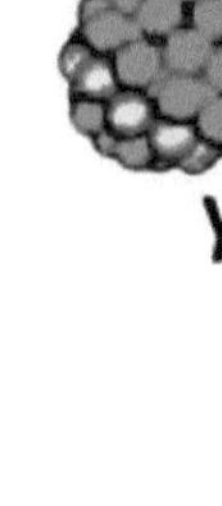

$$\rightarrow {}_{Z}^{A}X \longrightarrow {}_{Z-2}^{A-4}Y + {}_{2}^{4}He + \Delta E$$

$$\Delta E = \underbrace{(M_x - M_y - m_\alpha)}_{\text{in amu.}} \times 931.5 \, MeV$$

Shared as KE of Y and α.

$$M_y V_y = m_x V_\alpha$$

$$\Delta E = \tfrac{1}{2} M_y V_y^2 + \tfrac{1}{2} m_x V_\alpha^2$$

$$\Delta E = \tfrac{1}{2} m_x V_\alpha^2 \left[1 + \frac{m_\alpha}{m_y} \right]$$

$$K_\alpha = \Delta E \left[\frac{m_y}{m_y + m_\alpha} \right]$$

$$\boxed{K_\alpha = \Delta E \left(\frac{A-4}{A} \right)}$$

Module-12 Characteristics of Beta Decay

Characteristics of β-decay :

β-emission takes place to make the composition of Nu more stable in respect of balancing internal force.

There the 3 fundamental ways in which β-emission take place. These are –

(1) Beta - minus Emission (β^-) :

in this process β^- particle ($_{-1}^{0}e$) are emitted from Nu when inside a neutron decays to a proton acc. to reaction

$$_{0}^{1}n \longrightarrow {}_{1}^{1}p + {}_{-1}^{0}e \, (\beta^-)$$

$$_{Z}^{A}X \longrightarrow {}_{Z+1}^{A}Y + {}_{-1}^{0}e \, (\beta^-)$$

Module-12 Characteristics of Beta Decay

② <u>Beta plus emission</u>: β^+ particles are emitted from Nu when inside Nu a proton transforms into a neutron acc. to reaction –

$$_1^1 p \longrightarrow {}_0^1 n + {}_{+1}^0 e \ (\beta^+)$$

This reaction can only occur inside a Nu,

$$_Z^A X \longrightarrow {}_{Z-1}^A Y + {}_{+1}^0 e \ (\beta^+) \ \checkmark$$

③ <u>K-Capture</u>: This kind of β-decay is <u>similar to β^+ emission</u> in the Nu pulls the orbital e^- and capture it from k-shell and its one proton combine with this e^- and transform to a neutron acc. to reaction

$$_1^1 p + {}_{-1}^0 e \xrightarrow{\ \ \ K\text{-shell } e^-\ \ \ } {}_0^1 n$$

$$_Z^A X \longrightarrow {}_{Z-1}^A Y \ \checkmark$$

Module-13 Apparent Violation of Conservation Laws in Beta Decay

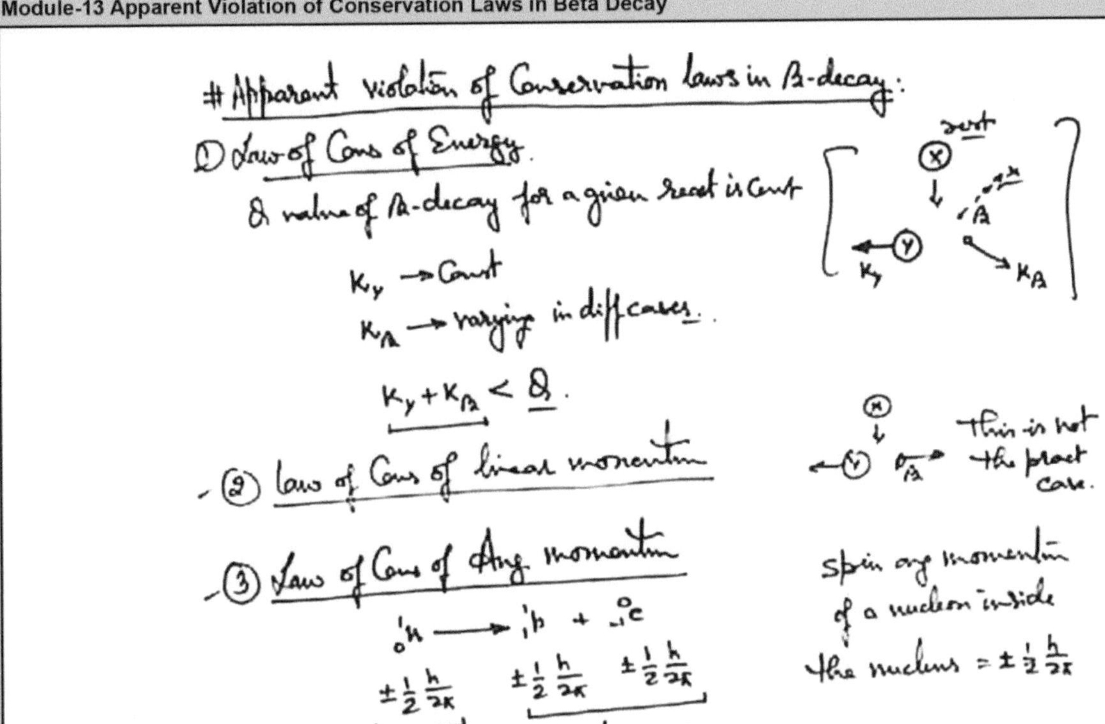

\# <u>Apparent violation of Conservation laws in β-decay</u>:

1) Law of Cons of Energy.

   Q value of β-decay for a given react is const

$$K_Y \to \text{Const}$$
$$K_\beta \to \text{varying in diff cases.}$$

$$\underline{K_Y + K_\beta < Q}$$

– ② <u>law of Cons of linear momentum</u>

– ③ <u>Law of Cons of Ang. momentum</u>

$$_0^1 n \longrightarrow {}_1^1 p + {}_{-1}^0 e$$
$$\pm\tfrac{1}{2}\tfrac{h}{2\pi} \qquad \pm\tfrac{1}{2}\tfrac{h}{2\pi} \quad \pm\tfrac{1}{2}\tfrac{h}{2\pi}$$
$$\pm\tfrac{h}{2\pi} \ \text{or } 0$$

spin ang momentum of a nucleon inside the nucleus $= \pm\tfrac{1}{2}\tfrac{h}{2\pi}$

This is not the exact case.

Pauli's Neutrino Hypothesis:

Pauli suggested that during β-decay an additional particle is also emitted called neutrino which is responsible of missing data in making Conservation laws valid in this process –

Acc. to Pauli, neutrino has the following characteristics –

1. Its charge is zero like a photon
2. It is an energy particle like a photon
3. Its rest mass is zero like a photon
4. It carries spin ang momentum like a nucleon $\pm\frac{1}{2}\frac{h}{2\pi}$
5. It carries linear momentum like a photon
6. In a β^+ decay a neutrino (ν) is emitted and in a β^- decay an antineutrino ($\bar{\nu}$) is emitted.

$$\beta^+ \text{ emission} \quad \left[{}^1_1p \longrightarrow {}^1_0n + {}^0_{+1}e\,(\beta^+) + \nu\right]$$

$$\text{for } \beta^- \text{ emission} \quad \left[{}^1_0n \longrightarrow {}^1_1p + {}^0_{-1}e\,(\beta^-) + \bar{\nu}\right]$$

Q-value of Beta minus Decay:

Reaction of β^- decay.

$$\underset{Z}{\overset{A}{}}X \longrightarrow \underset{Z+1}{\overset{A}{}}Y + {}^0_{-1}e\,(\beta^-) + \bar{\nu}$$

mass defect of reaction

$$\Delta m = \left[M_x - Z m_e\right] - \left[(M_y - (Z+1)m_e) + m_e\right]$$

$$\Delta m = M_x - M_y$$

$$Q = (M_x - M_y)c^2 = (M_x - M_y) \times 931.5 \text{ MeV}.$$

Module-16 Q-Value of Beta Plus Decay

Q-value of Beta plus Decay:

Reaction of β^+ decay

$$_{z}^{A}X \longrightarrow \ _{z-1}^{A}Y \ + \ _{+1}^{0}e(\beta^+) \ + \ \nu$$

mass defect

$$\Delta m = \left[M_x - z m_e \right] - \left[(M_y - (z-1)m_e) + m_e \right]$$

$$\Delta m = M_x - M_y - 2m_e$$

$$Q = (M_x - M_y - 2m_e) \times c^2$$

$$= (M_x - M_y - 2m_e) \times 931.5 \, meV$$

Scan for Video Explanation

Module-17 Q-Value of K-Capture Process

Q-value of K-Capture Process:

Reaction of K-capture

K-shell e^-

$$_{z}^{A}X \ + \ _{-1}^{0}e \longrightarrow \ _{z-1}^{A}Y \ + \ \nu$$

mass defect

$$\Delta m = \left[(M_x - z m_e) + m_e \right] - \left[M_y - (z-1)m_e \right]$$

$$= M_x - M_y$$

$$Q = (M_x - M_y)c^2$$

$$= (M_x - M_y) \times 931.5 \, meV$$

Scan for Video Explanation

Module-18 Characteristics of Gamma Emission

\# Characteristics of Gamma Emission:

Just like atoms, nucleus can also exist in diff excited states which are quantized. A Nu can also be excited to a higher Nu energy level by abs of quantum energy.

When a RA nu undergoes α or β emission, just after emission the daughter nucleus may remain in excited state and this excess energy can be released by this daughter Nu in form of γ-rays.

$$\left[\begin{array}{l} X \longrightarrow Y^* + \alpha \\ Y^* \longrightarrow Y + \gamma\text{-rays} \end{array} \right]$$

Module-19 Solved Example-3

Ex : Calculate how many α and β^- particles are emitted when $^{238}_{92}U$ decays to $^{206}_{82}Pb$.

Sol: If a and b are nos of α and β^- emitted then the reaction will be —

$$^{238}_{92}U \longrightarrow \,^{206}_{82}Pb + a\,^4_2He + b\,^0_{-1}e$$

Using Conservation of charge during reaction

$$\left. \begin{array}{l} 92 = 82 + 2a - b \\ 238 = 206 + 4a \end{array} \right\}$$

using Cons. of mass no.

on Solving we get
$$\left. \begin{array}{l} a = 8 \\ b = 6 \end{array} \right\} \text{Ans.}$$

Module-20 Solved Example-4

Ex : The nucleus $^{23}_{10}$Ne decays to $^{23}_{11}$Na by β^- emission. Calculate the maximum kinetic energy of the β particles emitted. Take mass of $^{23}_{10}$Ne is 22.994466 amu and that of $^{23}_{11}$Na is 22.989770 amu.

Sol^n: The reaction for this β-emission

$$^{23}_{10}Ne \longrightarrow \; ^{23}_{11}Na + \; ^{0}_{-1}e + \bar{\nu}$$

mass defect of β^- decay reaction is $\Delta m = M(^{23}Ne) - M(^{23}Na)$

$$= 22.994466 -$$
$$\quad 22.989770 \; amu$$
$$= 0.004696 \; amu$$

Q-value of React is $Q = \Delta m \times 931.5 \, MeV$
$$= 4.374 \, MeV$$

Most of this energy will be shared between A and $\bar{\nu}$, so kin energy of A part will be max when $E_\nu = 0$

$$\Rightarrow \; max \; KE_\beta = 4.374 \, MeV \; \underline{Ans}.$$

Module-21 Solved Example-5

Ex : Show that for a radionuclide $\left(^{55}_{26}Fe\right)$, k capture may be possible but β^+ decay is not possible. Given masses are :

$M\left(^{55}_{26}Fe\right) = 54.938298$ amu; $M\left(^{55}_{25}Mn\right) = 54.938050$ amu;

$m(e) = 0.000549$ amu

Sol^n: for k-capture reaction is $\quad ^{55}_{26}Fe \xrightarrow{(+\,^{0}_{-1}e)} \; ^{55}_{25}Mn + \nu$

mass defect of k-capture decay is $\Delta m = \left[M(Fe) - M(Mn)\right]$

$$Q = (54.938298 - 54.938050)$$
$$\times 931.5 \, MeV$$
$$= 0.23 \, MeV.$$

For β^+ decay reaction is $\quad ^{55}_{26}Fe \longrightarrow \; ^{55}_{25}Mn + \; ^{0}_{+1}e + \nu$

mass defect $\Delta m = M(Fe) - M(Mn) - 2m_e$

$$Q = \Delta m \times 931.5 \, MeV = -0.79 \, MeV \quad (not \; possible)$$

Ex : ^{228}Th emits alpha particles to reduces to ^{224}Ra. Calculate the kinetic energy of alpha particle emitted in the following reactions.

$$^{228}\text{Th} \longrightarrow {}^{224}\text{Ra}^{*} + \alpha$$

$$^{224}\text{Ra}^{*} \longrightarrow {}^{224}\text{Ra} + \gamma \ (217 \text{ keV})$$

Take masses : ^{228}Th = 228.028726 amu; ^{224}Ra = 224.020196 amu & ^{4}He = 4.00260 amu.

Sol: Q value of reaction is $Q = [M(Th) - M(Ra) - M(\alpha)] \times 931.5 \text{ MeV}$

$$= [228.028726 - 224.020196 - 4.0026] \times 931.5$$

$$= 5.524 \text{ MeV}$$

Energy diff betwⁿ $\underline{Ra}^{*}$ & $\underline{\alpha}$ is $\Delta E = 5.524 - 0.217 = \underline{5.307 \text{ MeV}}$

KE of emitted α-part is $K_{\alpha} = \dfrac{\Delta E (A-4)}{A} = \dfrac{5.307 \times 224}{228}$

$$= \underline{5.213 \text{ MeV}} \ Ans.$$

Chapter 16
Semiconductor & its Types

Lecture Notes Modules

Semiconductors:

- These are material used to design devices which
  Cortrol flow of charge particle inside the materials
- These devices based on S.C. materials can govern
  flow of charges for some specified process.
- Most of electronic equipments & gadgets are based
  Semiconductor devices.

Classification of materials:

3 types
1. Conductors → Conduct electricity $[\sigma = +ve]$
2. Insulators → No Conduction
3. Semiconductors → Conduct elect at room temp $[\alpha - ve]$

'Energy Band diagram' for an Atom:

Elect Pot. Energy of a two part. system

$$\left[U = \frac{k q_1 q_2}{r}\right]$$

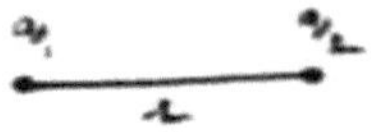

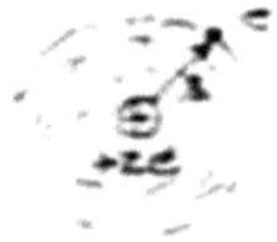

PE of e^- in an atom in the E.F. of Nu.

$$U = -\frac{k z e^2}{r}$$

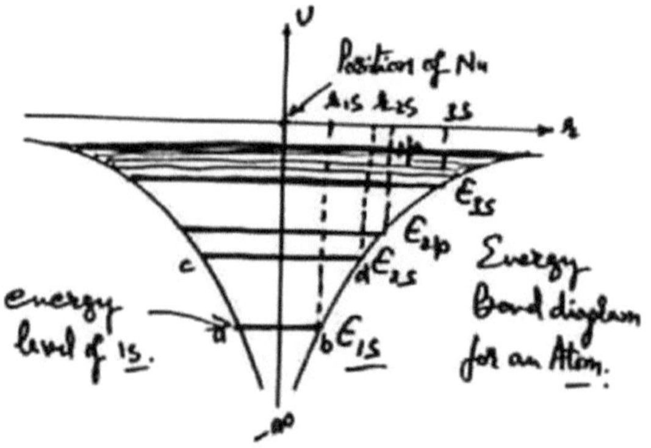

Energy Band diagram for an Atom.

Module-3 Energy Band Diagram of Two Closely Spaced Atoms

Energy Band Diagram of two closely spaced Atoms :

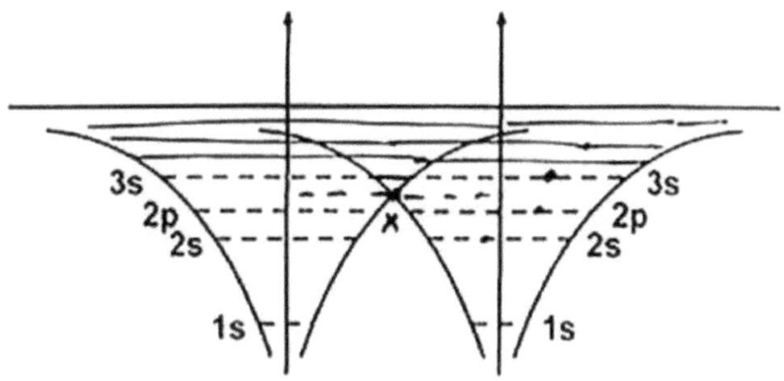

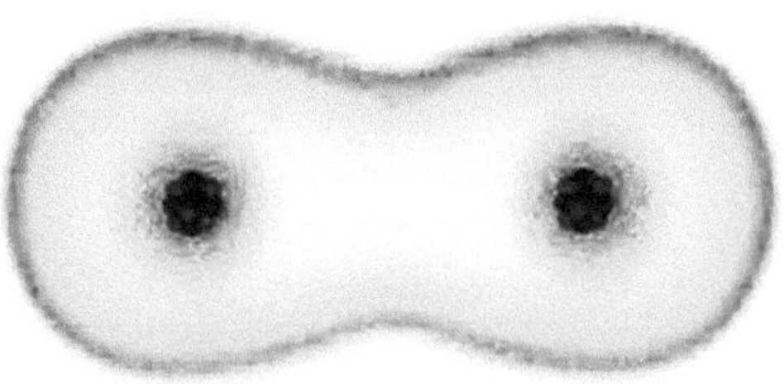

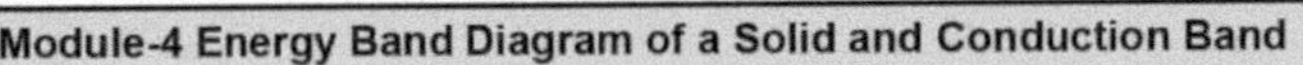

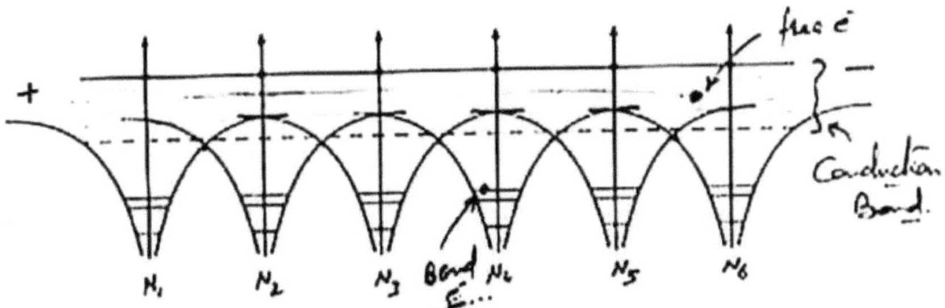

   Scan for Video Explanation

Module-4 Energy Band Diagram of a Solid and Conduction Band

Energy Band Diagram of a Solid and Conduction Band :

In a solid all atoms are arranged in a fixed lattice structure

All electrons in the overlapping region of orbits in lattice structure are free to move in whole lattice and those are called free e⁻.

   Scan for Video Explanation

Module-5 Energy Bands in Solid Lattice

Energy Bands In Solid Lattice:

In a single atome e occupy energy levels (Shells). In case of Solids an e of one atom is also in the influence of the other atoms in surrounding. Due to this energy levels ar modified.

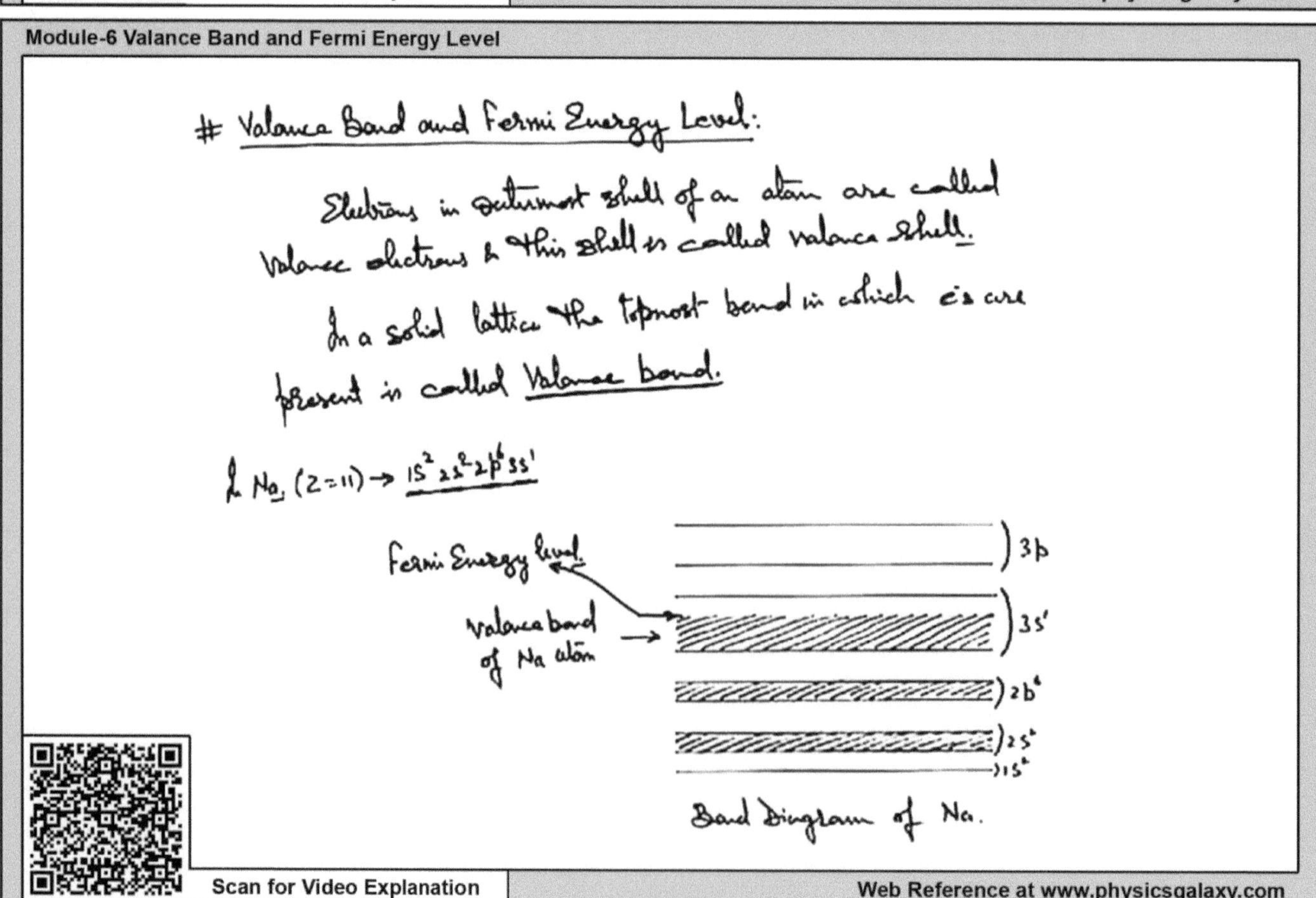

Module-6 Valance Band and Fermi Energy Level

Valance Band and Fermi Energy Level:

Electrons in outermost shell of an atom are called valance electrons & this shell is called valance shell.

In a solid lattice the topmost band in which e's are present is called Valance band.

Na $(Z = 11) \rightarrow 1s^2 2s^2 2p^6 3s^1$

Module-6 Valance Band and Fermi Energy Level

Fermi Energy Level :

At OK temp the topmost energy level upto which e^- are filled in Valance Band of a lattice is called Fermi Energy level.

At room temp (> OK), due to thermal agitation e^- are in energy level which is above the Fermi level.

at OK temp e^- exist only upto fermi level and all bands above this level are empty.

Module-7 Band Structure in Metals

Band Structure in Metals :

Conduction Band : The overlapped region of common orbitals of atoms in a lattice

Metals : These are substances in which their 'valence electrons' exist in their conduction band .   free e^-s.

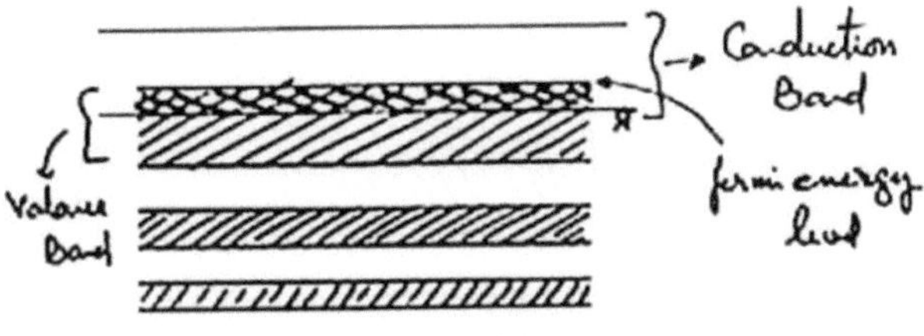

Band Structure in Non-metals:

When there is no overlapping betn VB and CB and CB exist high above the Fermi Level then in this substance e⁻s can not flow in VB. Only way to flow e⁻ is to transfer these e⁻ to CB.

Conduction Band {

$\Delta \mathcal{E}_g$

Valence Band {

Band Structure in Non metals

Fermi Level

$\Delta \mathcal{E}_g \rightarrow$ Fermi Energy Gap.

Fermi Energy Gap: Energy Reqd to excite e⁻ from Fermi level to CB. It is also called Forbidden Energy Gap.

for NM generally $\Delta \mathcal{E}_g > 5 eV$

Band Structure in Semiconductors:

Band Structure in S.C are similar to insulators but these have forbidden energy gap very small as CB is close to Fermi level in VB.

If $\Delta \mathcal{E}_g < 2 eV$, at room temp e⁻s gain this energy by thermal agitation and transfer to CB. (At very low temp S.C behave as Insulators)

Band Structure in Semiconductors

Conduction Band →

$\Delta \mathcal{E}_g < 2 eV$

Valence Band →

← e⁻s

← holes (+e) in VB

s.c at v. low temp   s.c. at Normal temp

Module-9 Band Structure in Semiconductors

In a SC, there are two possibilities of Conduction –

(1) By e^- in Conduction Band

(2) By holes (e^- deficient zones) in Valence Band

Conduction Band →

Valence Band →

with inc in temp. Conductivity of a.s.c increases hence its α^{is} – ve .

Module-10 Types of Semiconductors

Types of Semiconductors:

As discussed conductivity of sc inc with inc in temp. Conductivity of sc can be further increased by addition of impurities in lattice of sc. Addition of impurity in a sc is called 'Doping'.

On the Basis of Conductivity . s.c are classified in two catigories. –

(1) Intrinsic Semiconductors (Pure) – low conductivity

(2) Extrinsic Semiconductors (Doped) – relatively high conductivity

Module-11 Intrinsic Semiconductors

Intrinsic Semiconductors:

These are pure S.C. Substances. Generally IV gp elements Ge and Si are used as pure SC.

for Si $\Delta E_g = 1.14\,eV$

for Ge $\Delta E_g = 0.7\,eV$

In solid state of these elements all atoms form covalent bonds with neighbouring atoms and each atom behaves as if there are 8 e^-s in its valence shell

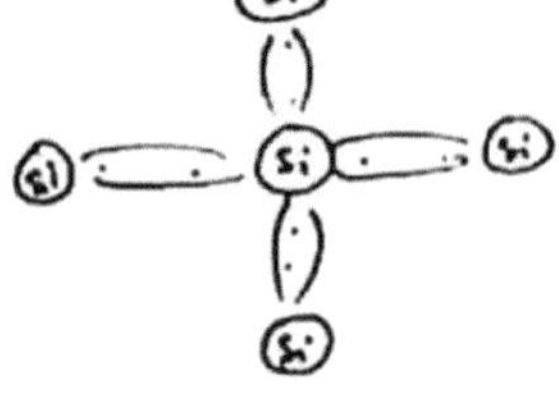

Module-11 Intrinsic Semiconductors

In general out of approx 10^8 Si atoms only one e–h pair is generated.

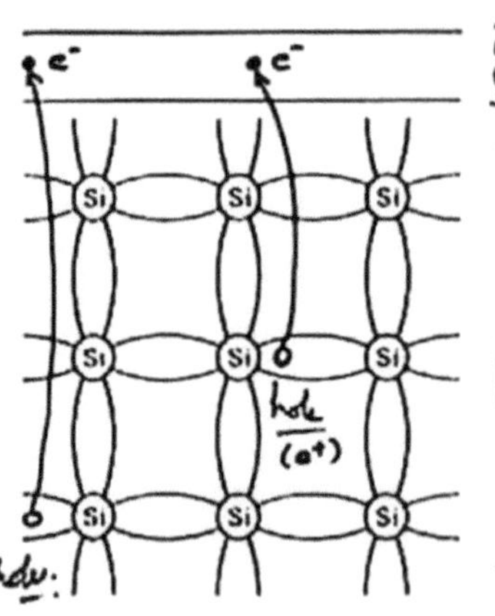

In Intrinsic S.C, free electron density 'n_e' in Cond. Band is equal to Concentration of holes 'n_h' in valence band & it is termed as intrinsic Concentration.

n_i depends on temp as

$$n_i = n_e = n_h$$

$$n_i = AT^3 e^{-\Delta E_g/kT} = n_0\, e^{-\Delta E_g/kT}$$

Module-12 Generation and Recombination of e-h Pairs

Generation and Recombination of e-h pairs :

In a pure S.C. $n_e = n_h$

Due to thermal agitation continuously new e-h pairs are generated per unit volume and other e-h pair disappears due to '<u>Recombination</u>'
↓
falling of an e^- from C.B. to a hole in VB to regenerate the covalent Bond again and release energy.

- At a given temp due to continuous generation & recombination of e-h pairs, avg Concentration of e's & holes remain Constant

- Thermal energy absorbed in generation of e-h pairs and released energy during recombination keeps the lattice in thermal equilibrium.

Scan for Video Explanation

Module-13 Mechanism of Conduction by Holes

Mechanism of Conduction by Holes :

Total Current in S.C $\boxed{I = I_e + I_h}$

Scan for Video Explanation

Module-14 Extrinsic Semiconductors

Extrinsic Semiconductors:

— In pure SC at room temp there exist free e^- and holes for conduction of elect but their qty is very less. It is abt 1 in 10^9 atms so conductivity of intrinsic SC is very low.

— When specified impurity atoms are added to a pure SC in low concentration of abt 1 in 10^8 to 1 in 10^5 atoms, SC conductivity can be significantly increase. Such SC after addition of impurity are called Doped S.c.   *(Doping)*

— There are two types of doping based on two types of impurities these are —

   ① P-type S.C — Trivalent impurity atoms are used
   ② N-type S.C. — Pentavalent imp atoms are used.

Module-15 N-Type Semiconductors

N-Type Semiconductor: In N-type S.c, pentavalent impurity atoms (P or As) are added, which are surrounded by Si/Ga.

   impurity Concentration $\simeq$ 1 in 10^7 atoms (these atoms replace Si atoms in lattice.)

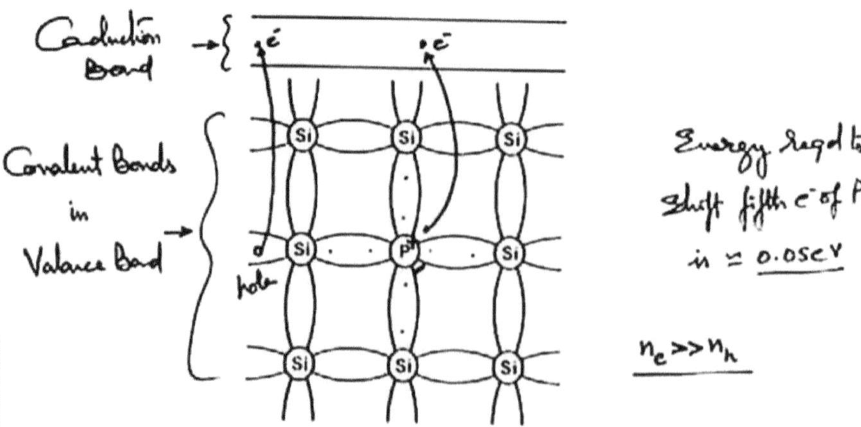

Module-15 N-Type Semiconductors

\# <u>Band Structure of N-type Semiconductor :</u>

Conduction Band →

0.05eV ←— Donor Energy level

Valence Band →

P ←— <u>Donor impurity</u>

$n_e >> n_h$

$e's →$ majority charge carriers.

$h_s →$ minority charge carriers.

Module-16 P-Type Semiconductors

\# <u>P-type Semiconductor :</u> In P-type S.C. trivalent impurity atoms (Al or In) are added and are surrounded by Si atoms.

impurity Conc $\simeq$ 1 in 10^7 atoms.

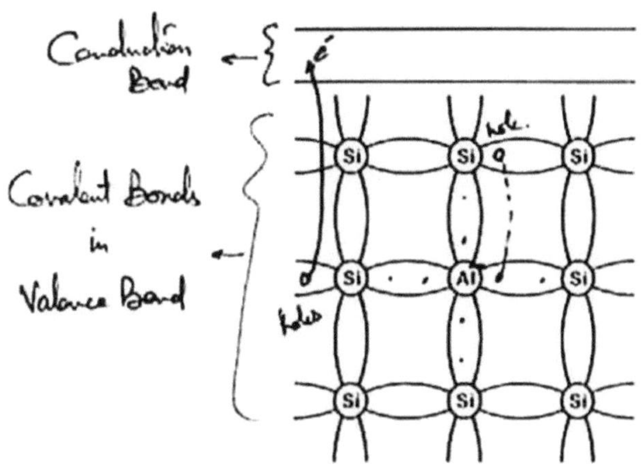

Energy reqd to transfer an $\bar{e}$ from a Si bond to Al is $\simeq 0.05$eV.

$n_h >> n_e$.

Module-16 P-Type Semiconductors

Band Structure of P-type Semiconductor:

Conduction Band → {

Valence Band → { (0.05 eV) — — — — — — — ← Acceptor Energy level

$n_h \gg n_e$

Al → Acceptor impurity

holes → majority charge carrier

e's → minority charge carrier

Module-17 Carrier Concentration in Extrinsic Semiconductors

Carrier Concentration in Extrinsic Semiconductors:

In ext sc. due to addition of impurity carriers conc changes.

- In N-type sc, e^- conc increases above the intrinsic conc and hole conc decreases below the intrinsic conc.

- In P-type sc, hole conc increases above the intrinsic conc and e^- conc decreases below the intrinsic conc.

It has also been proved that in thermal eq^n, the product of e^- and hole concentration does not depend on donor or acceptor doping and it is given as

$$n_e n_h = n_i^2$$ ← Mass Action law

Module-17 Carrier Concentration in Extrinsic Semiconductors

for a <u>P-type</u> S.c if $\underline{N_A}$ is the Conc. of acceptor impurity atoms

as $n_h >> n_e \Rightarrow n_h \simeq N_A$

e^- Conc $\quad n_e = \dfrac{n_i^2}{N_A}$

for a <u>N-type</u> S.c if N_D is the conc of donor imp atoms

as $n_e >> n_h \qquad n_e \simeq N_D$

h conc $\quad n_h = \dfrac{n_i^2}{N_D}$

Scan for Video Explanation

Module-18 Electrical Conduction in Metals

<u>Electrical Conduction in Metals</u>:

for current carrying Conductor current density J is related to drift speed of free e^-s as

$$J = ne\underline{v_d}$$

for a conductor $\qquad v_d \propto E \quad$ (applied E F in Conductor)

$$\underline{v_d = \mu E} \qquad \mu \leftarrow \text{mobility of charge carriers}$$

current density $\qquad \underline{J = ne\mu \underline{E}}$

$$\boxed{J = \sigma E}$$

where $\sigma = ne\underline{\mu}$ is called Conductivity of the metal

Scan for Video Explanation

Electrical Conduction in Semiconductors:

As we know that in a S.C. both $\bar{e}$s & holes contribute in conduction process so –

$$J = ne\mu \underline{E}$$

$$J = J_e + J_h$$

$$J = \underbrace{n_e e \mu_e E}_{\sigma_e} + \underbrace{n_h e \mu_h E}_{\sigma_h}$$

$$J = (\sigma_e + \sigma_h)E = \sigma_T E$$

Conductivity of a S.C. $\quad \sigma_T = \sigma_e + \sigma_h = (n_e \mu_e + n_h \mu_h)e$

for intrinsic S.C. $\quad n_e = n_h = n_i; \quad \sigma_T = n_i e(\mu_e + \mu_h)$

If in a S.C. I_e & I_h are the currents due to $\bar{e}$s & holes flow then

$$\text{Total Current} \quad \underline{I = I_e + I_h}.$$

Chapter 17
PN Junction & Semiconductor Diodes

Lecture Notes Modules

Module-1 Manufacturing P-type and N-type Semiconductors

Manufacturing P-type and N-type Semiconductors:

- Impurities of III gr and V gr elements are diffused to a pure semiconductor which result in P-type & N-type S.C. production.

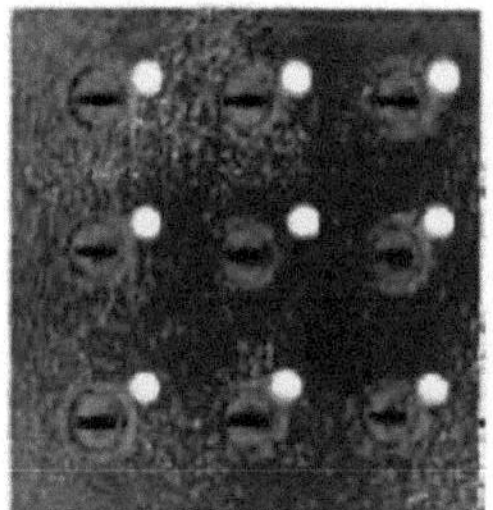

P-type

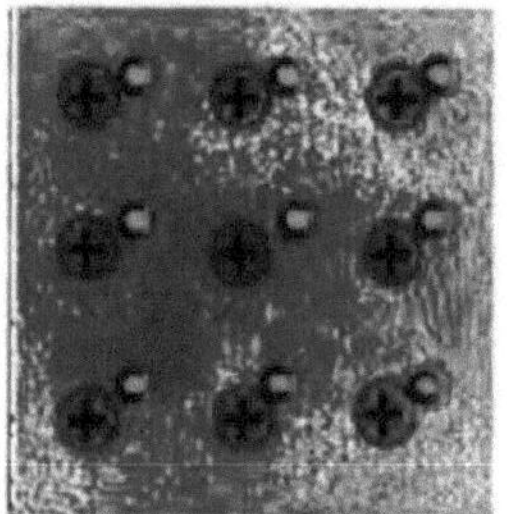

N-type

Module-2 Introduction to PN Junction

PN Junction:

- All major S.C. devices have one or more p-n junction
- It is a combination of a p-type & a n-type S.C.
- It is formed when a single semiconductor crystal is doped with acceptor atoms on one side and donor atoms on other side. The plane dividing these two zones is known as PN junction.

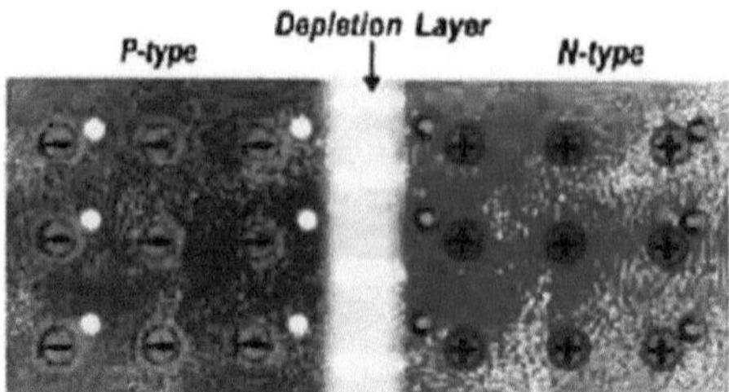

p-n junction Diode

Module-3 Mechanism of PN Junction Formation

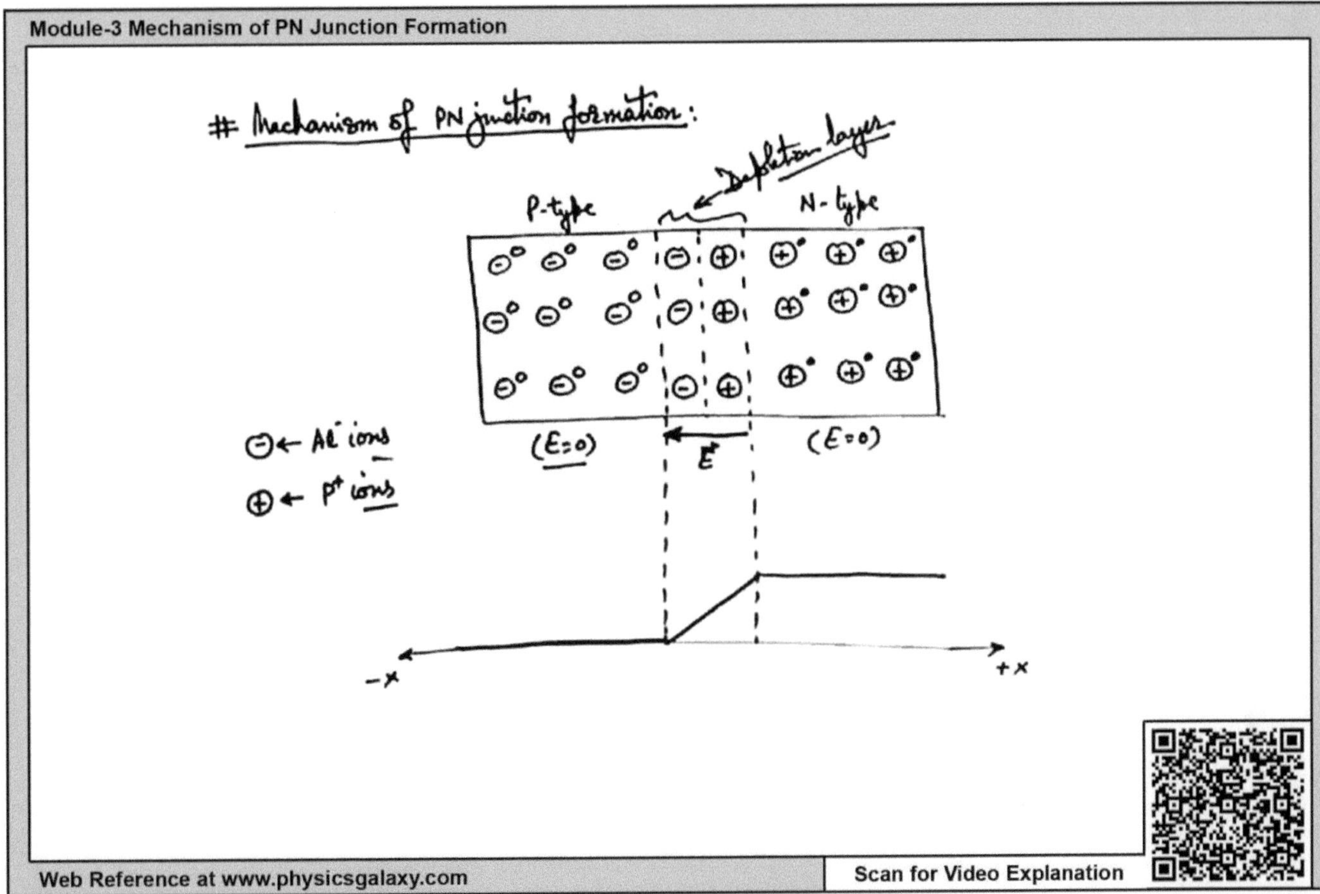

Module-3 Mechanism of PN Junction Formation

Important Points about formation of PN junction:

- When PN junction is formed e⁻s from N side and holes from P side diffuse into other regions

- Some of diffusing e⁻ combine with diffusing holes and the middle region becomes free from charge carriers. This region is called Depletion layer or Transition region.

- Due to +ve and −ve ions on the two sides of dep. layer an internal EF is setup which prevent further diffusion of carriers through dep layer.

- This int EF develops a potⁿ diff across junction, called junction voltage

- A common PN junction is called a "junction diode"

Module-3 Mechanism of PN Junction Formation

Circuit Symbol of a PN junction diode :

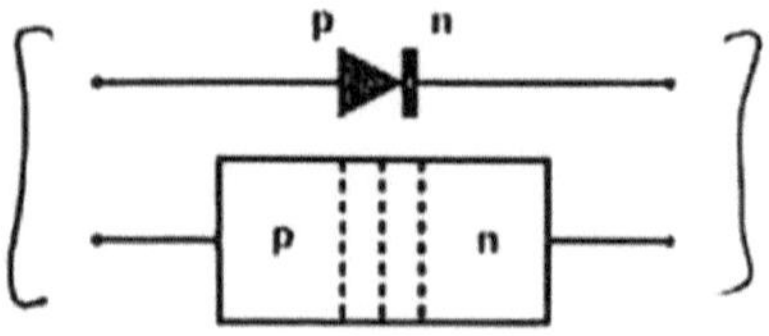

Scan for Video Explanation

Web Reference at www.physicsgalaxy.com

Module-4 Biasing of a PN Junction Diode

Biasing of a PN junction diode :

↓

Study of behaviour when a p.d. is applied across the device.

-> Most imp characteristic of a PN junction is that charge carriers are allowed to flow only in one direction not in opp dir.

-> When ext voltage is applied across a PN junction, its behaviour is studied in two ways -

① Forward Biasing

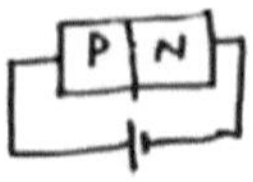

② Reverse Biasing

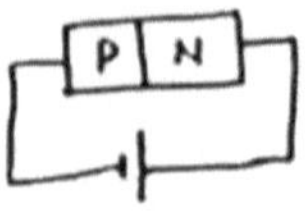

Scan for Video Explanation

Web Reference at www.physicsgalaxy.com

Module-5 Forward Biasing

Forward Biasing:

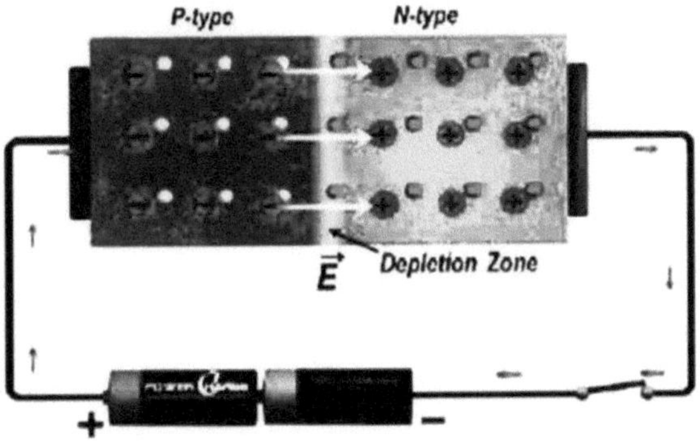

In FB external p.d. decreases the junction voltage (barrier p.d) and a current flows through the junction.

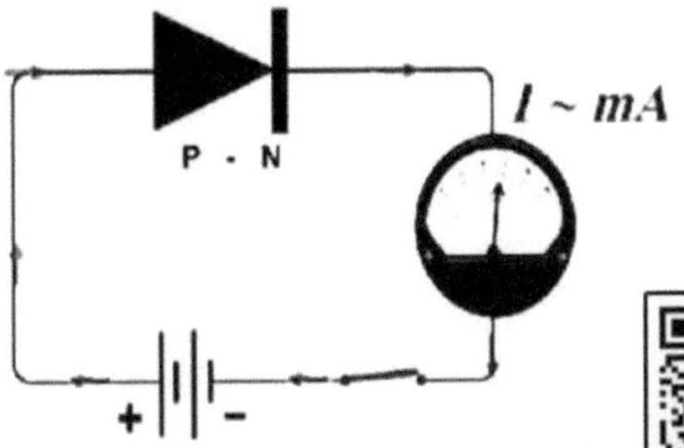

Web Reference at www.physicsgalaxy.com | Scan for Video Explanation

Module-6 Reverse Biasing

Reverse Biasing:

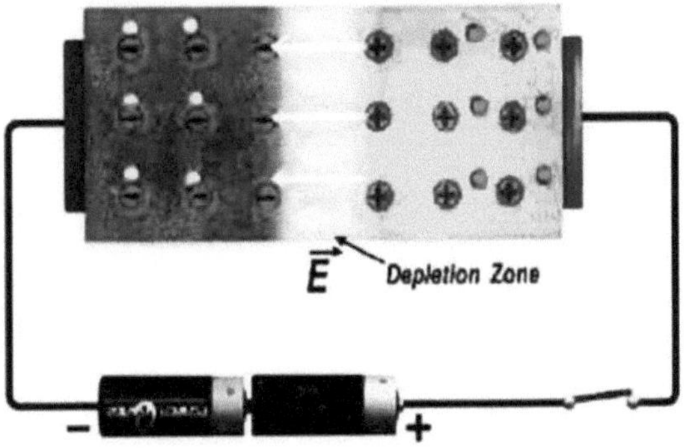

In RB external p.d. increases the barrier p.d. and both the sides e^- & holes are pulled in dir away from depletion layer.

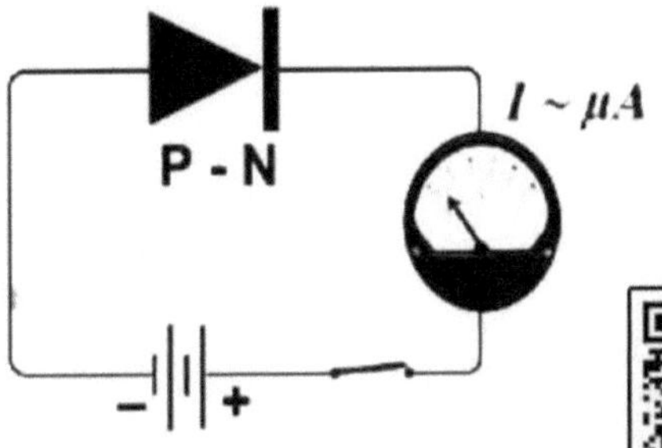

Web Reference at www.physicsgalaxy.com | Scan for Video Explanation

Volt-Ampere Characteristic of a PN Junction :

Nature of a PN junction diode is **Unilateral**

Current flows only in one dir from P to N side

Now we'll study the variation of current with p.d in both FB and RB situation & this is studied in two steps.

(1) Forward Bias Characteristics

(2) Reverse Bias Characteristics

V-I Curve for a PN Junction diode :

$$I = I_0 \left(e^{-V/kT} - 1 \right)$$

for high values of voltages $e^{V/kT} \gg 1$

I_0 → Rev saturation current

$$I = I_0 \, e^{V/kT}$$

Module-8 Resistance of PN Junction in Forward & Reverse Biasing

\# **Resistance of PN junction in Forward & Reverse Biasing:**

for a PN junction diode, its resistance is directly prop. to the thickness of depletion layer.

- **Forward Biasing:** During FB, ext EF reverses the dir of EF in dep layer due to which dep layer becomes thin.

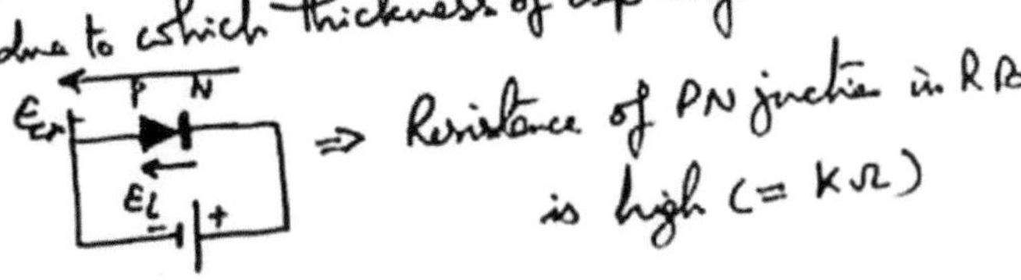

$\Rightarrow$ Resistance of PN junction in FB is low. $(\simeq \Omega$ only$)$

- **Reverse Biasing:** During RB, ext EF is in same dir of int EF due to which thickness of dep layer increases.

$\Rightarrow$ Resistance of PN junction in RB is high $(\simeq K\Omega)$

Scan for Video Explanation

Module-9 Dynamic Resistance of PN Junction

\# **Dynamic Resistance of PN junction:**

During FB, PN junction is a Non-ohmic device.

ohmic devices

$$\boxed{V = IR}$$

$$R = \frac{V}{I} = \frac{1}{\tan\theta} = \frac{1}{\text{slope}}$$

for non-ohmic devices, we define dynamic resistance as-

$$r_D = \frac{dV}{di} = \frac{1}{\tan\theta} = \frac{1}{\text{slope of v-i curve}}$$

Scan for Video Explanation

Module-10 Characteristics of an Ideal Diode

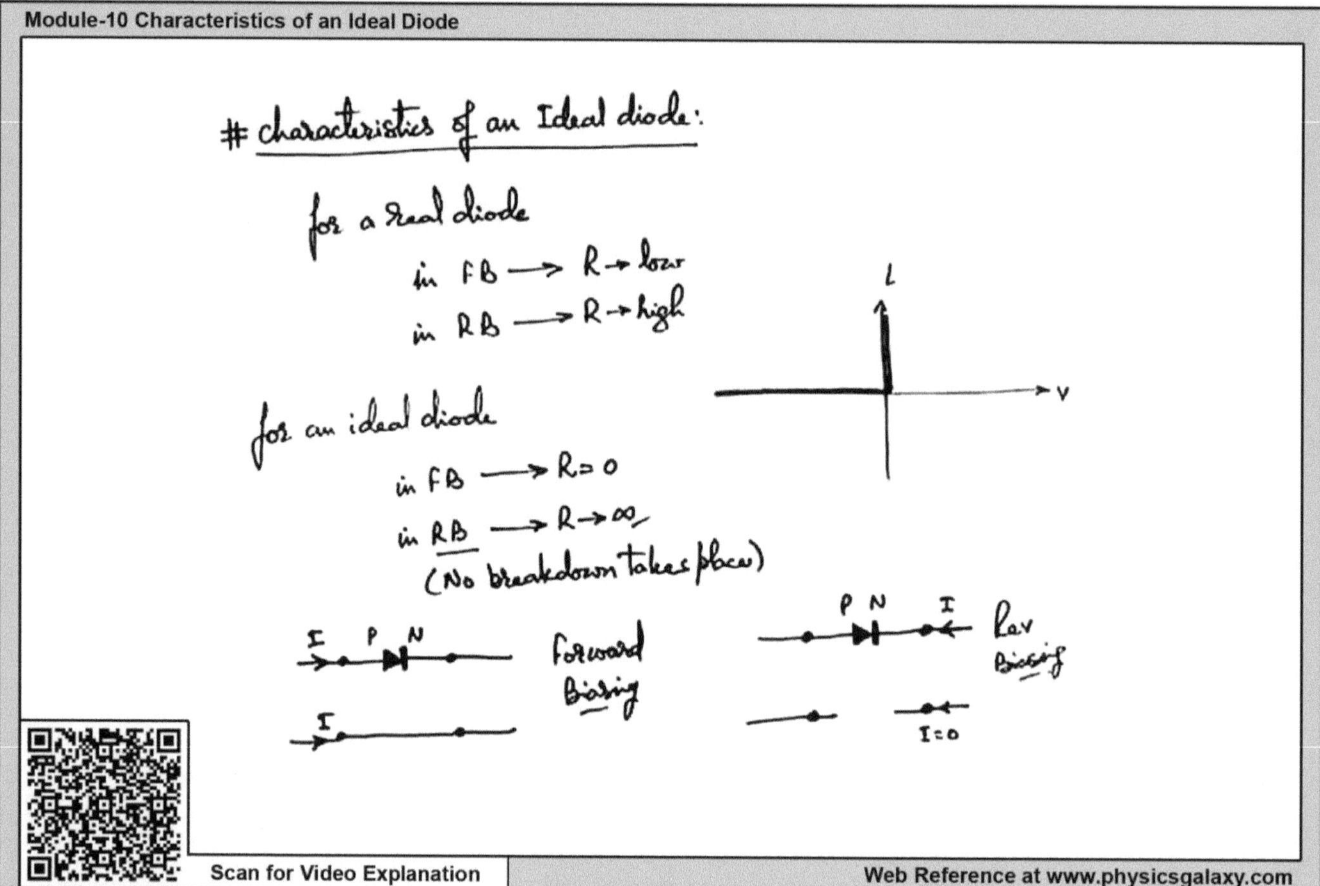

characteristics of an Ideal diode:

for a Real diode

$\quad$ in FB $\longrightarrow$ R $\to$ low

$\quad$ in RB $\longrightarrow$ R $\to$ high

for an ideal diode

$\quad$ in FB $\longrightarrow$ R = 0

$\quad$ in RB $\longrightarrow$ R $\to \infty$

$\quad$ (No breakdown takes place)

Module-11 Breakdown Mechanism of a PN Junction Diode in Reverse Biasing

Breakdown Mechanism of a PN junction diode in Reverse Biasing:

In RB, a constant current flows which is called rev saturation current due to minority carriers.

When V increases at a particular value V_z, covalent bonds near the junction start breaking due to high EF in the dep layer and suddenly large no of e-h pairs are generated and this suddenly increases the current in ckt.

This phenomenon is called breakdown of PN junction & V_z is called breakdown voltage or zener voltage.

Breakdown Mech is exp in two ways -

$\quad$ ① Zener Breakdown

$\quad$ ② Avalanche Breakdown

Module-12 Zener Breakdown

Zener Breakdown: It occurs when sc. are heavily doped and dep. layer is very thin.

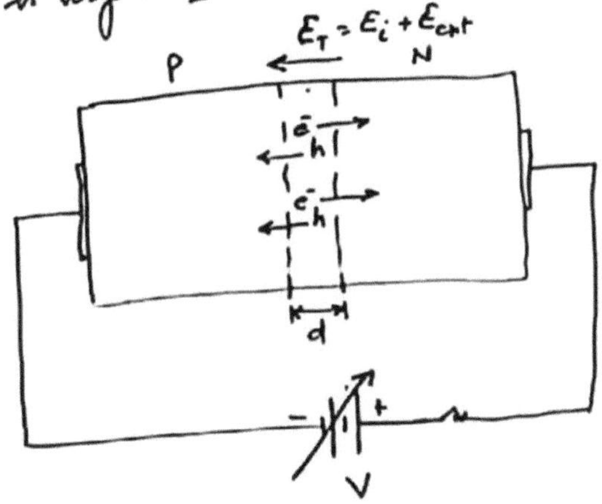

for small d

$E \uparrow$

$E = \frac{V}{d}$

Web Reference at www.physicsgalaxy.com

Scan for Video Explanation

Module-13 Avalance Breakdown

Avalance Breakdown: It occurs when P & N sides of a junction are moderately doped and dep. layer is thick

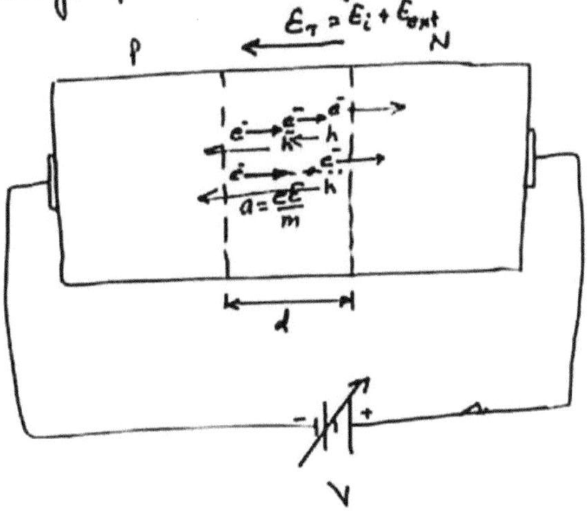

$E_{ext} = \frac{V}{d}$

$V_{B_{Av}} > V_{BZ}$

Web Reference at www.physicsgalaxy.com

Scan for Video Explanation

Module-14 Zener Diode

Zener Diode:

- This is also a pn junction diode formed between two heavily doped P-type and N-type S.c

- It is operated in R.B. region under breakdown & in FB region it acts like normal PN junction diode

- In a Zener diode even at very high currents voltage across diode remain Constant at V_z.

- ckt Symbol

- It is used to stabilize voltage in ckt across two terminals.

Module-15 Zener Diode as a Voltage Stabilizer

Zener Diode as a voltage Stabilizer:

In RB region at $V_{CM} = V_z$ across a PN junction, breakdown occurs and V_z is maintained across diode & current is increased to large values.

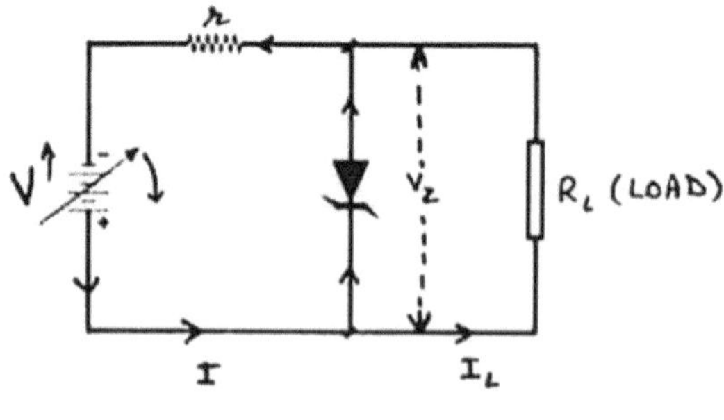

$$V_z = I_L R_L$$

Module-16 PN Junction Diode as a Rectifier

PN junction diode as a Rectifier :

A rectifier is a device used convert AC or voltage into unidirectional current or voltage.

Unilateral nature of a PN junction makes it useful tool to be used as a rectifier.

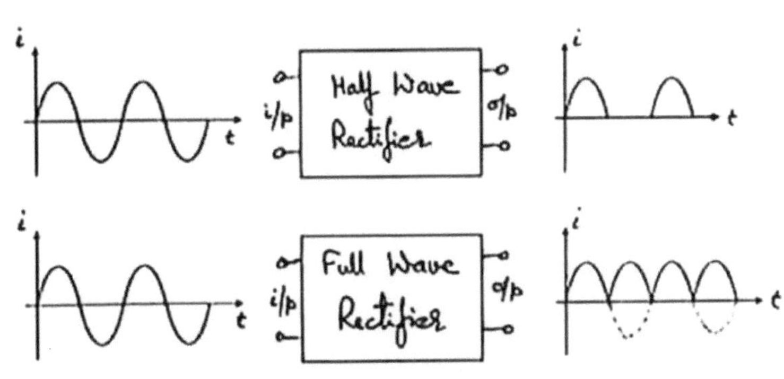

Module-17 Half Wave Rectifier

Half Wave Rectifier :

This is a device which converts AC voltage into pulsating unidirectional voltage for one half cycle of the AC Supply.

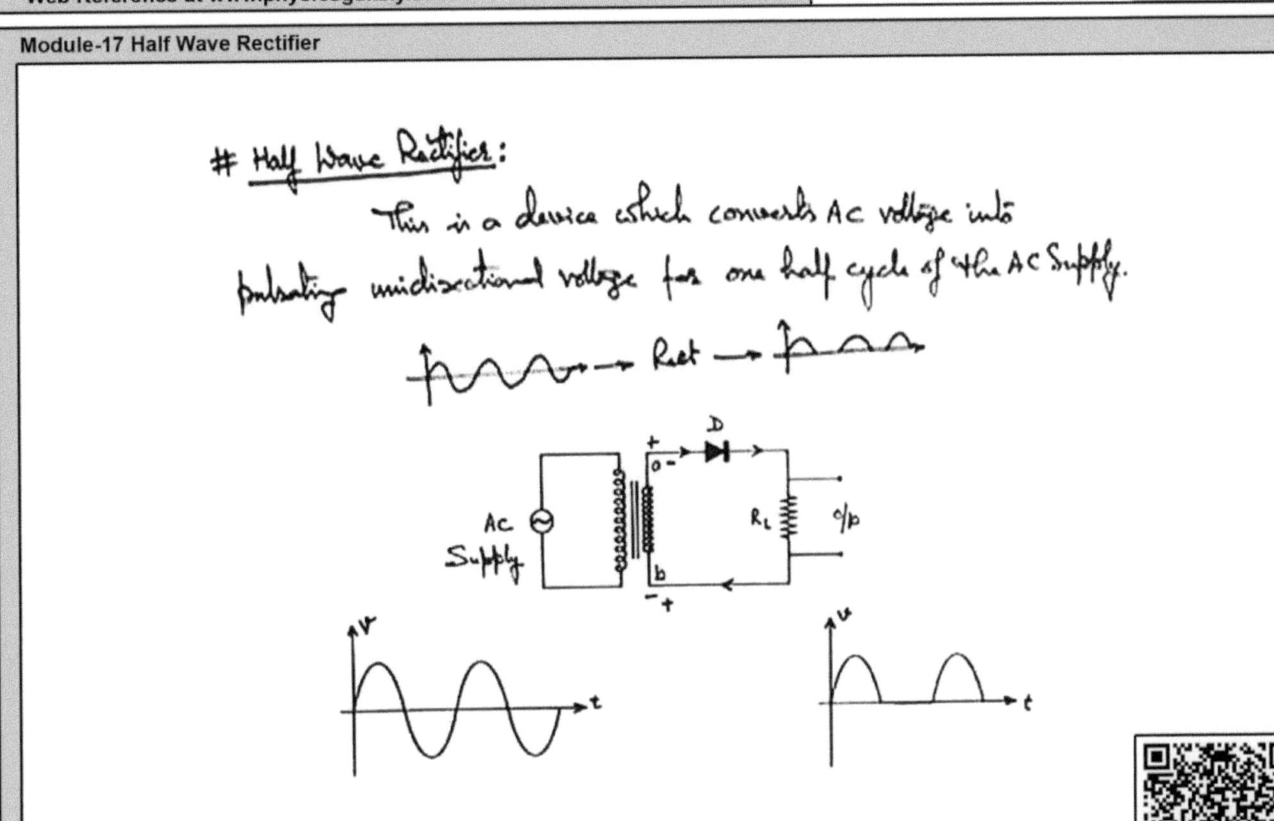

Full Wave Rectifier:

This is also called Centre tap rectifier. It allows +ve half cycles of AC as well as it reverses the dir of current during -ve half cycles also. It uses two diodes with secondary coil cut in two parts.

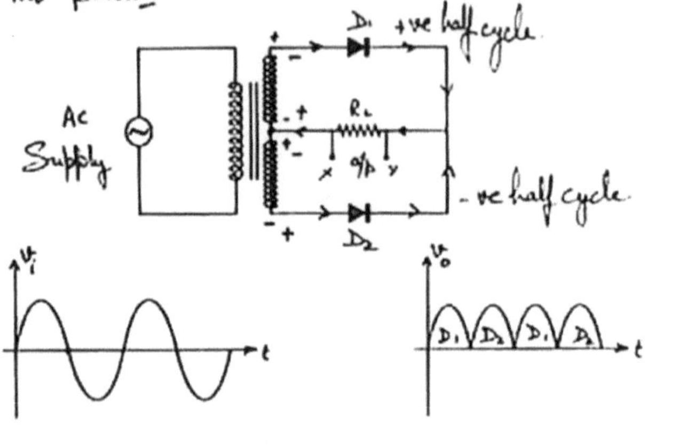

Average Current in Rectifiers:

- Half Wave Rectifier

avg current in o/p of the HW Rect.

$$i_{avg} = \frac{\text{Total charge flow in one cyc}}{\text{duration of cyc}}$$

$$i_{avg} = \frac{\int_0^{\pi/\omega} I_m \sin \omega t \, dt}{2\pi/\omega}$$

$$= \frac{I_m \omega}{2\pi} \left\{ -\frac{\cos \omega t}{\omega} \right\}_0^{\pi/\omega} = \frac{I_m}{2\pi} \left[(1) - (-1) \right]$$

$$\boxed{i_{avg} = \frac{I_m}{\pi}}$$

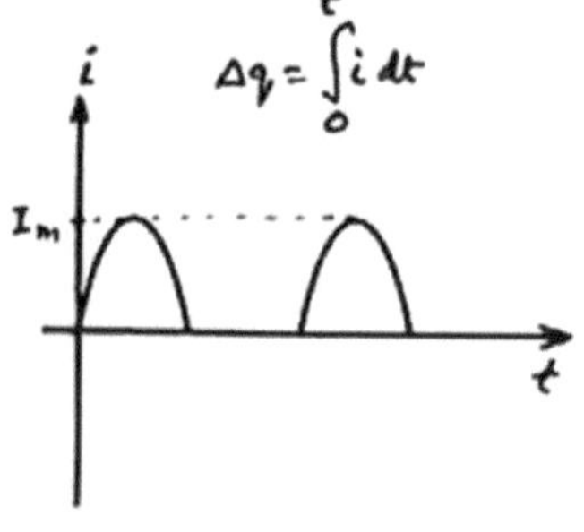

$i = I_m \sin \omega t \quad 0 < t \leq \pi/\omega$

$i = 0 \qquad \pi/\omega < t \leq 2\pi/\omega$

Module-19 Average Current in Rectifiers

— Full Wave Rectifier:

Avg current in a F.W. Rect.

$$i_{avg} = \frac{\text{Total ch. flow in one cyc}}{\text{duration of cyc}}$$

$$i_{avg} = \frac{2\int_0^{\pi/\omega} I_m \sin\omega t \, dt}{2\pi/\omega}$$

$$i_{avg} = \frac{I_m \omega}{\pi}\left[-\frac{\cos\omega t}{\omega}\right]_0^{\pi/\omega}$$

$$i_{avg} = \frac{I_m}{\pi}\left[(1)-(-1)\right]$$

$$\boxed{i_{avg} = \frac{2I_m}{\pi}}$$

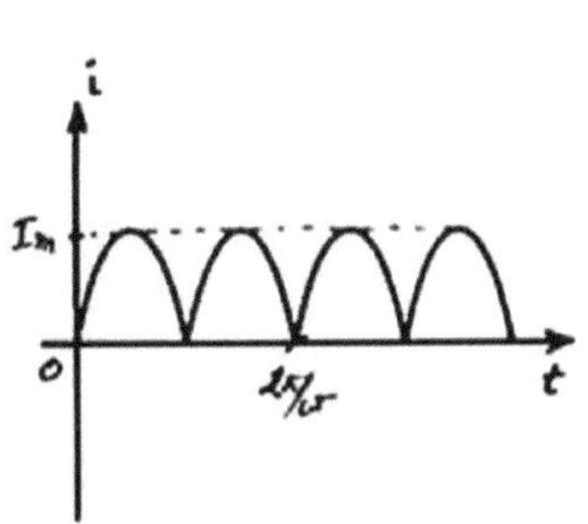

$i = I_m \sin\omega t \qquad 0 < t \le \pi/\omega$

$i = -I_m \sin\omega t \qquad \pi/\omega < t \le 2\pi/\omega$

Scan for Video Explanation

Module-20 RMS Value of Current in Rectifiers

\# RMS value of current in Rectifiers:

— Half Wave Rectifier:

$$I_{rms} = \sqrt{\frac{1}{T}\int_0^{\pi/\omega} I_m^2 \sin^2\omega t \, dt}$$

$$= \sqrt{\frac{1}{2\pi/\omega}\int_0^{\pi/\omega} I_m^2\left(\frac{1-\cos 2\omega t}{2}\right)dt}$$

$$= \sqrt{\frac{I_m^2\,\omega}{2\pi}\left[\frac{1}{2}t - \frac{\sin 2\omega t}{4\omega}\right]_0^{\pi/\omega}}$$

$$= \sqrt{\frac{I_m^2\,\omega}{2\pi}\left[\frac{\pi}{2\omega}\right]}$$

$$\boxed{I_{rms} = \frac{I_m}{2}}$$

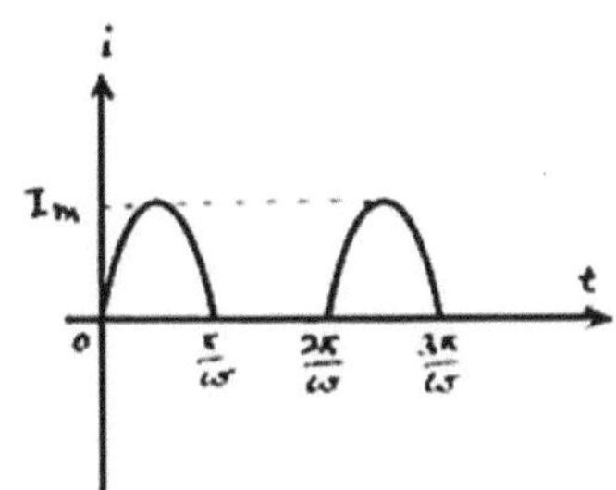

$i = I_m \sin\omega t \qquad 0 < t \le \pi/\omega$

$i = 0 \qquad \pi/\omega < t \le 2\pi/\omega$

Scan for Video Explanation

Module-20 RMS Value of Current in Rectifiers

— __Full Wave Rectifier:__

$$I_{rms} = \sqrt{\frac{1}{T} \int_0^T i_{(t)}^2 \, dt}$$

$$= \sqrt{\frac{1}{\pi/\omega} \int_0^{\pi/\omega} I_m^2 \sin^2 \omega t \, dt}$$

$$= \sqrt{\frac{I_m^2 \omega}{\pi} \int_0^{\pi/\omega} \left(\frac{1 - \cos 2\omega t}{2} \right) dt}$$

$$= \sqrt{\frac{I_m^2 \omega}{\pi} \left[\frac{1}{2}t - \frac{\sin 2\omega t}{4\omega} \right]_0^{\pi/\omega}}$$

$$= \sqrt{\frac{I_m^2 \omega}{\pi} \left[\frac{\pi}{2\omega} \right]}$$

$$\boxed{I_{rms} = \frac{I_m}{\sqrt{2}}}$$

$$i = I_m \sin \omega t \qquad 0 < t \le \pi/\omega$$

$$i = -I_m \sin \omega t \qquad \pi/\omega < t \le 2\pi/\omega$$

Module-21 Efficiency of a Rectifier

__Efficiency of a Rectifier:__

Efficiency

$$\eta = \frac{\text{Power Output}}{\text{Ac Power input}}$$

AC input Power $\qquad P_{in} = I_{rms}^2 (r_d + R_L)$

Output Power $\qquad P_{out} = I_{avg}^2 R_L$

Rectifier Efficiency $\qquad \boxed{\eta = \frac{I_{avg}^2 R_L}{I_{rms}^2 (r_d + R_L)} = \frac{I_{avg}^2 / I_{rms}^2}{\left(1 + \frac{r_d}{R_L}\right)}}$

Module-21 Efficiency of a Rectifier

– for a half wave rectifier $I_{avg} = \dfrac{I_m}{\pi}$ & $I_{rms} = \dfrac{I_m}{2}$

Efficiency of HW Rect $\eta = \dfrac{\left(I_m/\pi\right)^2 / \left(I_m/2\right)^2}{\left(1 + \dfrac{r_d}{R_L}\right)} = \dfrac{4/\pi^2}{\left(1 + r_d/R_L\right)}$

$$\boxed{\eta = \dfrac{0.406}{\left(1 + \dfrac{r_d}{R_L}\right)}}$$

for an ideal diode $r_d = 0$ $\Rightarrow$ $\boxed{\eta = 0.406 \text{ or } 40.6\%}$

– for a full wave rect. $I_{avg} = \dfrac{2 I_m}{\pi}$ & $I_{rms} = I_m/\sqrt{2}$

Efficiency of FW Rect $\eta = \dfrac{\left(2 I_m/\pi\right)^2 / \left(I_m/\sqrt{2}\right)^2}{1 + \dfrac{r_d}{R_L}} = \dfrac{8/\pi^2}{1 + \dfrac{r_d}{R_L}}$ $\boxed{\dfrac{0.812}{\left(1 + \dfrac{r_d}{R_L}\right)}}$

for an ideal diode $r_d = 0$ $\Rightarrow$ $\boxed{\eta = 0.812 \text{ or } 81.2\%}$

Scan for Video Explanation

Module-22 Bridge Rectifier

\# __Bridge Rectifier:__

This is a modified FW rectifier which has several adv over a common centre tap rectifier. It uses 4 diodes for its rectification mechanism.

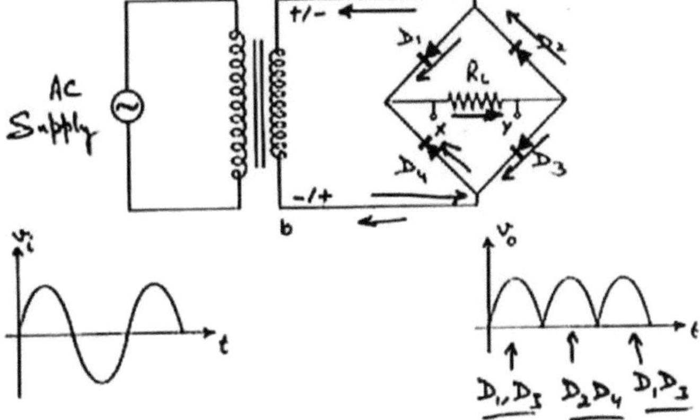

Scan for Video Explanation

Module-23 Photo Diode

Photo Diode:

A junction diode manufactured by using a light sensitive Semiconductor.

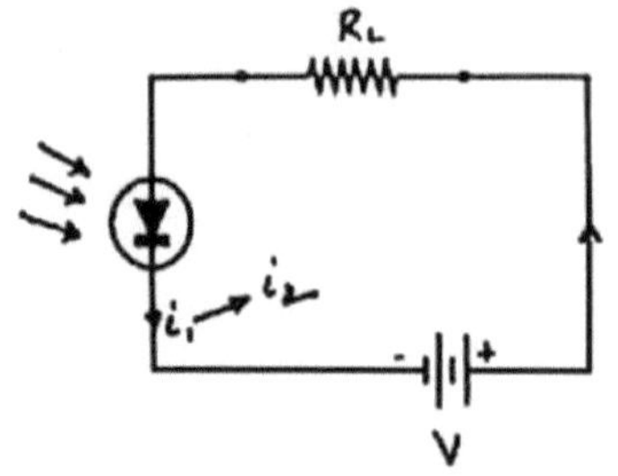

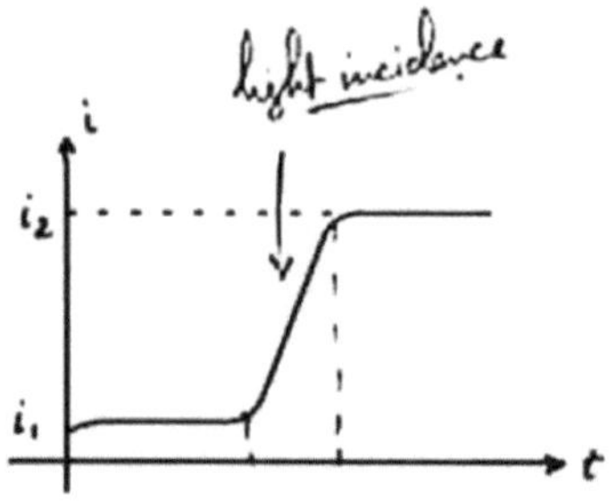

photon energy $= h\nu > \Delta E_g$

$i_1 \rightarrow$ dark current

$i_2 \rightarrow$ bright current

Scan for Video Explanation

Web Reference at www.physicsgalaxy.com

Module-23 Photo Diode

Working of a Photo diode:

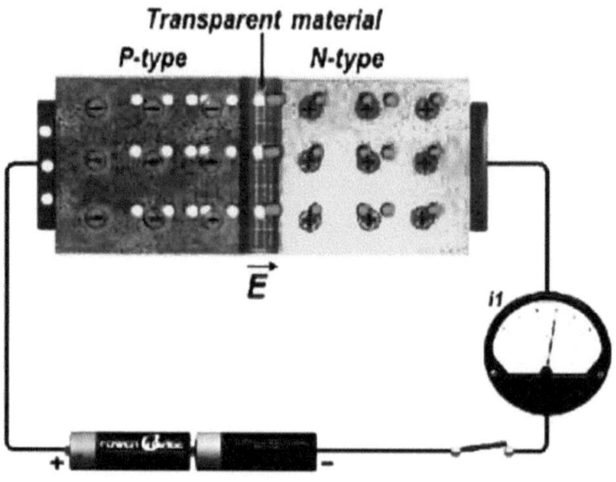

Scan for Video Explanation

Web Reference at www.physicsgalaxy.com

Light Emitting Diode:
(LED)

In a PN junction, in FB above knee voltage current flows because in dep layer e^-s from N side & holes from P side combine & constitute current.

When e^-s & holes recombine in dep layer, photons of energy equal to ΔE_g is released.

for Si $\Delta E_g = 1.14\,eV$ $\Rightarrow$ wl of ph. $\lambda = \dfrac{hc}{\Delta E_g} = \dfrac{12423}{1.14} = 10898\,\overset{\circ}{A}$ IR region

for a GaAsP $\Delta E_g = 1.9\,eV$ $\Rightarrow$ wl of ph $\lambda = \dfrac{hc}{\Delta E_g} = \dfrac{12423}{1.9}$

$$\lambda = 6538\,\overset{\circ}{A}$$
green color.

Scan for Video Explanation

Working of LED:

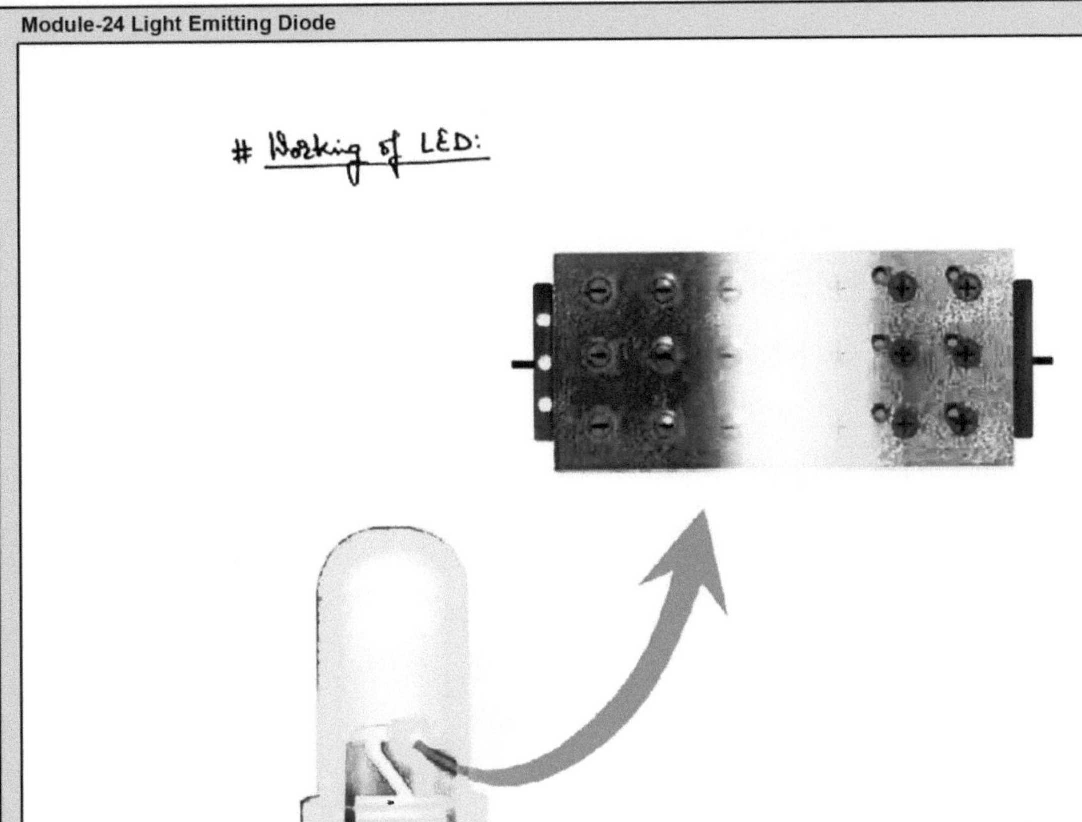

Scan for Video Explanation

Module-25 Solved Example-1

Ex : A silicon diode is connected to a resistance R and a battery of voltage V_B as shown. The knee point of its I-V curve is at 0.7 volt. Given that the diode requires a minimum current of 1 mA to attain a value higher than the knee point. If $V_B = 5V$, what should be the maximum value of resistance R so that voltage across diode is above knee point ?

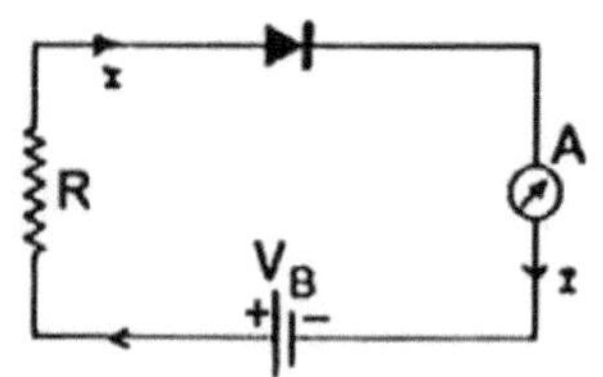

Sol: By KVL for the loop

$$V_B = IR + V_K$$

$$I = \frac{V_B - V_K}{R}$$

$$R = \frac{V_B - V_K}{I} = \frac{5 - 0.7}{10^{-3}} = 4.3 \times 10^3$$

$$R = 4300 \,\Omega \quad \underline{Ans}.$$

Module-26 Solved Example-2

Ex : The forward biased resistance of a PN junction diode is 10Ω and its knee point voltage is 0.7 volt. This diode is connected across a load resistance of 500Ω and an AC supply of peak voltage 20V. Find the peak current through the diode and peak voltage across the load.

Sol: When diode is FB, current in ckt will be

$$I = \frac{20 - 0.7}{510} = 0.0378 A \quad \underline{Ans}.$$

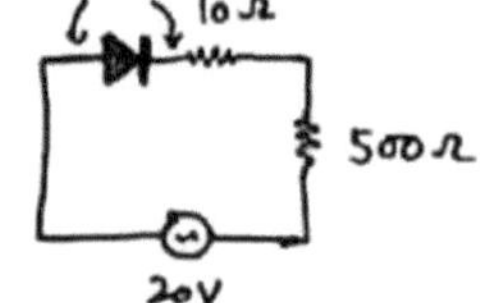

Peak voltage across load –

$$V_L = I_{peak} \times R_L = 0.0378 \times 500$$

$$= 18.9 \, V \quad \underline{Ans}.$$

Module-27 Solved Example-3

Ex : In the circuit shown in figure find the current flowing through battery. Assume diodes are ideal.

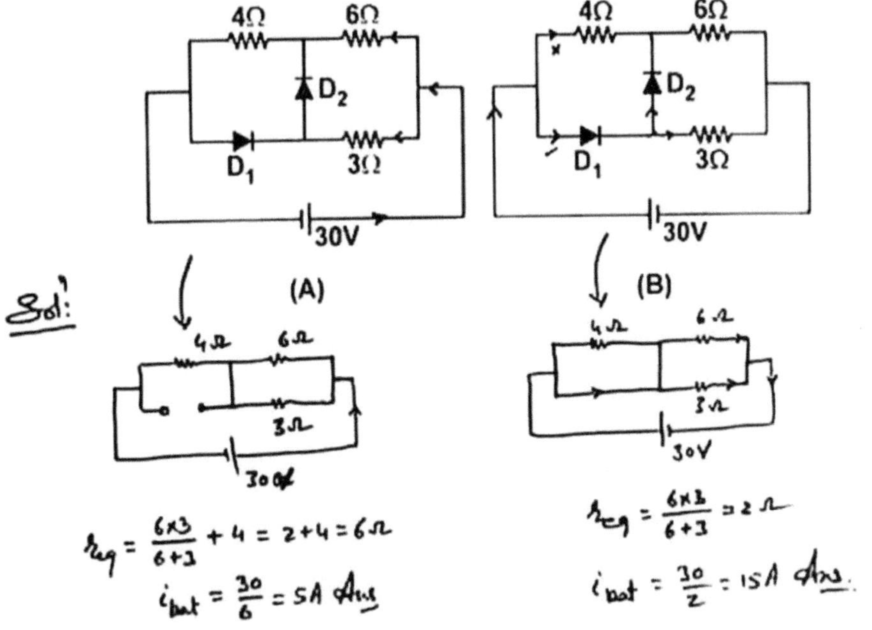

Sol:

(A)

$$\eta_{eq} = \frac{6 \times 3}{6+3} + 4 = 2+4 = 6\,\Omega$$

$$i_{bat} = \frac{30}{6} = 5A \text{ Ans}$$

(B)

$$\eta_{eq} = \frac{6 \times 3}{6+3} = 2\,\Omega$$

$$i_{bat} = \frac{30}{2} = 15A \text{ Ans.}$$

Scan for Video Explanation

Module-28 Solved Example-4

Ex : In the circuit shown in figure a zener diode of voltage $V_Z = 6V$ is used to maintain a constant load voltage across a resistance

of $1000\,\Omega$ with a series resistance $100\,\Omega$. If the emf of source is 9V, calculate the current in series resistance and zener diode. Also calculate power dissipated in zener diode.

Sol:

current in R_2 : $i = \dfrac{V_2}{R_2} = \dfrac{6}{1000} = 6\,mA$ Ans.

Current in R : $i_R = \dfrac{V_{xy}}{R} = \dfrac{9-6}{100} = 0.03A$ Ans.

Current in Zener Diode is $i_z = i_R - i = (0.006 - 0.03) = 0.024A$ Ans.

$$P_D = i_z \cdot V_z = 0.024 \times 6 = 0.144W \text{ Ans.}$$

Scan for Video Explanation

Ex : In the circuit shown in figure, find the equivalent resistance across the battery when switch is closed. Assume diode is ideal.

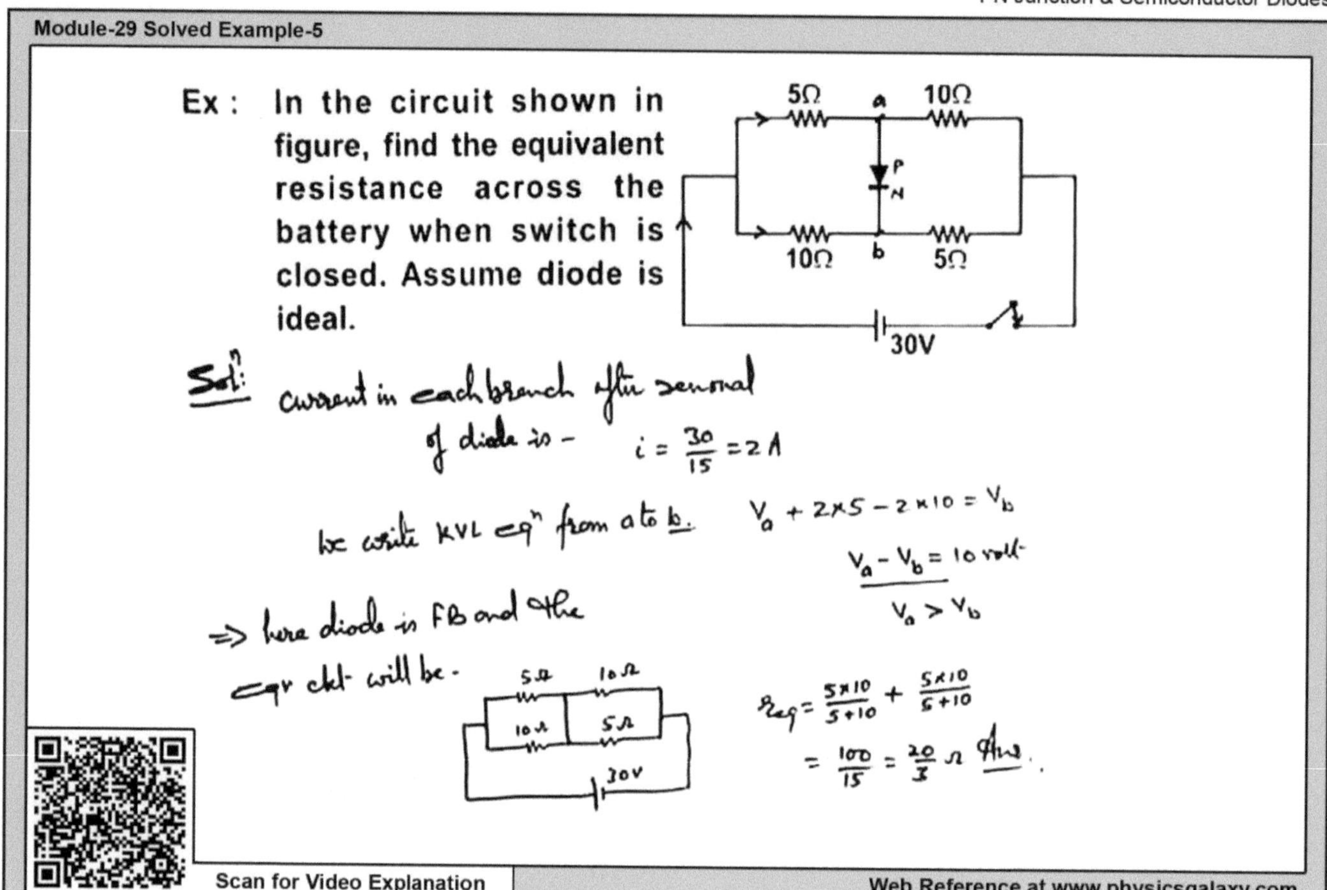

Sol: current in each branch after removal of diode is —

$$i = \frac{30}{15} = 2\,A$$

be write KVL eq^n from a to b.

$$V_a + 2\times5 - 2\times10 = V_b$$

$$V_a - V_b = 10\ volt$$

$$V_a > V_b$$

$\Rightarrow$ here diode is FB and the eqv ckt will be —

$$R_{eq} = \frac{5\times10}{5+10} + \frac{5\times10}{5+10}$$

$$= \frac{100}{15} = \frac{20}{3}\,\Omega\ \text{Ans}.$$

Chapter 18
Transistor and its Application

Transistor:

It is a 2-junction s.c device & it is made in two ways.

① n-p-n transistor

② p-n-p transistor

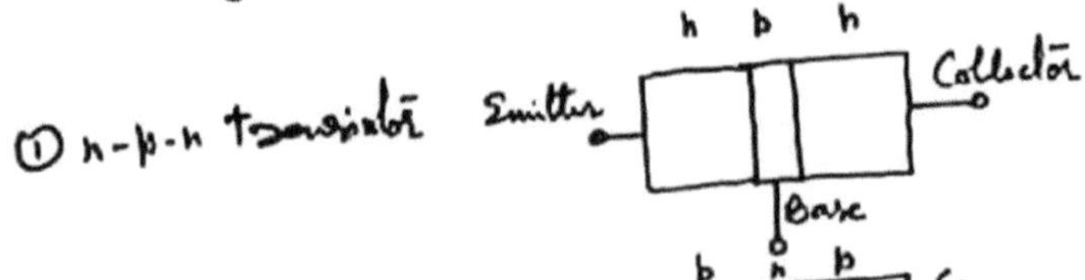

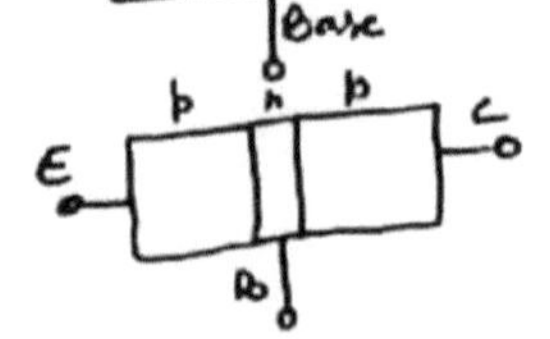

The three terminals of a transistor are called Emitter, Base and Collector.

① **Emitter:** It is one of the side sections of the transistor & it is heavily doped relative to other sections, in a ckt emitter emits majority carriers to the other parts of transistor

② **Base:** It is middle section of tr. It is very thin & very lightly doped.

③ **Collector:** It is the side section on other side of base.

Majority carriers emitted by emitter are collected by Collector.

NOTE: In normal operation of a tr, its BE junction is forward biased and its BC junction is reverse biased.

Module-2 Circuit Symbols of a Transistors

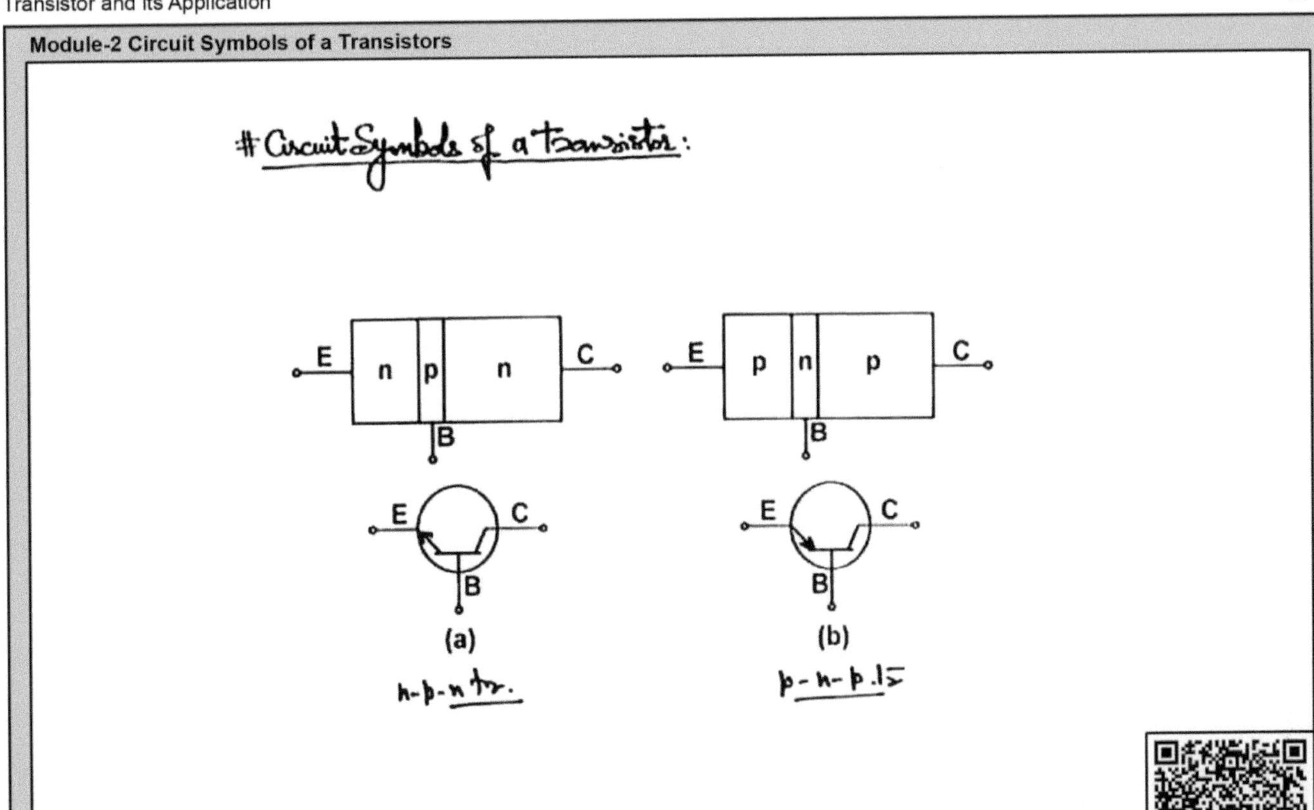

Scan for Video Explanation

Module-3 Working of a Transistor

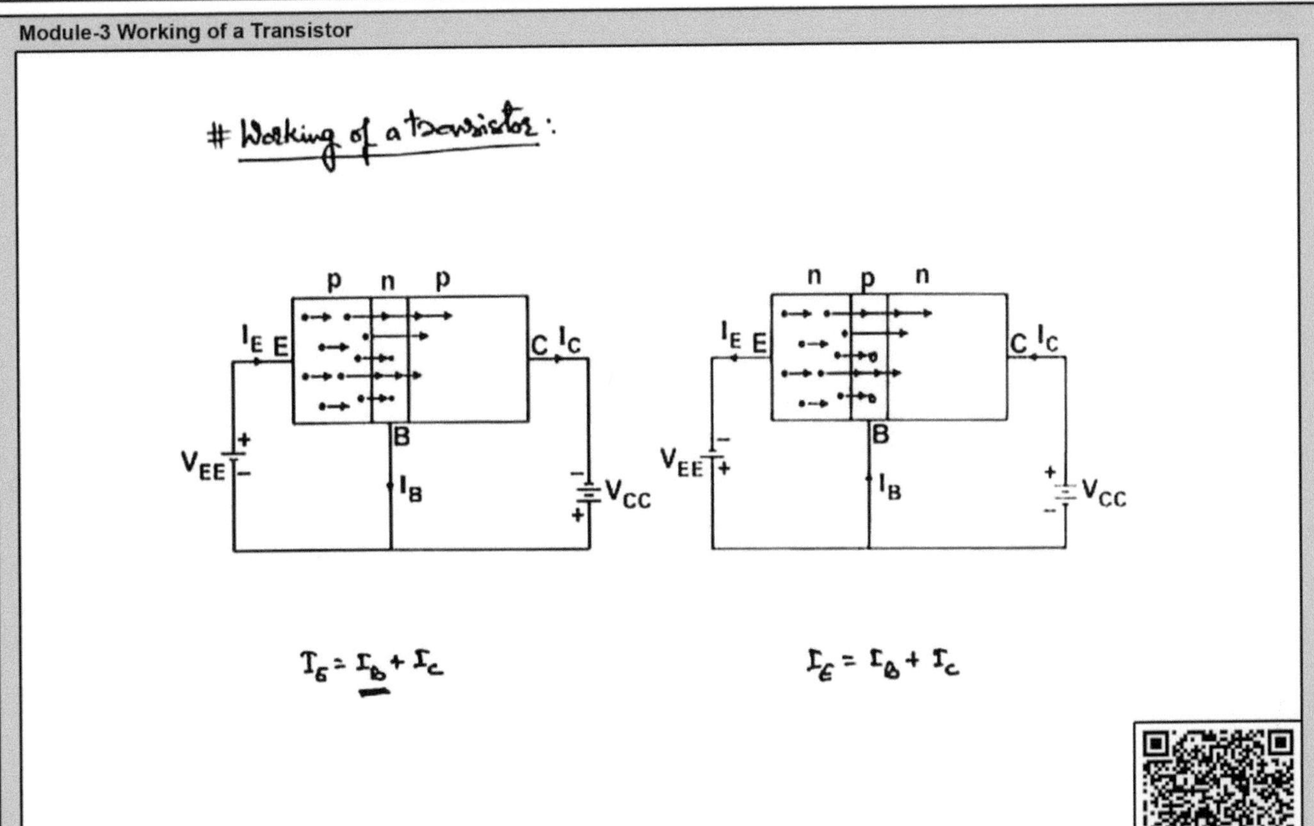

Scan for Video Explanation

Module-4 DC Current Gains of a Transistor

DC Current Gains of a Transistor:

DC current gains are characteristic const of a tr and for every tr two current gains are defined. These are -

① Base current Amplification factor

$$\beta = \frac{I_c}{I_B}$$

② Emitter Current Amplification factor

$$\alpha = \frac{I_c}{I_E}$$

for a tr.

$$I_E = I_B + I_c$$

$$\frac{I_c}{\alpha} = \frac{I_c}{\beta} + I_c$$

$$\frac{1}{\alpha} = \frac{1}{\beta} + 1 \qquad \Rightarrow \qquad \boxed{\begin{array}{c} \alpha = \dfrac{\beta}{1+\beta} \\[2mm] \beta = \dfrac{\alpha}{1-\alpha} \end{array}}$$

Scan for Video Explanation

Web Reference at www.physicsgalaxy.com

Module-5 Amplifier

Amplifier:

- An Amp is a device which increases the strength of a time varying signal

- To inc the strength of a signal, Amp extracts the energy from an external source and add it into the signal to amplify its strength.

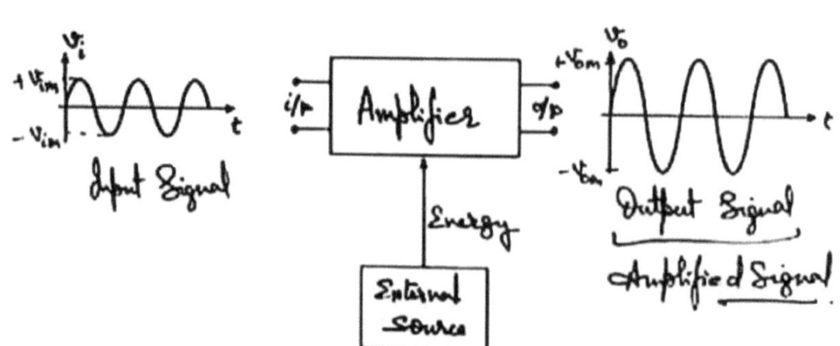

Scan for Video Explanation

Web Reference at www.physicsgalaxy.com

Module-6 Transistor as an Amplifier

Transistor as an Amplifier :

When a transistor is biased such that —

(i) — its BE junction is FB. $\Rightarrow r_{BE}\downarrow \Rightarrow$ high value of $\underline{I_E}$

(ii) — its BC junction is RB $\Rightarrow \underline{r_{BC}}\uparrow$

As majority of carriers from Emitter are passed to Collector side. A high pot^n drop takes place across BC junction.

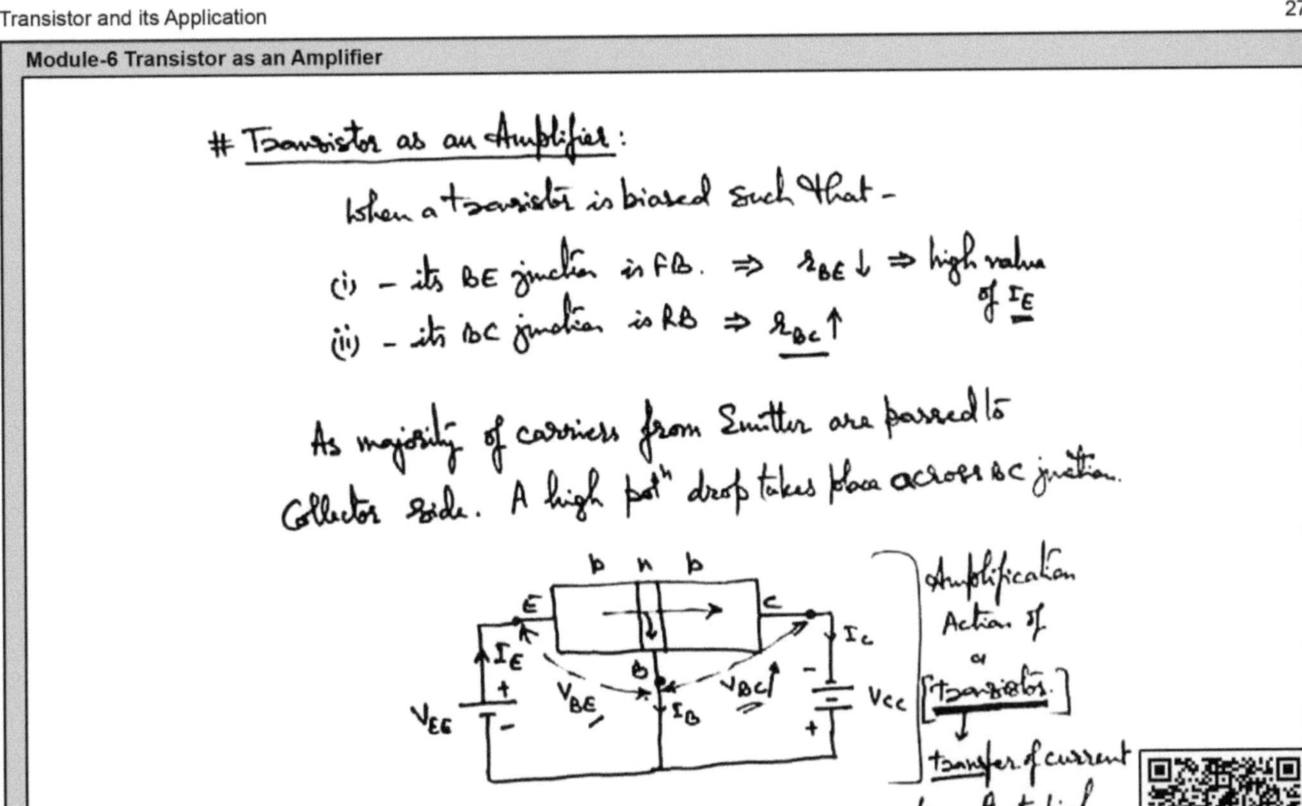

Scan for Video Explanation

Module-7 Transistor Connections as Amplifier

Transistor Connections as Amplifiers :

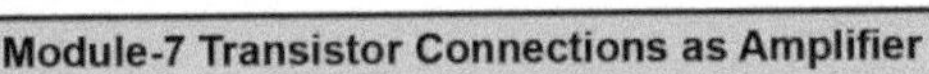

A transistor has only 3 term & to be used as an amplifier its one term must be common to i/p & o/p terminals of the amp.

A transistor can be used as an Amp in 3 ways —

① Common Base Connection

② Common Emitter Connection

③ Common Collector Connection

Scan for Video Explanation

Module-8 Study of Common Base Connections of a Transistor

Study of Common Base Connections of a Transistor:

Base term is common for both i/p & o/p term.

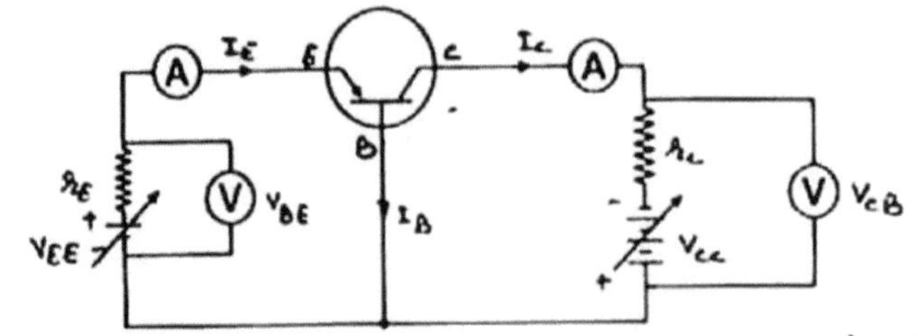

Input Characteristic: (I_E & V_{BE})

Output Characteristic: (I_C & V_{CB})

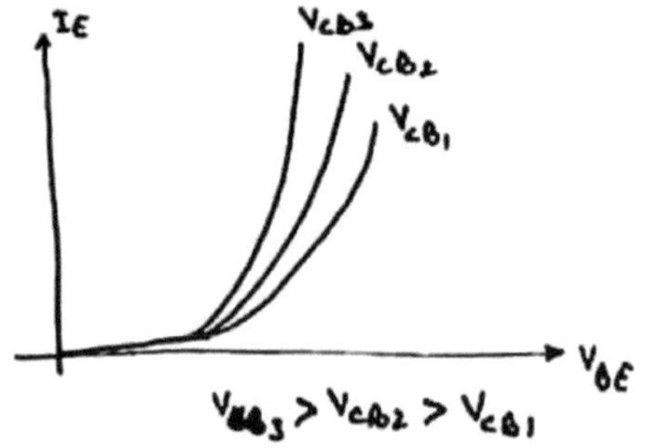

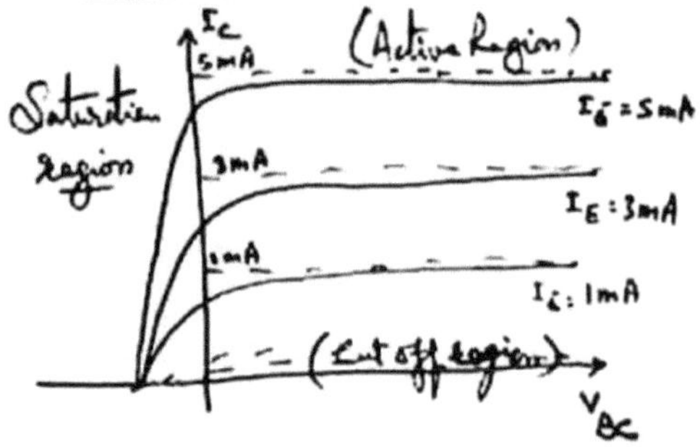

$V_{CB3} > V_{CB2} > V_{CB1}$

Module-9 Operating Regions of a Transistor in Common Base Connections

Operating Regions of a Transistor in Common Base Connections:

characteristics of a tr has 3 regions under which a tr is operated

(1) **Active Region:** BE junction is FB and BC junction is reversed biased

This is the normal operation mode of a tr.

(2) **Cut off Region:** When both BE and BC junction are rev. biased.

$$I_C = I_E = 0$$

Gen tr is not operated in this mode.

(3) **Saturation Region:** when both BE and BC junction are Forward Biased.

In this case a slight variation in V_{CB} causes large variation in I_C.

Module-10 Output Resistance of a Common Base Circuit

Output Resistance of a Common Base Circuit:

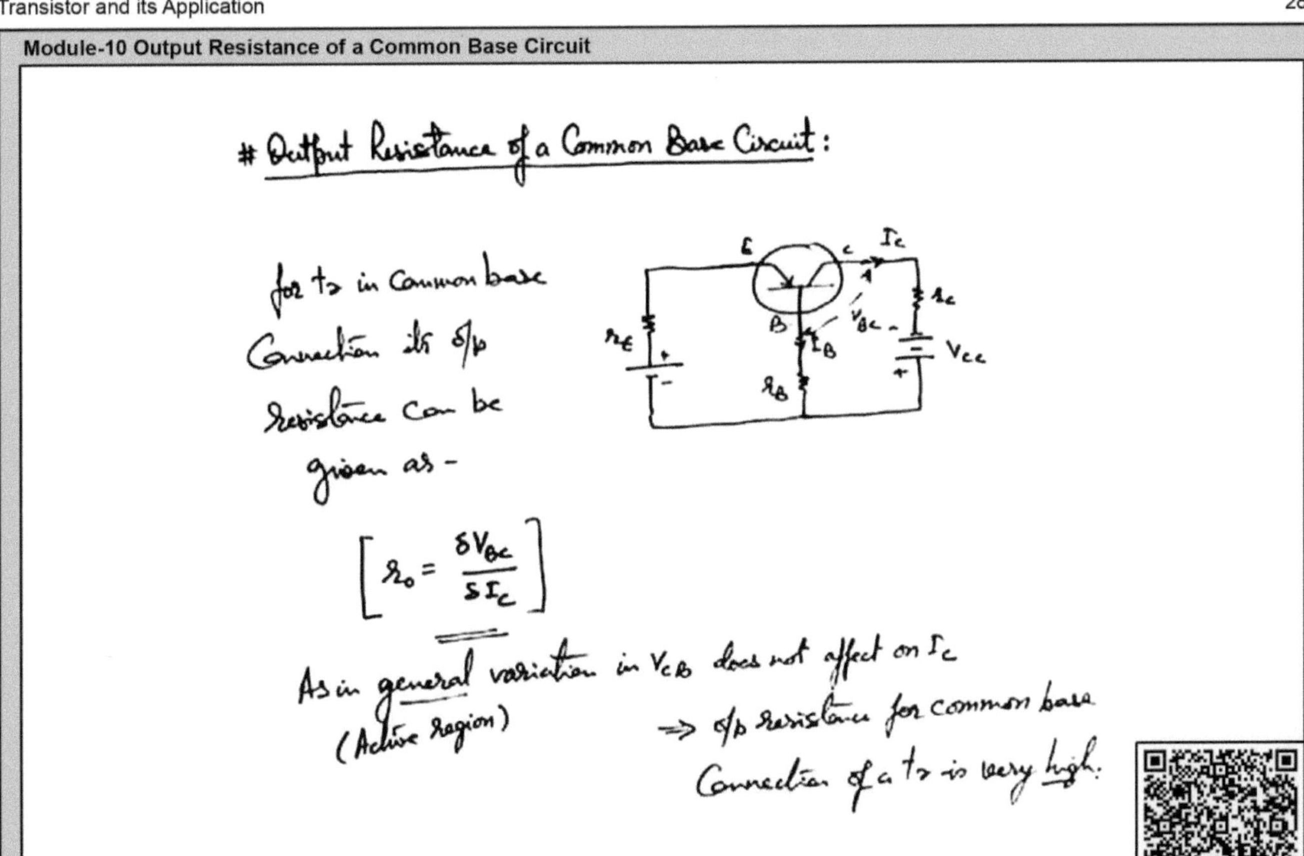

for a t₂ in Common base Connection its o/p resistance can be given as –

$$\left[\, r_0 = \frac{\delta V_{BC}}{\delta I_C} \,\right]$$

As in general variation in V_{CB} does not affect on I_C (Active region)

⟹ o/p resistance for common base Connection of a t₂ is very high.

Scan for Video Explanation

Module-11 Study of Common Emitter Connections of a Transistor

Study of Common Emitter Connections of a Transistor:

Emitter terminal is common for i/p & o/p terminals.

Input characteristic: (I_B and V_{BE})

Output characteristic: (I_C & V_{CE})

Scan for Video Explanation

Module-12 Operating Regions of a Transistor in Common Emitter Connections

\# <u>Operating Regions of a Transistor in Common Emitter Connections</u>:

A transistor is operated under 3 possible regions. These are-

① <u>Active Region</u>: Collector junction is rev biased and emitter junction is forward biased.

for low I_B, variation in I_C with V_{CE} is very small

for high I_B, this variation is large

② <u>Saturation Region</u>: both junctions are FB

    in this region $V_{CE} \approx 0$ and small variation I_B does not affect I_C.

③ <u>Cut off Region</u>: both junctions are Rev. biased.

    in this mode very small collector current flows due to leakage of charge carriers from emitter to collector. This is denoted by I_{CEo}

　　　　　　　　　　Web Reference at www.physicsgalaxy.com

Module-13 Output Resistance of a Common Emitter Circuit

\# <u>Output Resistance of Common Emitter circuit</u>:

i/p → B & E   and   o/p → C & E

$$r_0 = \frac{\delta V_{CE}}{\delta I_C}$$

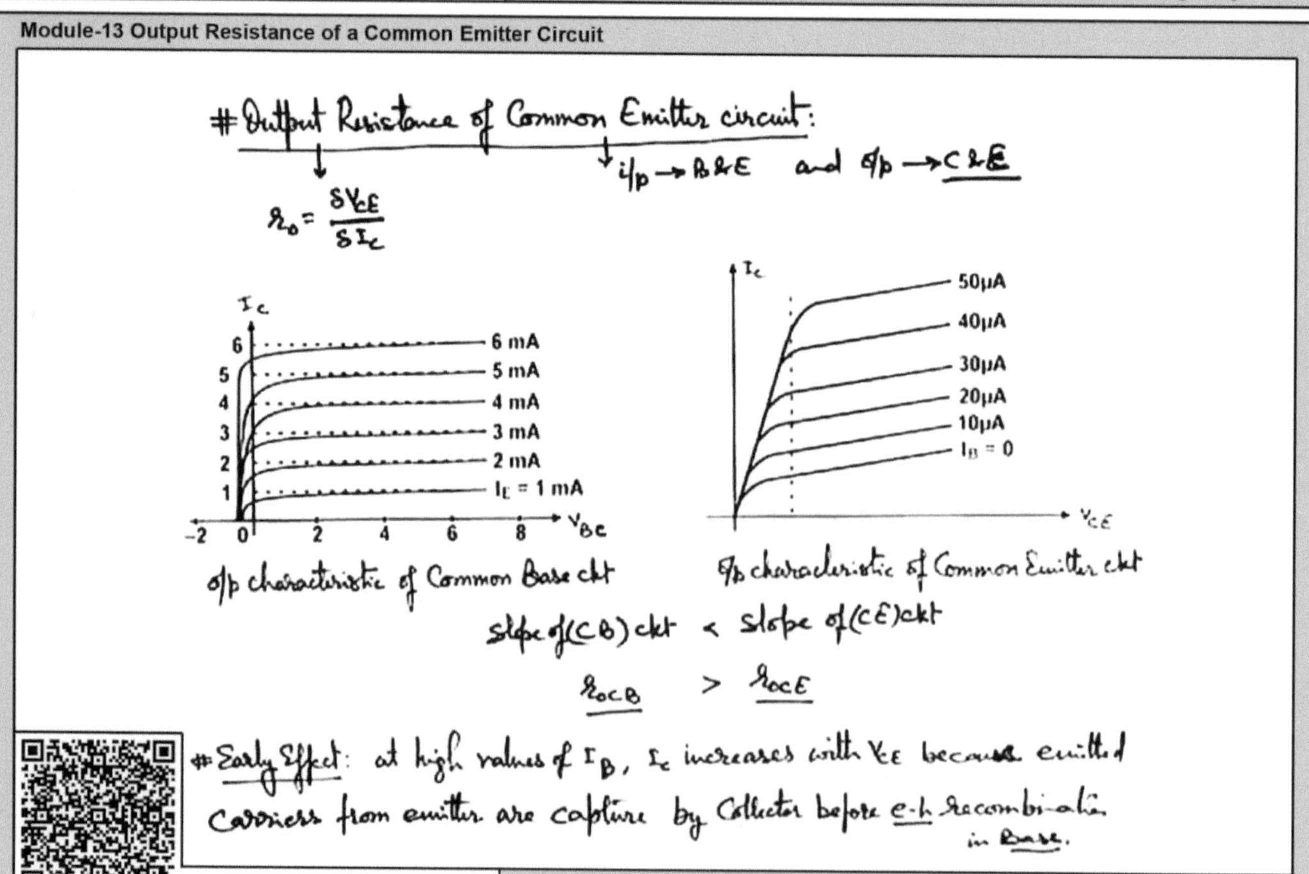

o/p characteristic of Common Base ckt   o/p characteristic of Common Emitter ckt

slope of (CB) ckt < slope of (CE) ckt

r_{oCB} > r_{oCE}

\# <u>Early Effect</u>: at high values of I_B, I_C increases with V_{CE} because emitted carriers from emitter are capture by collector before e-h recombination in Base.

　　　　　　　　　　Web Reference at www.physicsgalaxy.com

Module-14 Use of a Transistor as an Amplifier

Transistor as an Amplifier:

In o/p ch. of Common Emitter & Common Base connection of a tr such that in active region, small variation in i/p current to tr causes large variation in o/p current.

Due to this prop, Transistor can be used as an Amplifier.

On the basis of diff connections of a tr, it can be used as an amplifier in 3 ways -

    ✓ ① Common Base Amplifier
    ✓ ② Common Emitter Amplifier
    ✗ ③ Common Collector Amplifier

Module-15 Common Base Amplifier

Common Base Amplifier:

In this we connect an input signal to the i/p side of the Common base connection of a transistor.

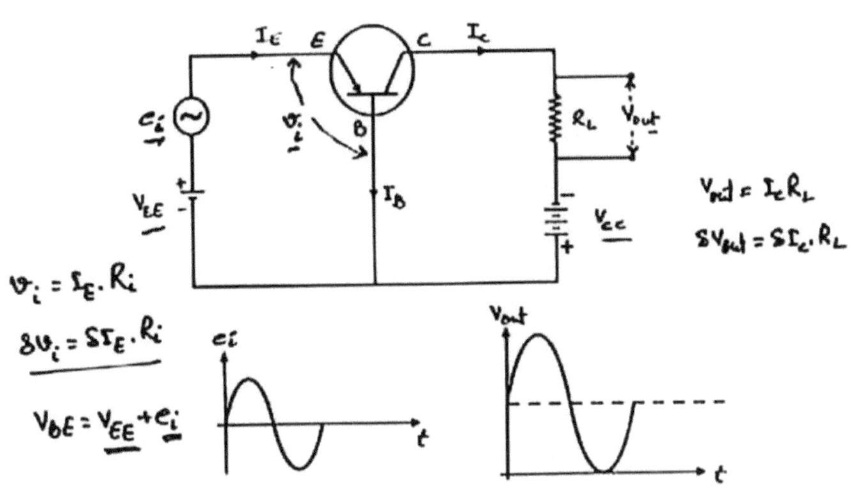

Module-15 Common Base Amplifier

\# <u>Various Gains in Common Base Amplifier</u>:

(1) <u>AC current Gain</u>:

$$\text{Dc current gain} \quad \alpha_{dc} = \frac{I_c}{I_E}$$

$$\text{Ac current gain} \quad \boxed{\alpha_{AC} = \frac{\delta I_c}{\delta I_E}}$$

(2) <u>AC voltage Gain</u>:

$$A_v = \frac{\delta V_{out}}{\delta V_{in}} \qquad \text{here} \quad \delta V_{out} = \delta I_c \cdot R_L$$
$$\& \quad \delta V_i = \delta I_E \cdot R_i$$

$$A_v = \frac{\delta I_c}{\delta I_E} \times \frac{R_L}{R_i}$$

$$\boxed{A_v = \alpha_{AC} \cdot \left(\frac{R_L}{R_i}\right)}$$

Ac Voltage Gain = Ac current Gain × Resistance Gain.

Module-15 Common Base Amplifier

(3) <u>AC Power Gain</u>:

$$G_{AC} = \frac{P_{out}}{P_{in}}$$

$$G_{AC} = \frac{(\delta I_c)^2 R_L}{(\delta I_E)^2 R_i}$$

$$G_{AC} = \alpha_{AC}^2 \times \frac{R_L}{R_i}$$

$$\boxed{G_{AC} = \alpha_{AC} \times A_v} \qquad A_v = \alpha_{AC} \cdot \frac{R_L}{R_i}$$

Ac Power Gain = Ac current gain × Ac voltage gain.

Module-16 Common Emitter Amplifier

\# <u>Common Emitter Amplifier</u>:

In this we connect a signal at i/p terminals of the Common Emitter connection of a transistor.

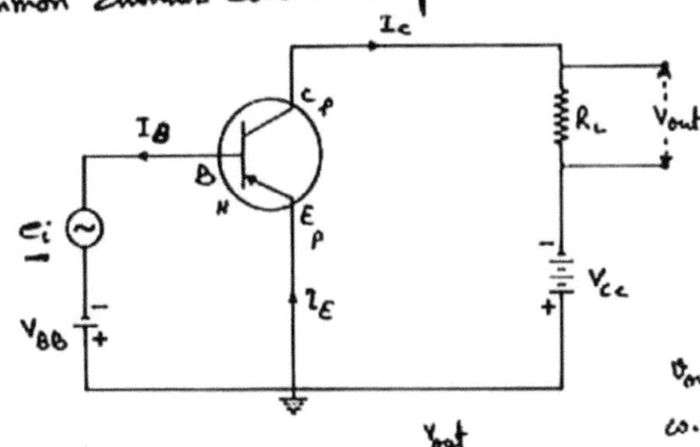

V_{out} is <u>Out of phase</u> w.r.t. c_i ($180°$)

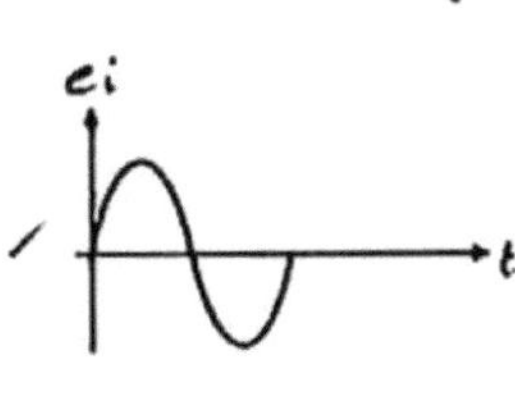

Module-16 Common Emitter Amplifier

\# <u>Various Gains in Common Emitter Amplifier</u>:

① <u>AC Current Gain</u>:

$$\text{Dc current Gain} \quad \beta_{DC} = \frac{I_C}{I_B}$$

$$\text{AC Current Gain} \left[\beta_{AC} = \frac{\delta I_C}{\delta I_B} \right]$$

② <u>AC Voltage Gain</u>:

$$A_V = \frac{\delta V_{out}}{\delta V_{in}} \qquad \text{here} \quad \delta V_{out} = \delta I_C \cdot R_L$$
$$\delta V_{in} = \delta I_B \cdot R_i$$

$$A_V = \frac{\delta I_C \cdot R_L}{\delta I_B \cdot R_i}$$

$$\left[A_V = \beta_{AC} \cdot \frac{R_L}{R_i} \right]$$

As $\beta_{AC} > \alpha_{AC} \Rightarrow$ Voltage gain of <u>CE amp</u> is very large Compared to a <u>CB amp</u>.

Module-16 Common Emitter Amplifier

(3) __AC Power Gain__ :

$$G_{AC} = \frac{P_{out}}{P_{in}} = \frac{(\delta I_c)^2 \cdot R_L}{(\delta I_B)^2 \cdot R_i}$$

$$G_{AC} = \beta_{AC}^2 \cdot \frac{R_L}{R_i}$$

$$\boxed{G_{AC} = \beta_{AC} \times A_v}$$

(4) __Transconductance__ :

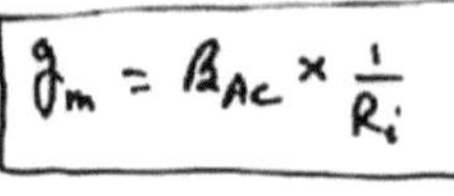

$$g_m = \frac{\delta I_c}{\delta V_{BE}} = \frac{\text{Small var in o/p current}}{\text{Small var in i/p voltage}}$$

$$g_m = \frac{\delta I_c}{\delta I_B} \times \frac{\delta I_B}{\delta V_{BE}}$$

$$R_i = \frac{\delta V_{i \to BE}}{\delta I_{i \to B}}$$

$$\boxed{g_m = \beta_{AC} \times \frac{1}{R_i}}$$

Module-17 Oscillator

__Oscillator__ :

Electrically an osc is a device which generates ac output signal without any external input signal.

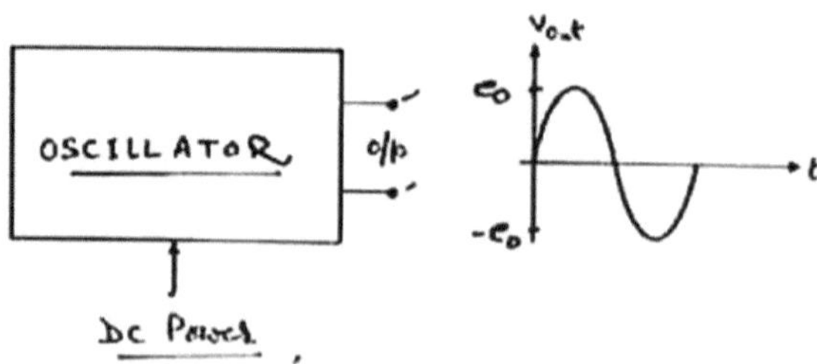

Module-18 Transistor as an Oscillator

Transistor as an Oscillator :

A t.r. can be used in a ckt s.t. it can't produces undamped oscillations at the o/p terminals of ckt.

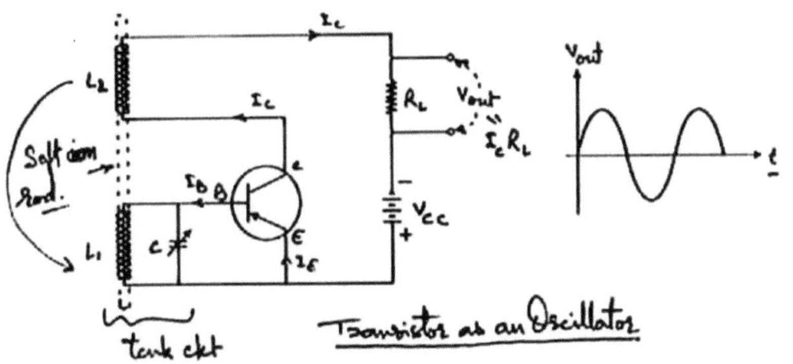

Transistor as an Oscillator

The ckt of oscillator consist of 3 parts

① Tank Ckt.   ② Amplifier ckt.   ③ Feedback ckt.
                                         ↓
                                      +ve feedback.

Module-18 Transistor as an Oscillator

(1) **Tank Ckt** : It is an LC Osc unit

$$f_{osc} = \frac{1}{2\pi \sqrt{LC}}$$

This osc voltage across tank ckt act as i/p signal for Amp ckt.

(2) **Amplifier ckt :**

It amplifies the osc voltage of the tank ckt.

(3) **Feedback ckt :** This section supplies a part of o/p energy from collector ckt to the tank ckt. The o/p osc are in o/p phase w.r.to osc. of i/p voltage and due to mutual induction again a phase shift of 180° occurs and hence the energy supplied to tank ckt is in same phase of its osc.

This is called positive feedback.

Module-19 Solved Example-1

Ex : In a transistor circuit its base current is 105µA and collector current is 2.05 mA. Determine the value of I_E and $\underline{\alpha}$.

Sol^n: Given that $I_B = 105 \times 10^{-6}$ A

$$I_C = 2.05 \times 10^{-3}\, A$$

Base current gain $\beta = \dfrac{I_c}{I_B} = \dfrac{2.05 \times 10^{-3}}{105 \times 10^{-6}} = \underline{19.5}$.

$$\alpha = \dfrac{\beta}{1+\beta} = \dfrac{19.5}{20.5} = 0.95 \text{ Ans.}$$

also $\alpha = \dfrac{I_c}{I_E} \Rightarrow I_E = \dfrac{I_c}{\alpha} = \dfrac{2.05 \times 10^{-3}}{0.95} = 2.155\, mA$ Ans.

or. $I_E = I_c + I_B = 0.105\, mA +$
$$2.05\, mA + 0.105\, mA = 2.155\, mA \text{ Ans}$$

Module-20 Solved Example-2

Ex : In a junction transistor operating under common emitter connections, the base current is changed by 20µA. Due to this base-emitter voltage is changed by 0.02 volt and collector changed by 2mA. Find :
(a) Input resistance & β_{AC} of circuit
(b) Voltage gain of amplifier if $R_L = 5000\Omega$.

Sol^n. (a) As we know $\beta_{AC} = \dfrac{\delta I_c}{\delta I_B} = \dfrac{2 \times 10^{-3}}{20 \times 10^{-6}} = 100$ Ans.

(b) $A_v = \beta_{AC} \times \dfrac{R_L}{R_i}$

i/p resistance $R_i = \dfrac{\delta V_{BE}}{\delta I_B} = \dfrac{0.02}{20 \times 10^{-6}} = 1000\,\Omega = 1k\Omega$

$$A_v = 100 \times \dfrac{5000}{1000} = 500 \text{ Ans.}$$

Module-21 Solved Example-3

Ex : An NPN transistor is connected in common emitter configuration in which collector supply is 8V and the voltage drop across the load resistance of 800Ω connected in the collector circuit is 0.8V. Determine the collector emitter voltage and collector current.

Sol.:

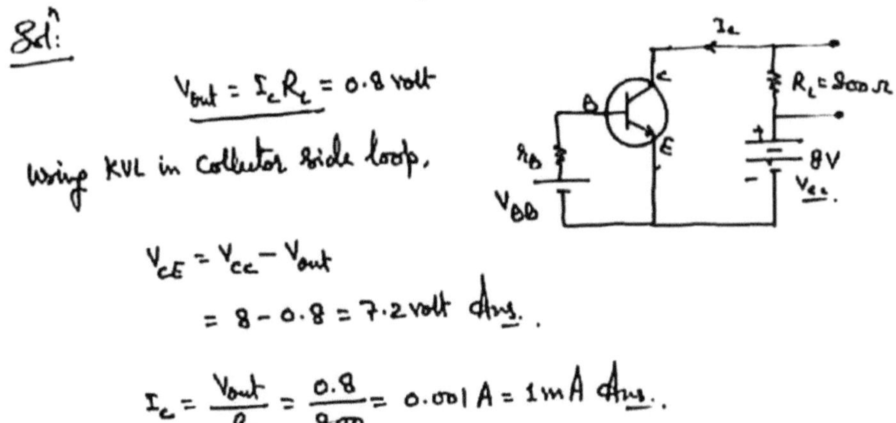

$$V_{out} = I_c R_L = 0.8 \text{ volt}$$

Using KVL in collector side loop,

$$V_{CE} = V_{cc} - V_{out}$$
$$= 8 - 0.8 = 7.2 \text{ volt} \quad \text{Ans.}$$

$$I_c = \frac{V_{out}}{R_L} = \frac{0.8}{800} = 0.001 \text{ A} = 1 \text{ mA} \quad \text{Ans.}$$

Module-22 Solved Example-4

Ex : The input resistance of a silicon transistor is 665Ω. A change of 15μA in the base current produces a change of 2mA in the collector current. This transistor is used as a common emitter amplifier with a load resistance of 5kΩ. Find the voltage gain of the amplifier.

Sol.:

As we know

$$\beta_{AC} = \frac{\delta I_c}{\delta I_B} = \frac{2 \times 10^{-3}}{15 \times 10^{-6}} = \frac{400}{3}$$

Voltage gain

$$A_v = \beta_{AC} \times \frac{R_L}{R_i}$$
$$= \frac{400}{3} \times \frac{5000}{665}$$
$$= 1000 \quad \text{Ans.}$$

Chapter 19
Logic Gates

Digital Signals and Logic Gates :

Signals which are composed by comb^n of only two state of elect pot^n → High & Low.

Analog signal

Digital Signal

High → +5V

Low → 0V

The fundamental electronic ckt which are used in various analysis of digital signals are called 'Logic Gates'

Logic gates are the basic building blocks of digital electronics

Logic Gates :

- LG is an elec ckt which follows a certain logical relation between i/p and o/p voltages.

- These are used to Control the flow of information (via voltage) in electronic ckt.

- There are 5 commonly use LG. These are —

- Each logic gate is indicated by a symbol & its function is given by its 'Truth Table'
  ↓
  i/p & o/p Relationship.

$$\begin{bmatrix} \text{(1) NOT Gate} \\ \text{(2) AND Gate} \\ \text{(3) OR Gate} \end{bmatrix}$$

$$\begin{bmatrix} \text{(4) NOR Gate} \\ \text{(5) NAND Gate} \end{bmatrix}$$

Module-3 Truth Table of Logic Gates

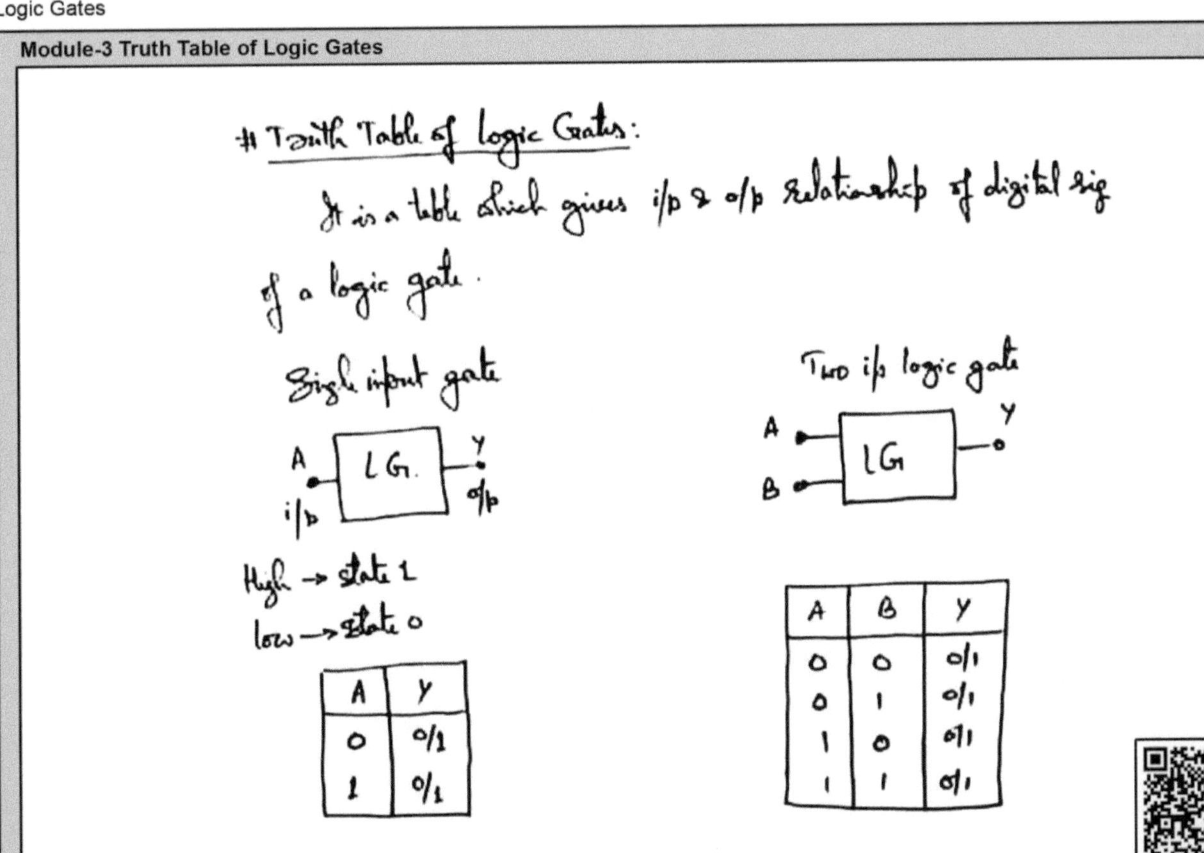

\# Truth Table of Logic Gates:

It is a table which gives i/p & o/p relationship of digital sig of a logic gate.

Single input gate

A — [L G] — Y
i/p   o/p

Two i/p logic gate

A — [L G] — Y
B —   o/p

High → state 1
low → state 0

A	Y
0	0/1
1	0/1

A	B	Y
0	0	0/1
0	1	0/1
1	0	0/1
1	1	0/1

Scan for Video Explanation

Module-4 NOT Gate

\# NOT Gate: (also called an inverter gate)

- This is a basic gate with 1 i/p & 1 o/p.
- This reverses the voltage level of i/p as o/p.

i/p High ——→ o/p low

o/p low ——→ o/p High

Symbol.

A —▷○— Y
i/p   o/p

Truth Table.

A	Y
0	1
1	0

Waveform analysis of NOT Gate:

V_A

i/p waveform.

o/p waveform

Scan for Video Explanation

Module-5 OR Gate

OR Gate: It has 2 or more i/p & 1 o/p.

- It produces High o/p(1) when any of its i/p is High(1) and it produces low o/p(0) when (only) all its i/p are low(0)

Symbol

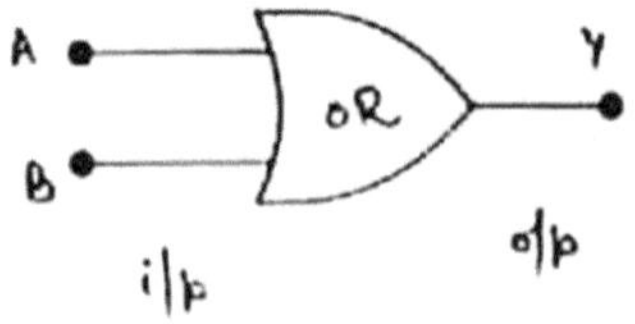
A
B
OR
Y
i/p
o/p

Truth Table

A	B	Y
0	0	0
0	1	1
1	0	1
1	1	1

Eq ckt for an OR Gate:

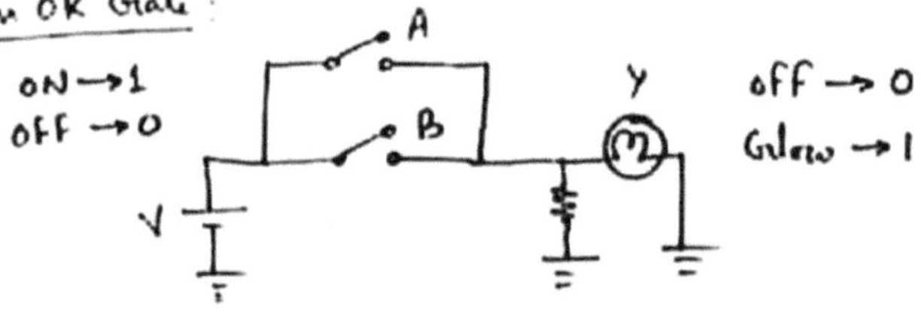
ON → 1
OFF → 0
A
B
V
Y
off → 0
Glow → 1

Scan for Video Explanation

Web Reference at www.physicsgalaxy.com

Module-6 Waveform Analysis of OR Gate

Waveform Analysis of OR Gate:

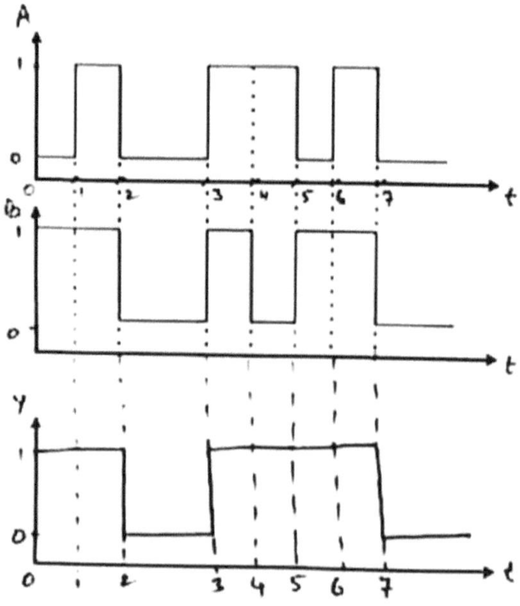
A
B
Y
t

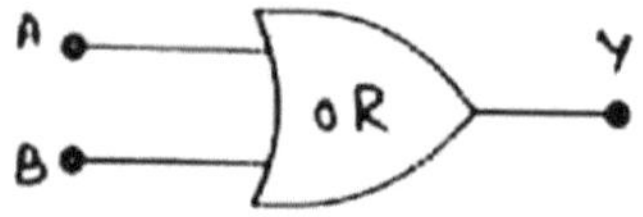
A
B
OR
Y

A	B	Y
0	0	0
0	1	1
1	0	1
1	1	1

Scan for Video Explanation

Web Reference at www.physicsgalaxy.com

Module-7 AND Gate

\# __AND Gate__ : It has 2 or more i/p and 1 o/p.

— Its o/p is High (1) when (only) all of its i/p are High (1) and its o/p is Low(0) when any of its i/p is Low(0).

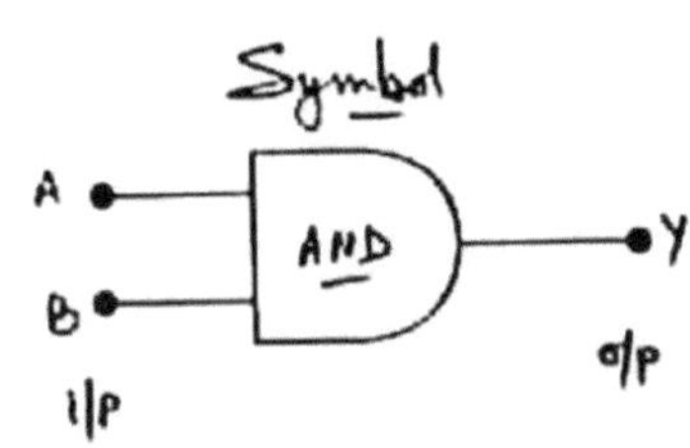

Eg ckt to understand AND gate

Truth Table

A	B	Y
0	0	0
0	1	0
1	0	0
1	1	1

Module-8 Waveform Analysis of AND Gate

\# __Waveform Analysis of AND Gate__ :

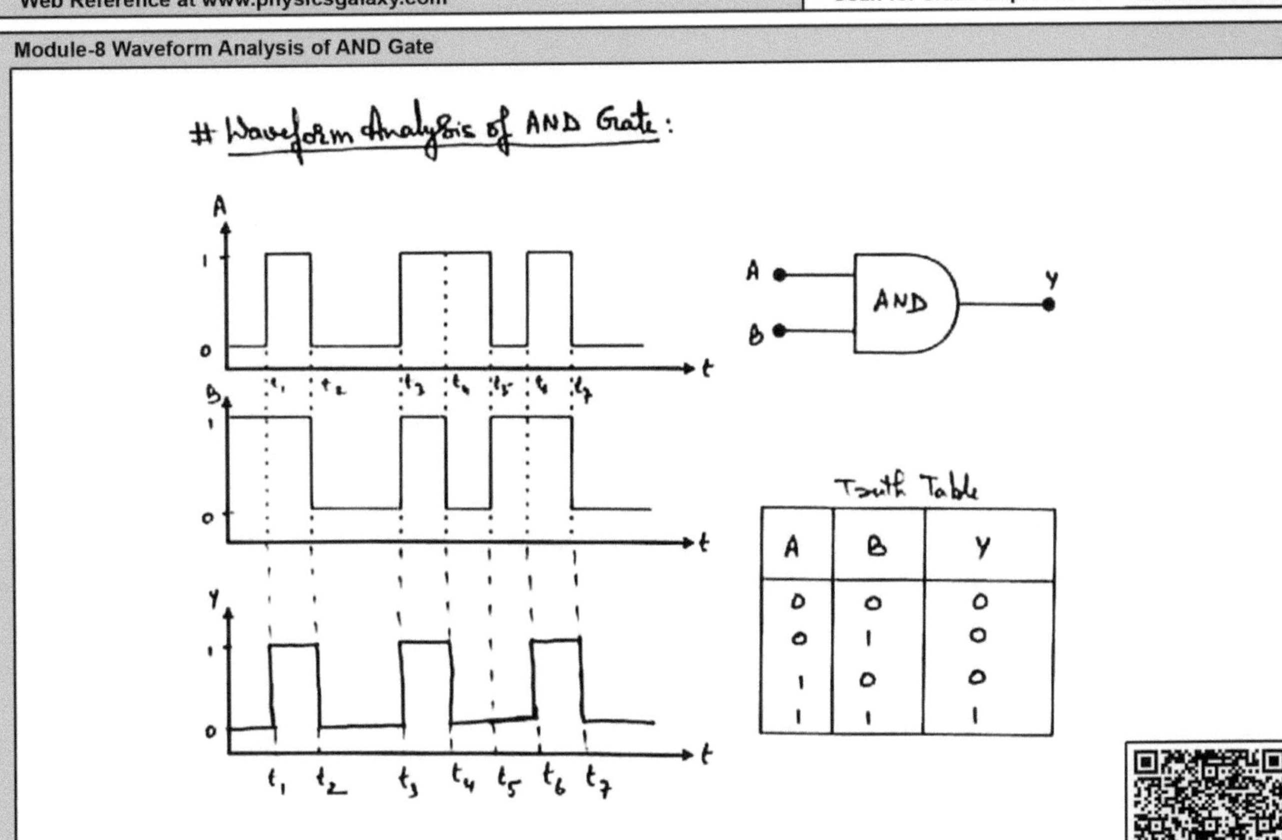

Truth Table

A	B	Y
0	0	0
0	1	0
1	0	0
1	1	1

Module-9 Input-Output Relationship for Basic Gates

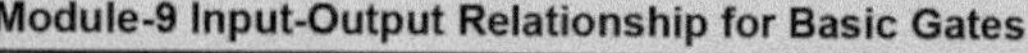

Input - Output relationship for Basic Gates:

NOT   OR   AND

$Y = A'$ or $\bar{A}$

NOT

$Y = A + B$

OR

$Y = AB$

AND

A, B → OR gate → $(A+B)$ → NOT → $(A+B)'$ → AND gate (with C) → Y

final output

$$Y = (A+B)' \cdot C$$

Module-10 NAND Gate

NAND Gate: This is an AND gate followed by a NOT gate

— It has 2 or more i/p & 1 o/p.

→ Its o/p is low (0) when all inputs are in High (1) state & its o/p is high (1) when any of its i/p is low (0)

Symbol

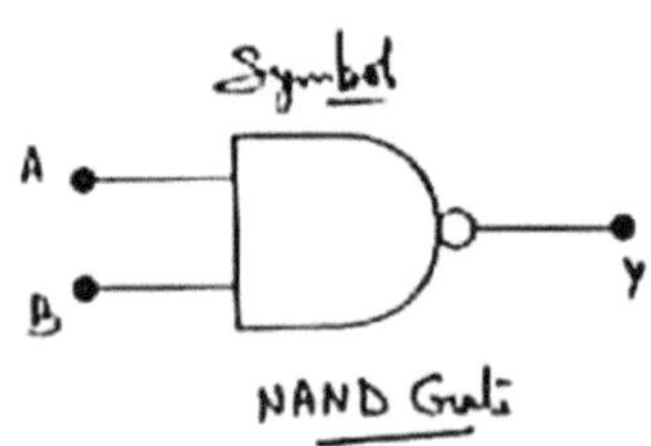

NAND Gate

Truth Table

A	B	Y
0	0	1
0	1	1
1	0	1
1	1	0

— NAND Gate is also called __universal gate__ because using this all Basic Gates — OR, AND and NOT can be realized.

Module-11 Waveform Analysis of NAND Gate

Waveform Analysis of NAND Gate:

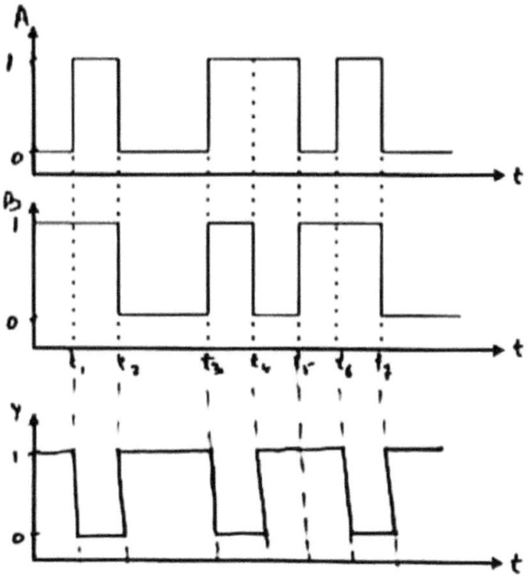

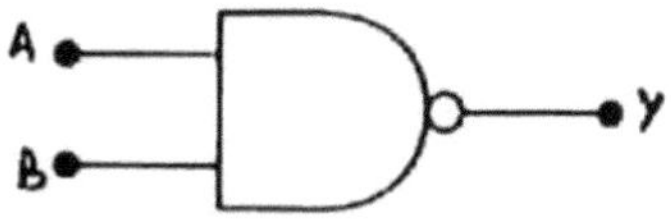

NAND Gate

Truth Table.

A	B	Y
0	0	1
0	1	1
1	0	1
1	1	0

Scan for Video Explanation

Module-12 Implementing NOT Gate using NAND Gate

Implementing NOT Gate using NAND Gate:

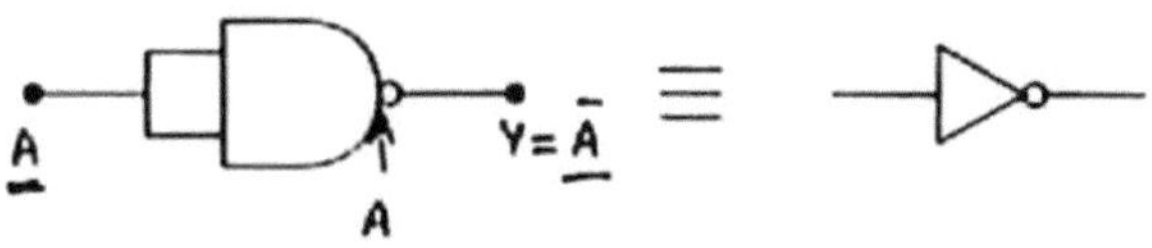

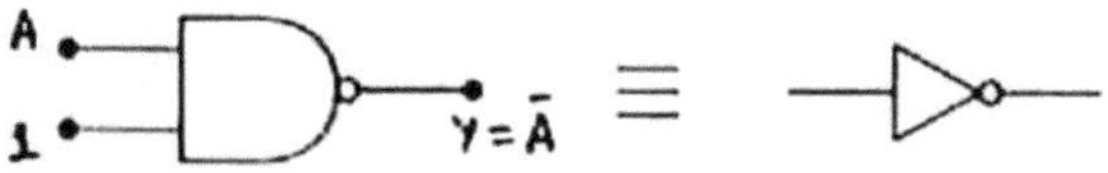

$Y = \bar{A}$

$Y = \bar{A}$

Scan for Video Explanation

Module-13 Implementing AND Gate using NAND Gates

Implementing AND Gate using NAND Gate :

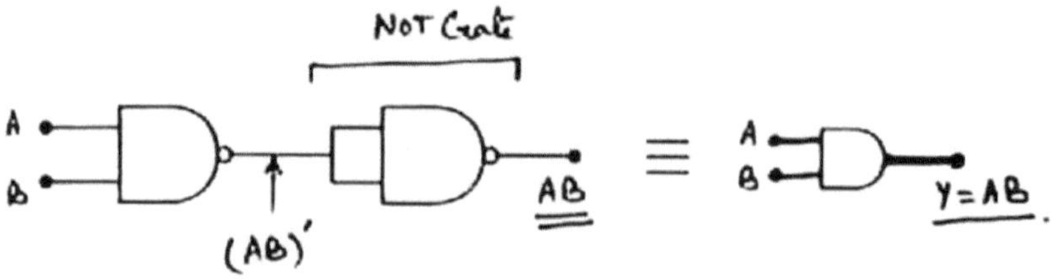

Module-14 Implementing OR Gate using NAND Gates

Implementing OR gate using NAND gates :

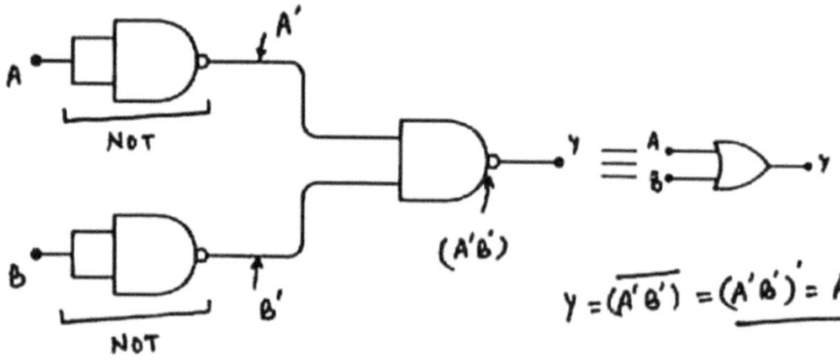

$$y = \overline{(A'B')} = (A'B')' = A + B$$

A	B	Y
0	0	0
0	1	1
1	0	1
1	1	1

← Truth Table of OR Gate

Module-15 NOR Gate

\# <u>NOR Gate</u>: This is an OR Gate followed by NOT Gate

- It has 2 or more i/p & 1 o/p
- Its o/p is High (1) only when both of its i/p are low(0) & Its o/p is low(0) when any of its i/p is High.(1)

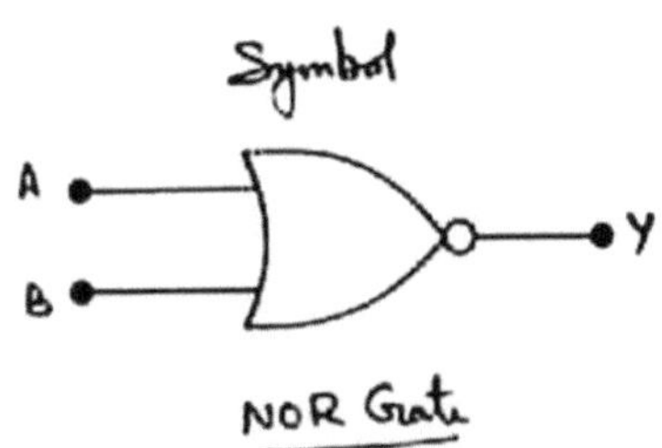

Truth Table

A	B	Y
0	0	1
0	1	0
1	0	0
1	1	0

- This gate is also considered as a <u>universal gate</u> as all basic gates NOT, OR & AND can be realized using 1 or more. NOR Gates.

Module-16 Waveform Analysis of NOR Gate

\# <u>Waveform Analysis of NOR Gate</u>:

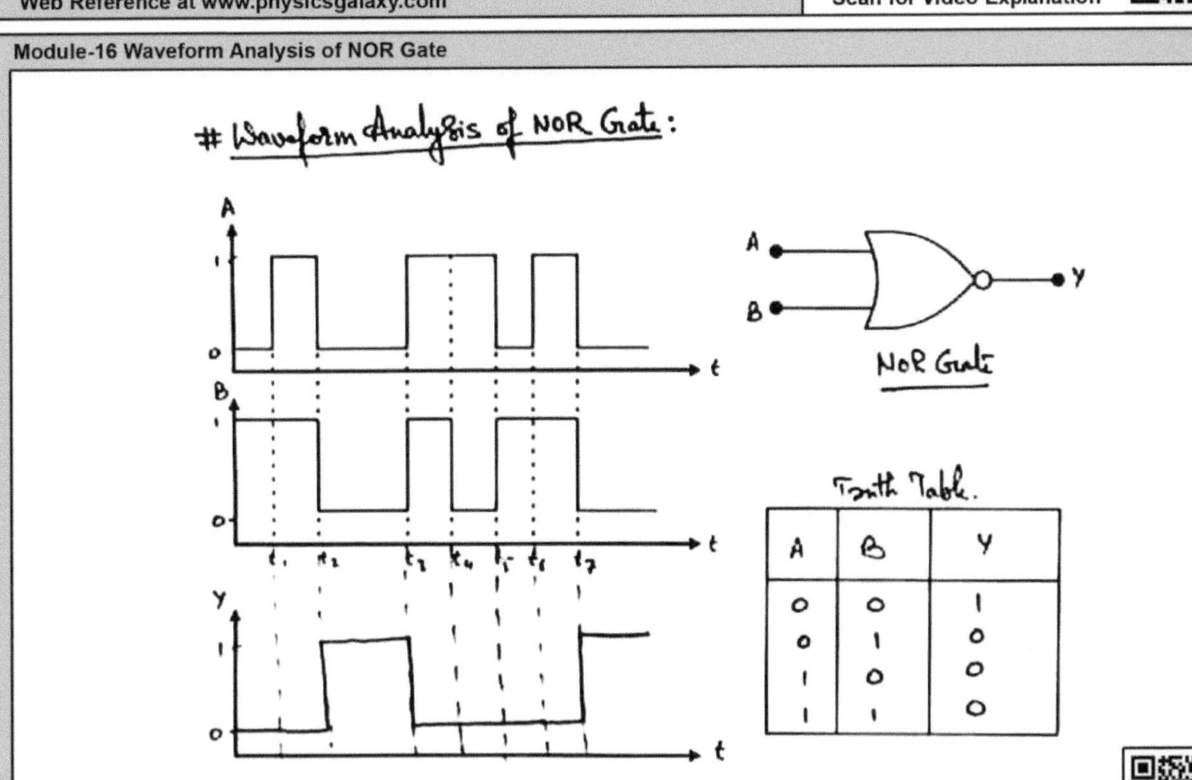

Truth Table.

A	B	Y
0	0	1
0	1	0
1	0	0
1	1	0

Module-17 Implementing NOT Gate using NOR Gate

Implementing NOT Gate using NOR Gate :

$$Y = \bar{A}$$

$$\equiv$$

$$Y = \bar{A}$$

$$\equiv$$

Module-18 Implementing OR Gate using NOR Gates

Implementing OR Gate using NOR Gates :

$$Y = A + B$$

Module-19 Implementing AND Gate using NOR Gates

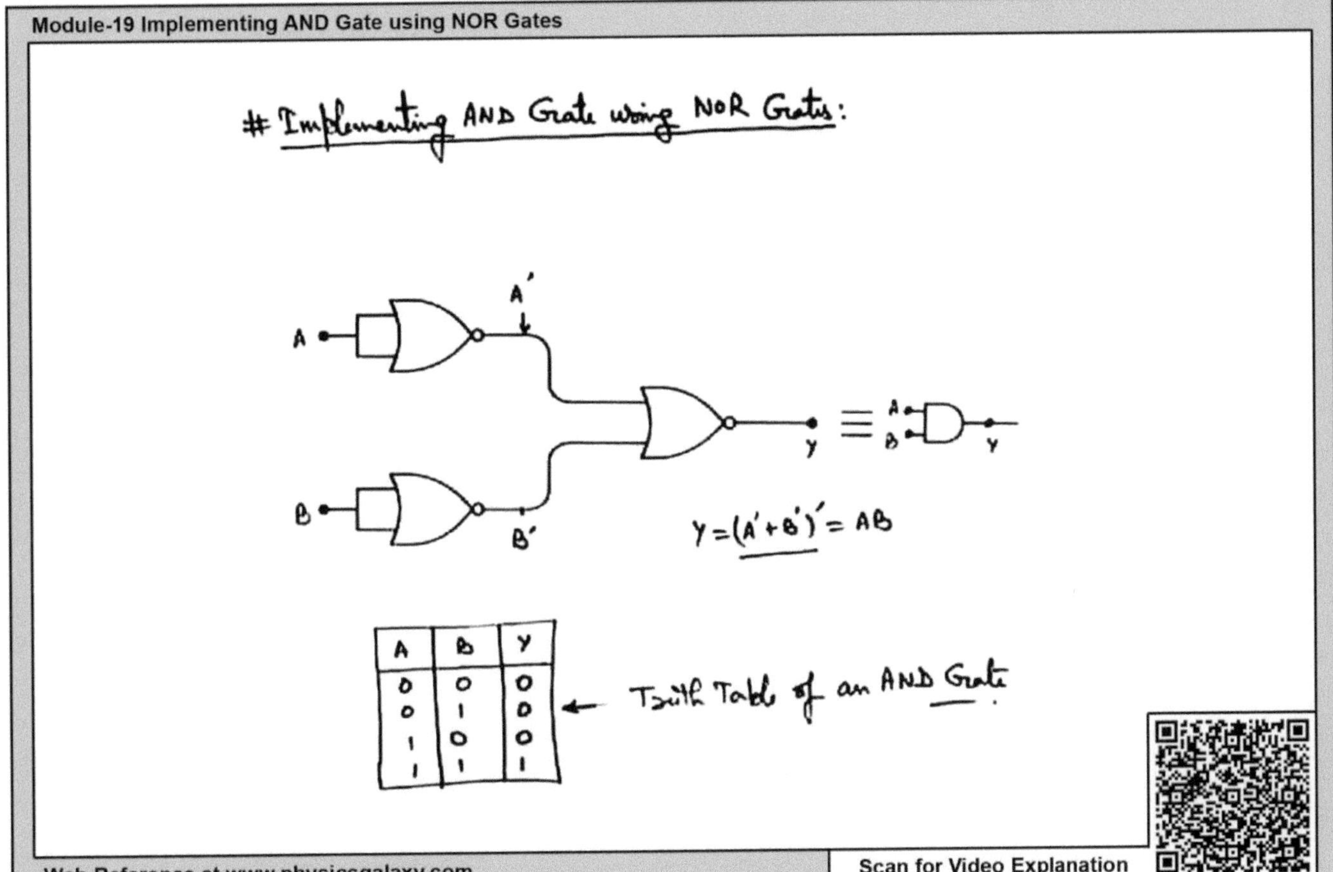

A	B	Y
0	0	0
0	1	0
1	0	0
1	1	1

← Truth Table of an AND Gate.

Scan for Video Explanation

Chapter 20
Communication Systems

Module-1 Introduction to Communication Systems

\# <u>Communication Systems</u> :

→ there are used to send information from one pt to another.

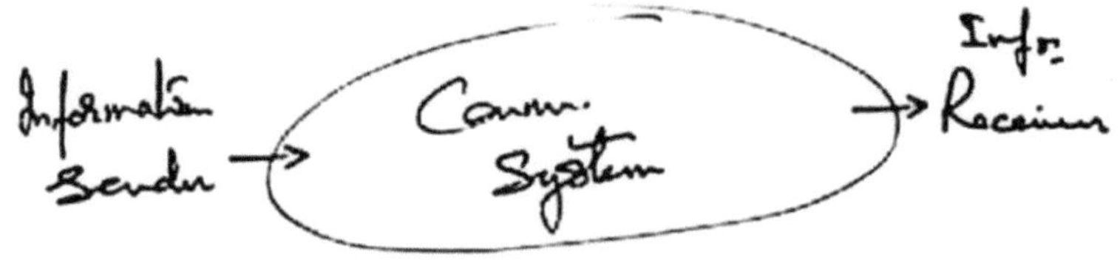

Information Sender → (Comm. System) → Info. Receiver

1835	→ Telegraphy.
1876	→ Telephones.
1895	→ Wireless telegraphy
1936	→ Television
1955	→ Fax.
1968	→ Arpanet (Internet)
1990	→ www. (World Wide Web)

Module-2 Elements of a Common Communication System

\# <u>Elements of a common Communication System</u> :

A common Com System has 3 main elements —

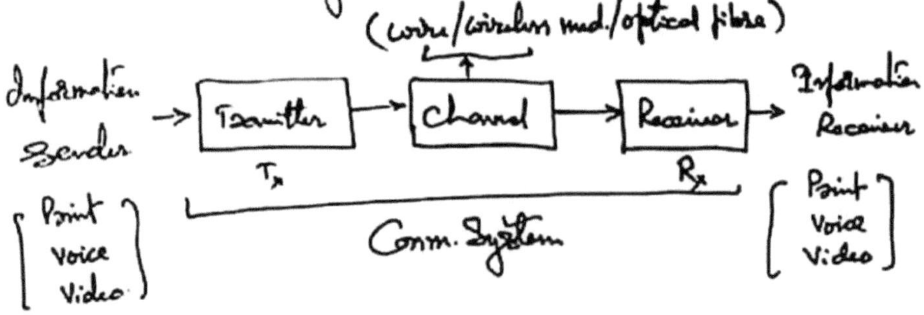

(wire / wireless med. / optical fibre)

Information Sender → [Transmitter T_x] → [Channel] → [Receiver R_x] → Information Receiver

[Print / Voice / Video]   Comm. System   [Print / Voice / Video]

There are two basic modes of Comm of Information —

① Point to point $1 T_x \longrightarrow 1 R_x$

② Broadcasting $1 T_x \longrightarrow$ many R_x

Module-3 Transducers and Signals in Communication Systems

Transducers and Signals in 'Communication Systems':

These are devices which converts energy from one form to another..

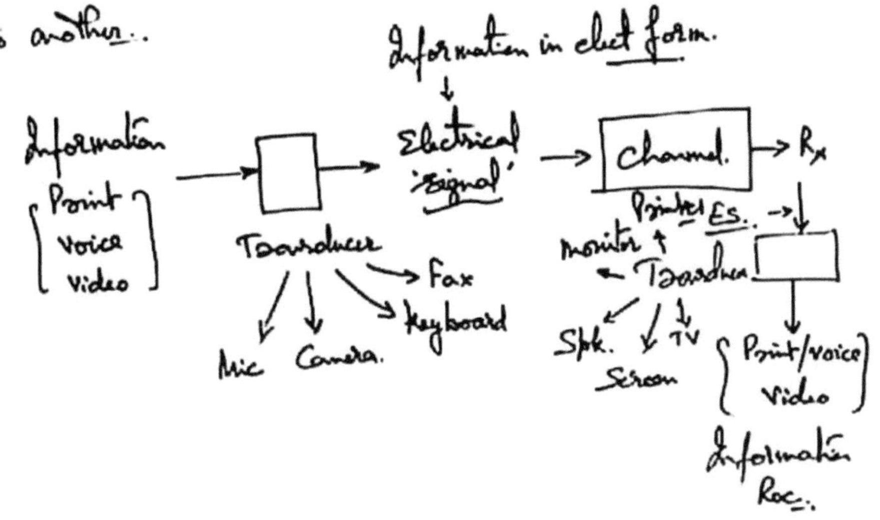

Web Reference at www.physicsgalaxy.com

Scan for Video Explanation

Module-4 Noise in Communication Systems

Noise in Communication Systems:

unwanted elect impulses caught by or induced in/ signal over the channel.

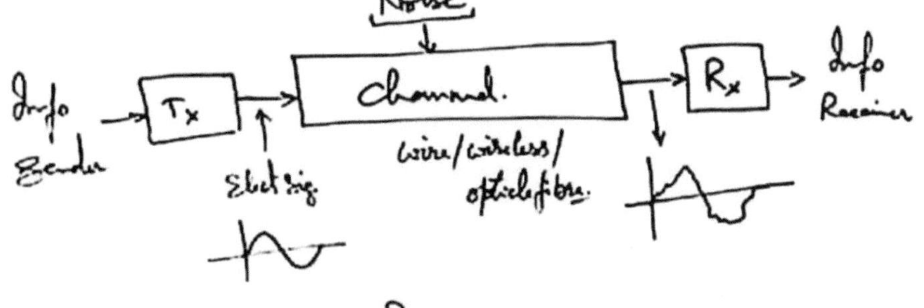

Receiver

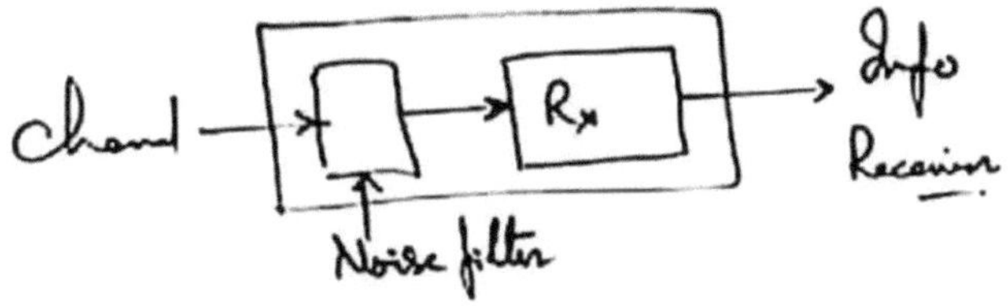

Web Reference at www.physicsgalaxy.com

Scan for Video Explanation

Module-5 Transmitters and Receiver in Communication Systems

Transmitter and Receiver in Communication Systems :

T_x : it converts the info signal into a suitable form which can be transmitted over the channel.

R_x : It receives the signal from channel and extracts the info signal from the received signal.

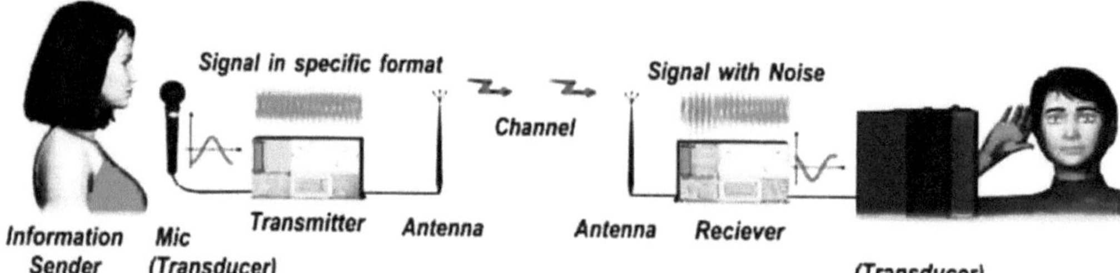

Module-6 Attenuation and Amplification in Communication Systems

Attenuation and Amplification in Communication Systems :

When a signal propagates through a channel, some energy is dissipated in the medium due to which signal intensity decreases, this loss is called Attenuation :

Amplifiers are used to compensate the attenuation of signal

Module-7 Range of a Communication System and Repeaters

 # Range of a Communication System and Repeaters :

Range is the largest dist over which the signal can be transmitted from source pt to the destination point with sufficient signal strength.

To increase the range of a Comm Sys, Repeaters are used.

Comb^n of T_x & R_x

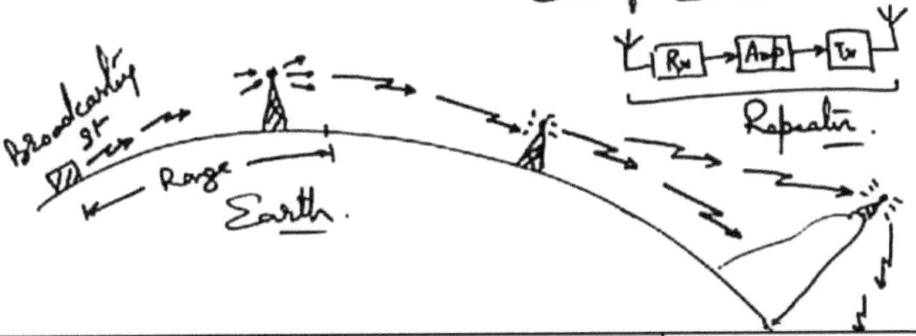

Rx → Amp → Tx
Repeater.
Broadcasting st
Range
Earth.

Scan for Video Explanation

Module-8 Bandwidth of Signals

 # Bandwidth of Signals :

BW is the range of freq which are used for the informal signals.

Voice Signal → 20Hz to 20kHz

Speech (300Hz to 3000Hz)
BW = 2700 Hz

Music (20Hz to 20kHz)
BW = 20kHz

Video Signal → BW = 4 to 4.5 MHz

TV Signals Broadcasting → 6 to 7 MHz.

Scan for Video Explanation

Module-9 Operating Frequencies of Transmission Medium

Operating Frequencies of Transmission Medium (channel):

Commonly use channels are → wire → Coaxial Cable, parallel Trans line.
→ free space (wireless)
→ fibre optic cable.

A particular channel can only transmit signals of specific freq range which is called operating freq of that trans medium.

	op. freq.
wire line →	10^9 to 10^{10} Hz
free space →	10^3 Hz to 10^{10} Hz
fibre optic →	10^{12} Hz to 10^{15} Hz

Scan for Video Explanation

Module-10 Transmission of Electromagnetic Signals Through Space

Transmission of EM Signals through Space:

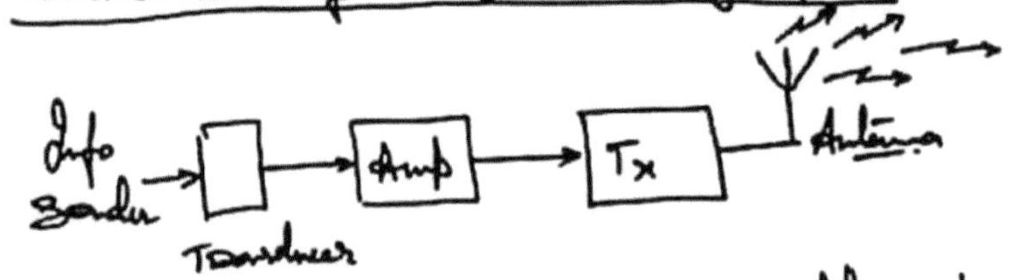
Info Sender
Transducer
Amp
Tx
Antenna

Analysis of antenna shows that for optimum power transmission of signals the size of antenna must be at least $\lambda/4$. (λ ← W/L of EM waves)

for a sound signal of 3000Hz $\longrightarrow \lambda = c/n = \frac{3\times10^8}{3000} = 10^5 m = 100 km$.

Size of Ant req ≃ 25 km or more.
not practical.

for a HF wave of freq ≃ 1000MHz $\longrightarrow \lambda = c/n = \frac{3\times10^8}{10^9} = 0.3 m$
$\simeq 30 cm$.

Size of Ant req. ≥ 7.5cm ✓

Scan for Video Explanation

Module-11 Power of Electromagnetic Signals Through Space

Power of EM Signals through space:

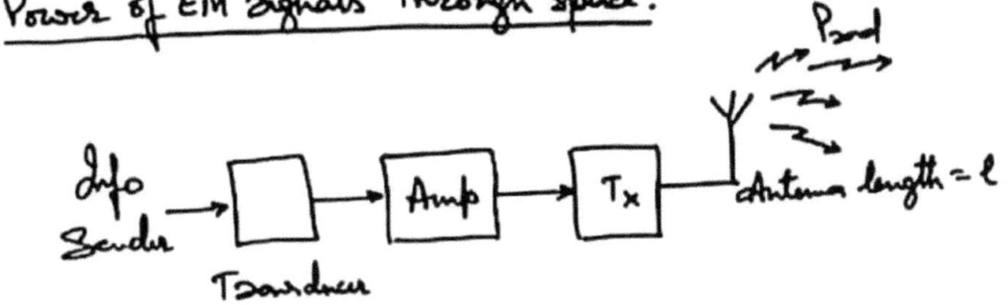
Info
Sender
Transducer
Amp
Tx
Antenna length = l
Prad

Various analysis shows that the radiation power from antenna is $P_{rad} \propto (l/\lambda)^2$

As $\lambda \uparrow$ (for LF waves) $\Rightarrow P_{rad} \downarrow$

$\Rightarrow$ for good range of transmission λ should be low
thus for HF power transmission will be high

Web Reference at www.physicsgalaxy.com

Scan for Video Explanation

Module-12 Electromagnetic Wave Propagation in Space

EM Wave Propagation in space:

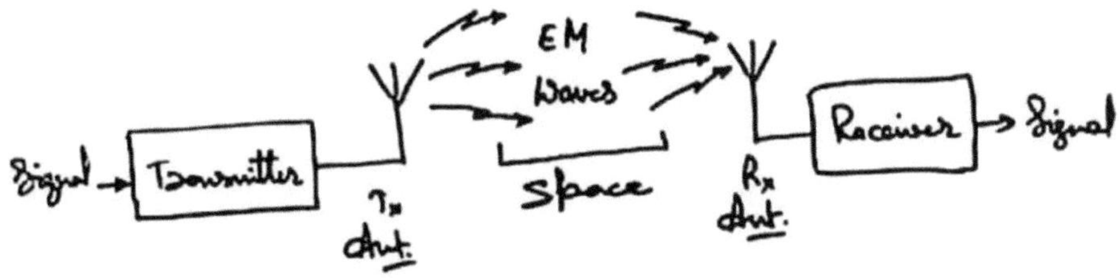
Signal
Transmitter
Tx
Ant.
EM
Waves
Space
Rx
Ant.
Receiver
Signal

There are 3 general ways in which EM wave propagation take place in space -

1. Ground Waves ~ less than 2MHz
2. Sky Waves ~ 3MHz to 30MHz
3. Space Waves ~ more than 40MHz

Web Reference at www.physicsgalaxy.com

Scan for Video Explanation

Module-13 Ground Wave Propagation

Ground Wave Propagation :

At low freq when large Ant are used, the signal EM waves spreads out along the Earth Surface by inducing EM currents on earth surface. These waves are called ground waves or Surface waves.

Due to abs of energy by earth surface the wave is attenuated and range of such waves is vel less.

Module-14 Sky Wave Propagation

Sky Wave Propagation :

long dist prop of signals are done by ionospheric reflection of waves, called sky waves

Ionosphere ~ 60 to 500km abv earth surface in which degree of ionization varies with height

for EM waves of freq upto 30MHz are reflected by ionospheric layers. Here we must know that freq > 40MHz are able to penetrate the ionosphere.

Module-15 Space Wave Propagation

Space Wave Propagation :

EM waves of freq abv $40 MHz$ are use for space wave prop. in which the line of sight communication is done.

Here LOS must be clear for T_x and R_x Antennas.

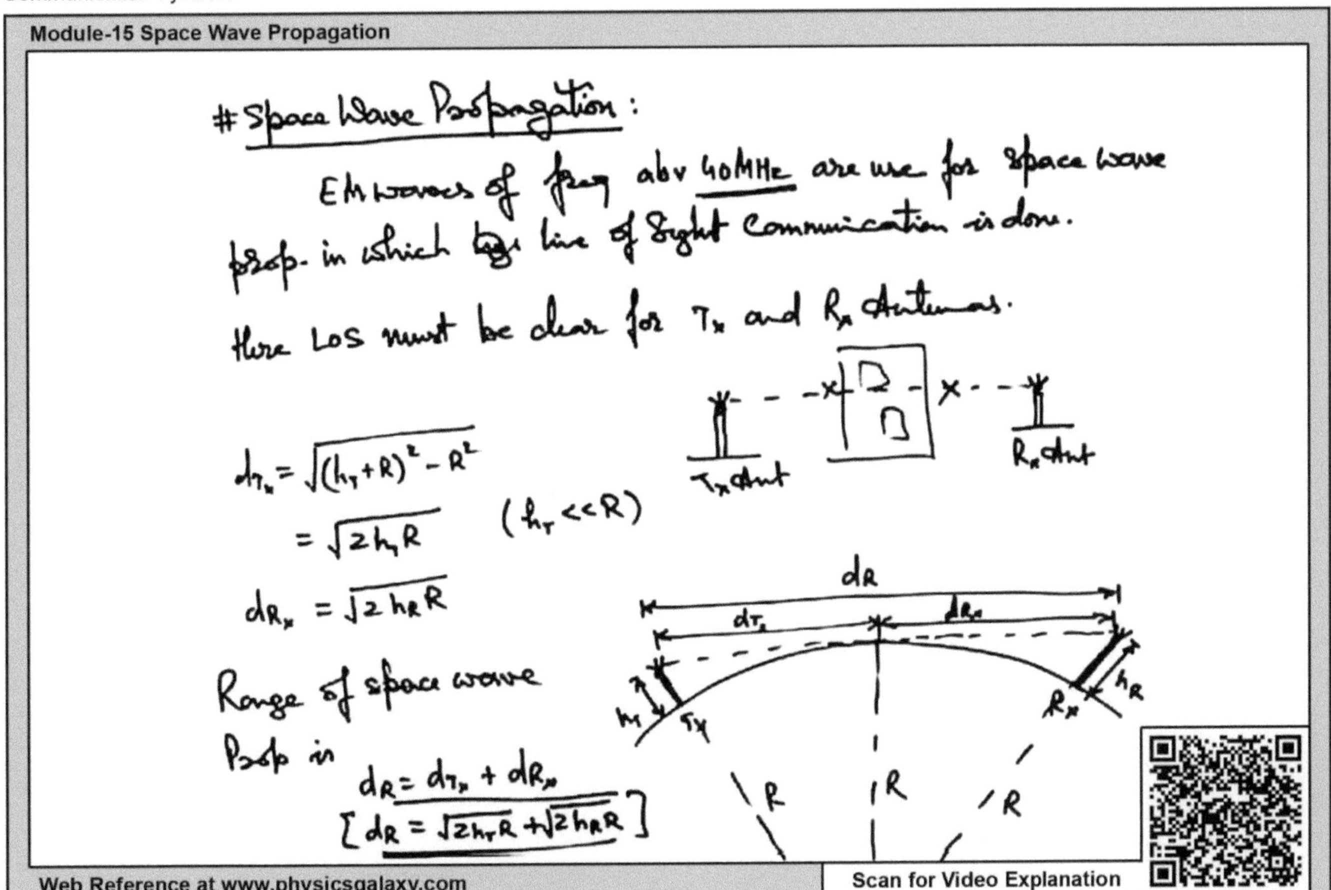

$$d_{T_x} = \sqrt{(h_T + R)^2 - R^2}$$
$$= \sqrt{2 h_T R} \qquad (h_T << R)$$

$$d_{R_x} = \sqrt{2 h_R R}$$

Range of space wave Prop in

$$d_R = d_{T_x} + d_{R_x}$$
$$\boxed{d_R = \sqrt{2 h_T R} + \sqrt{2 h_R R}}$$

Scan for Video Explanation

Chapter 21
Modulation and Demodulation

Problems in Transmission of Baseband Signals :

(low freq Signals)

If dir voice or video sig are transmitted there are several factor due to which the effective transmission fails.

(1) <u>Size of Antenna</u> : As disc that at low freq (high λ) antenna size req is very large so it becomes impractical to transmit such sign.

(2) <u>Radiation Power</u> : for low freq rad power is very low so reception is very weak.

(3) <u>Mixing of channel</u> : If several voice channels (songs/news/drama) are broadcasted together, receiver will catch all together and it will result in channel mix as all are at same freq range.

Modulation of Signals & Carrier Frequency :

As discussed for effective signal tx high freq are much more effective & feasible over low freq hence for wireless tans of signals it is req to superimpose baseband signals (low freq) with a high freq signal (carrier wave) then this mixed signal can be transmitted efficiently.

The superimposition of Baseband signal with carrier freq wave is called modulation.

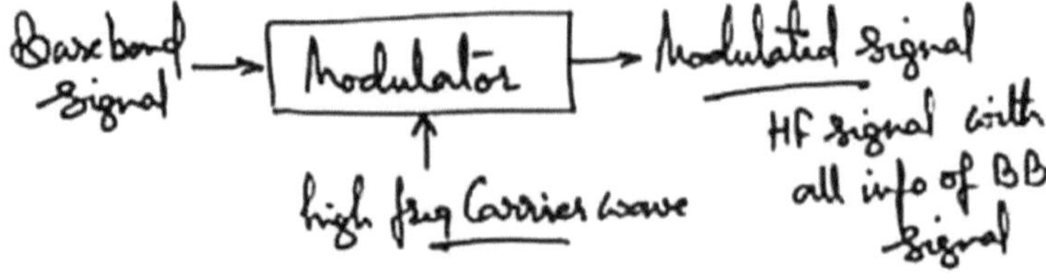

Module-3 Demodulation at the Receiving End

\# _Demodulation at the Receiving end:_

BB Signal (LF) → MOD → Amp → Tx

Carrier (HF) Wave

Modulated Signal (HF)

Amp (Rx) → DE MOD → BB Signal

Modulated Signal (HF)

Carrier (HF) Wave

Transmission End

Reception End

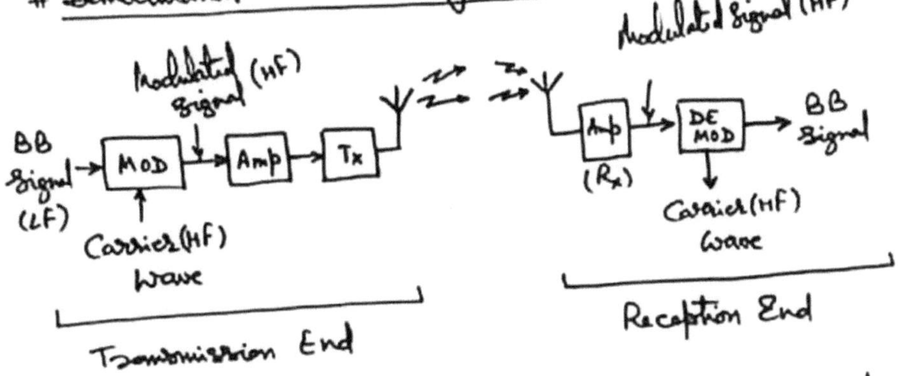

Demodulation : The process of recovering Baseband Signal from HF modulated Signal is called demodulation.

Scan for Video Explanation

Module-4 Types of Modulation of Baseband Signals

\# _Types of Modulation of Baseband Signals:_

Mod is the process of attaching baseband signals with a specific HF carrier wave. Carrier wave is generally used is of two types —

① Sinusoidal Carrier Wave

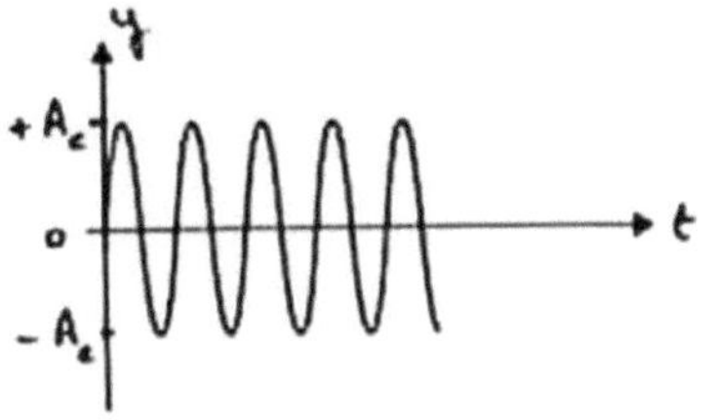

② Pulsating Carrier Wave

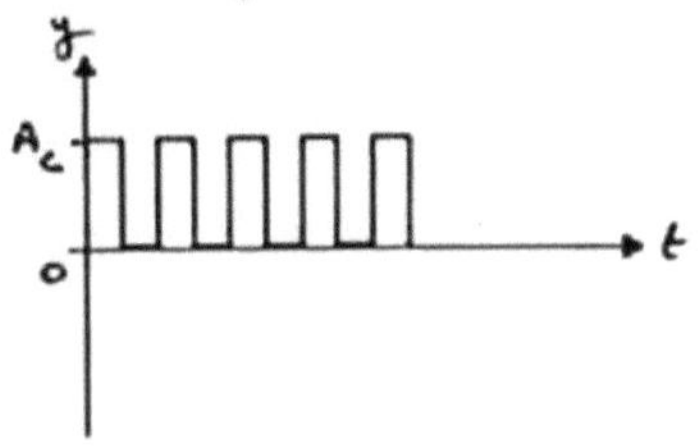

$$y_c = A_c \sin(\omega_c t + \phi_c)$$

Scan for Video Explanation

Carrier Wave $\quad y_c = \underline{A_c} \sin(\underline{\omega_c} t + \underline{\phi_c})$

by mod either of A_c, ω_c and ϕ_c of carrier wave can be modified by mixing BB signal so all the inf in BB signal will be contained in carrier wave by variation of A_c, ω_c or ϕ_c.

In gen^l there are 3 types of modulations of carrier wave —

① Amplitude Modulation (AM)

② Frequency Modulation (FM)

③ Phase Modulation (PM)

Amplitude Modulation (AM):

In AM, amplitude of carrier wave is varied acc to the baseband signal.

$$\text{BB Signal} \longrightarrow \boxed{AM - MOD} \longrightarrow AM \text{ Signal}$$

$y_m = A_m \sin \omega_m t$
(Modulating Signal)

$y_{AM} = \underline{R} \sin \underline{\omega_c} t$

Carrier Wave
$y_c = \underline{A_c} \sin \underline{\omega_c} t$

$\omega_c \gg \omega_m$

Amp of AM wave is $\quad R = A_c + A_m \sin \omega_m t$

AM wave is $\quad y_{AM} = (A_c + A_m \sin \omega_m t) \sin \omega_c t$

Module-5 Amplitude Modulation (AM)

$$y_{AM} = \left(A_c + A_m \sin \omega_m t\right) \sin \omega_c t$$

$$y_{AM} = A_c \left(1 + \frac{A_m}{A_c} \sin \omega_m t\right) \sin \omega_c t$$

$$\mu = \frac{A_m}{A_c} \longrightarrow \text{Modulation Index}$$

$$y_{AM} = A_c \sin \omega_c t + \frac{\mu A_c}{2} \cos(\omega_c - \omega_m) t - \frac{\mu A_c}{2} \cos(\omega_c + \omega_m)$$

AM signal consist of 3 freq $\longrightarrow$ ω_c, $\omega_c - \omega_m$, $\omega_c + \omega_m$.

Carrier freq   lower side freq   upper side freq.

Freq Spectrum of AM wave:

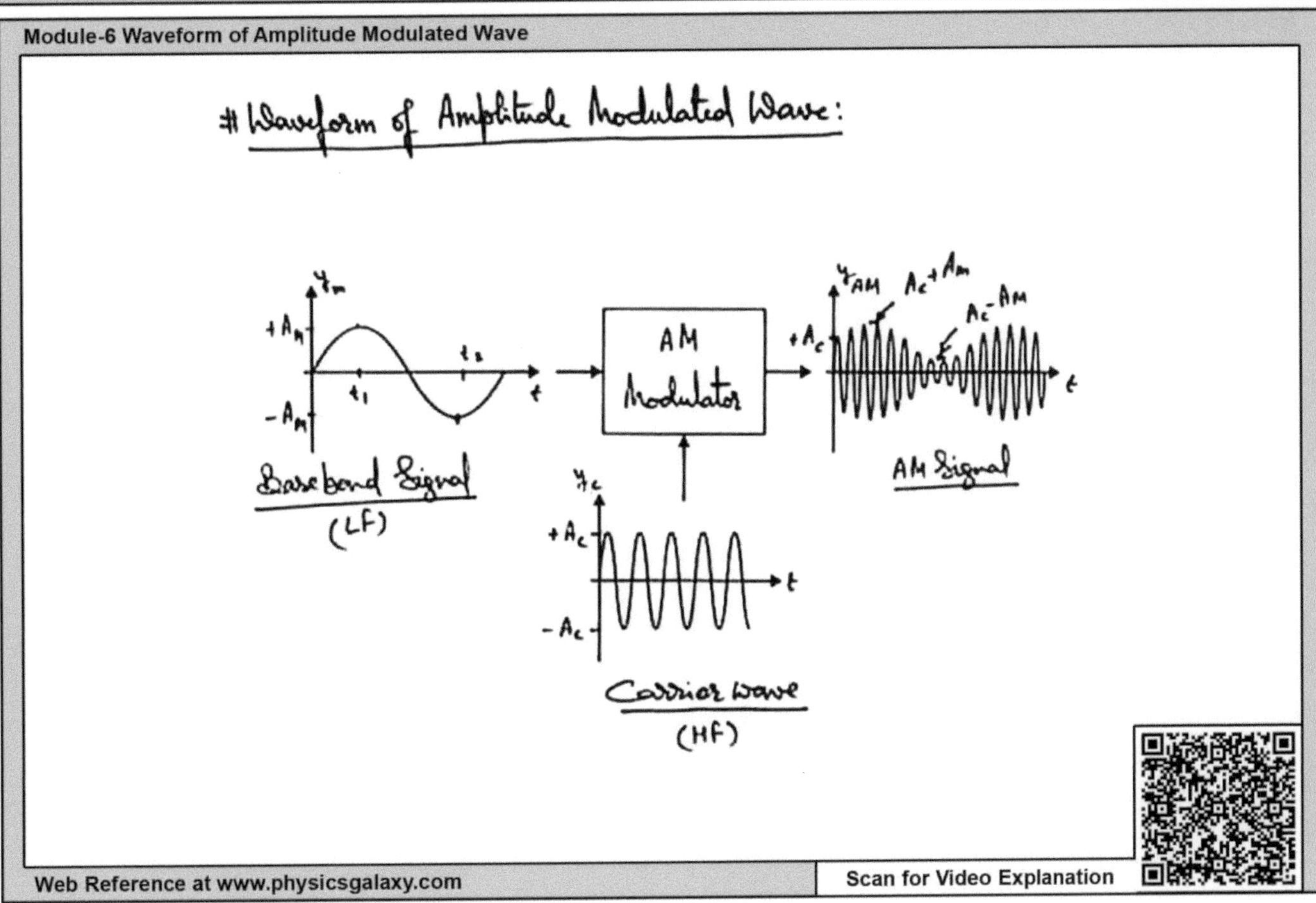

Module-6 Waveform of Amplitude Modulated Wave

 # Waveform of Amplitude Modulated Wave:

Module-6 Waveform of Amplitude Modulated Wave

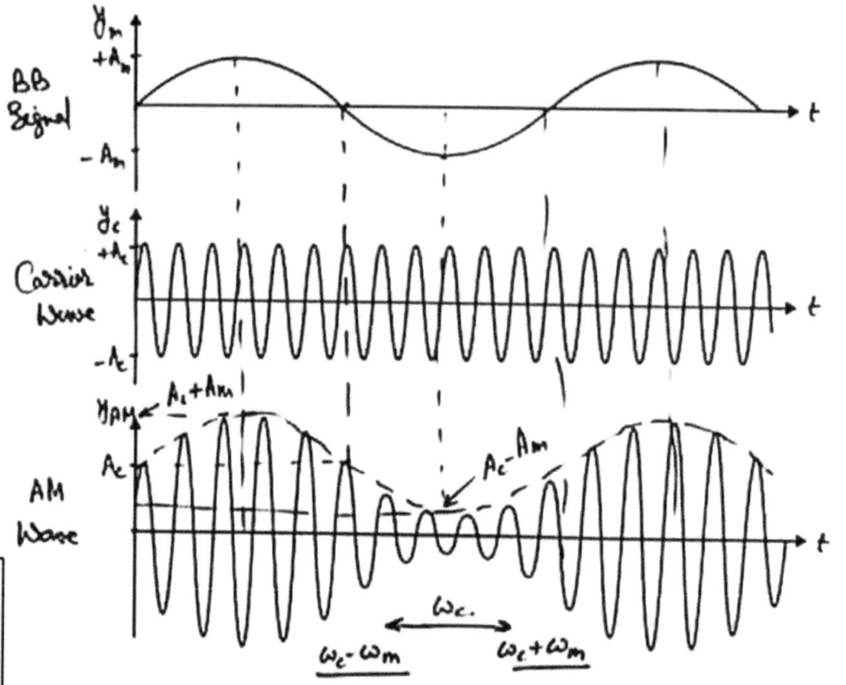

Scan for Video Explanation

Web Reference at www.physicsgalaxy.com

Module-7 Frequency Modulation (FM)

Frequency Modulation (FM):

In FM, freq of carrier wave is varied acc to the base band signal.

LF BB Signal $y_m = A_m \sin \omega_m t$

HF Carrier wave $y_c = A_c \sin \omega_c t$ $\quad \omega_c = 2\pi f_c$

FM → $y_{FM} = A_c \sin [2\pi [f_c + k_f A_m \sin \omega_m t] t]$

FM index.

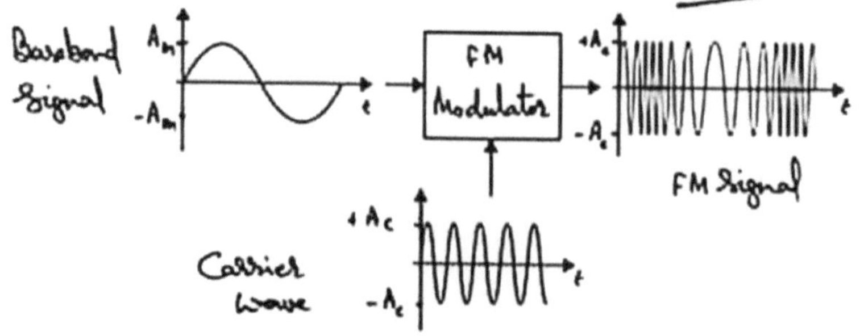

Scan for Video Explanation

Web Reference at www.physicsgalaxy.com

Module-7 Frequency Modulation (FM)

Waveform of Frequency Modulated Wave:

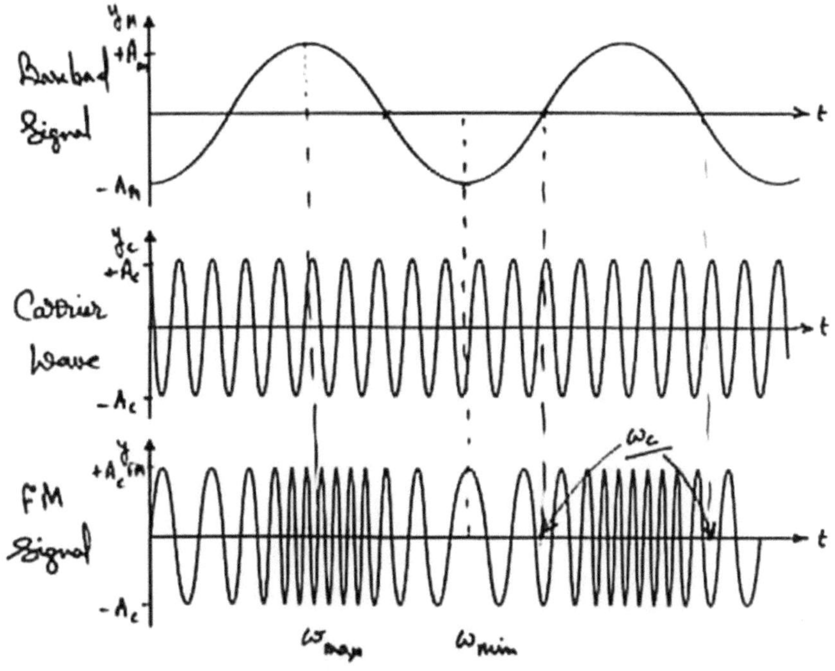

Web Reference at www.physicsgalaxy.com

Scan for Video Explanation

Module-8 Comparison of AM and FM Waveforms

Comparison of AM and FM Waveforms:

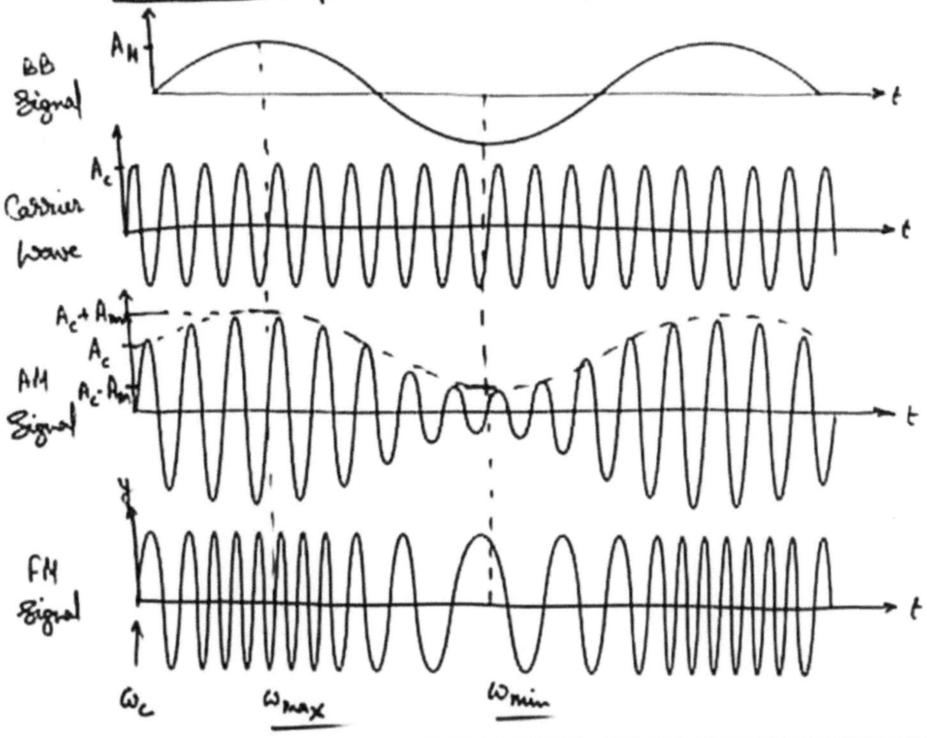

Web Reference at www.physicsgalaxy.com

Scan for Video Explanation

Phase Modulation (PM):

In PM, phase of carrier wave is varied acc[to] the baseband informational signal.

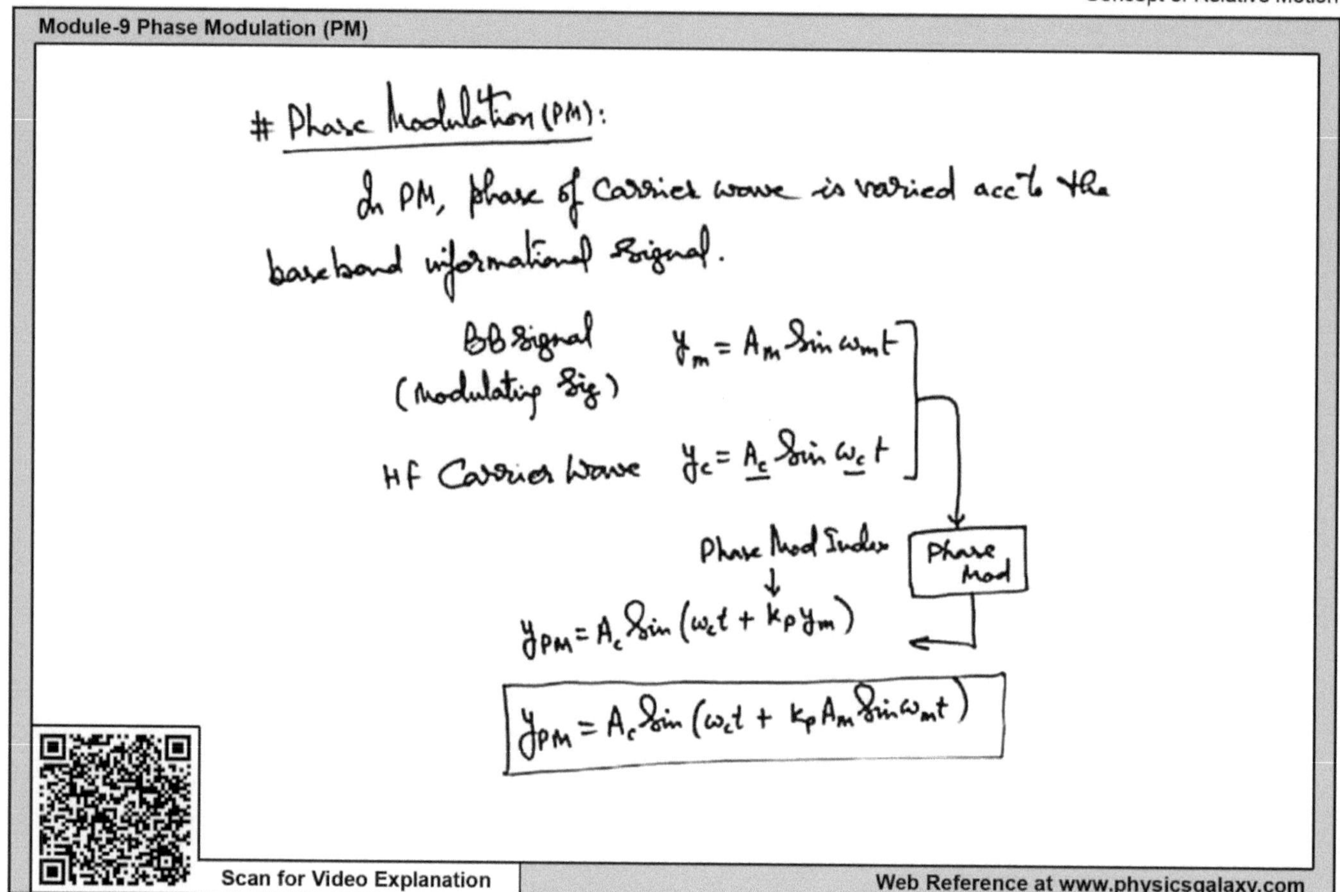

Printed by Libri Plureos GmbH in Hamburg,
Germany